Shojo Beat

Aishiteruze BABY

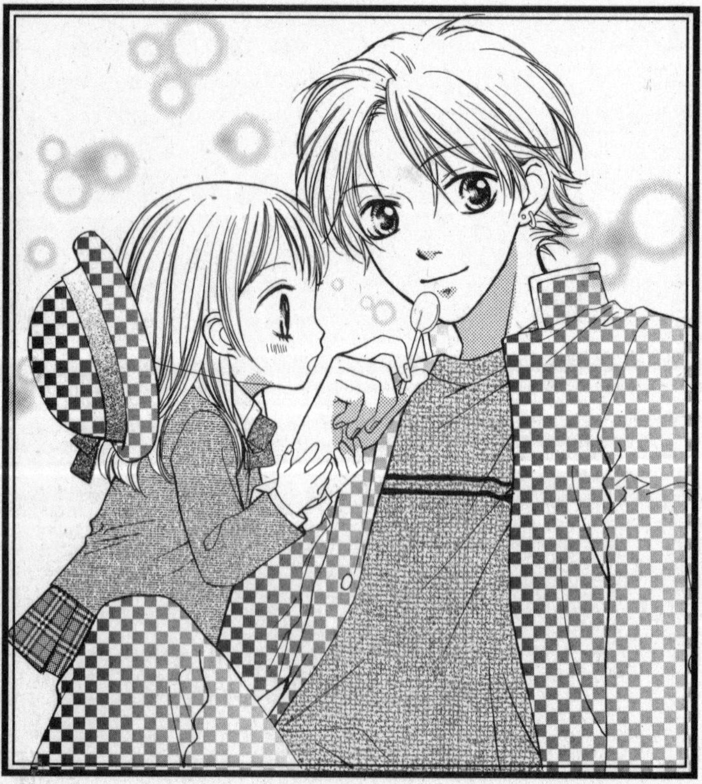

1

Story & Art by Yoko Maki

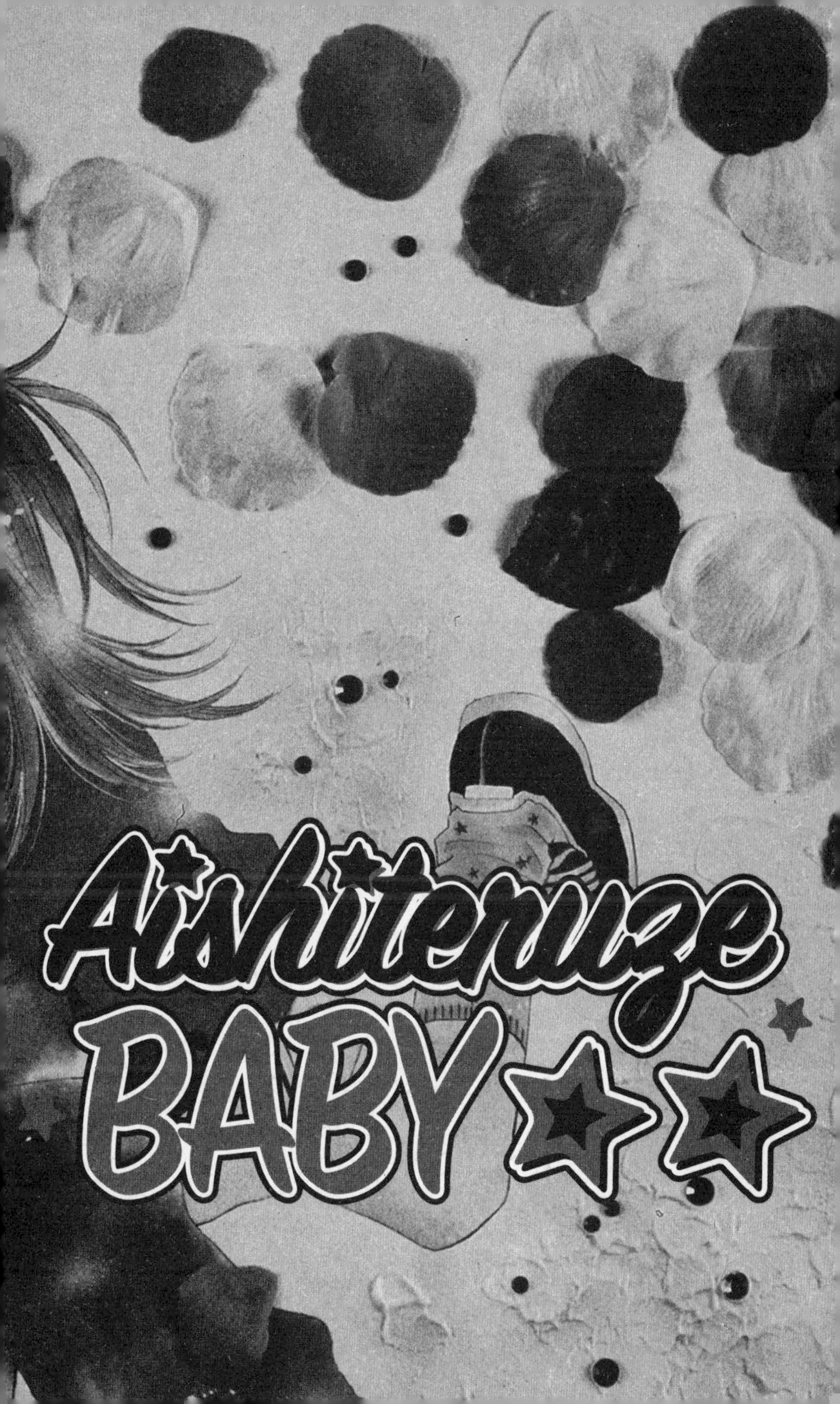
Aishiteruze
BABY★★

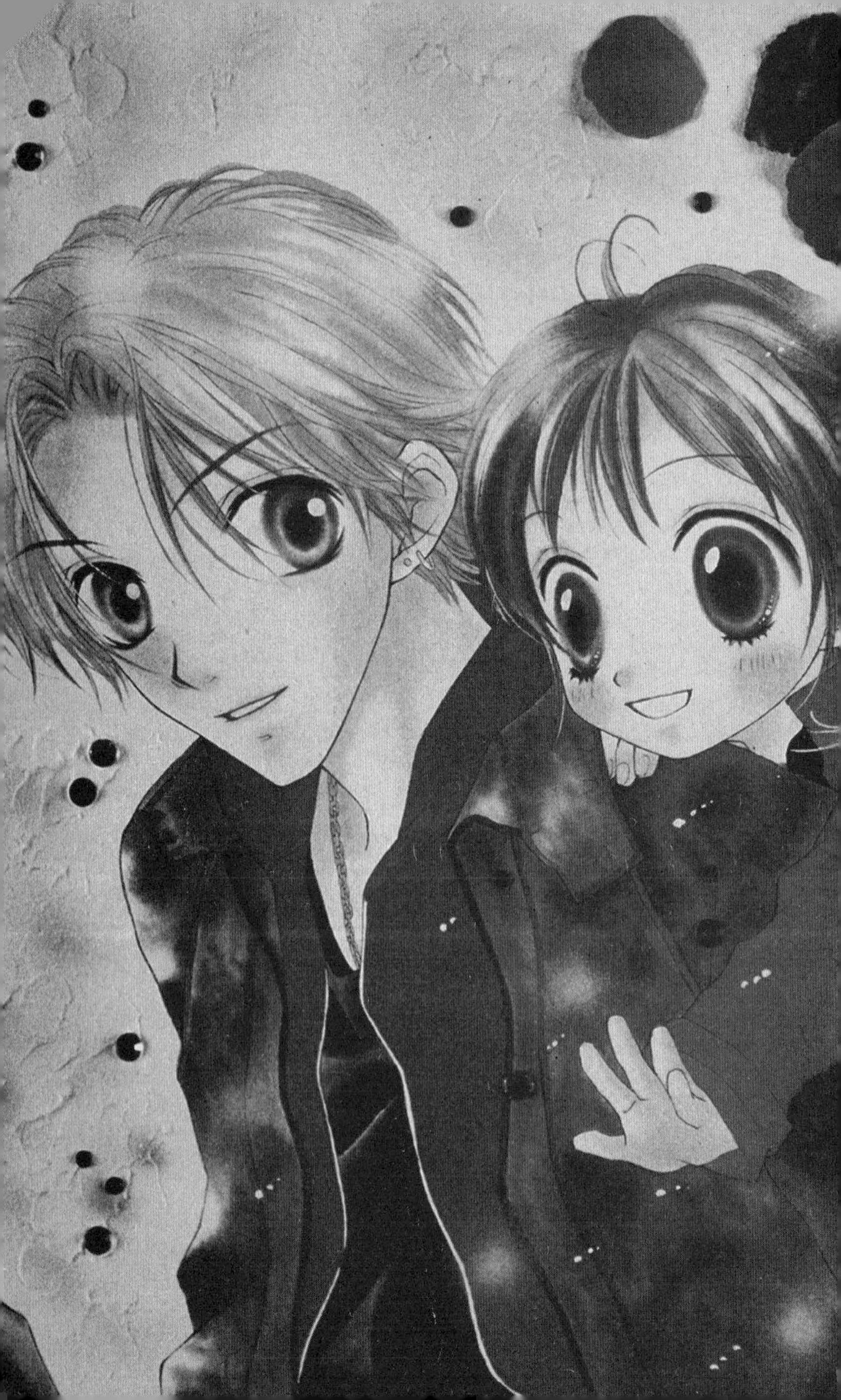

Contents

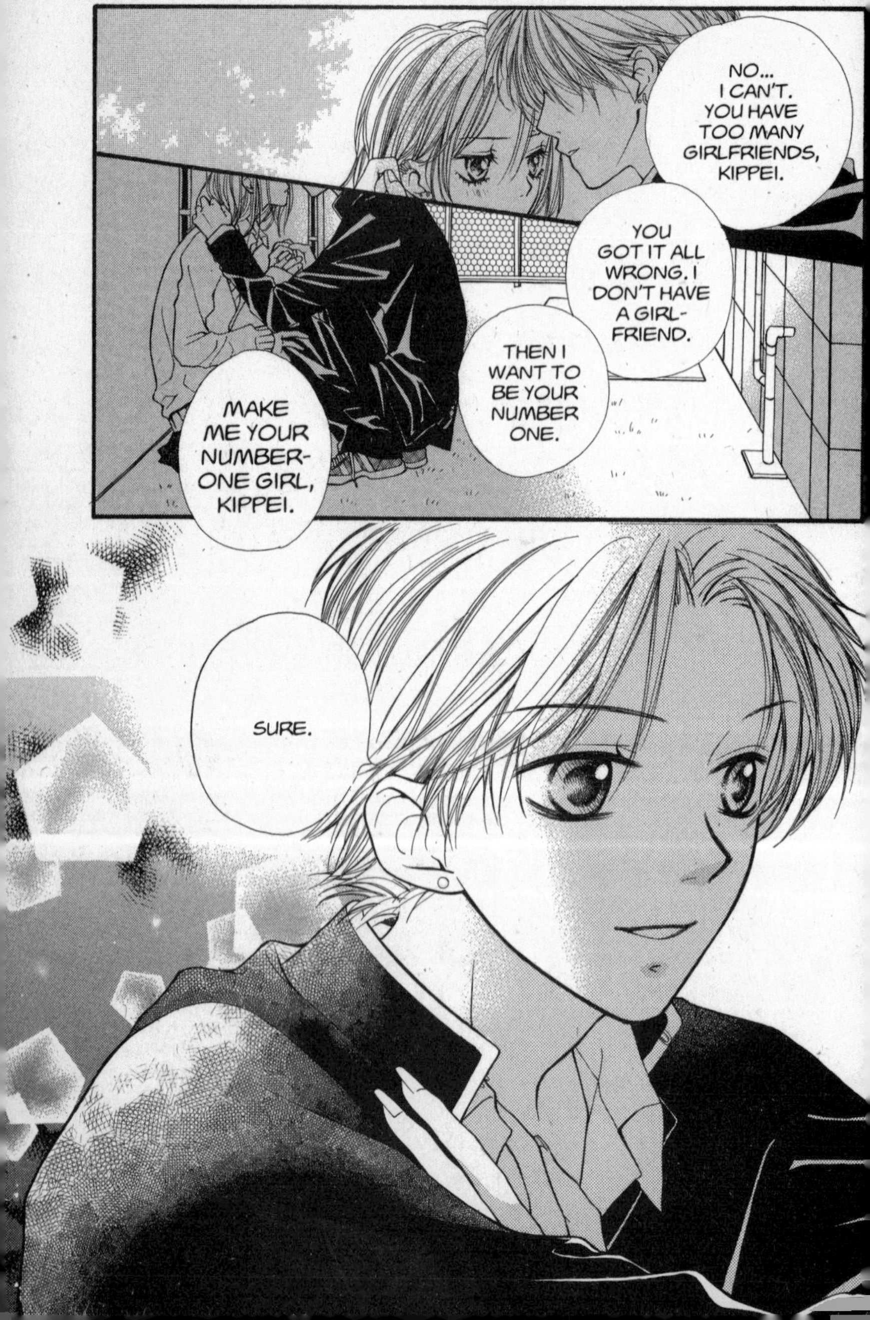
NO... I CAN'T. YOU HAVE TOO MANY GIRLFRIENDS, KIPPEI.
YOU GOT IT ALL WRONG. I DON'T HAVE A GIRL-FRIEND.
THEN I WANT TO BE YOUR NUMBER ONE.
MAKE ME YOUR NUMBER-ONE GIRL, KIPPEI.
SURE.

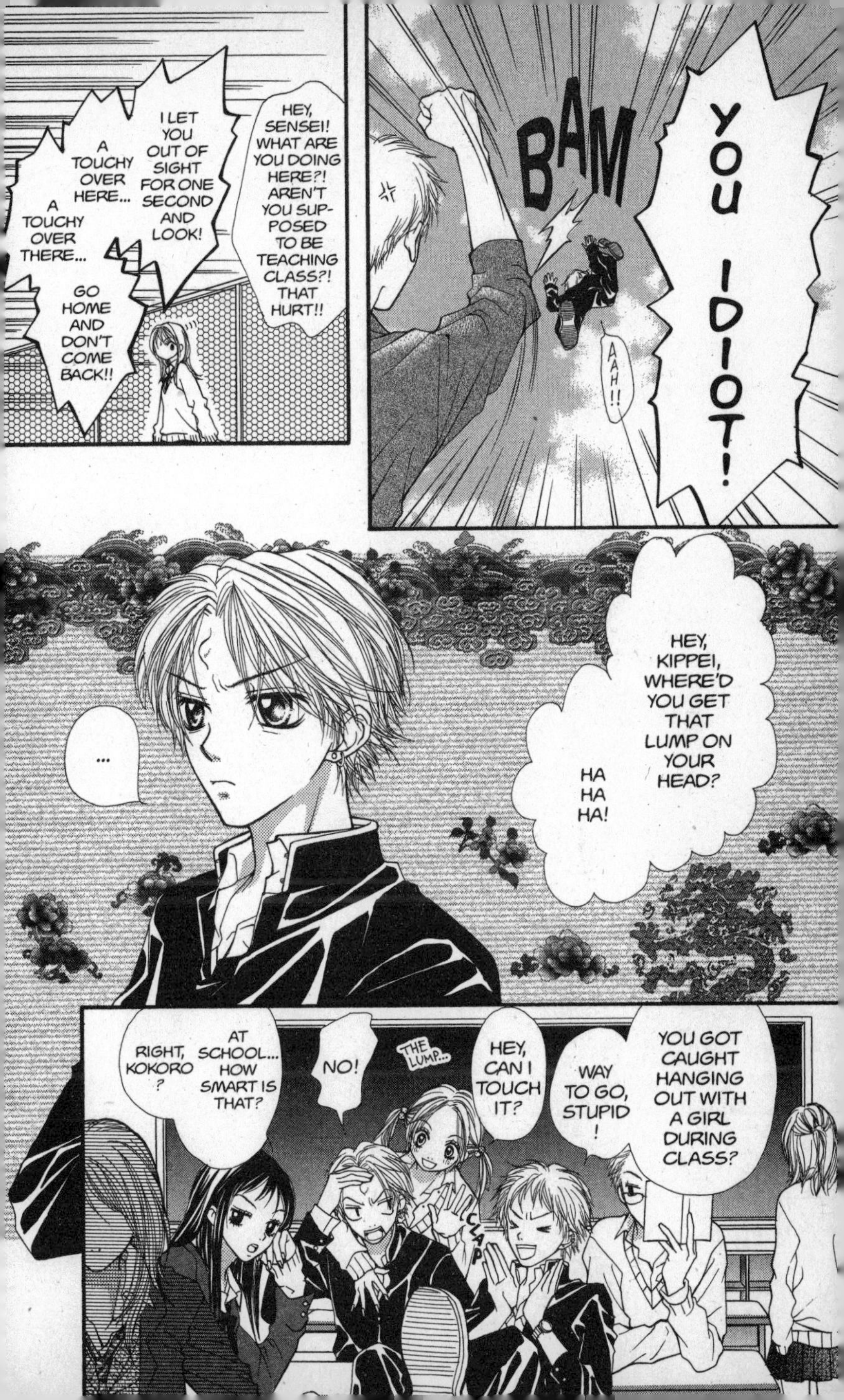
YOU IDIOT!
BAM
AAH!!
HEY, SENSEI! WHAT ARE YOU DOING HERE?! AREN'T YOU SUPPOSED TO BE TEACHING CLASS?! THAT HURT!!
I LET YOU OUT OF SIGHT FOR ONE SECOND AND LOOK!
A TOUCHY OVER HERE...
A TOUCHY OVER THERE...
GO HOME AND DON'T COME BACK!!
HEY, KIPPEI, WHERE'D YOU GET THAT LUMP ON YOUR HEAD?
HA HA HA!
...
YOU GOT CAUGHT HANGING OUT WITH A GIRL DURING CLASS?
WAY TO GO, STUPID!
HEY, CAN I TOUCH IT?
THE LUMP...
NO!
CLAP
AT SCHOOL... HOW SMART IS THAT?
RIGHT, KOKORO?

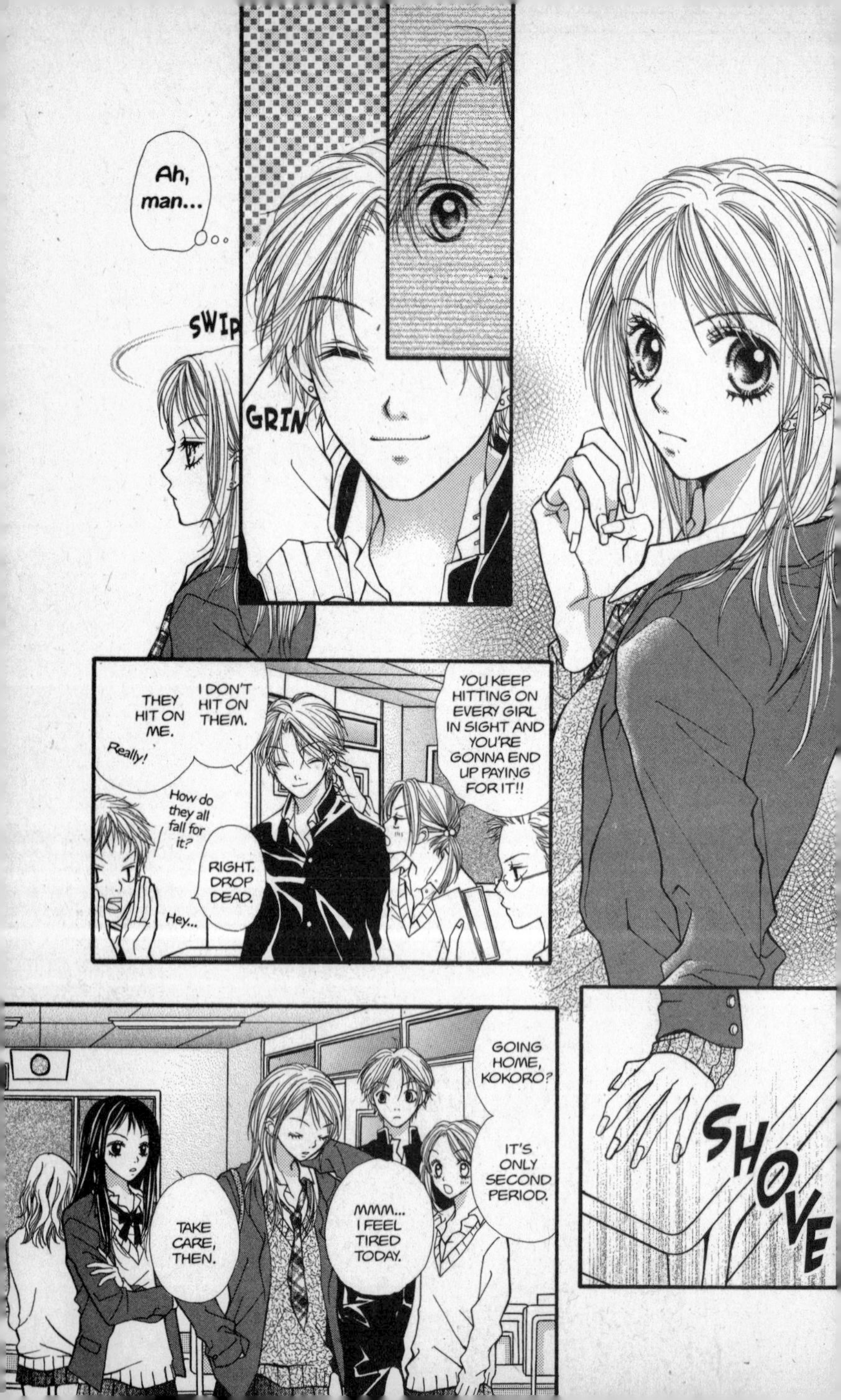
GRIN
SWIP
Ah, man...
YOU KEEP HITTING ON EVERY GIRL IN SIGHT AND YOU'RE GONNA END UP PAYING FOR IT!!
I DON'T HIT ON THEM.
THEY HIT ON ME.
Really!
How do they all fall for it?
RIGHT. DROP DEAD.
Hey...
SHOVE
GOING HOME, KOKORO?
IT'S ONLY SECOND PERIOD.
MMM... I FEEL TIRED TODAY.
TAKE CARE, THEN.

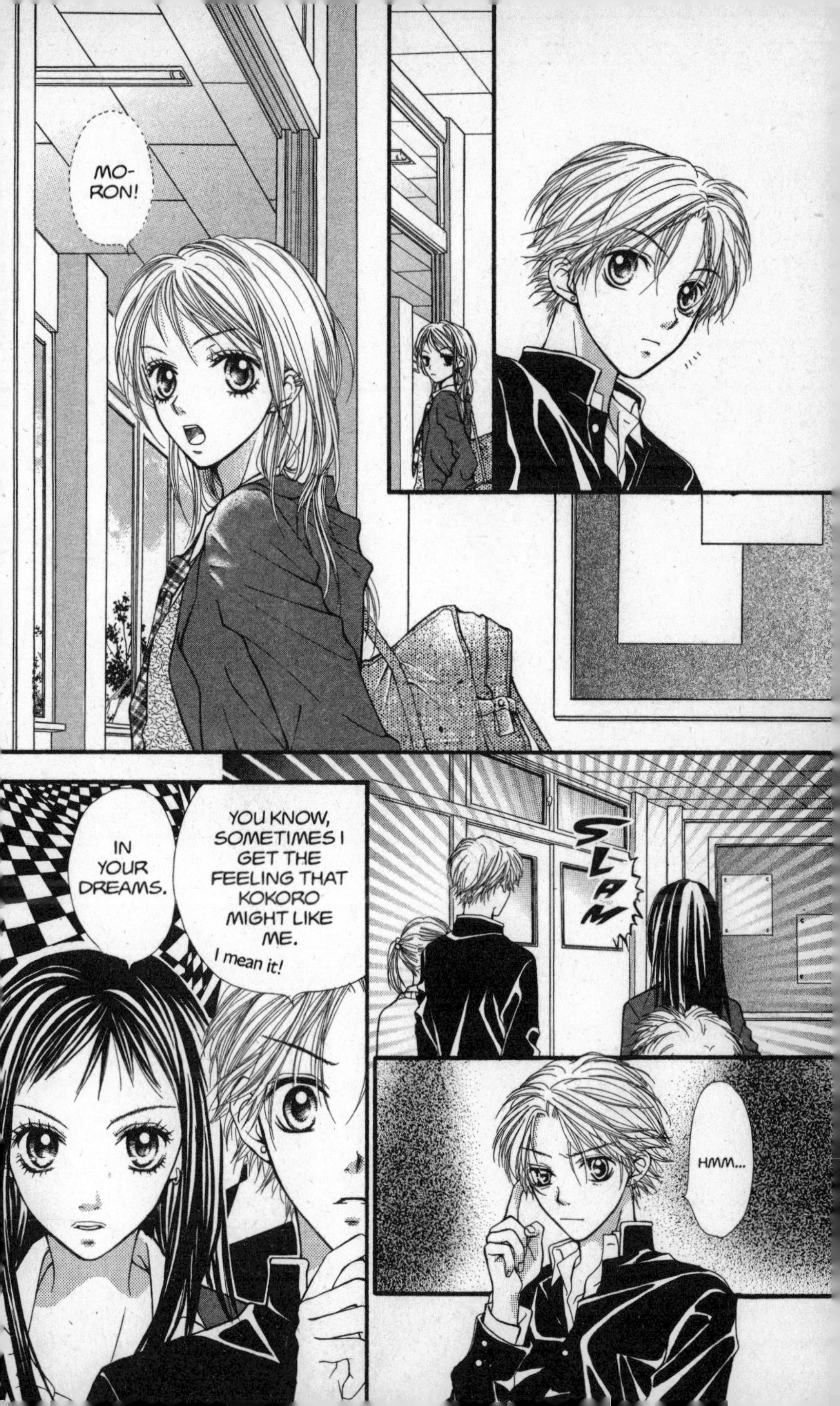
MO-RON!
SLAM
HMM...
YOU KNOW, SOMETIMES I GET THE FEELING THAT KOKORO MIGHT LIKE ME.
I mean it!
IN YOUR DREAMS.

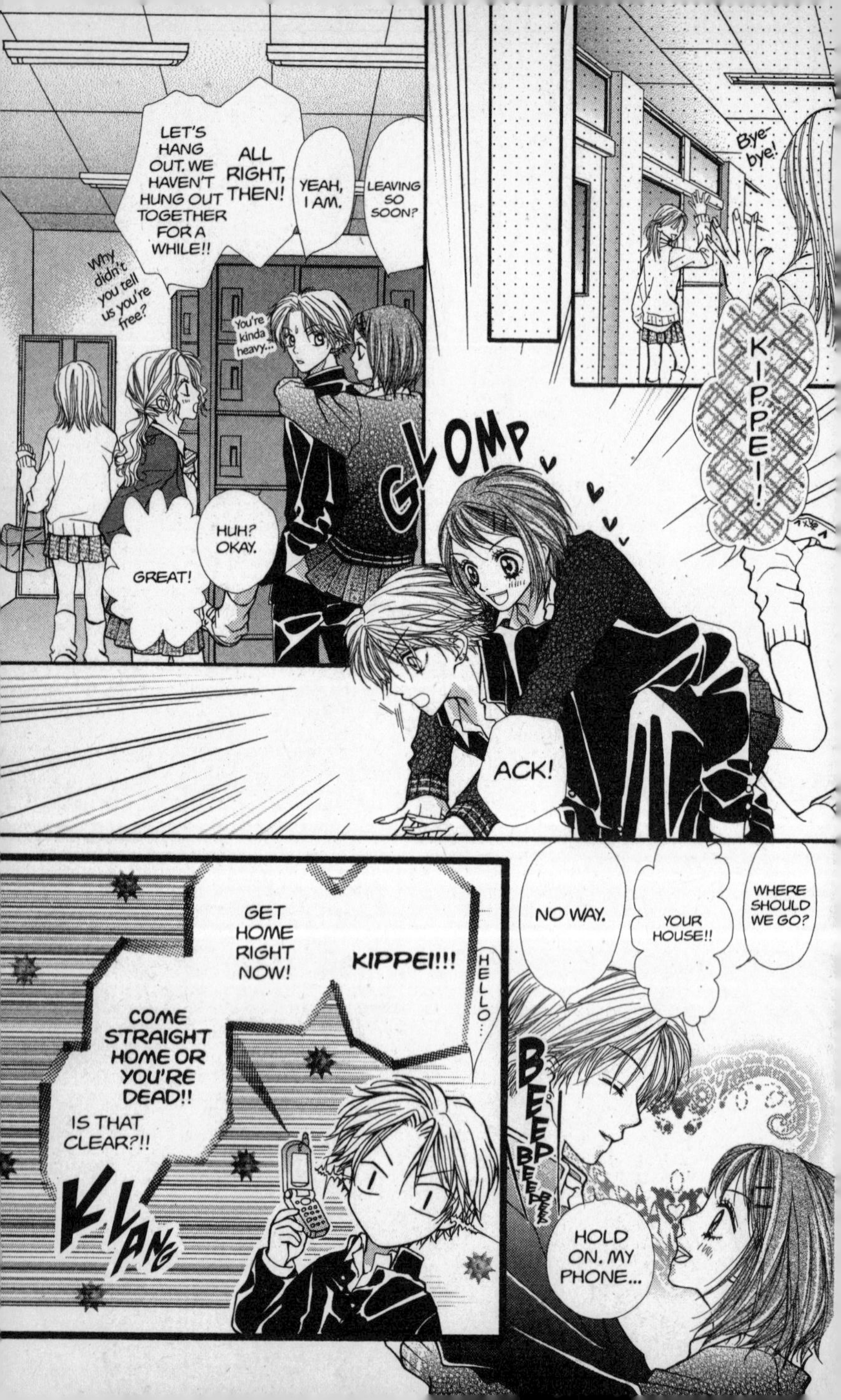
Bye-bye!
LEAVING SO SOON?
YEAH, I AM.
ALL RIGHT, THEN!
LET'S HANG OUT. WE HAVEN'T HUNG OUT TOGETHER FOR A WHILE!!
Why didn't you tell us you're free?
You're kinda heavy...
HUH? OKAY.
GREAT!
KIPPEI!!
GLOMP
ACK!
WHERE SHOULD WE GO?
YOUR HOUSE!!
NO WAY.
BEEP BEEP BEEP
HOLD ON. MY PHONE...
HELLO...
KIPPEI!!!
GET HOME RIGHT NOW!
COME STRAIGHT HOME OR YOU'RE DEAD!!
IS THAT CLEAR?!!
KLANG

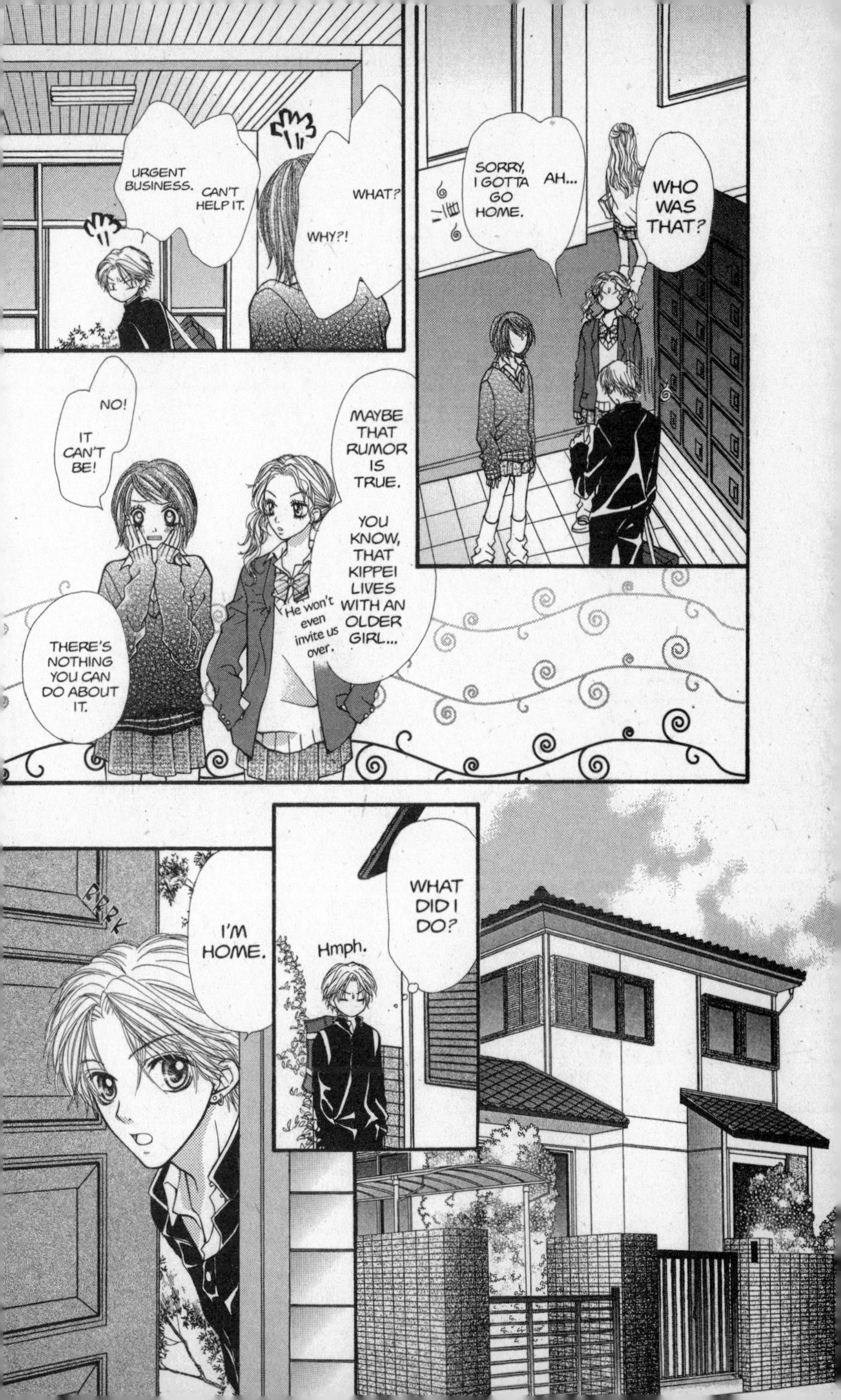

WHO WAS THAT?
AH...
SORRY, I GOTTA GO HOME.
WHAT?
WHY?!
URGENT BUSINESS.
CAN'T HELP IT.
MAYBE THAT RUMOR IS TRUE.
YOU KNOW, THAT KIPPEI LIVES WITH AN OLDER GIRL...
He won't even invite us over.
NO!
IT CAN'T BE!
THERE'S NOTHING YOU CAN DO ABOUT IT.
WHAT DID I DO?
Hmph.
BRRK
I'M HOME.

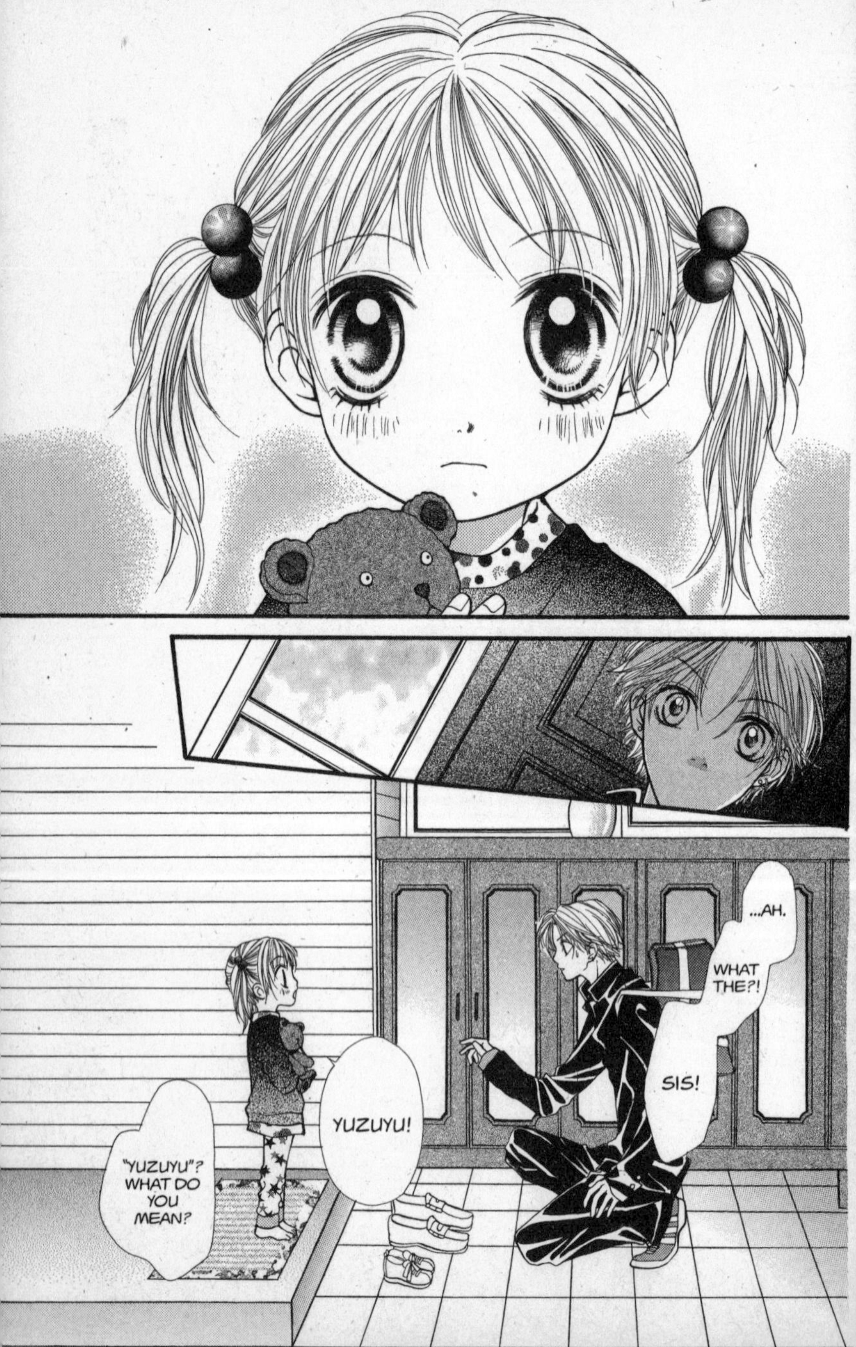
...AH. WHAT THE?! SIS!
YUZUYU!
"YUZUYU"? WHAT DO YOU MEAN?

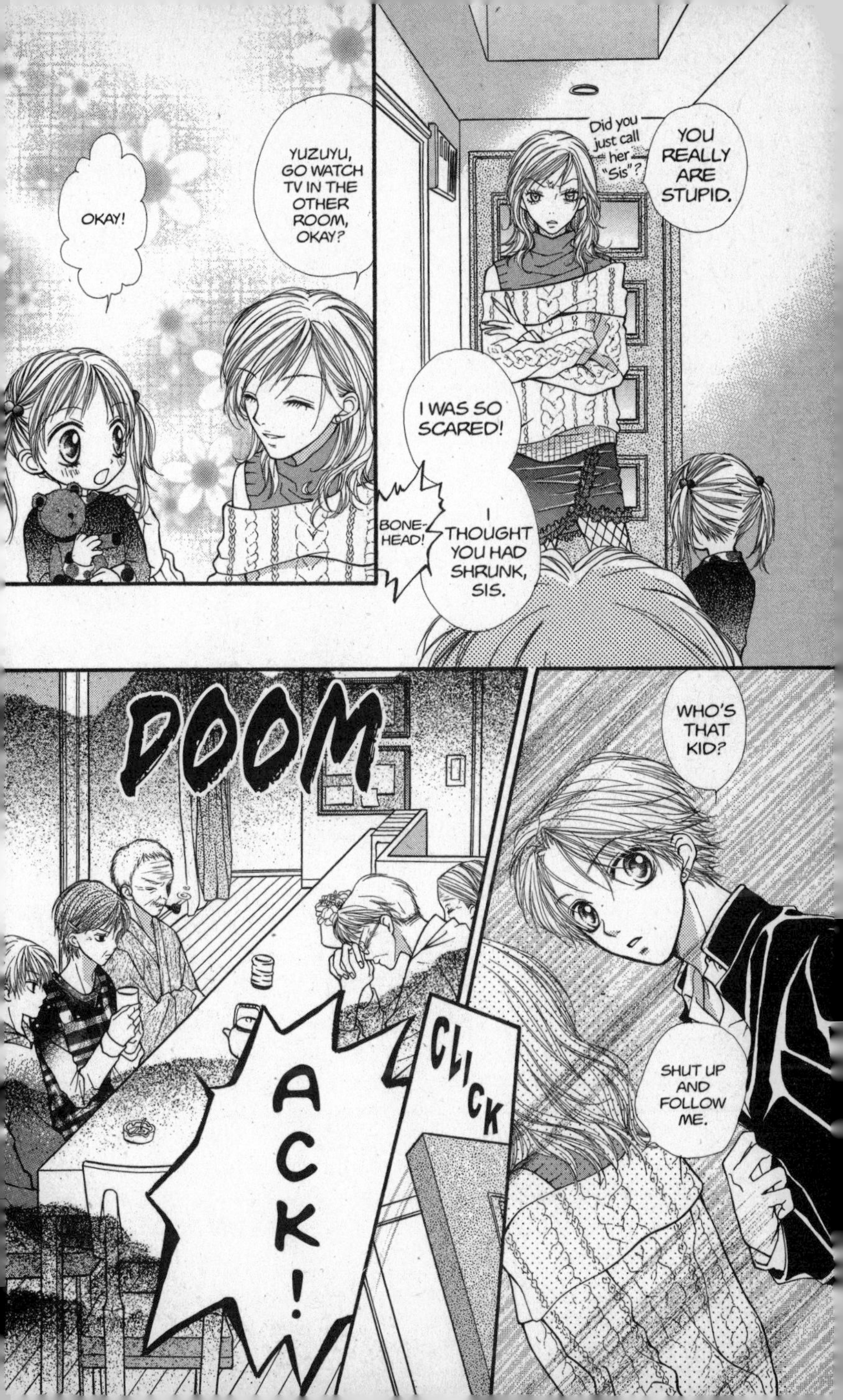
YOU REALLY ARE STUPID.
Did you just call her "Sis"?
I WAS SO SCARED!
I THOUGHT YOU HAD SHRUNK, SIS.
BONE-HEAD!
YUZUYU, GO WATCH TV IN THE OTHER ROOM, OKAY?
OKAY!
WHO'S THAT KID?
SHUT UP AND FOLLOW ME.
CLICK
DOOM
ACK!

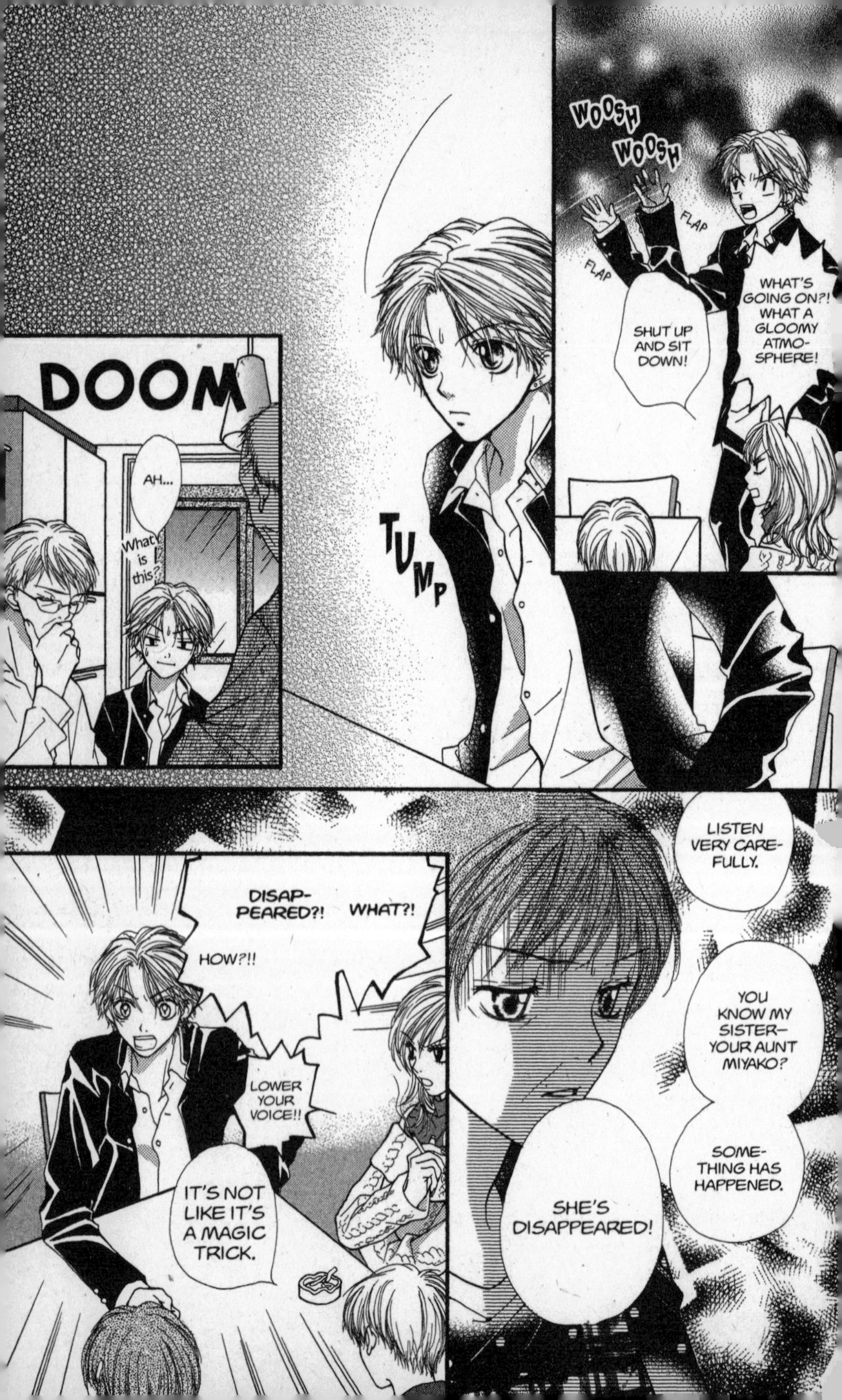
WOOSH
WOOSH
FLAP
FLAP
WHAT'S GOING ON?! WHAT A GLOOMY ATMO-SPHERE!
SHUT UP AND SIT DOWN!
TUMP
DOOM
AH...
What is this?
LISTEN VERY CARE-FULLY.
YOU KNOW MY SISTER—YOUR AUNT MIYAKO?
SOME-THING HAS HAPPENED.
SHE'S DISAPPEARED!
WHAT?!
DISAP-PEARED?!
HOW?!!
LOWER YOUR VOICE!!
IT'S NOT LIKE IT'S A MAGIC TRICK.

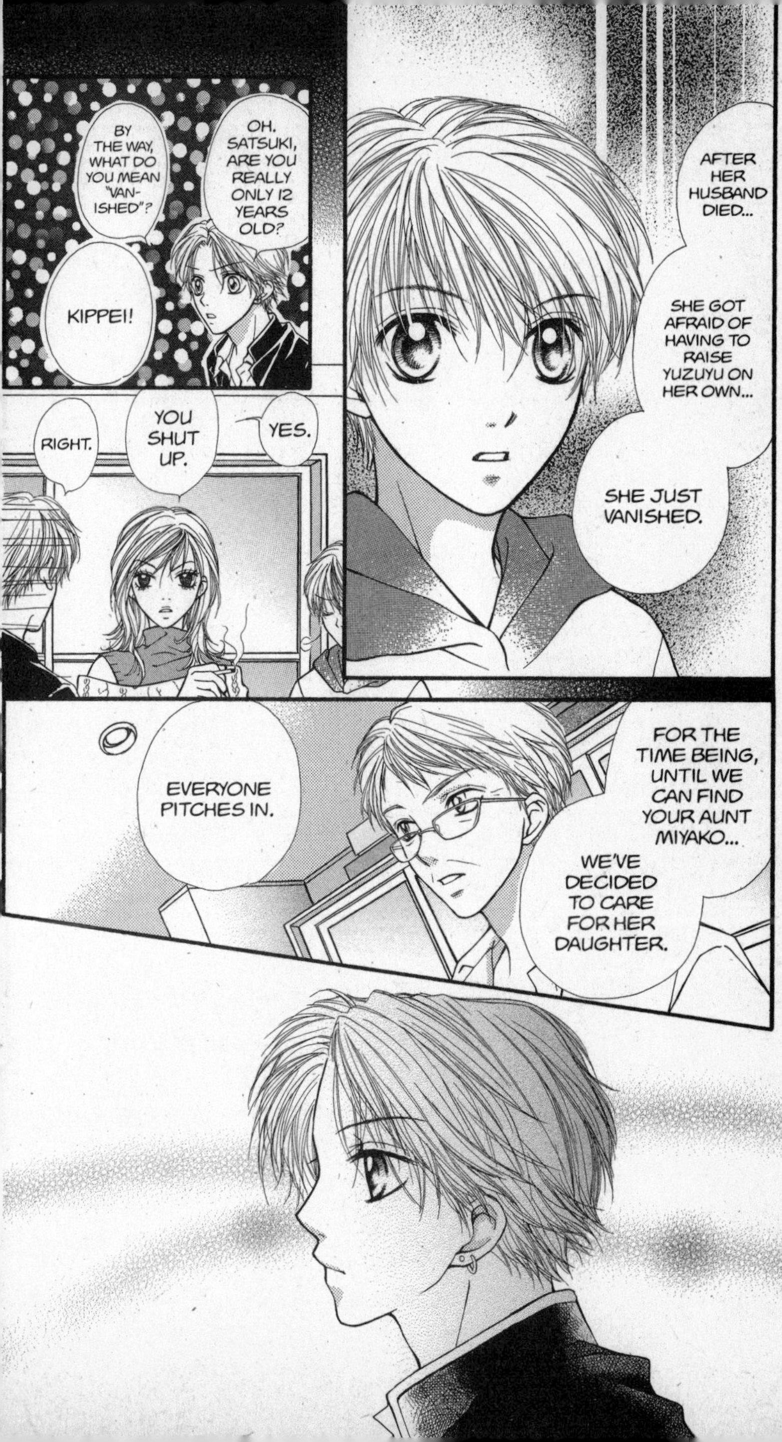
AFTER HER HUSBAND DIED...
SHE GOT AFRAID OF HAVING TO RAISE YUZUYU ON HER OWN...
SHE JUST VANISHED.
OH. SATSUKI, ARE YOU REALLY ONLY 12 YEARS OLD?
BY THE WAY, WHAT DO YOU MEAN "VAN-ISHED"?
KIPPEI!
YES.
YOU SHUT UP.
RIGHT.
FOR THE TIME BEING, UNTIL WE CAN FIND YOUR AUNT MIYAKO...
WE'VE DECIDED TO CARE FOR HER DAUGHTER.
EVERYONE PITCHES IN.

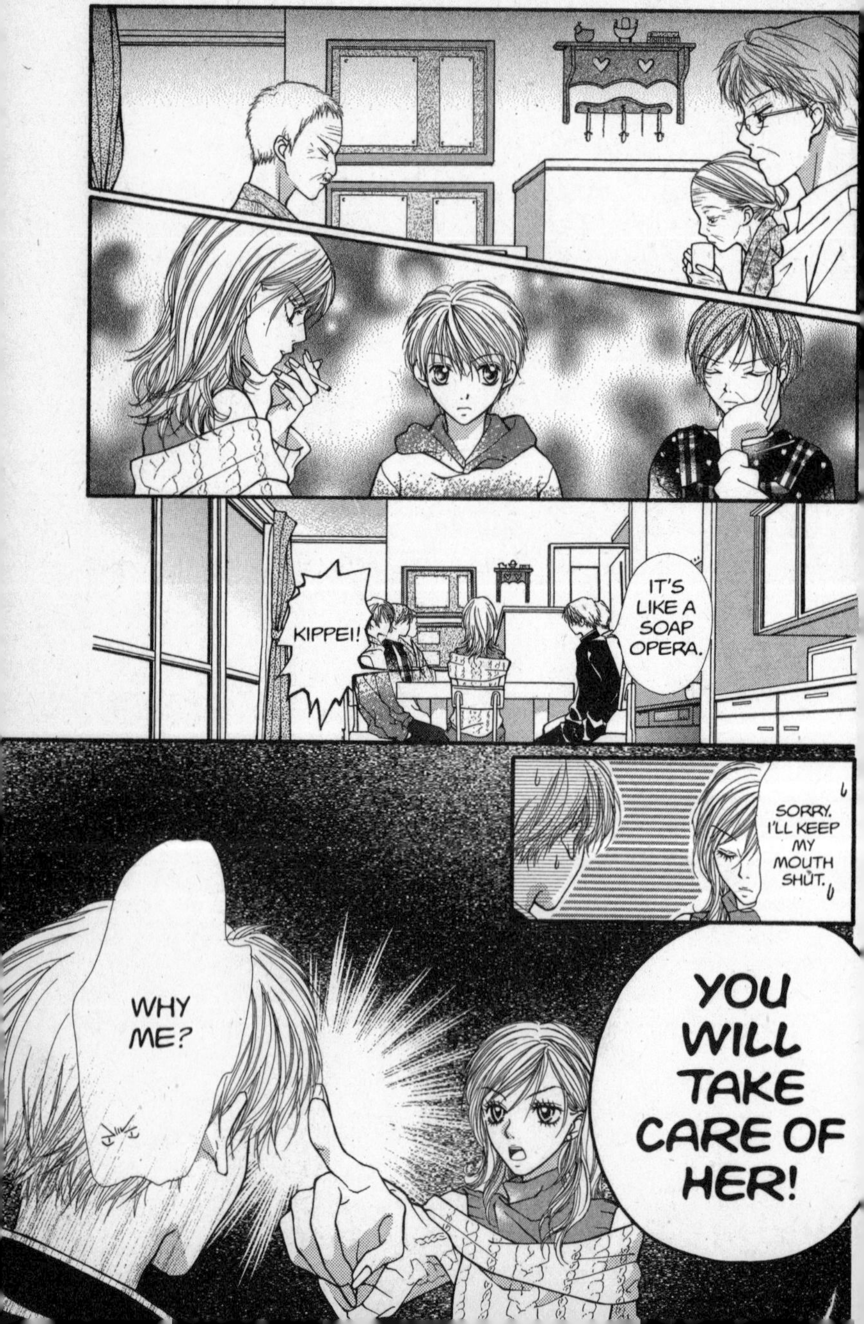
IT'S LIKE A SOAP OPERA.
KIPPEI!
SORRY. I'LL KEEP MY MOUTH SHUT.
YOU WILL TAKE CARE OF HER!
WHY ME?

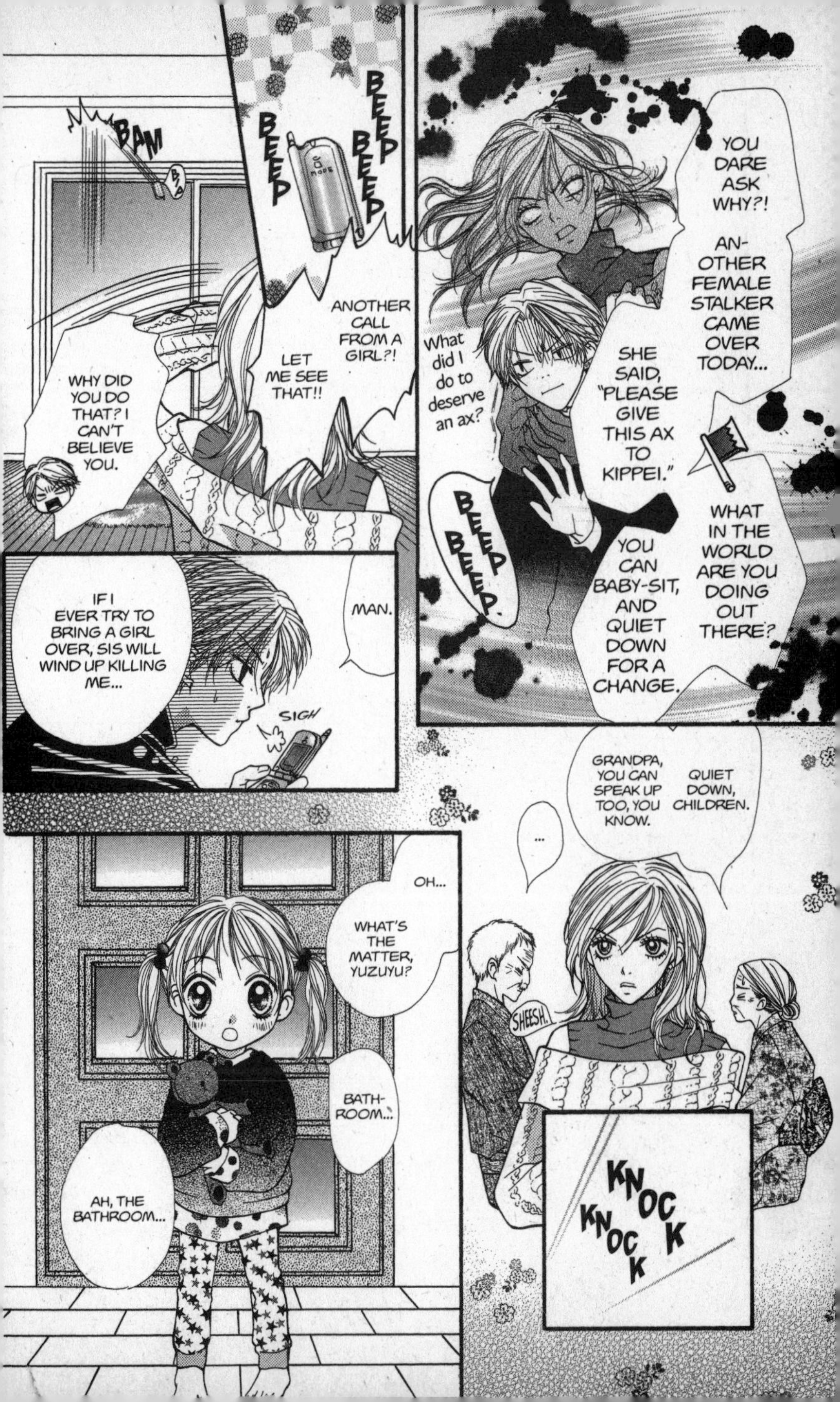
YOU DARE ASK WHY?!
AN-OTHER FEMALE STALKER CAME OVER TODAY...
SHE SAID, "PLEASE GIVE THIS AX TO KIPPEI."
What did I do to deserve an ax?
WHAT IN THE WORLD ARE YOU DOING OUT THERE?
YOU CAN BABY-SIT, AND QUIET DOWN FOR A CHANGE.
BEEP BEEP
BEEP BEEP BEEP BEEP
ANOTHER CALL FROM A GIRL?!
LET ME SEE THAT!!
BAM
WHY DID YOU DO THAT? I CAN'T BELIEVE YOU.
MAN.
IF I EVER TRY TO BRING A GIRL OVER, SIS WILL WIND UP KILLING ME...
SIGH
QUIET DOWN, CHILDREN.
GRANDPA, YOU CAN SPEAK UP TOO, YOU KNOW.
...
SHEESH.
KNOCK KNOCK
OH...
WHAT'S THE MATTER, YUZUYU?
BATH-ROOM...
AH, THE BATHROOM...

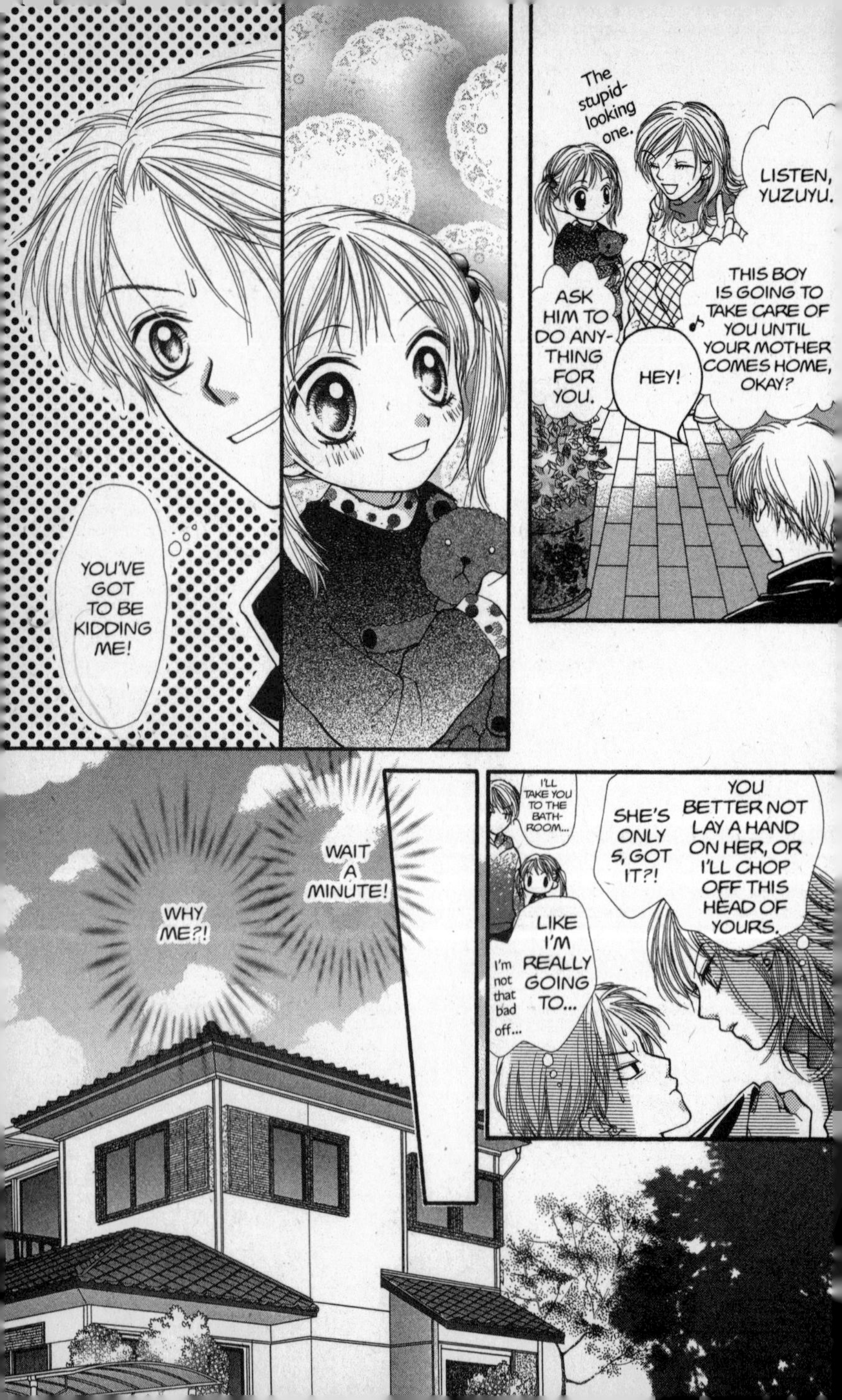
LISTEN, YUZUYU.
The stupid-looking one.
THIS BOY IS GOING TO TAKE CARE OF YOU UNTIL YOUR MOTHER COMES HOME, OKAY?
HEY!
ASK HIM TO DO ANY-THING FOR YOU.
YOU'VE GOT TO BE KIDDING ME!
YOU BETTER NOT LAY A HAND ON HER, OR I'LL CHOP OFF THIS HEAD OF YOURS.
SHE'S ONLY 5, GOT IT?!
I'LL TAKE YOU TO THE BATH-ROOM...
LIKE I'M REALLY GOING TO...
I'm not that bad off...
WAIT A MINUTE!
WHY ME?!

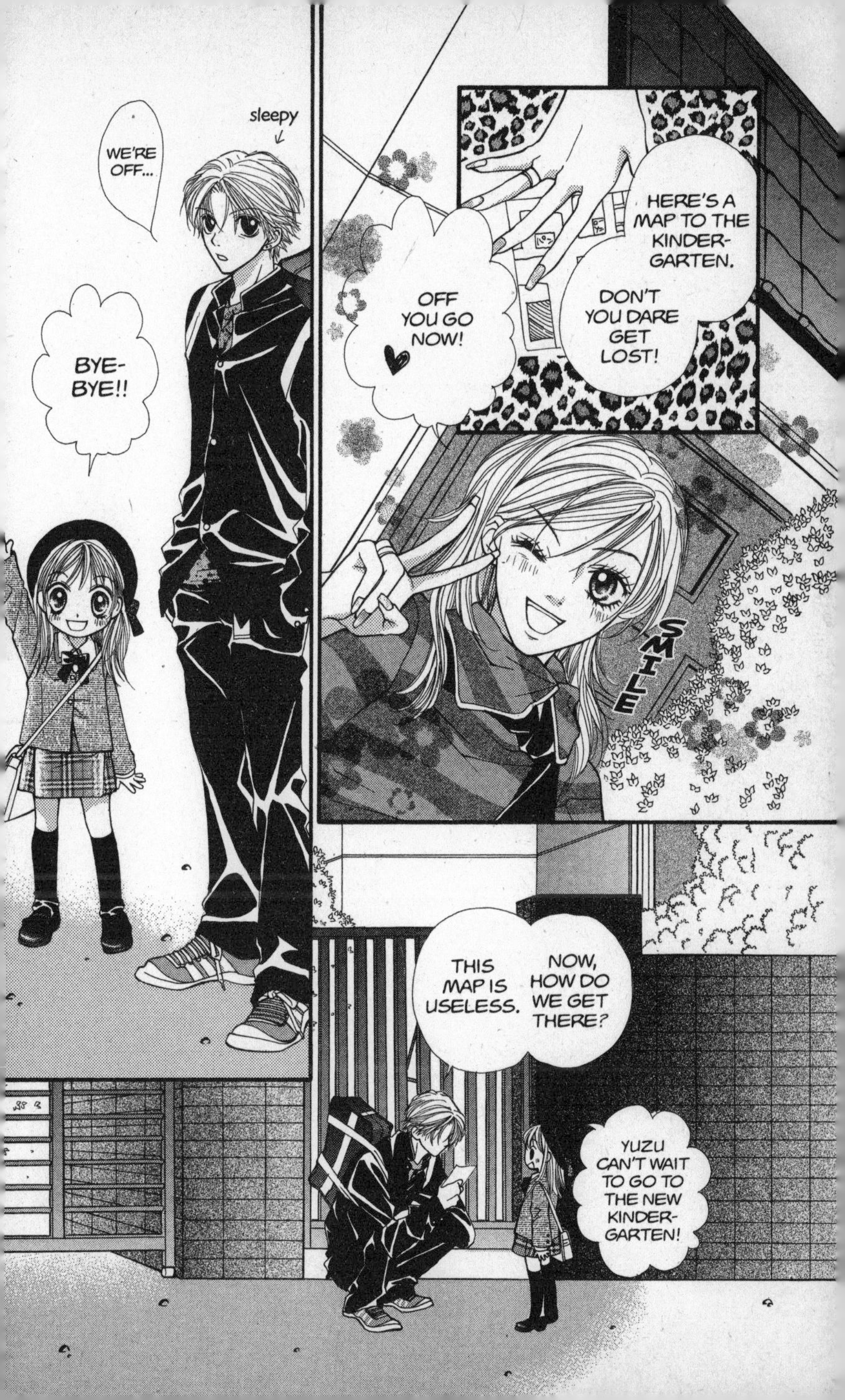
HERE'S A MAP TO THE KINDER-GARTEN.
DON'T YOU DARE GET LOST!
OFF YOU GO NOW!
SMILE
sleepy
WE'RE OFF...
BYE-BYE!!
NOW, HOW DO WE GET THERE?
THIS MAP IS USELESS.
YUZU CAN'T WAIT TO GO TO THE NEW KINDER-GARTEN!

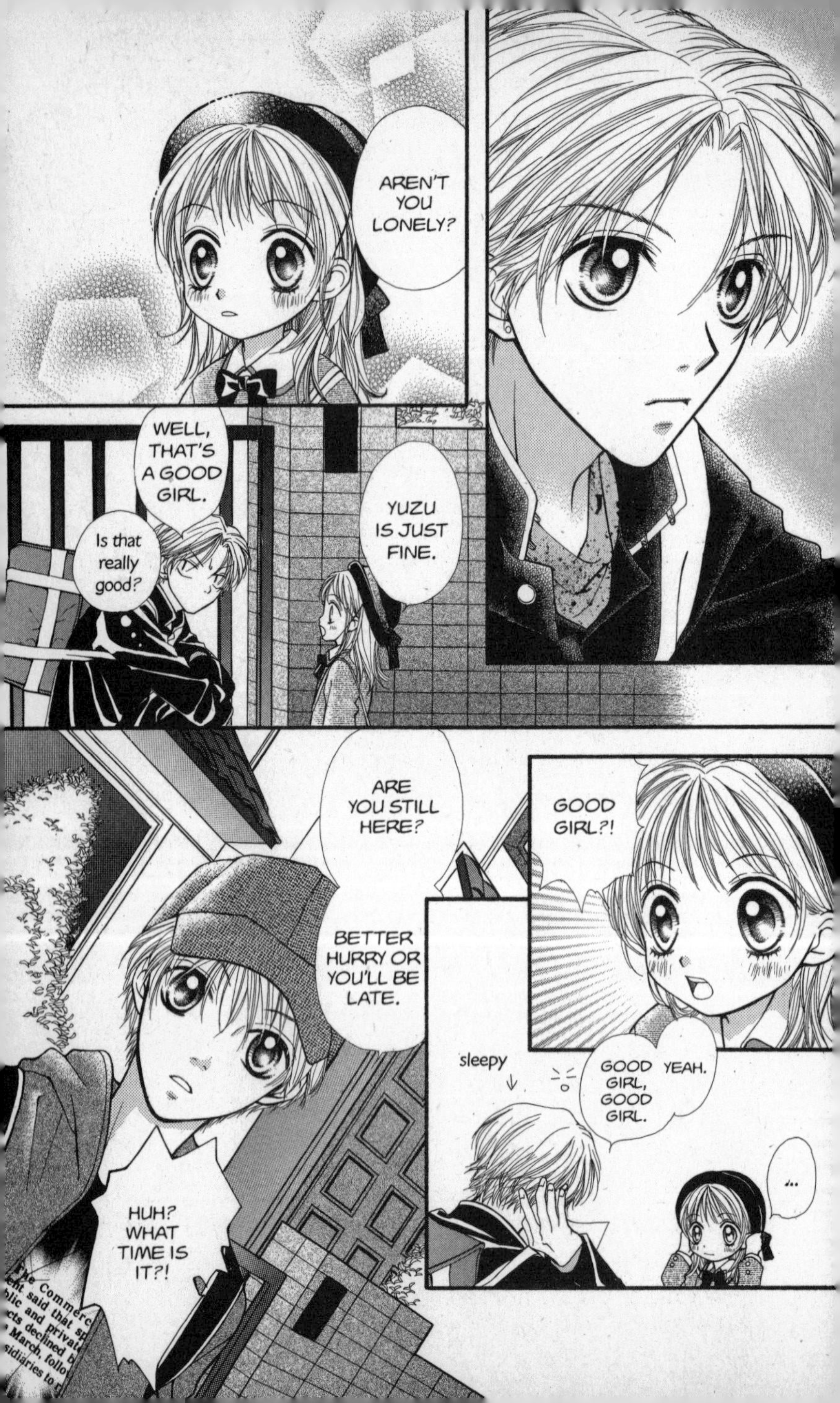

AREN'T YOU LONELY?
YUZU IS JUST FINE.
WELL, THAT'S A GOOD GIRL.
Is that really good?
GOOD GIRL?!
YEAH.
GOOD GIRL, GOOD GIRL.
sleepy
...
ARE YOU STILL HERE?
BETTER HURRY OR YOU'LL BE LATE.
HUH? WHAT TIME IS IT?!

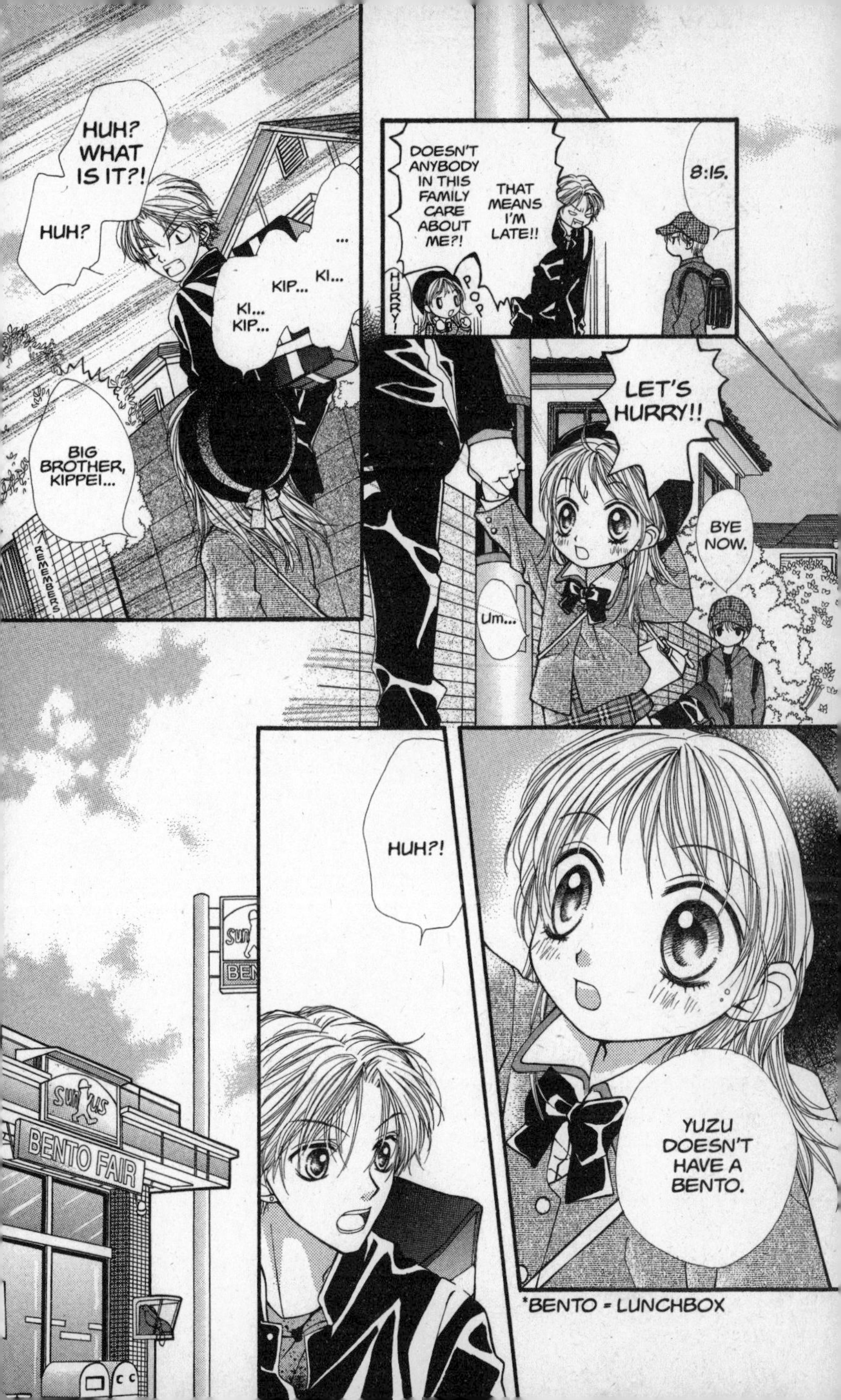
8:15.
THAT MEANS I'M LATE!!
DOESN'T ANYBODY IN THIS FAMILY CARE ABOUT ME?!
POP
HURRY!
LET'S HURRY!!
BYE NOW.
Um...
...
KI... KIP...
KIP... KI...
HUH? WHAT IS IT?!
HUH?
BIG BROTHER, KIPPEI...
REMEMBERS
YUZU DOESN'T HAVE A BENTO.
*BENTO = LUNCHBOX
HUH?!
BENTO FAIR

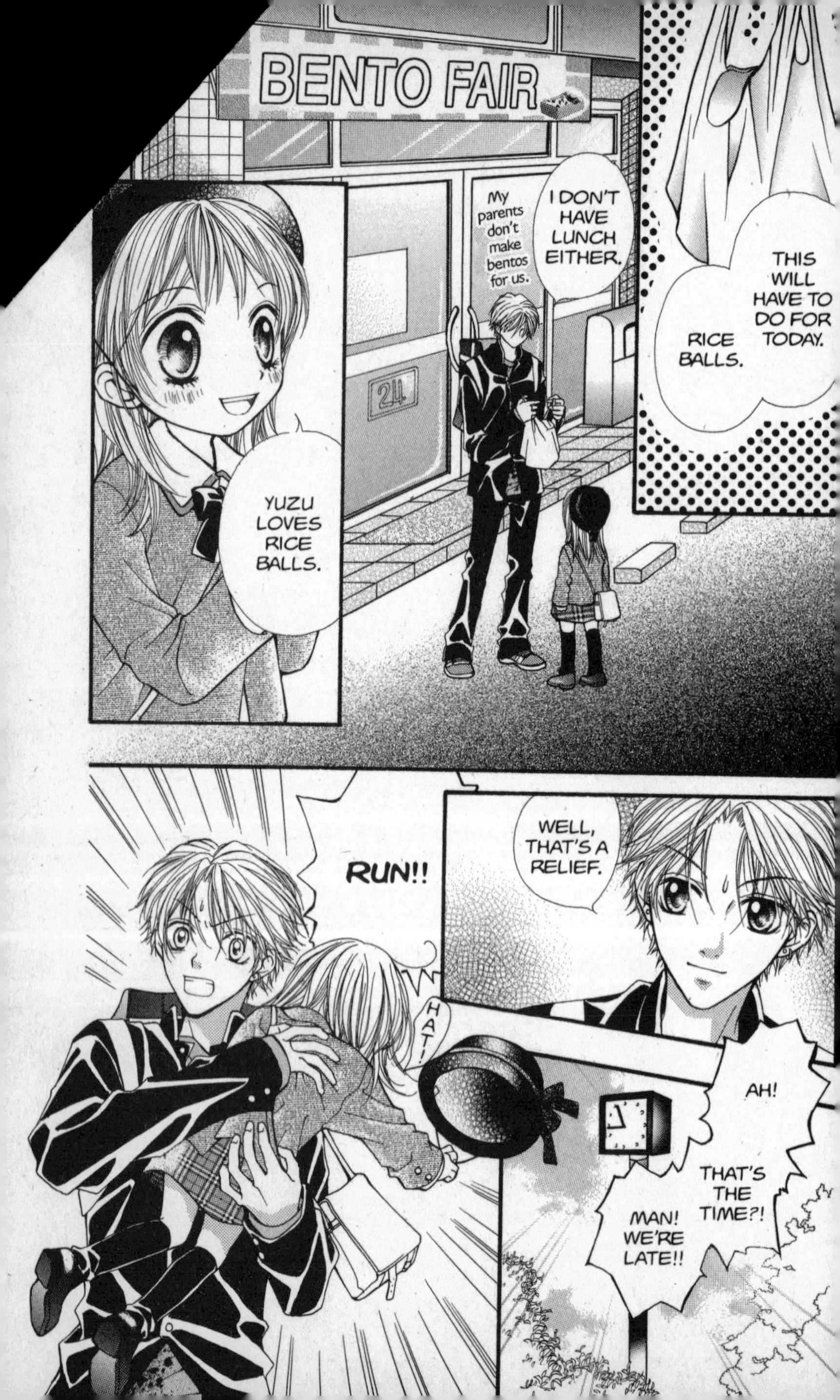
RICE BALLS.
THIS WILL HAVE TO DO FOR TODAY.
BENTO FAIR
I DON'T HAVE LUNCH EITHER.
My parents don't make bentos for us.
24
YUZU LOVES RICE BALLS.
WELL, THAT'S A RELIEF.
AH!
THAT'S THE TIME?!
MAN! WE'RE LATE!!
RUN!!
HAT!

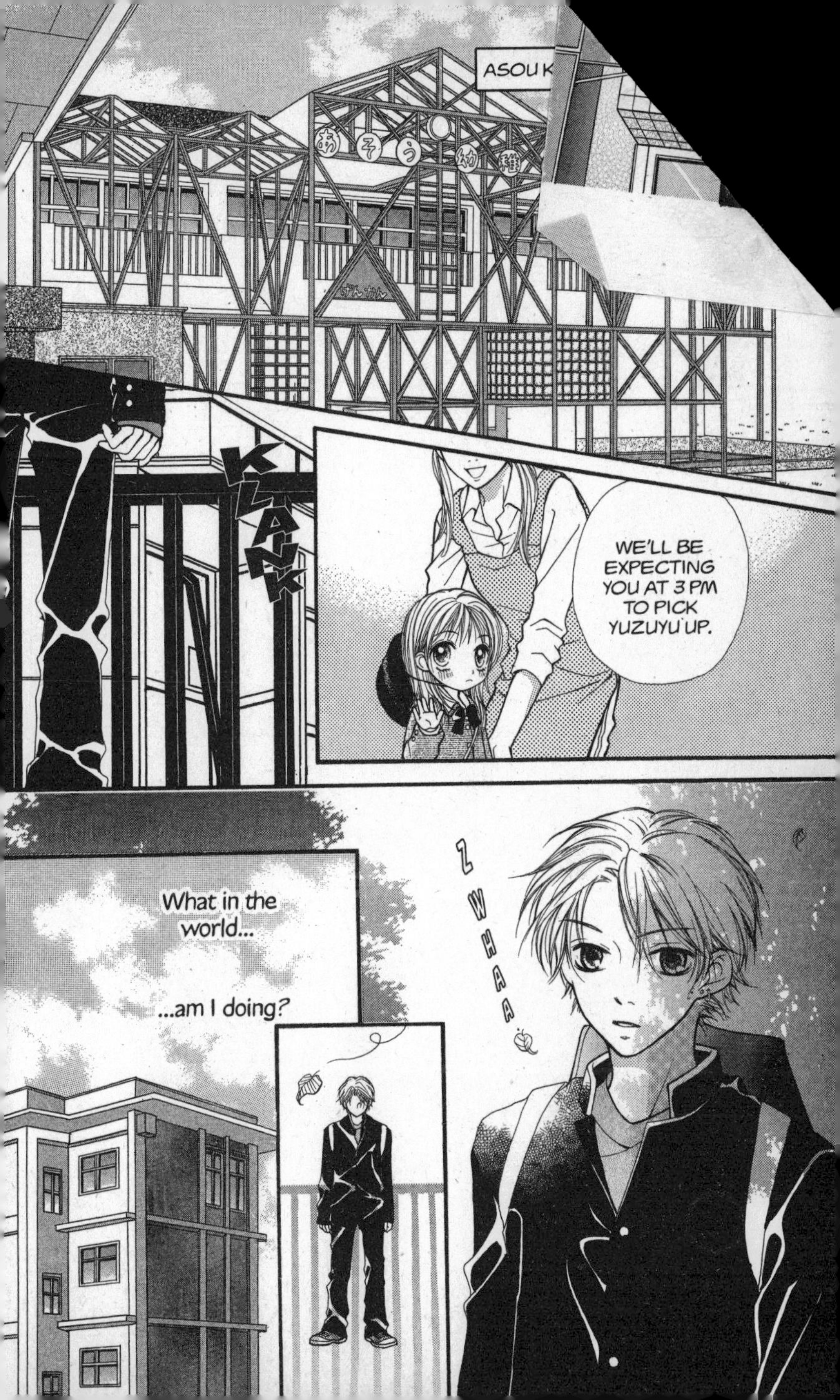

ASOU K
あそう幼稚
WE'LL BE EXPECTING YOU AT 3 PM TO PICK YUZUYU UP.
KLANK
ZWHAAA
What in the world...
...am I doing?

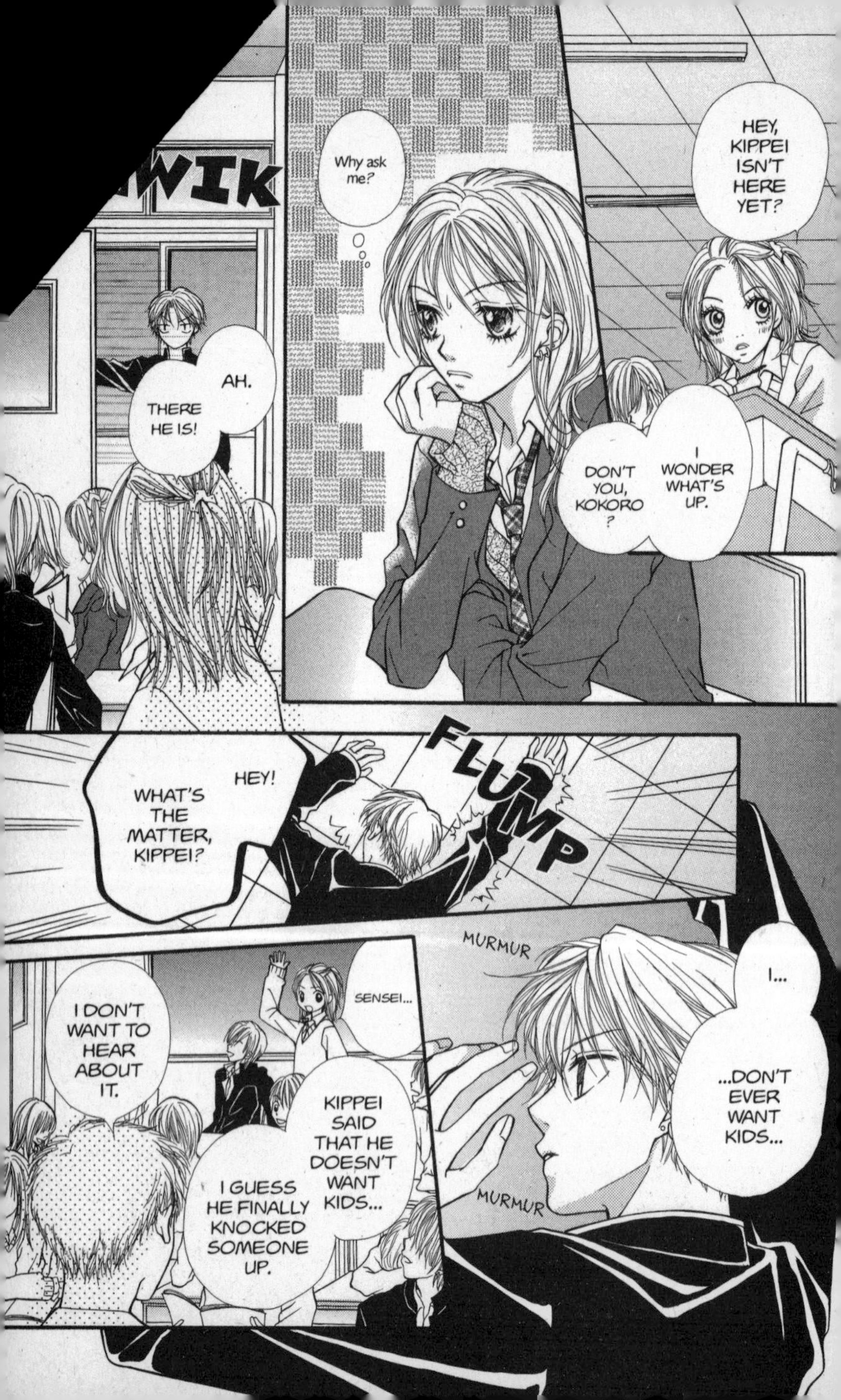
HEY, KIPPEI ISN'T HERE YET?
I WONDER WHAT'S UP.
DON'T YOU, KOKORO?
Why ask me?
WIK
AH.
THERE HE IS!
FLUMP
HEY!
WHAT'S THE MATTER, KIPPEI?
MURMUR
I...
...DON'T EVER WANT KIDS...
MURMUR
SENSEI...
KIPPEI SAID THAT HE DOESN'T WANT KIDS...
I GUESS HE FINALLY KNOCKED SOMEONE UP.
I DON'T WANT TO HEAR ABOUT IT.

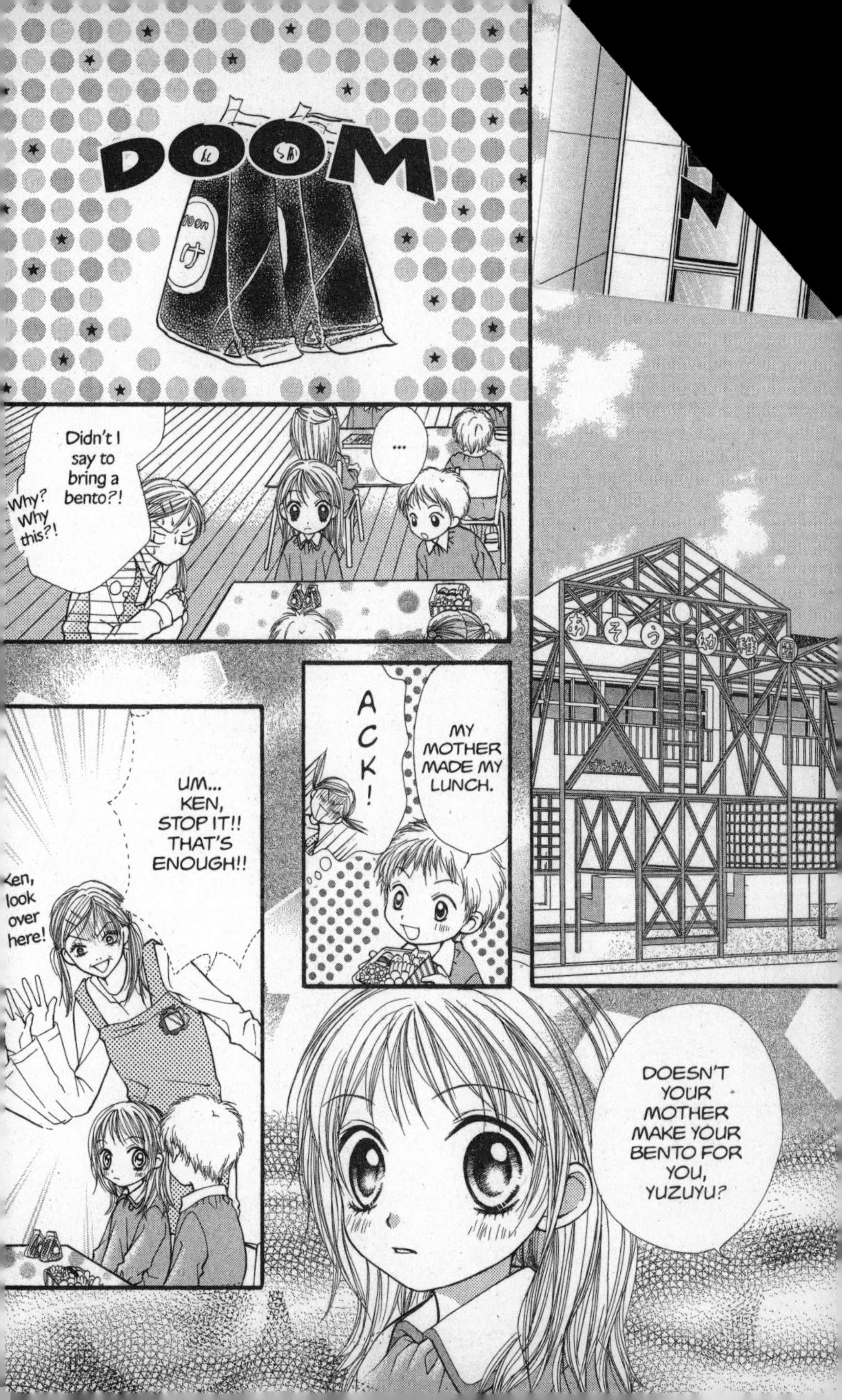

あそう幼稚園
DOOM
Didn't I say to bring a bento?!
Why? Why this?!
...
MY MOTHER MADE MY LUNCH.
ACK!
DOESN'T YOUR MOTHER MAKE YOUR BENTO FOR YOU, YUZUYU?
UM... KEN, STOP IT!! THAT'S ENOUGH!!
Ken, look over here!

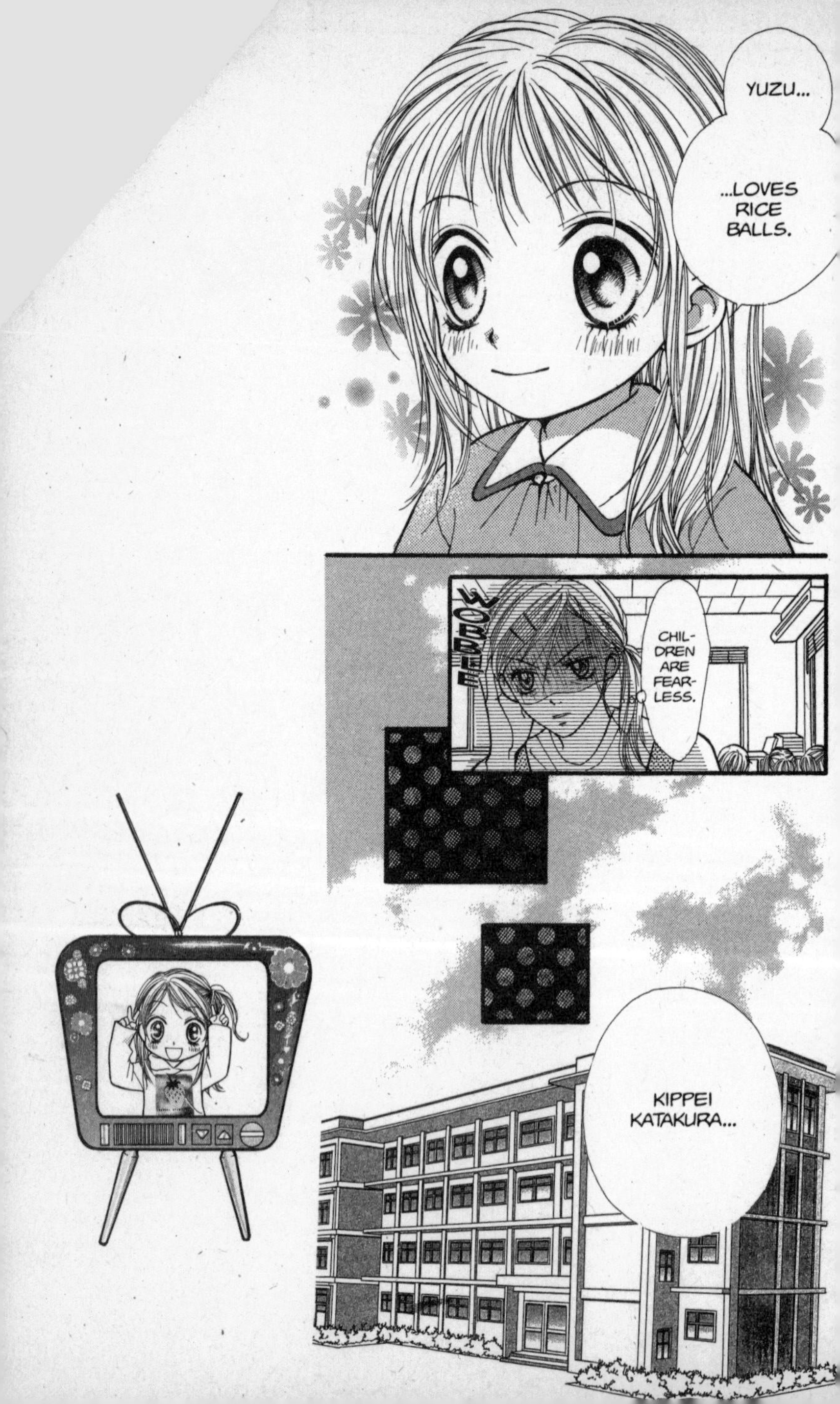
YUZU...
...LOVES RICE BALLS.
WOBBLE
CHIL-DREN ARE FEAR-LESS.
KIPPEI KATAKURA...

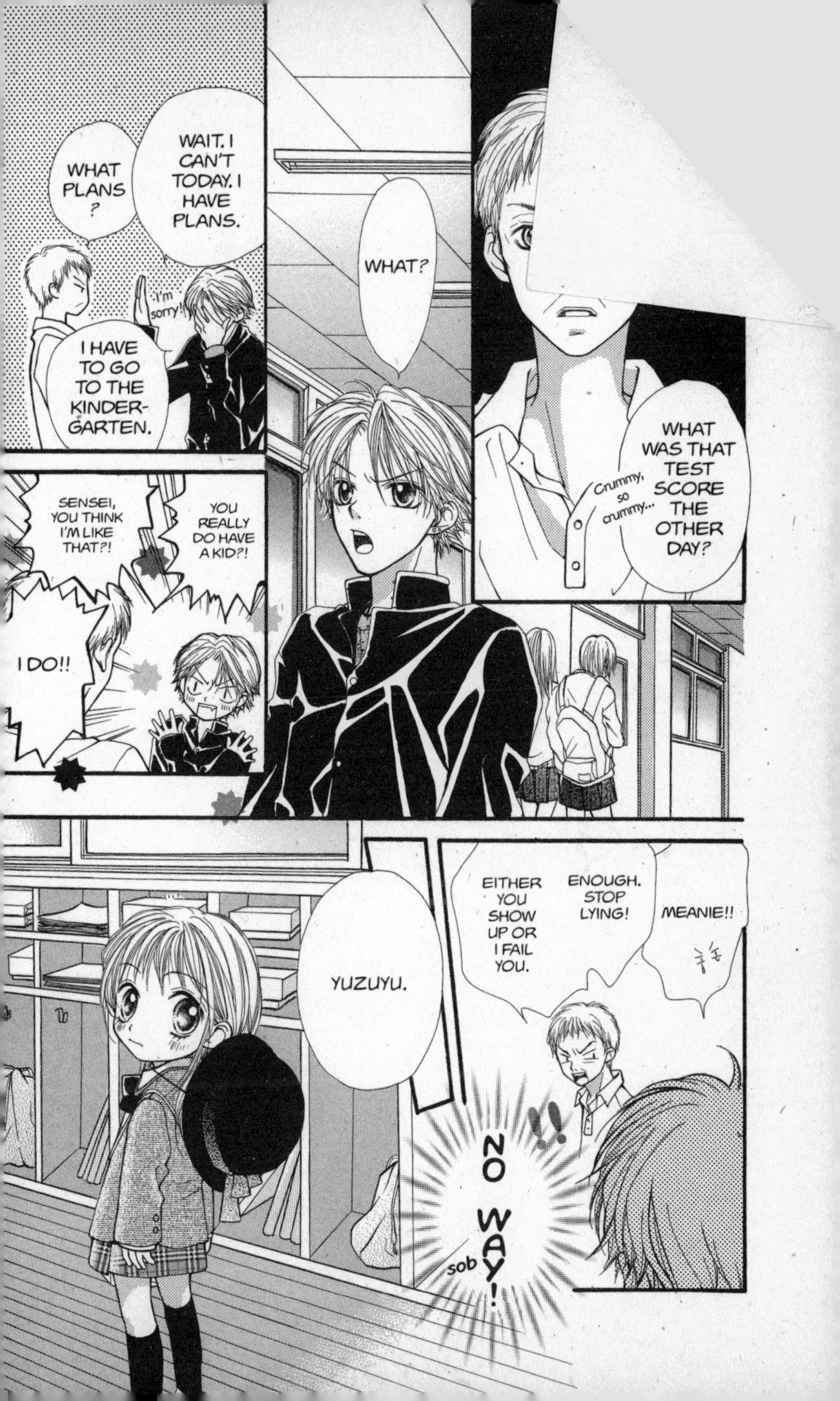

WHAT WAS THAT TEST SCORE THE OTHER DAY?
Crummy, so crummy...
WHAT?
WAIT. I CAN'T TODAY. I HAVE PLANS.
WHAT PLANS?
I'm sorry!
I HAVE TO GO TO THE KINDER-GARTEN.
YOU REALLY DO HAVE A KID?!
SENSEI, YOU THINK I'M LIKE THAT?!
I DO!!
MEANIE!!
ENOUGH. STOP LYING!
EITHER YOU SHOW UP OR I FAIL YOU.
NO WAY!
sob
YUZUYU.

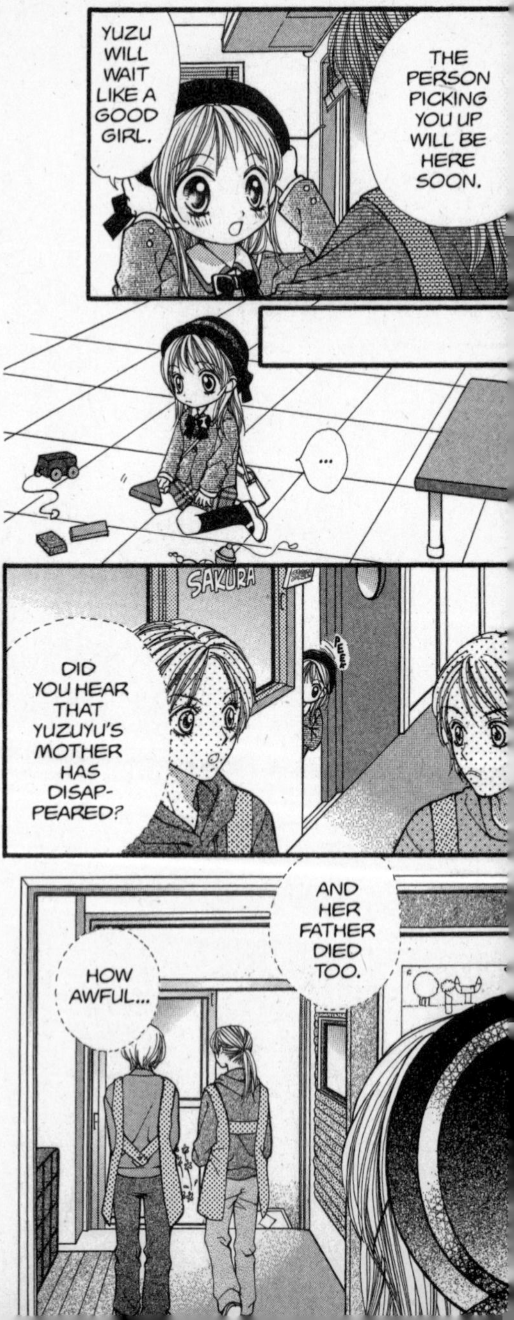
THE PERSON PICKING YOU UP WILL BE HERE SOON.
YUZU WILL WAIT LIKE A GOOD GIRL.
...
SAKURA
PEEK
DID YOU HEAR THAT YUZUYU'S MOTHER HAS DISAP-PEARED?
AND HER FATHER DIED TOO.
HOW AWFUL...

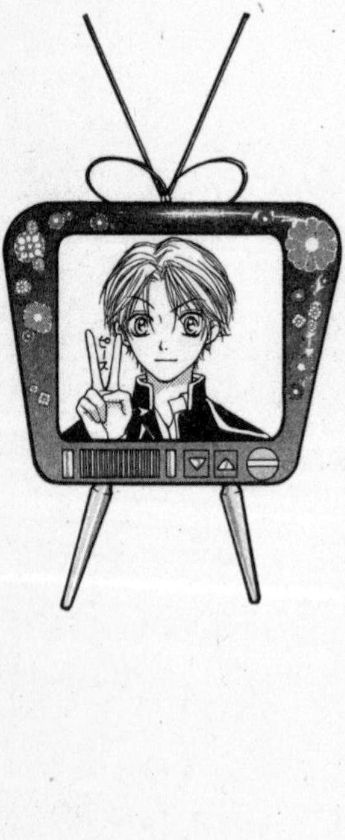

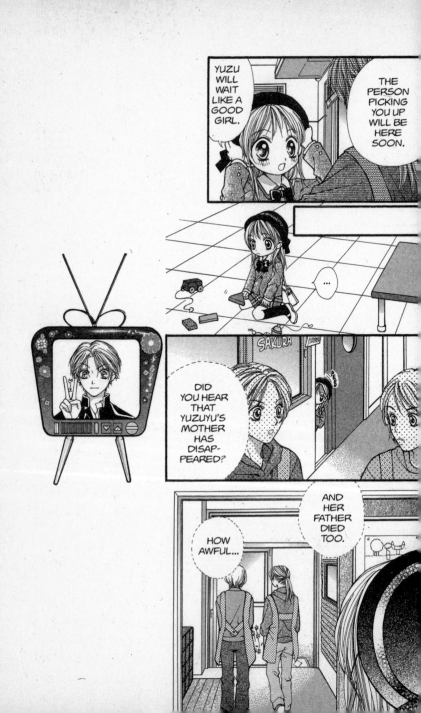

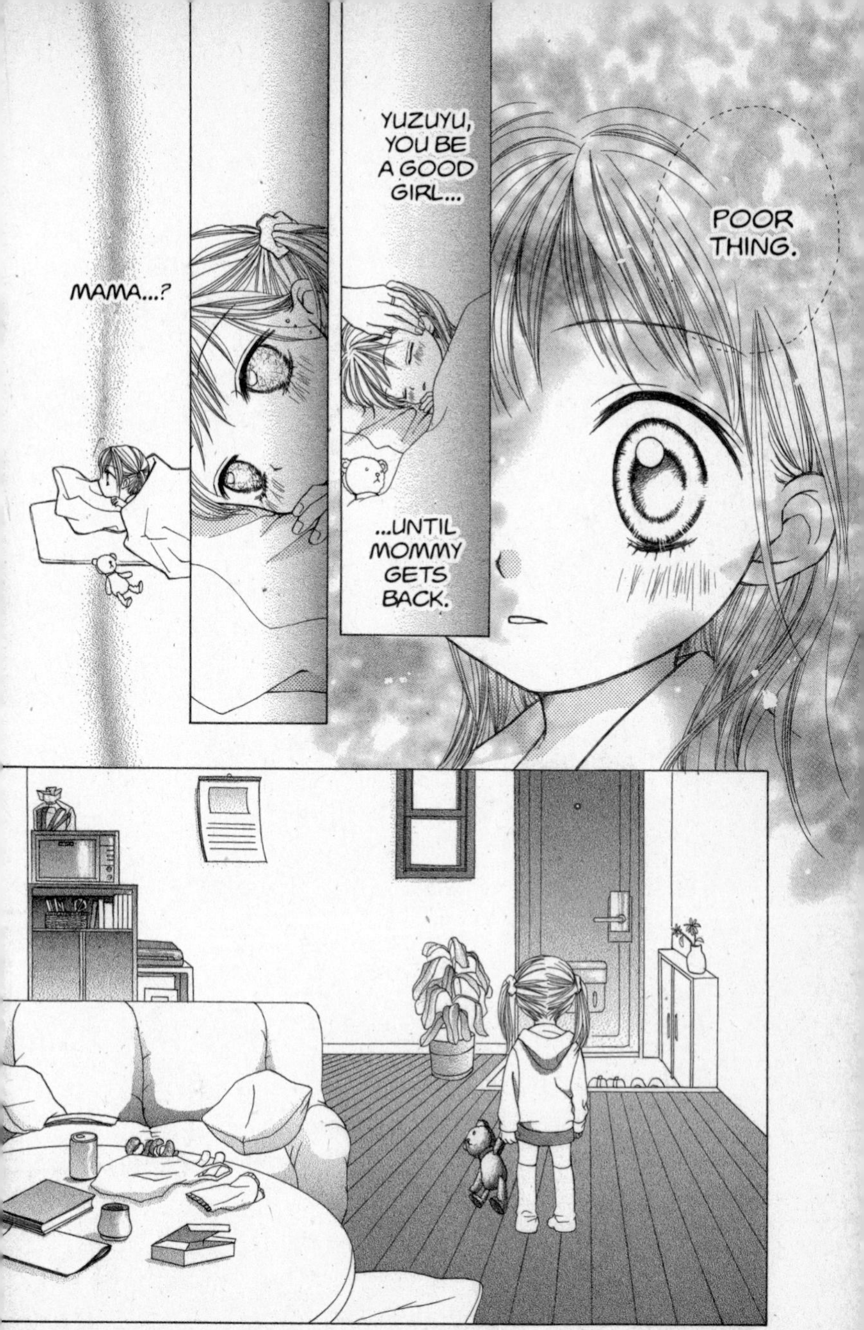
POOR THING.
YUZUYU, YOU BE A GOOD GIRL...
...UNTIL MOMMY GETS BACK.
MAMA...?

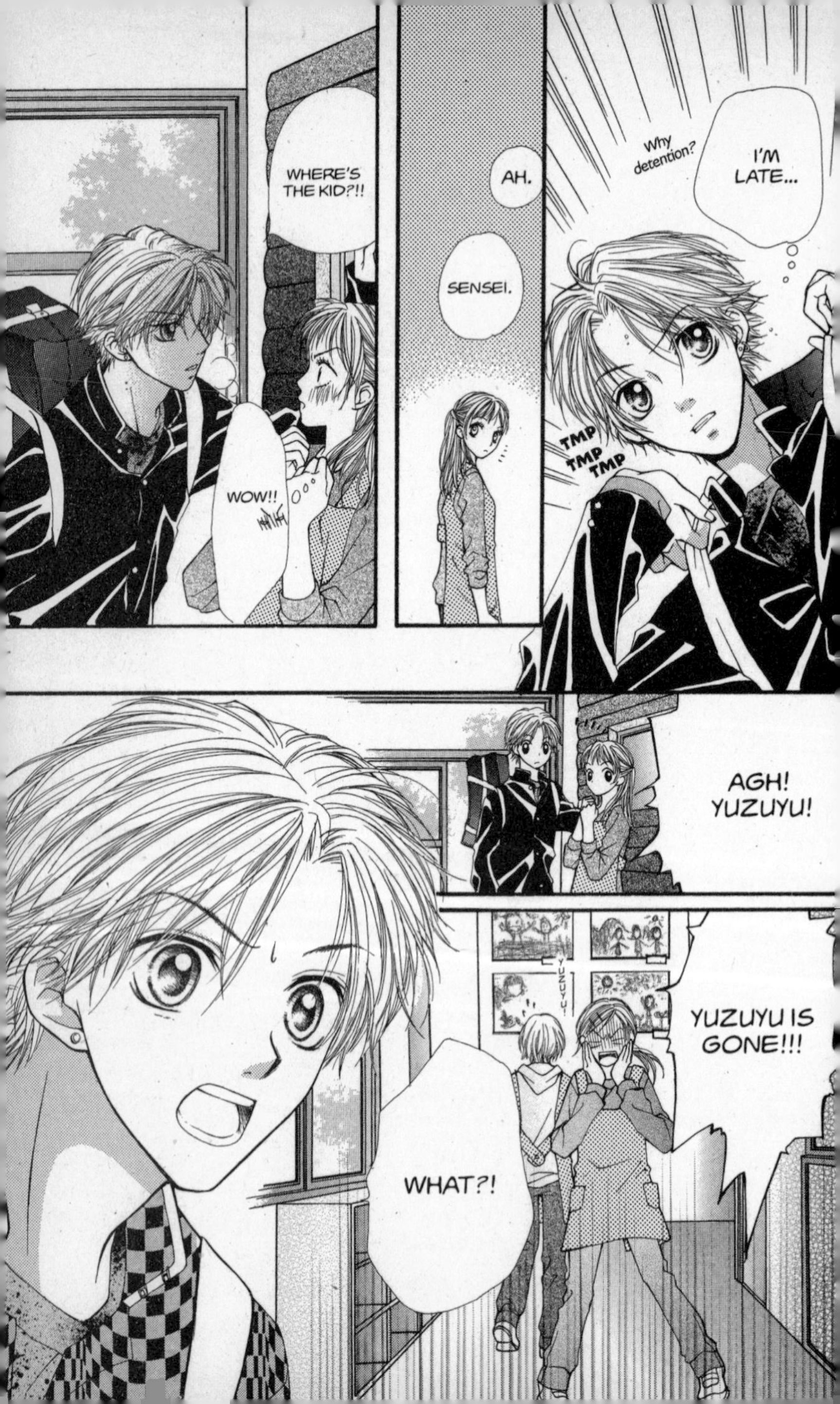
I'M LATE...
Why detention?
TMP TMP TMP
AH.
SENSEI.
WHERE'S THE KID?!!
WOW!!
AGH! YUZUYU!
YUZUYU IS GONE!!!
YUZUYU!
WHAT?!

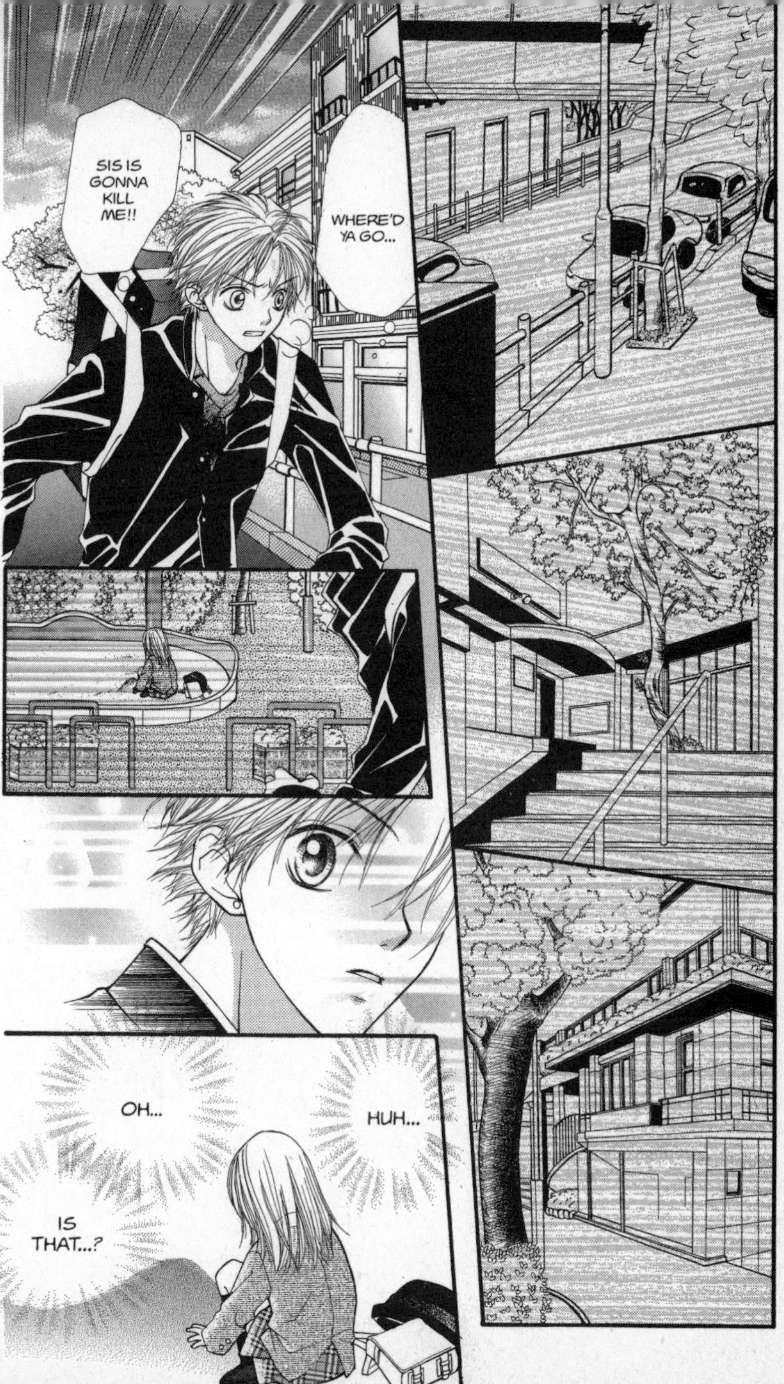
WHERE'D YA GO...
SIS IS GONNA KILL ME!!
HUH...
OH...
IS THAT...?

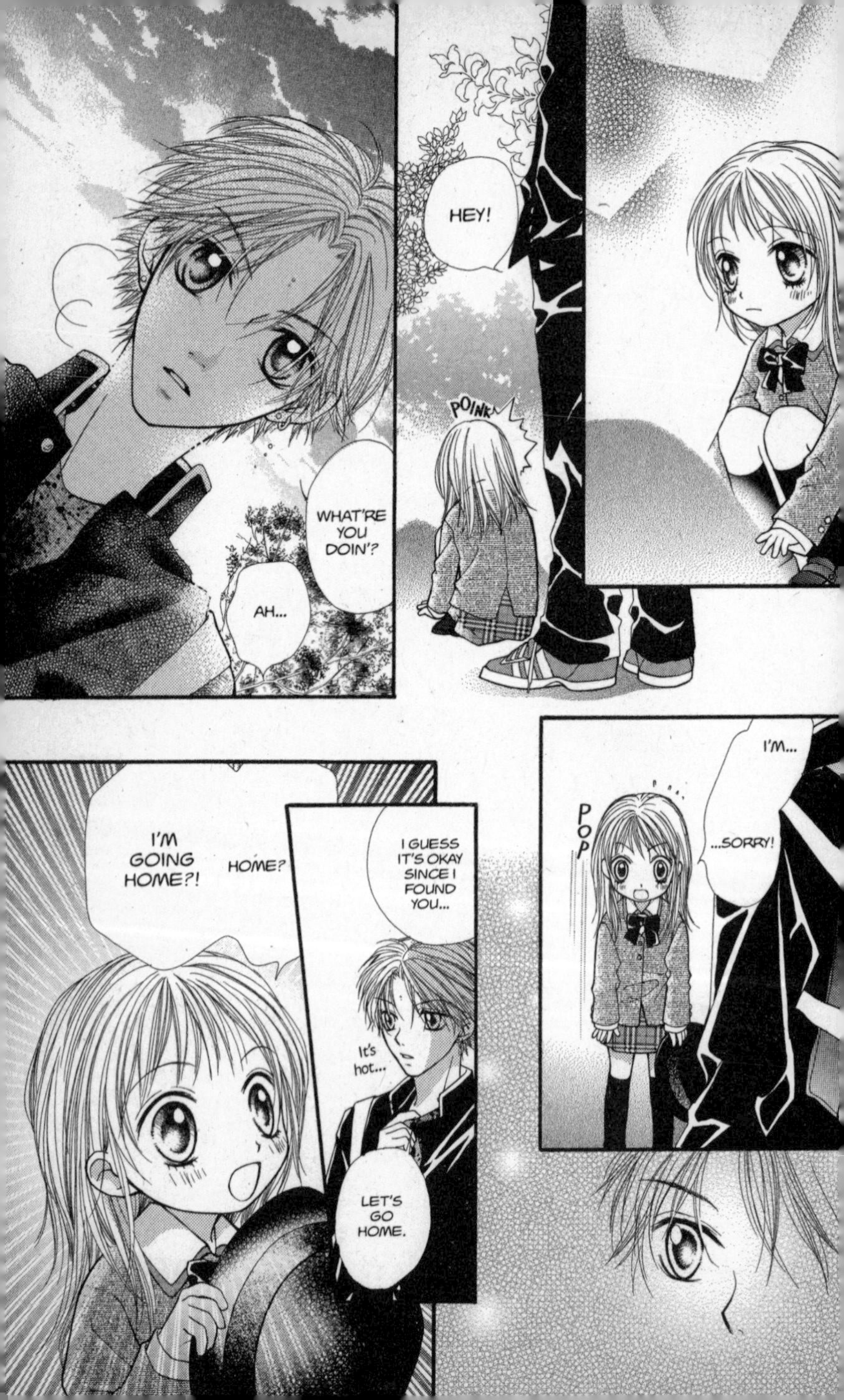
HEY!
POINK
WHAT'RE YOU DOIN'?
AH...
I'M...
POP
...SORRY!
I GUESS IT'S OKAY SINCE I FOUND YOU...
It's hot...
LET'S GO HOME.
HOME?
I'M GOING HOME?!

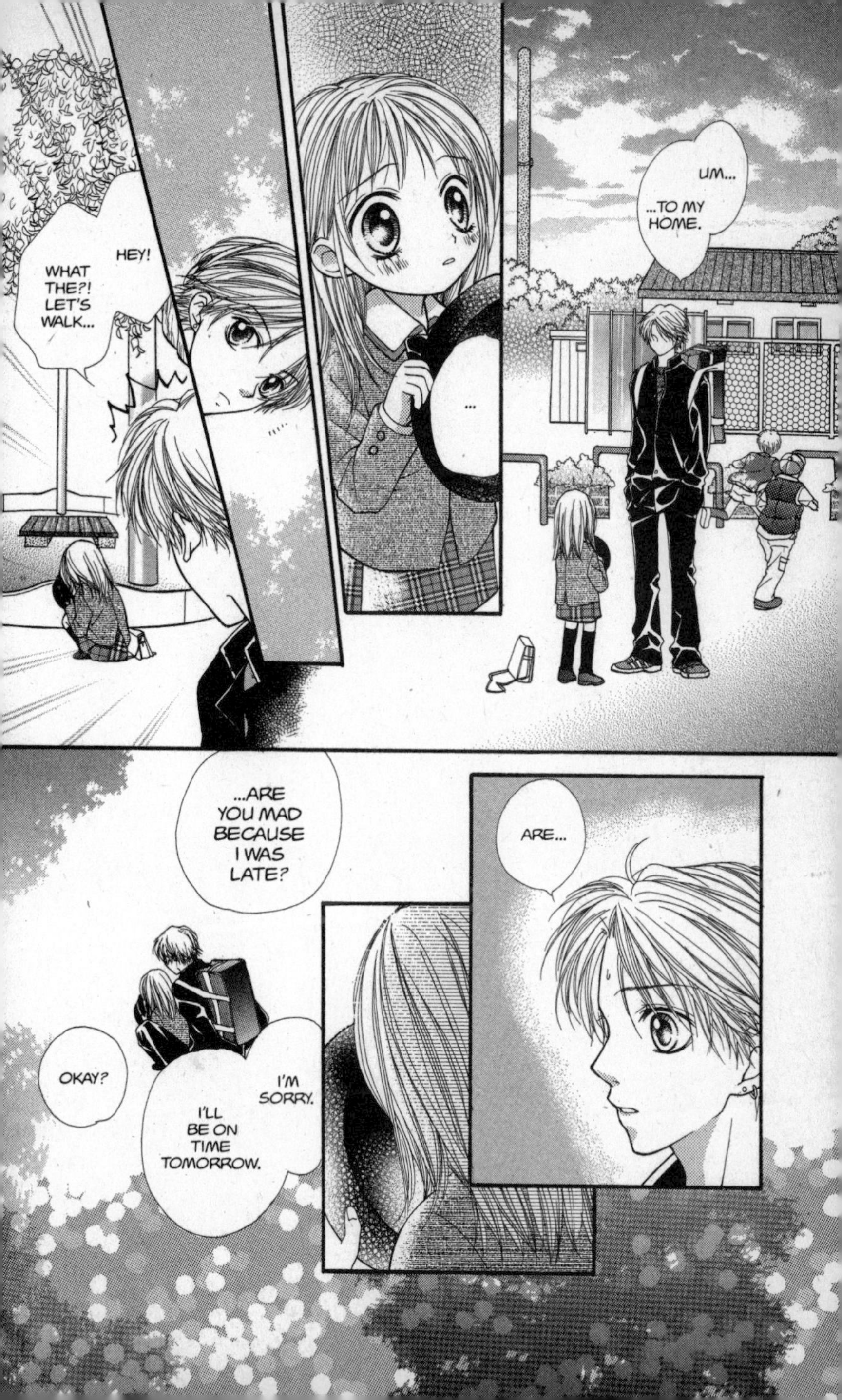
UM...
...TO MY HOME.
...
HEY!
WHAT THE?! LET'S WALK...
ARE...
...ARE YOU MAD BECAUSE I WAS LATE?
I'M SORRY.
I'LL BE ON TIME TOMORROW.
OKAY?

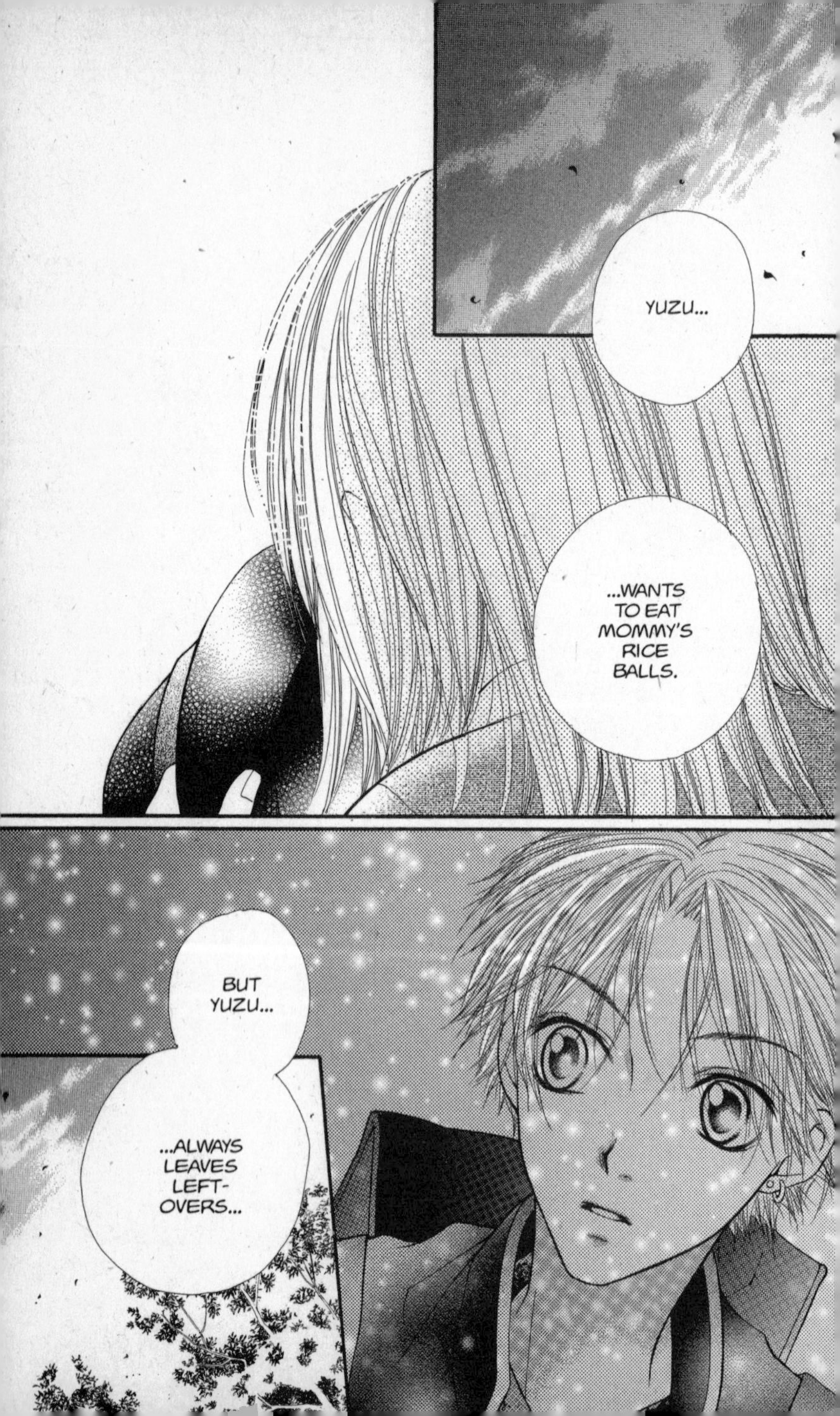
YUZU...
...WANTS TO EAT MOMMY'S RICE BALLS.
BUT YUZU...
...ALWAYS LEAVES LEFT-OVERS...

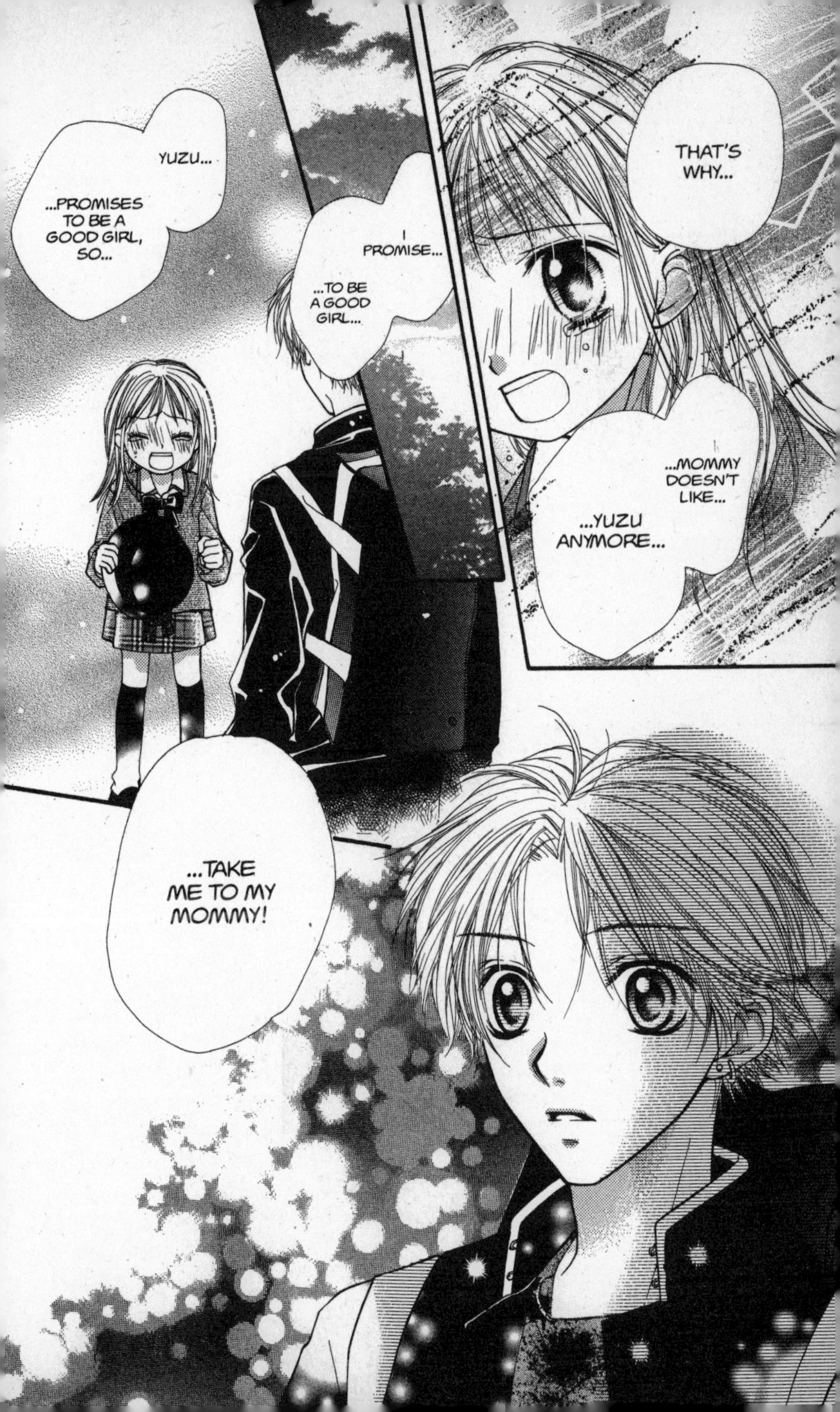
THAT'S WHY...
...MOMMY DOESN'T LIKE...
...YUZU ANYMORE...
I PROMISE...
...TO BE A GOOD GIRL...
YUZU...
...PROMISES TO BE A GOOD GIRL, SO...
...TAKE ME TO MY MOMMY!

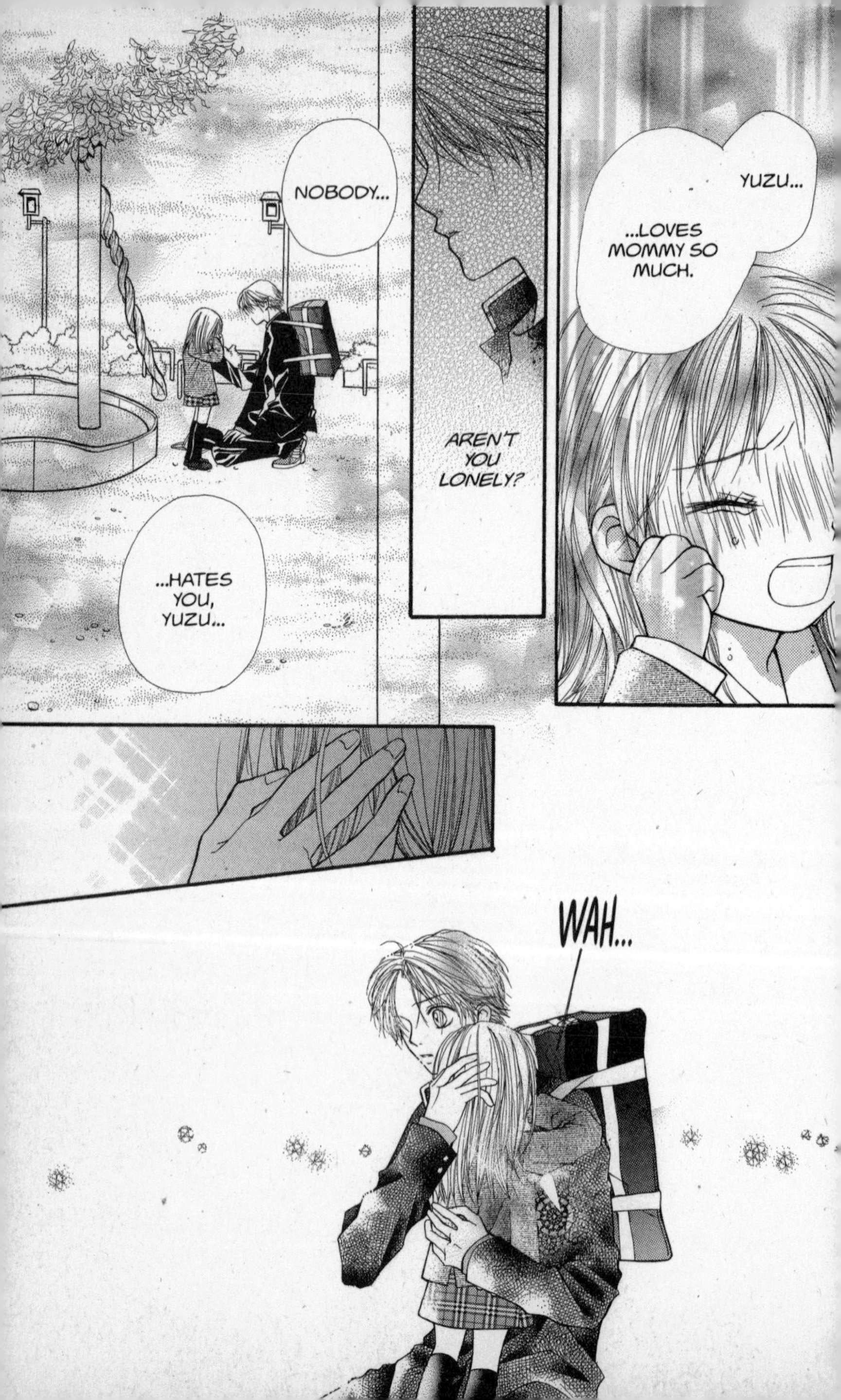
YUZU...
...LOVES MOMMY SO MUCH.
AREN'T YOU LONELY?
NOBODY...
...HATES YOU, YUZU...
WAH...

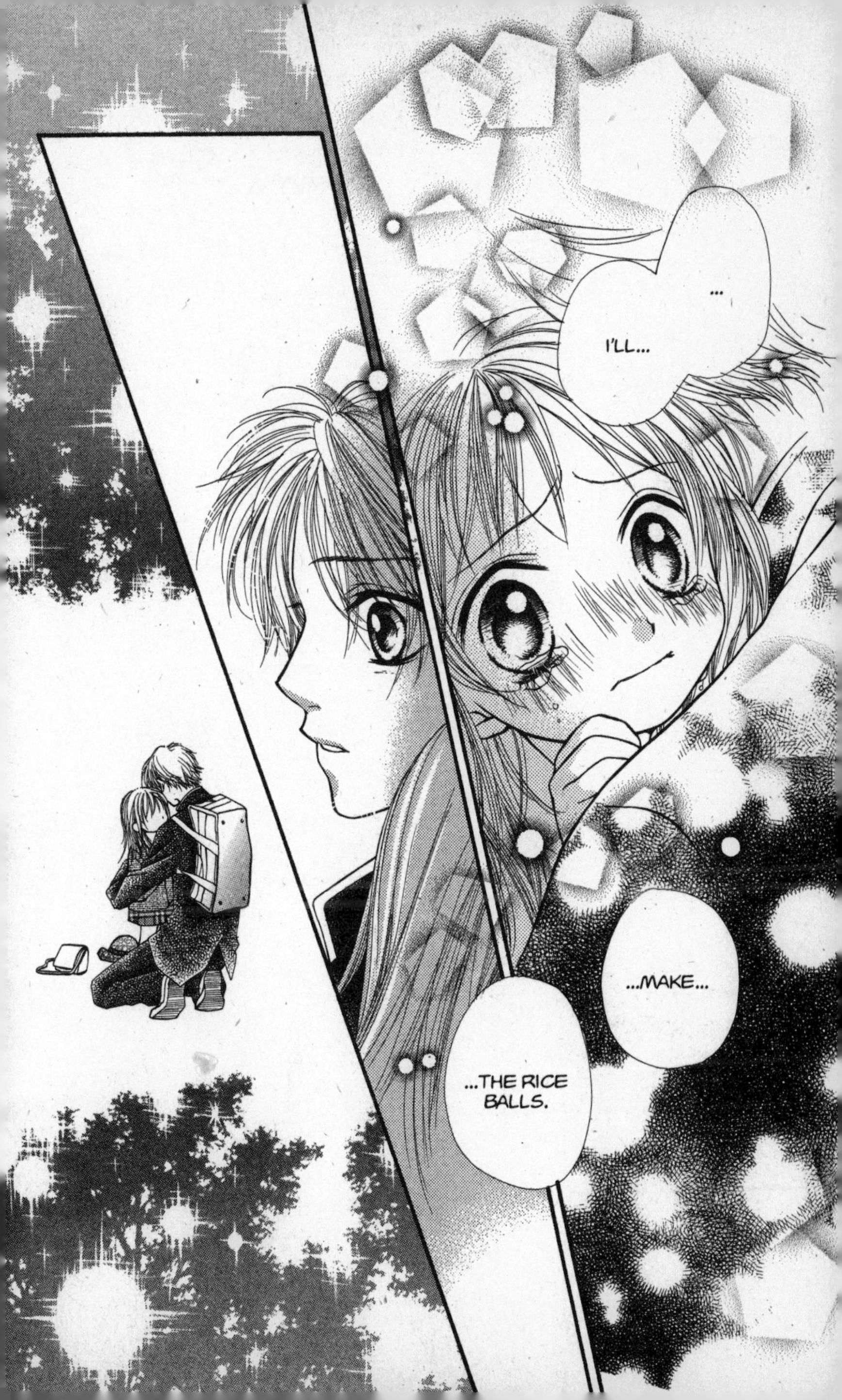
...
I'LL...
...MAKE...
...THE RICE BALLS.

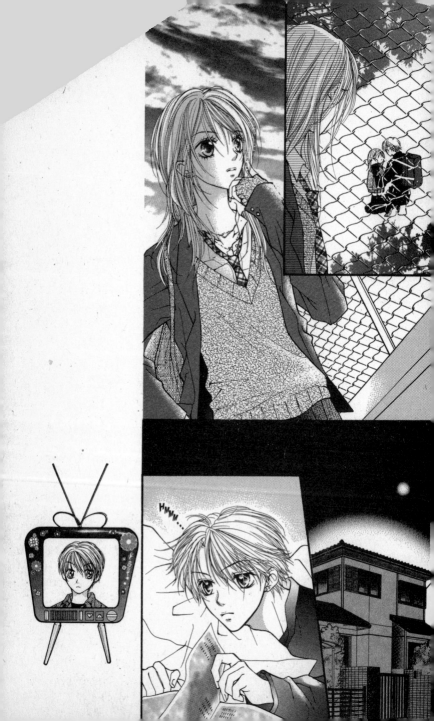

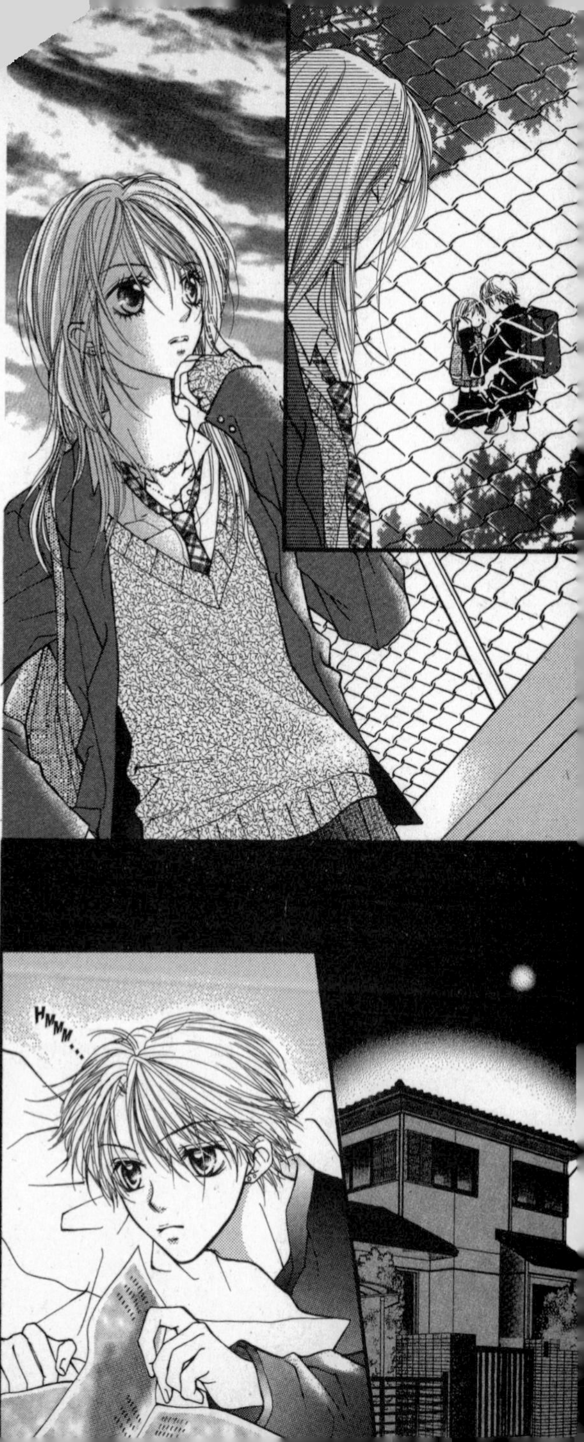
HMMM...
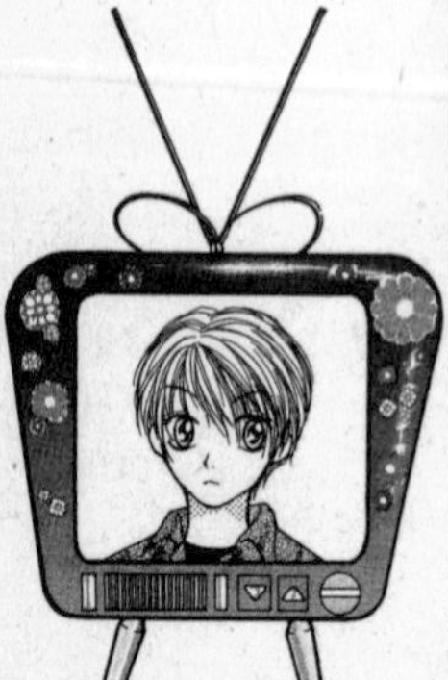

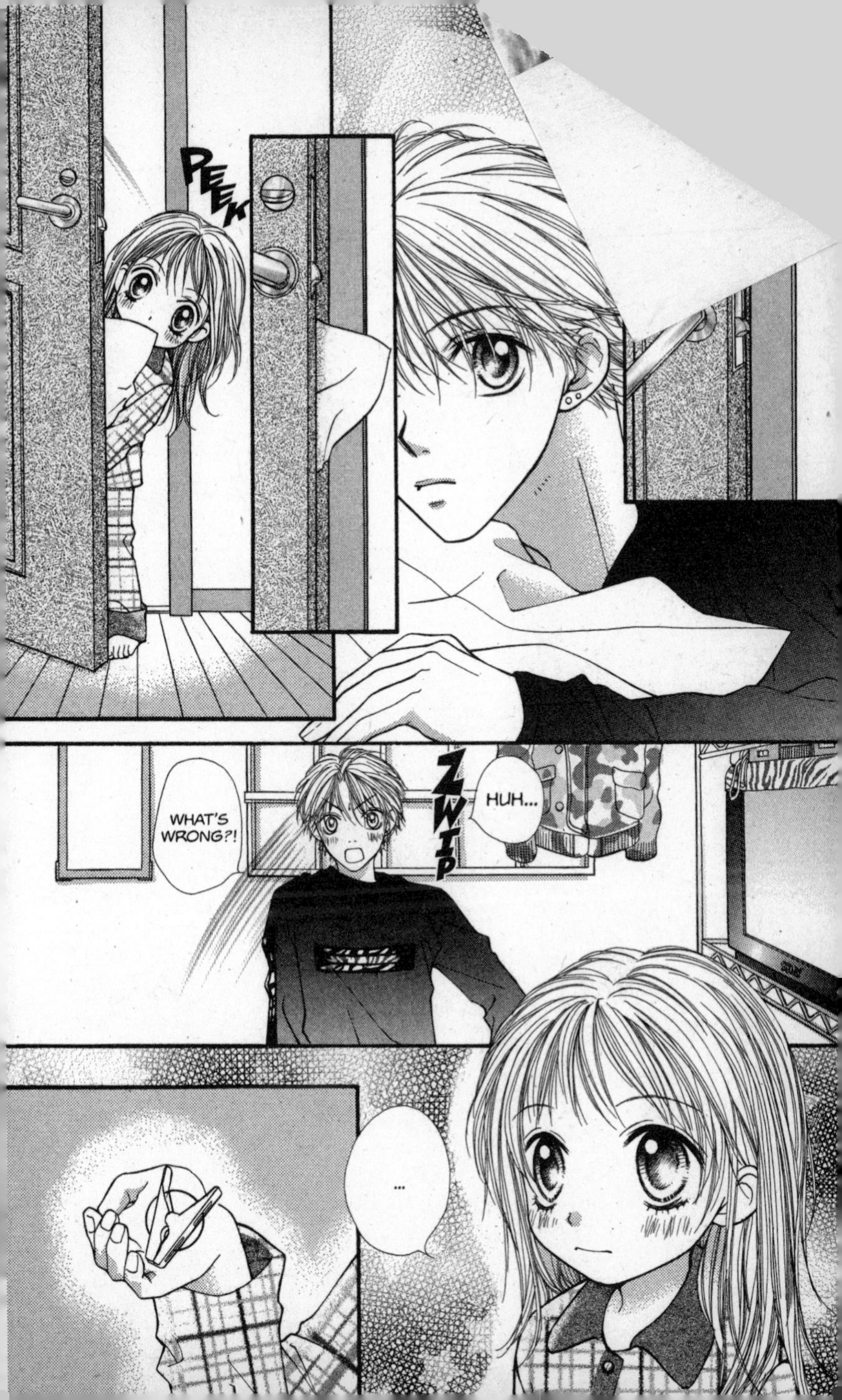
PEEK
HUH...
ZWIP
WHAT'S WRONG?!
...

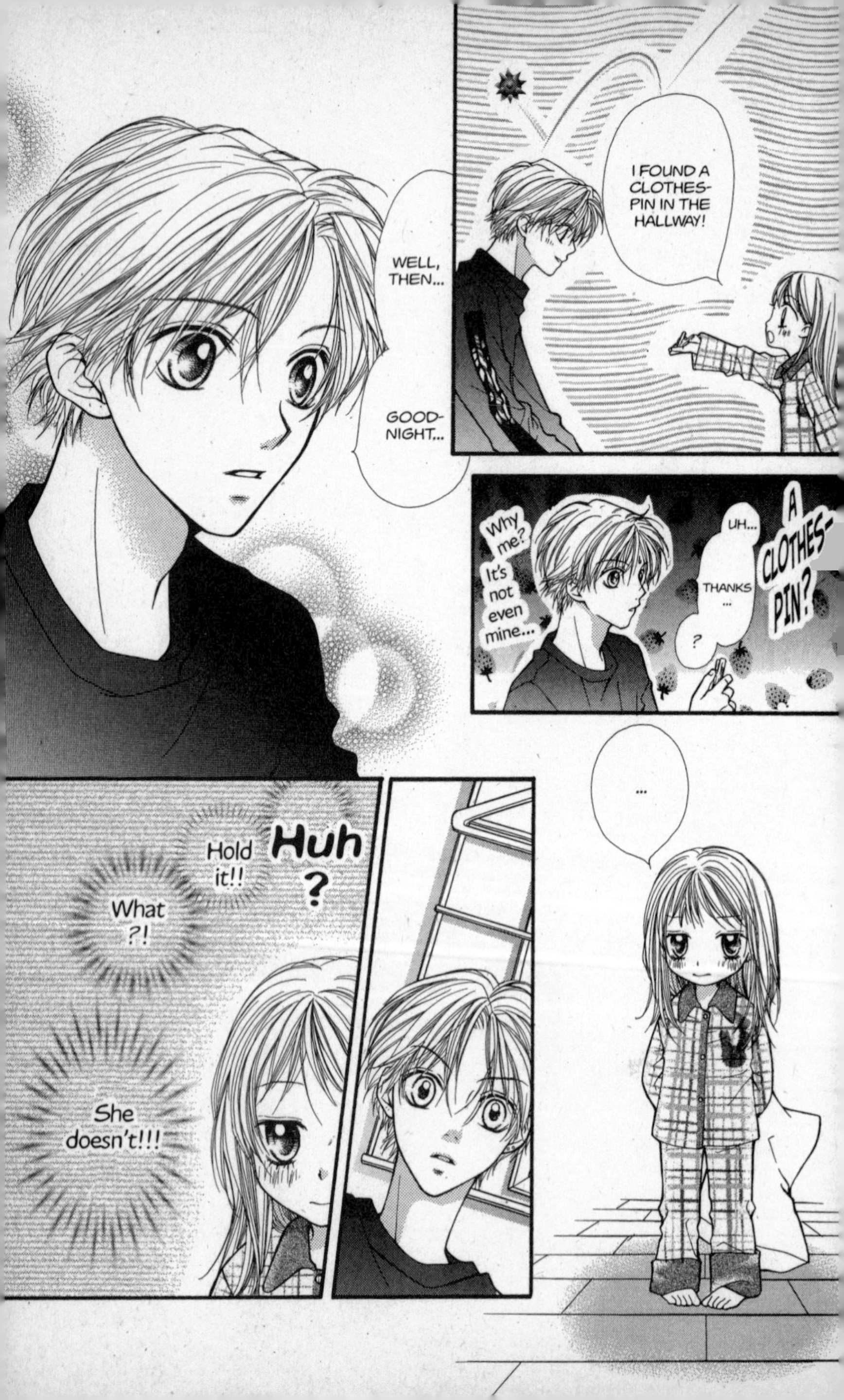
I FOUND A CLOTHES-PIN IN THE HALLWAY!
A CLOTHES-PIN?
UH... THANKS... ?
Why me? It's not even mine...
WELL, THEN...
GOOD-NIGHT...
...
Huh ?
Hold it!!
What ?!
She doesn't!!!

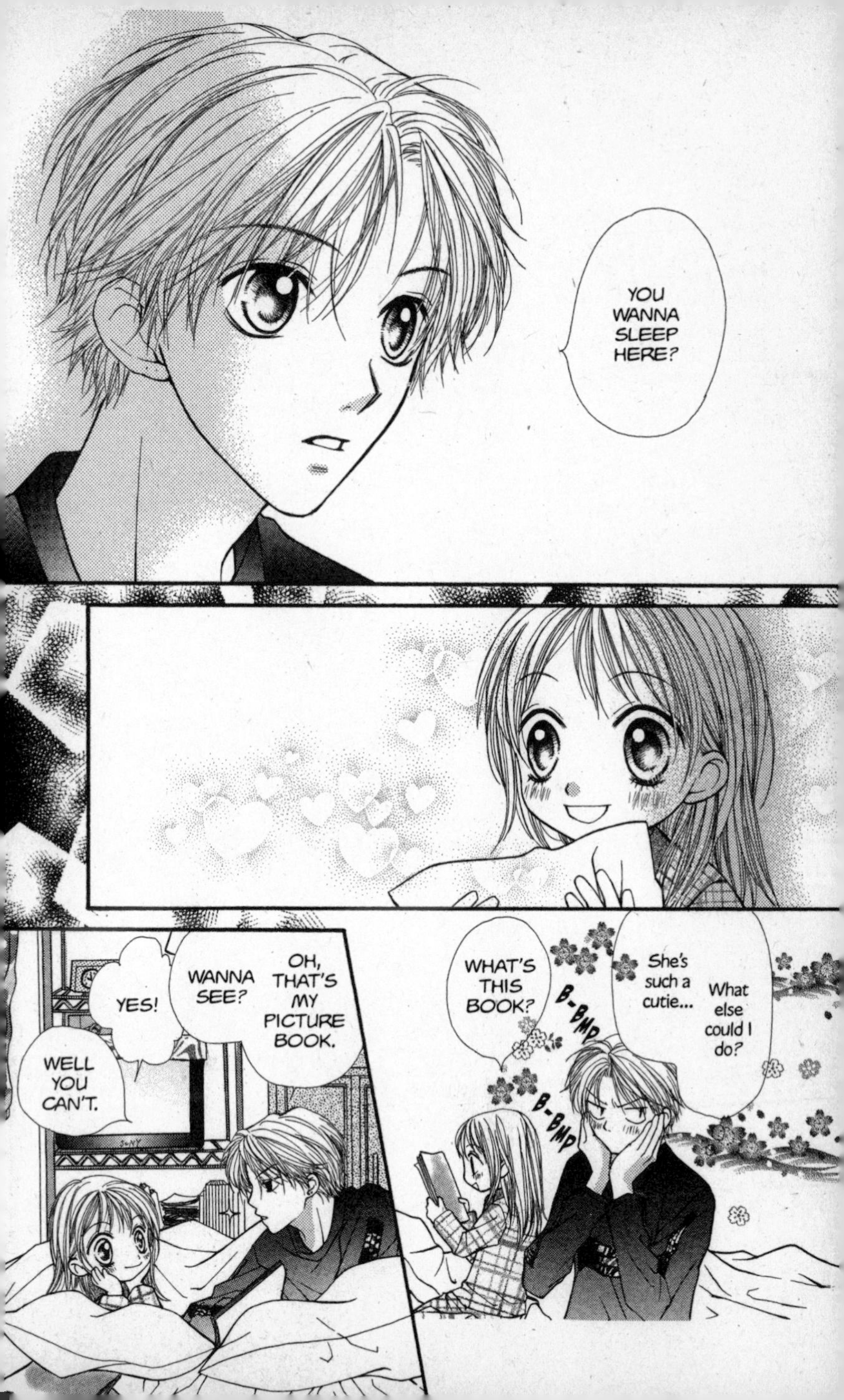
YOU WANNA SLEEP HERE?
She's such a cutie...
What else could I do?
WHAT'S THIS BOOK?
B-BMP
B-BMP
OH, THAT'S MY PICTURE BOOK.
WANNA SEE?
YES!
WELL YOU CAN'T.

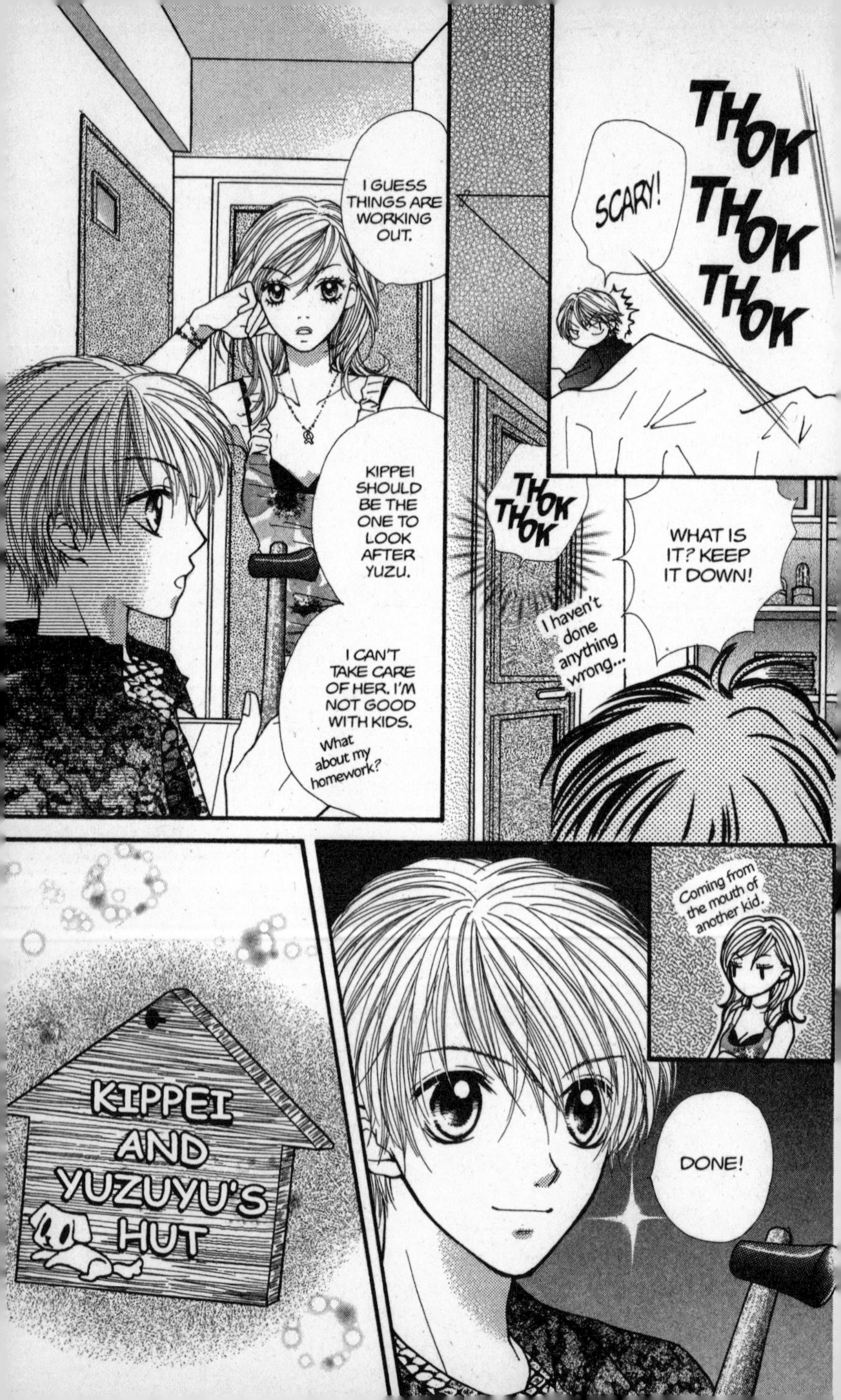
THOK
THOK
THOK
SCARY!
THOK THOK
WHAT IS IT? KEEP IT DOWN!
I haven't done anything wrong...
I GUESS THINGS ARE WORKING OUT.
KIPPEI SHOULD BE THE ONE TO LOOK AFTER YUZU.
I CAN'T TAKE CARE OF HER. I'M NOT GOOD WITH KIDS.
What about my homework?
Coming from the mouth of another kid.
DONE!
KIPPEI AND YUZUYU'S HUT

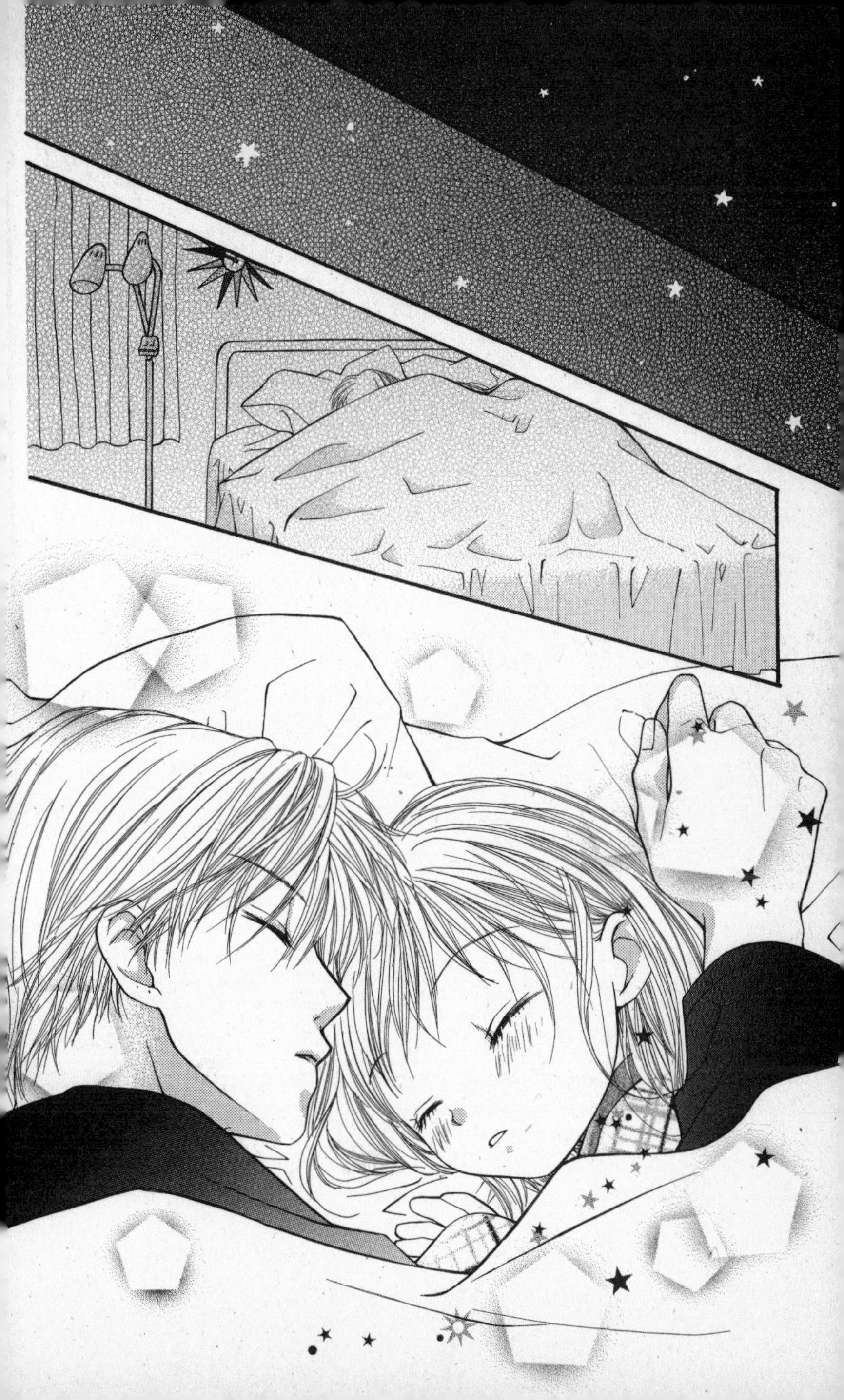

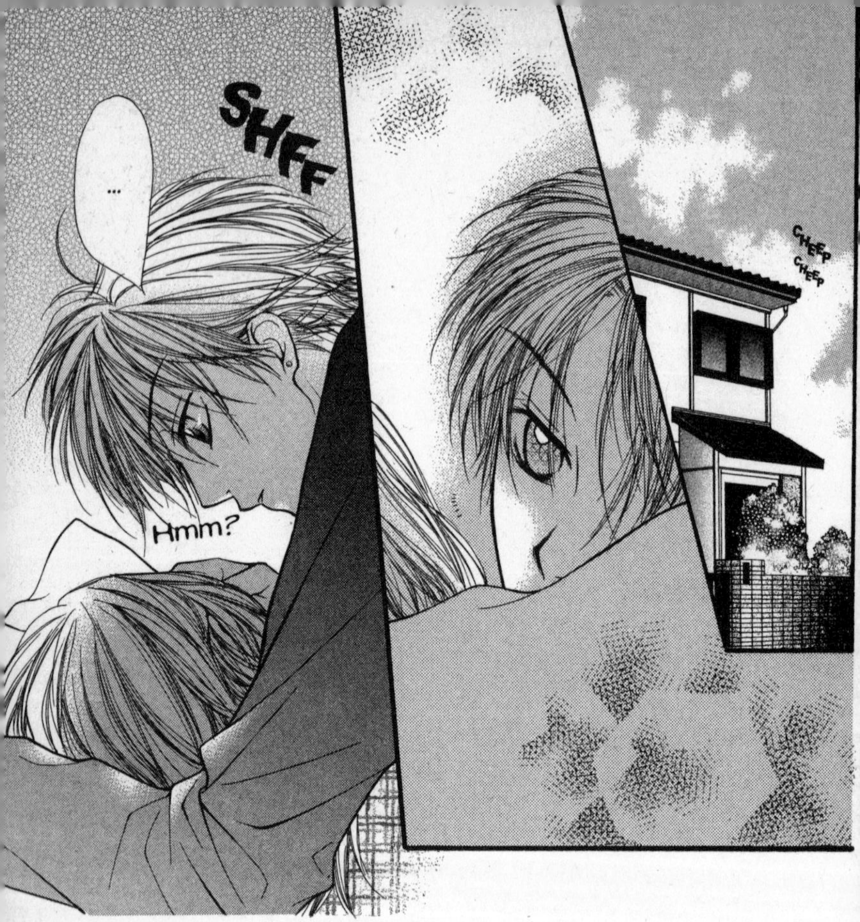
CHEEP
CHEEP
SHFF
...
Hmm?

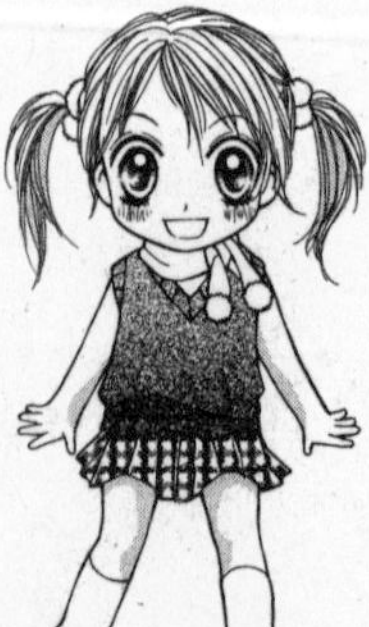

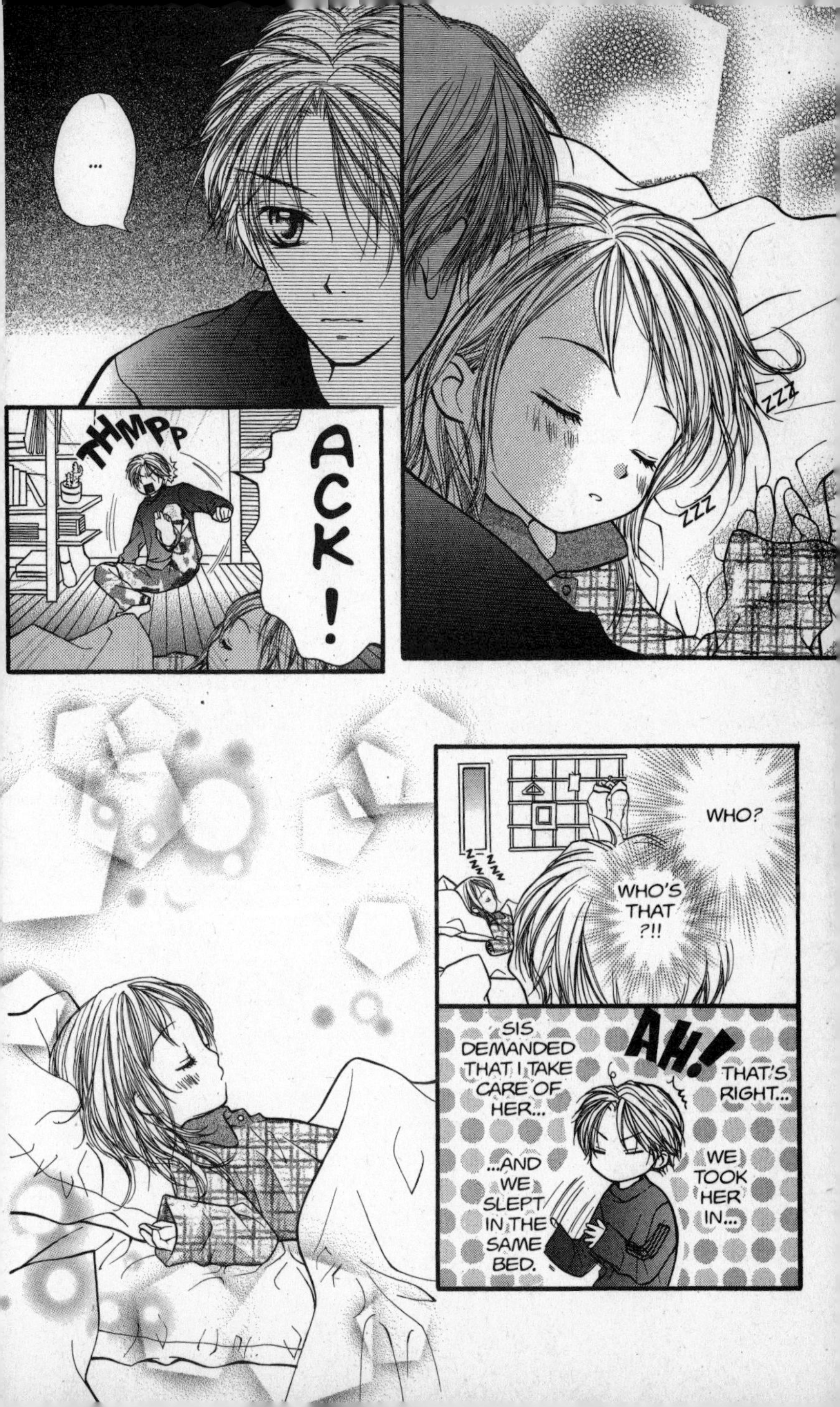
ZZZ
ZZZ
...
THMPP
ACK!
WHO?
WHO'S THAT ?!!
AH!
THAT'S RIGHT...
WE TOOK HER IN...
SIS DEMANDED THAT I TAKE CARE OF HER...
...AND WE SLEPT IN THE SAME BED.

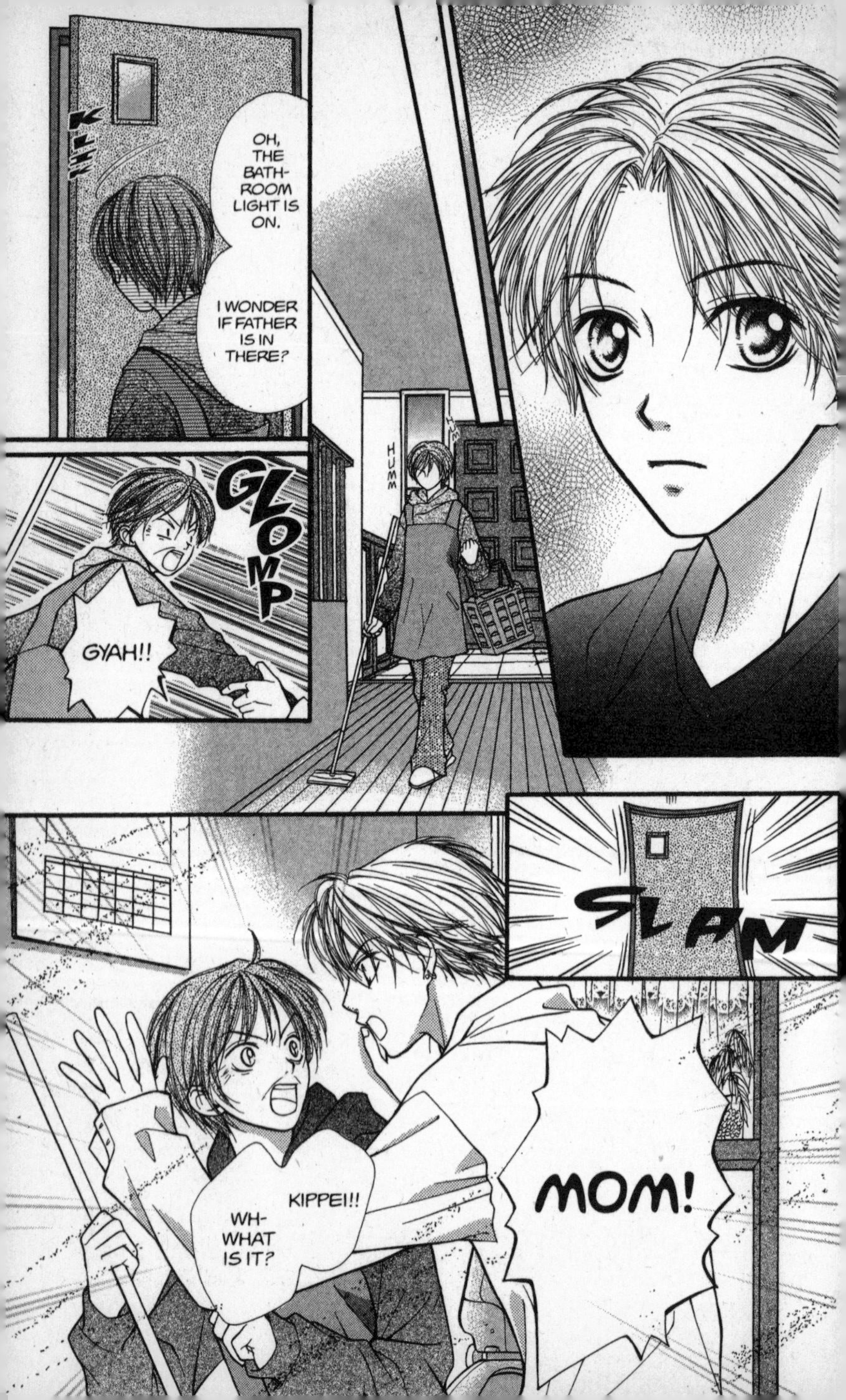
HUMM
OH, THE BATH-ROOM LIGHT IS ON.
KLIK
I WONDER IF FATHER IS IN THERE?
GLOMP
GYAH!!
SLAM
MOM!
KIPPEI!!
WH-WHAT IS IT?

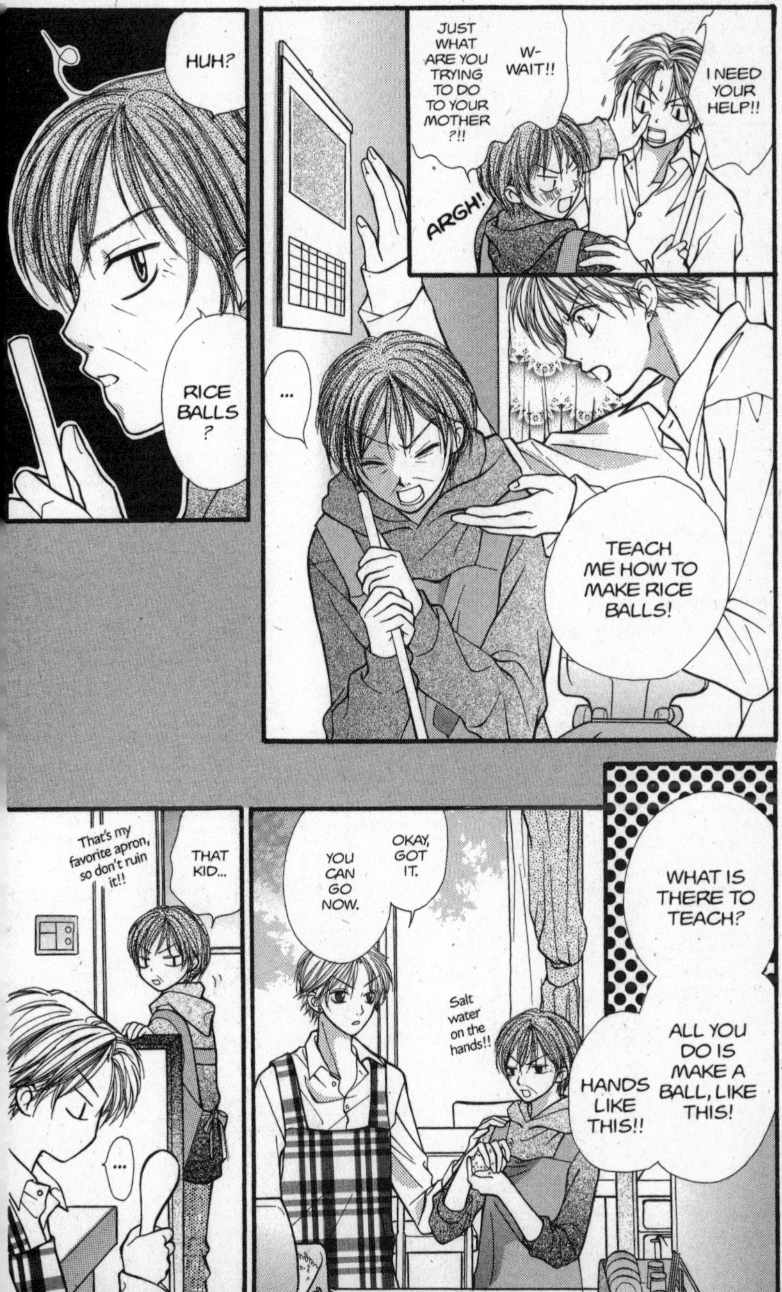

I NEED YOUR HELP!!
W-WAIT!!
JUST WHAT ARE YOU TRYING TO DO TO YOUR MOTHER?!!
ARGH!
TEACH ME HOW TO MAKE RICE BALLS!
...
HUH?
RICE BALLS?
WHAT IS THERE TO TEACH?
ALL YOU DO IS MAKE A BALL, LIKE THIS!
HANDS LIKE THIS!!
OKAY, GOT IT.
YOU CAN GO NOW.
Salt water on the hands!!
THAT KID...
That's my favorite apron, so don't ruin it!!
...

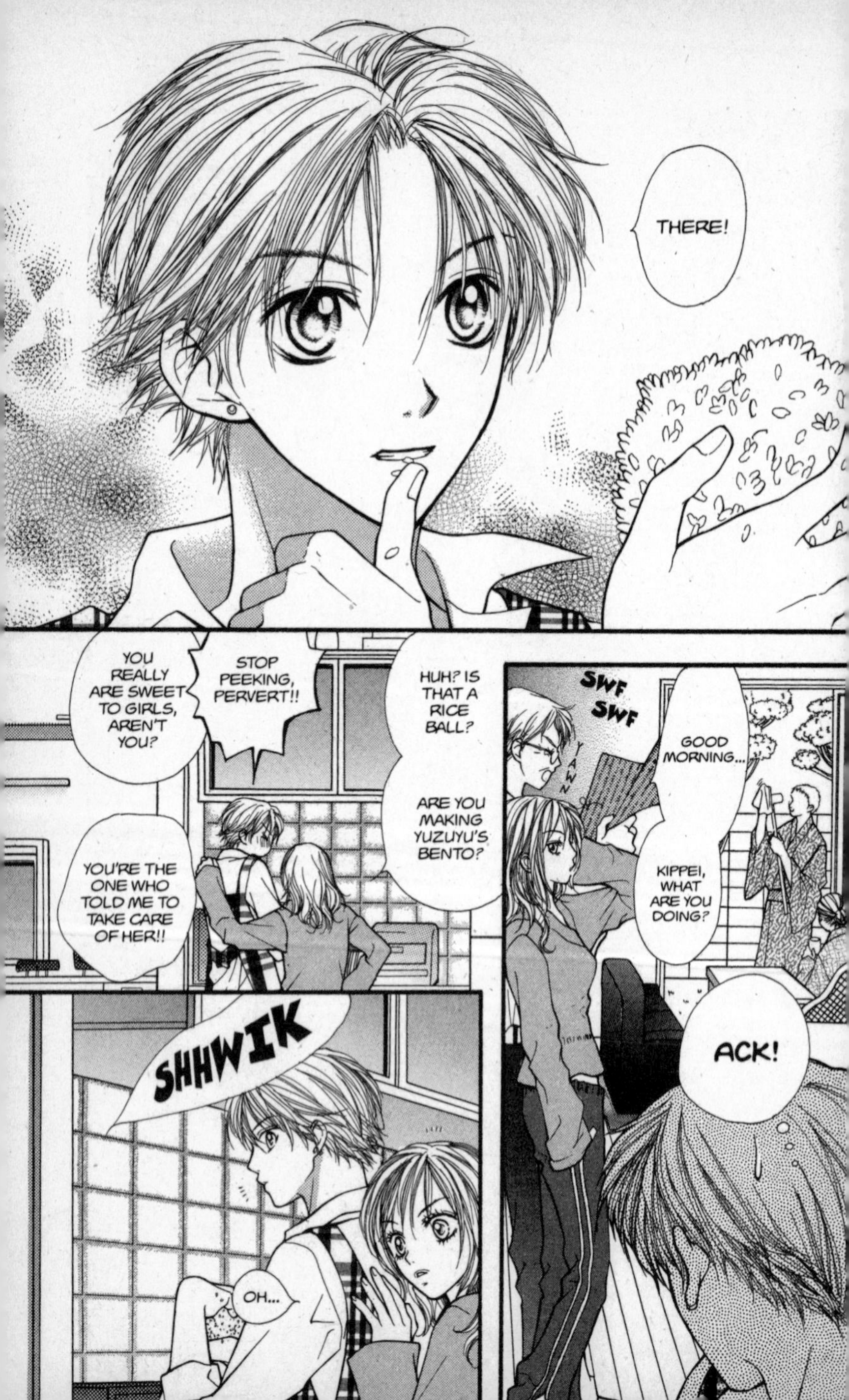
THERE!
SWF SWF
YAWN
GOOD MORNING...
KIPPEI, WHAT ARE YOU DOING?
ACK!
HUH? IS THAT A RICE BALL?
ARE YOU MAKING YUZUYU'S BENTO?
STOP PEEKING, PERVERT!!
YOU REALLY ARE SWEET TO GIRLS, AREN'T YOU?
YOU'RE THE ONE WHO TOLD ME TO TAKE CARE OF HER!!
SHHWIK
OH...

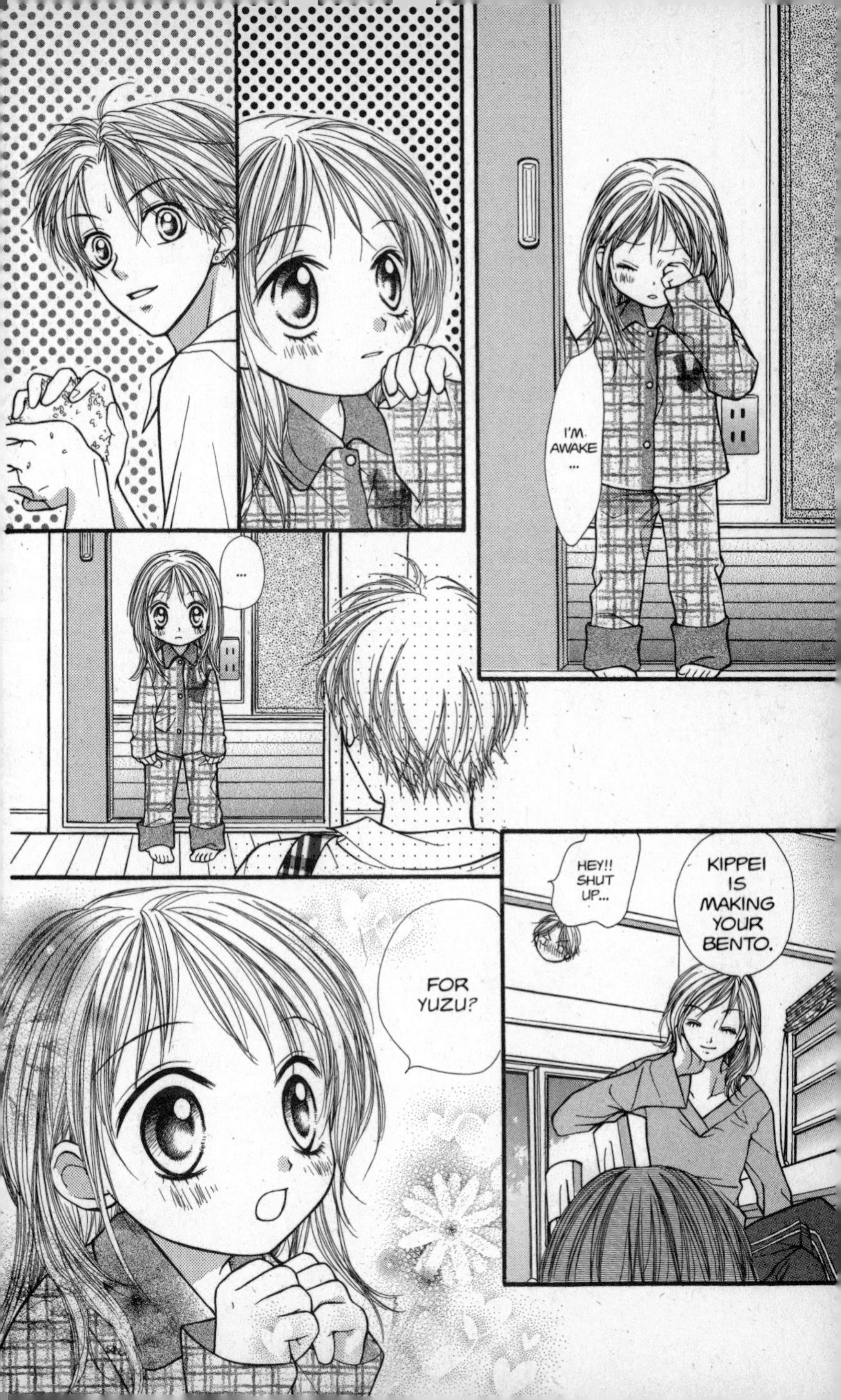
I'M AWAKE ...
...
KIPPEI IS MAKING YOUR BENTO.
HEY!! SHUT UP...
FOR YUZU?

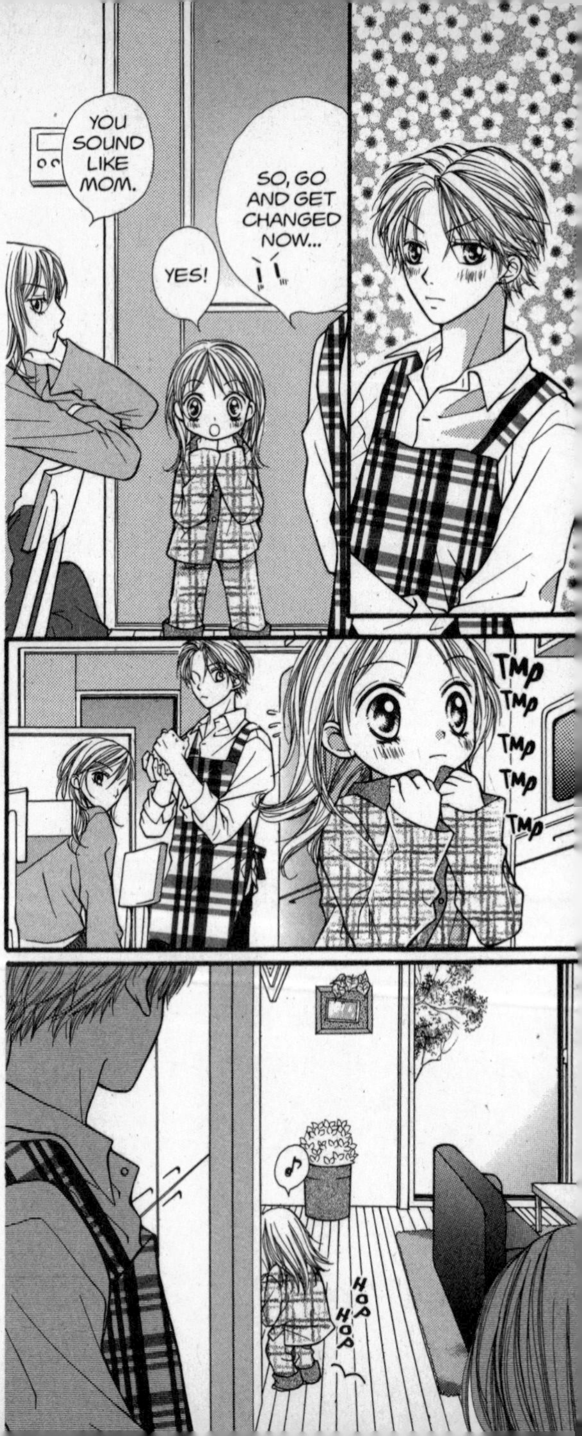
SO, GO AND GET CHANGED NOW...
YES!
YOU SOUND LIKE MOM.
TMP TMP TMP TMP TMP
HOP HOP
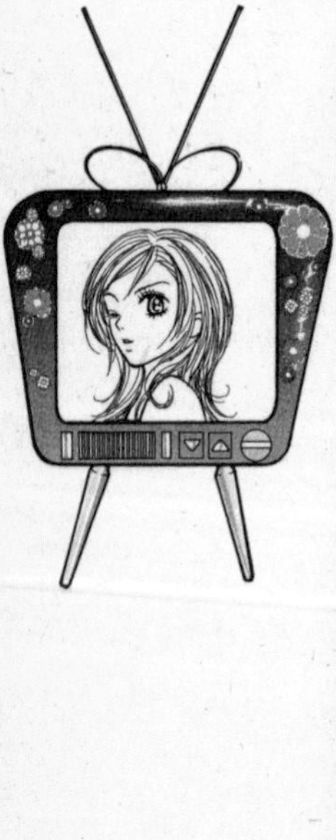

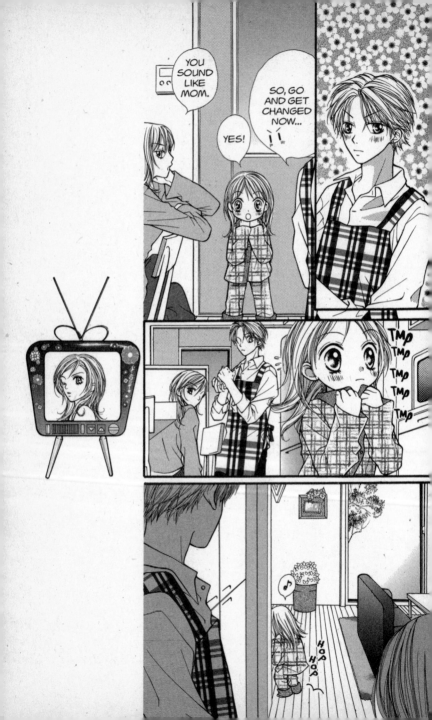

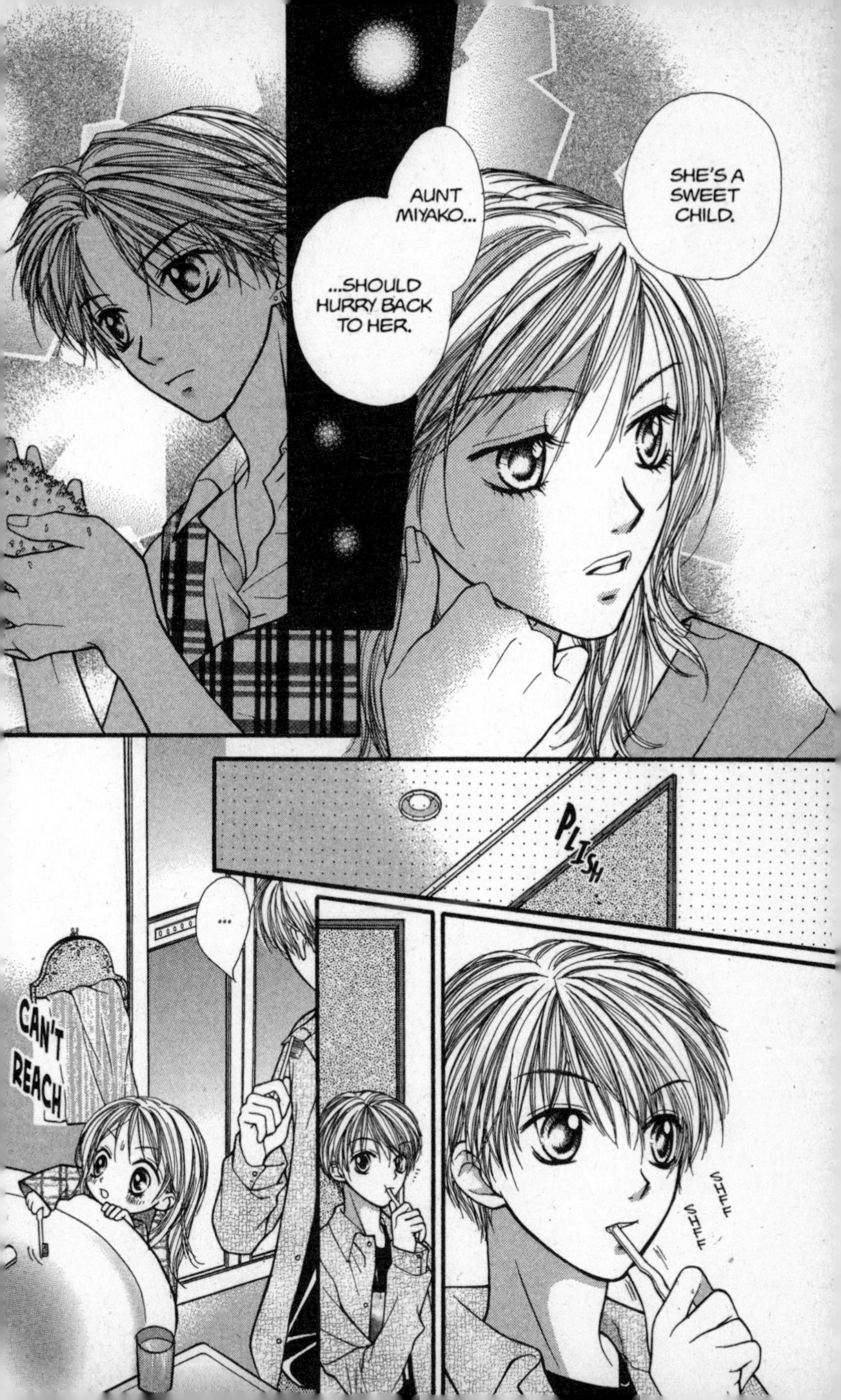
SHE'S A SWEET CHILD.
AUNT MIYAKO...
...SHOULD HURRY BACK TO HER.
PLISH
SHEFF SHEFF
...
CAN'T REACH

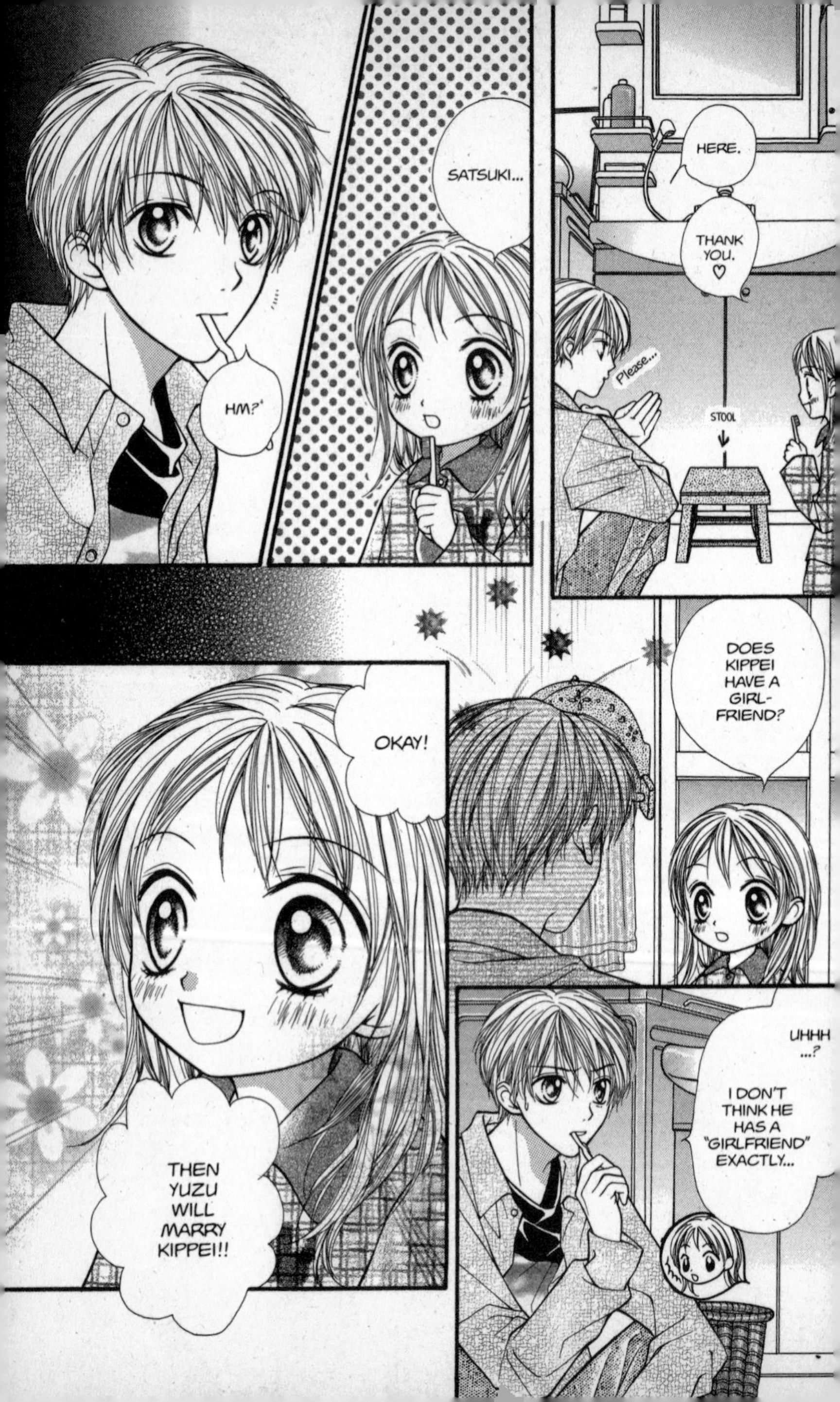
HERE.
THANK YOU. ♡
Please...
STOOL
SATSUKI...
HM?'
DOES KIPPEI HAVE A GIRL-FRIEND?
UHHH ...?
I DON'T THINK HE HAS A "GIRLFRIEND" EXACTLY...
OKAY!
THEN YUZU WILL MARRY KIPPEI!!

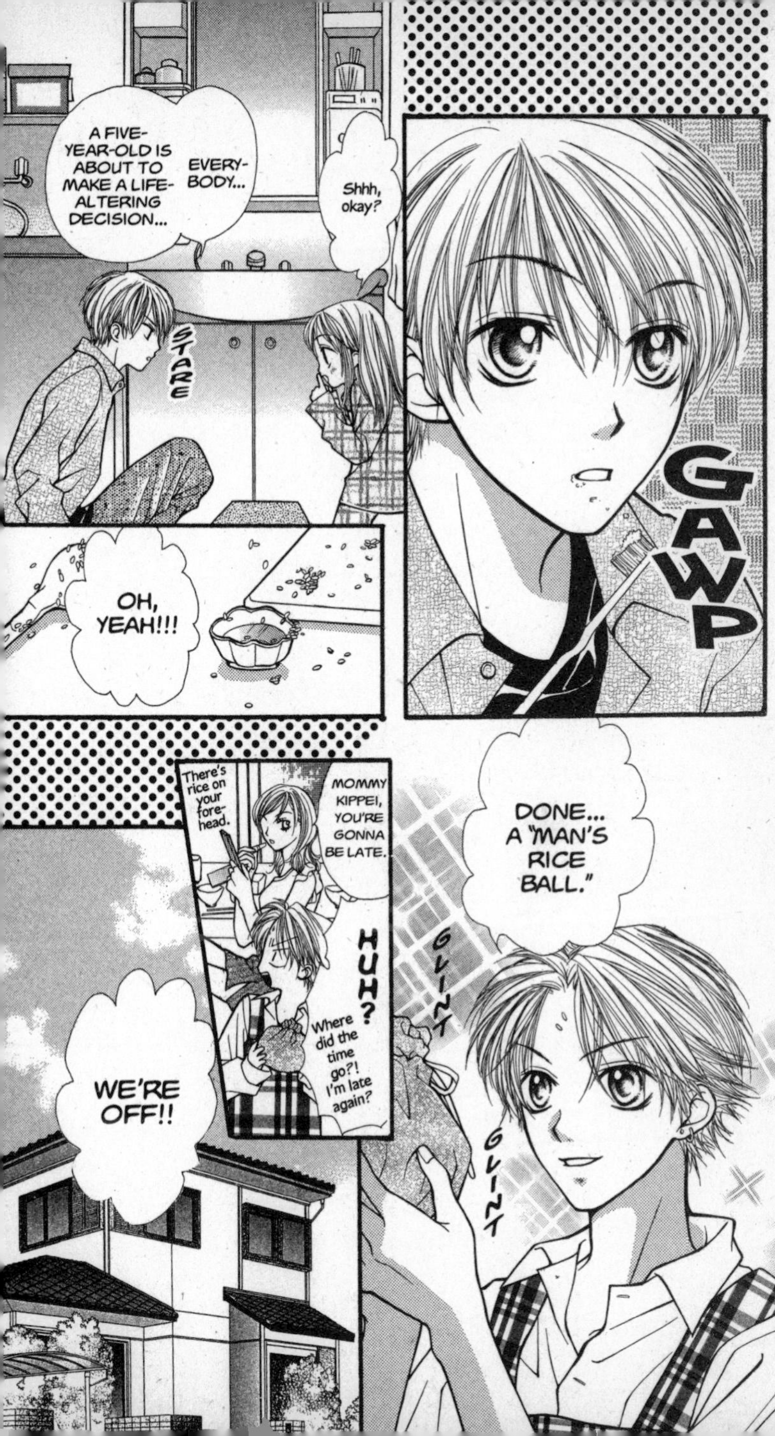
GAWP
Shhh, okay?
EVERYBODY...
A FIVE-YEAR-OLD IS ABOUT TO MAKE A LIFE-ALTERING DECISION...
STARE
OH, YEAH!!!
DONE... A "MAN'S RICE BALL."
GLINT
GLINT
MOMMY KIPPEI, YOU'RE GONNA BE LATE.
There's rice on your forehead.
HUH?
Where did the time go?! I'm late again?
WE'RE OFF!!

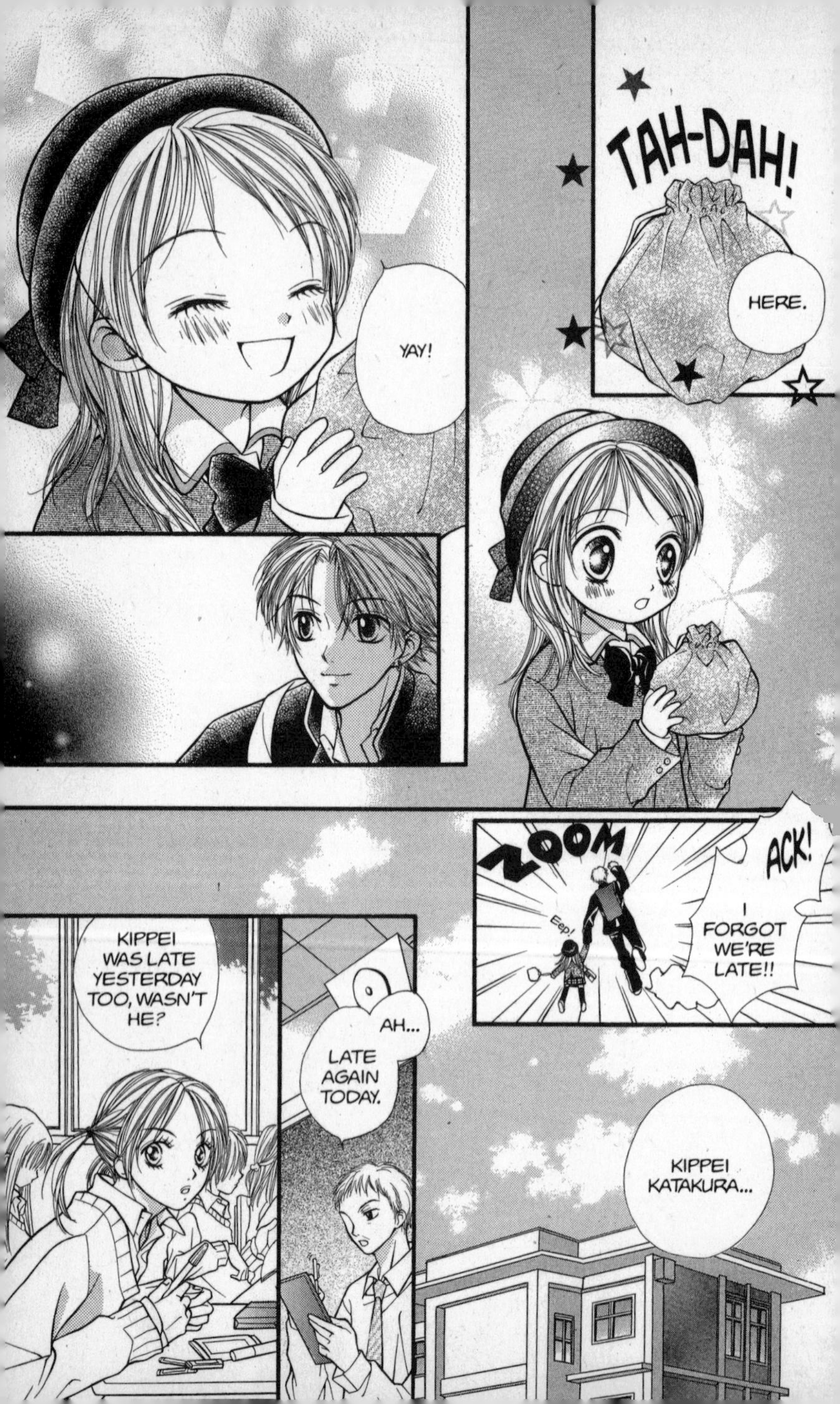
TAH-DAH!
HERE.
YAY!
ZOOM
ACK!
Eep!
I FORGOT WE'RE LATE!!
KIPPEI KATAKURA...
AH...
LATE AGAIN TODAY.
KIPPEI WAS LATE YESTERDAY TOO, WASN'T HE?

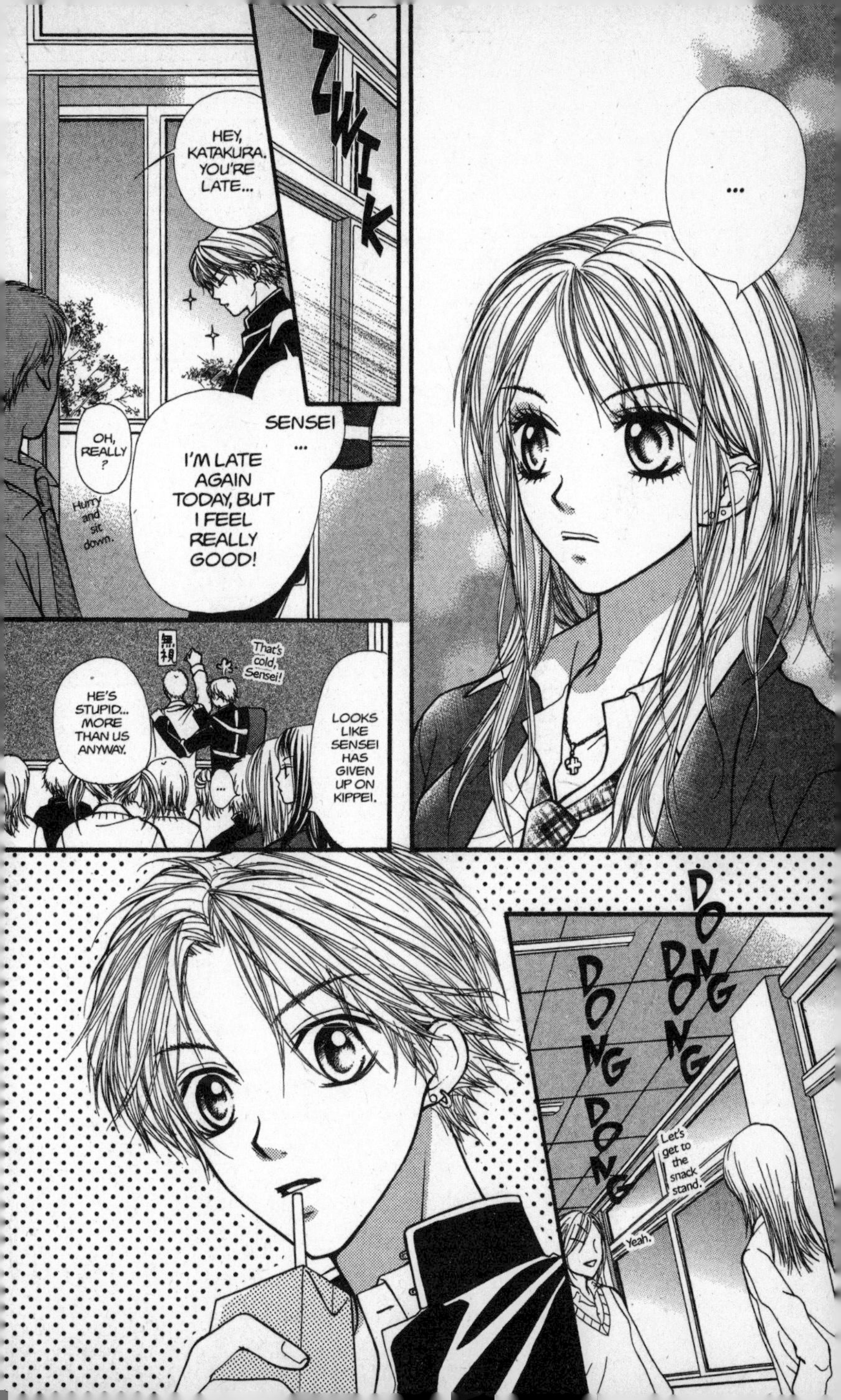
...
ZWIK
HEY, KATAKURA. YOU'RE LATE...
SENSEI... I'M LATE AGAIN TODAY, BUT I FEEL REALLY GOOD!
OH, REALLY?
Hurry and sit down.
LOOKS LIKE SENSEI HAS GIVEN UP ON KIPPEI.
That's cold, Sensei!
無視
HE'S STUPID... MORE THAN US ANYWAY.
...
DONG DONG DONG DONG DONG DONG
Let's get to the snack stand.
Yeah.

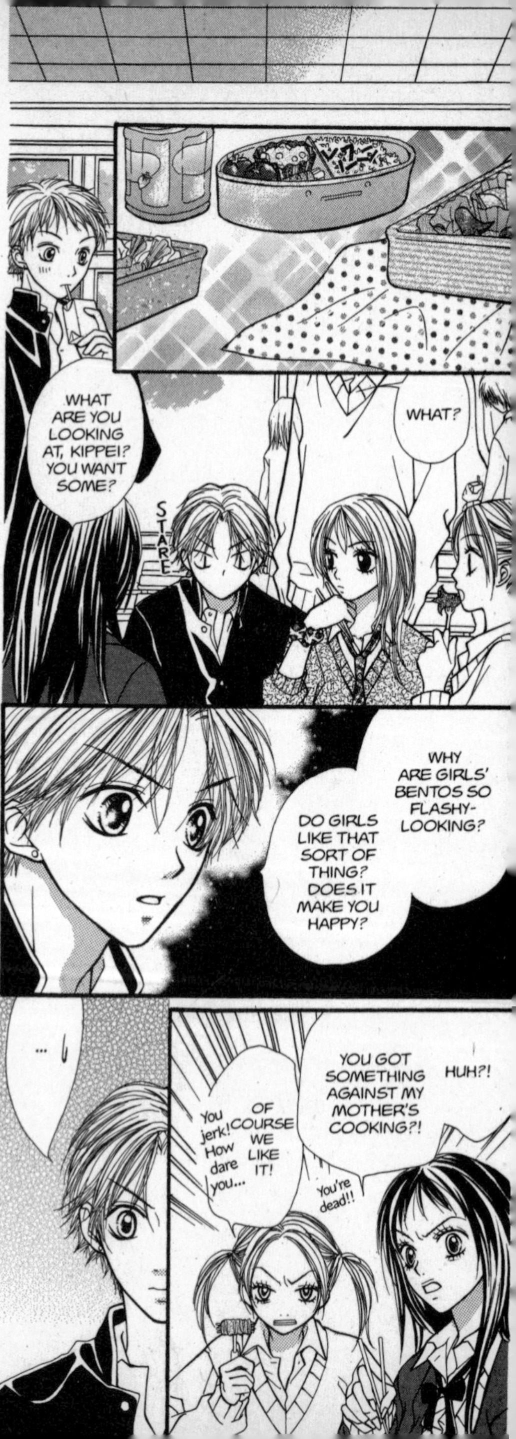
WHAT?
WHAT ARE YOU LOOKING AT, KIPPEI? YOU WANT SOME?
STARE
WHY ARE GIRLS' BENTOS SO FLASHY-LOOKING?
DO GIRLS LIKE THAT SORT OF THING? DOES IT MAKE YOU HAPPY?
HUH?!
YOU GOT SOMETHING AGAINST MY MOTHER'S COOKING?!
You're dead!!
OF COURSE WE LIKE IT!
You jerk! How dare you...
...
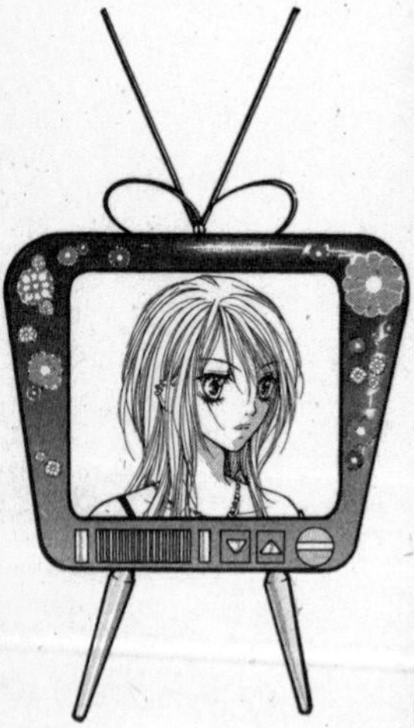

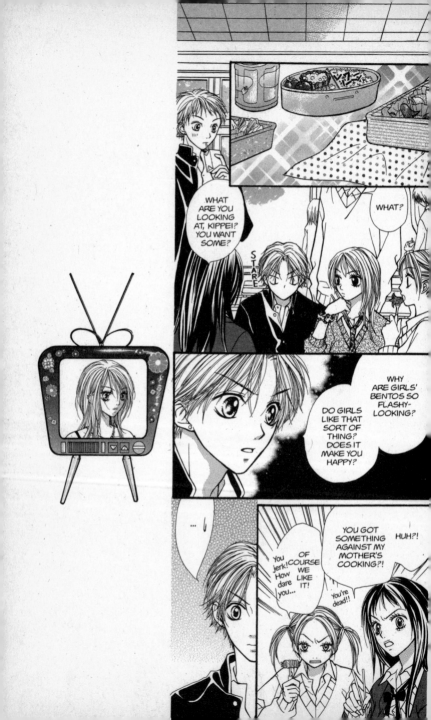

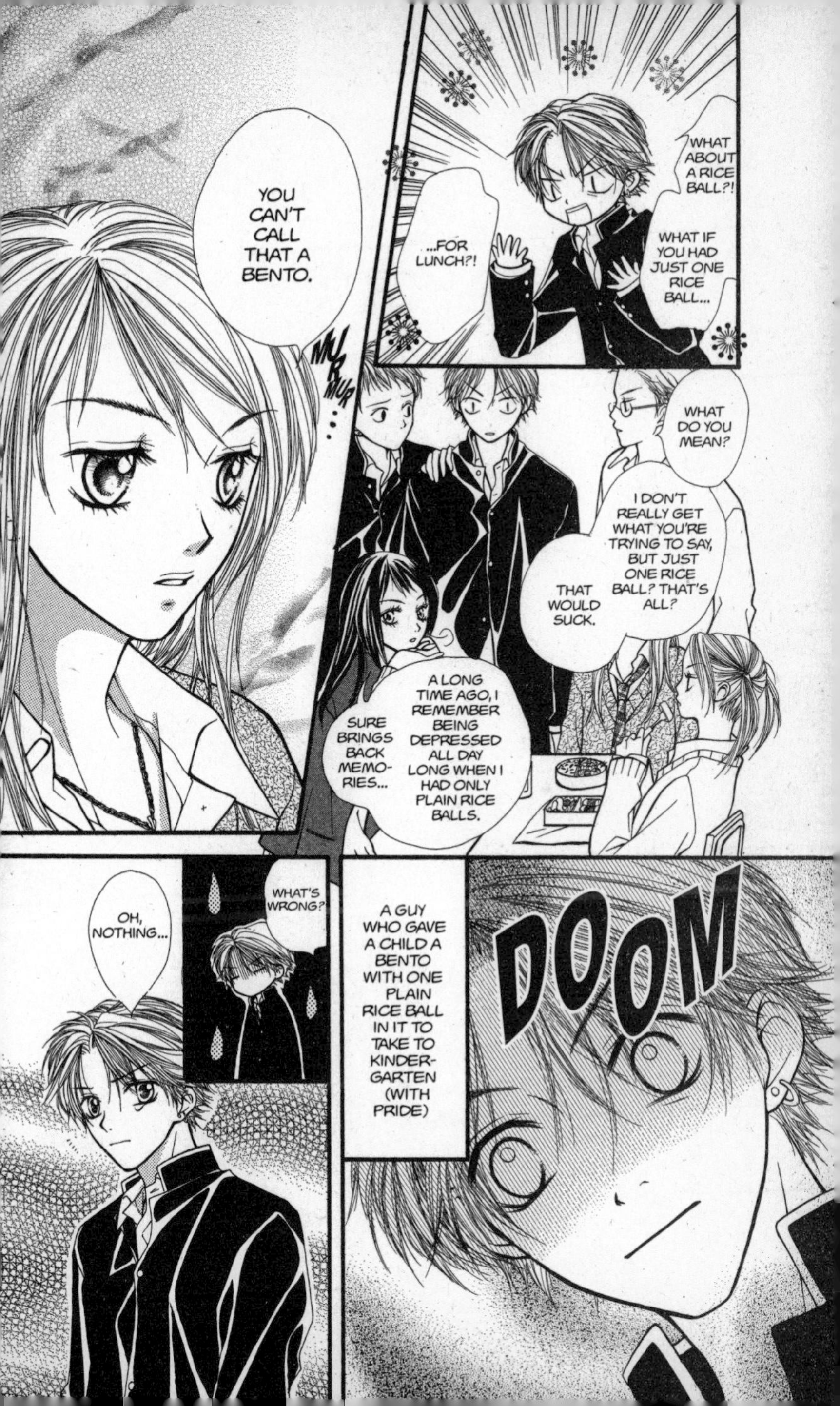
WHAT ABOUT A RICE BALL?!
WHAT IF YOU HAD JUST ONE RICE BALL...
...FOR LUNCH?!
WHAT DO YOU MEAN?
I DON'T REALLY GET WHAT YOU'RE TRYING TO SAY, BUT JUST ONE RICE BALL? THAT'S ALL?
THAT WOULD SUCK.
A LONG TIME AGO, I REMEMBER BEING DEPRESSED ALL DAY LONG WHEN I HAD ONLY PLAIN RICE BALLS.
SURE BRINGS BACK MEMO-RIES...
YOU CAN'T CALL THAT A BENTO.
MURMUR...
A GUY WHO GAVE A CHILD A BENTO WITH ONE PLAIN RICE BALL IN IT TO TAKE TO KINDER-GARTEN (WITH PRIDE)
DOOM
WHAT'S WRONG?
OH, NOTHING...

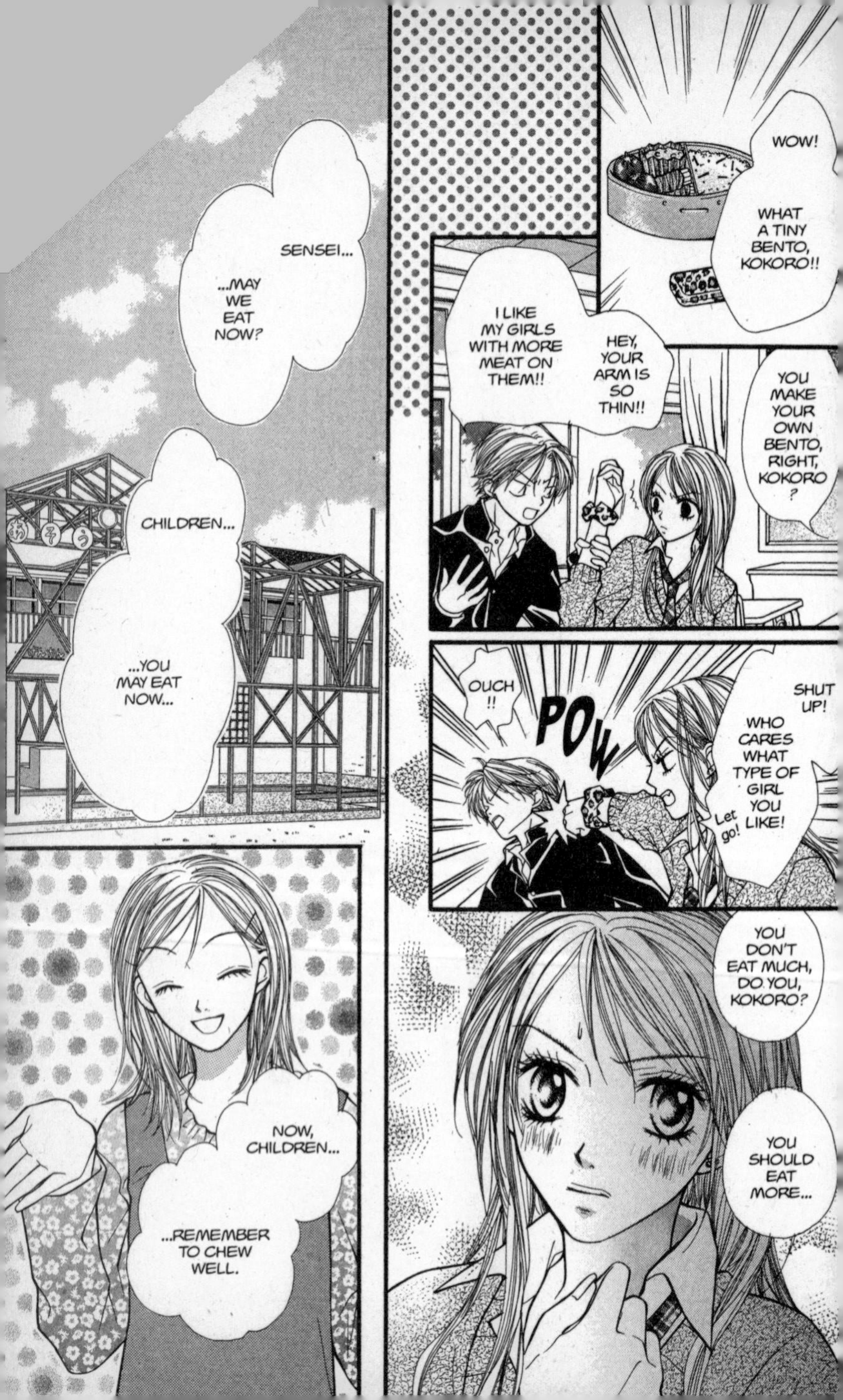
WOW!
WHAT A TINY BENTO, KOKORO!!
YOU MAKE YOUR OWN BENTO, RIGHT, KOKORO?
HEY, YOUR ARM IS SO THIN!!
I LIKE MY GIRLS WITH MORE MEAT ON THEM!!
SHUT UP! WHO CARES WHAT TYPE OF GIRL YOU LIKE!
Let go!
POW
OUCH!!
YOU DON'T EAT MUCH, DO YOU, KOKORO?
YOU SHOULD EAT MORE...
SENSEI...
...MAY WE EAT NOW?
CHILDREN...
...YOU MAY EAT NOW...
NOW, CHILDREN...
...REMEMBER TO CHEW WELL.

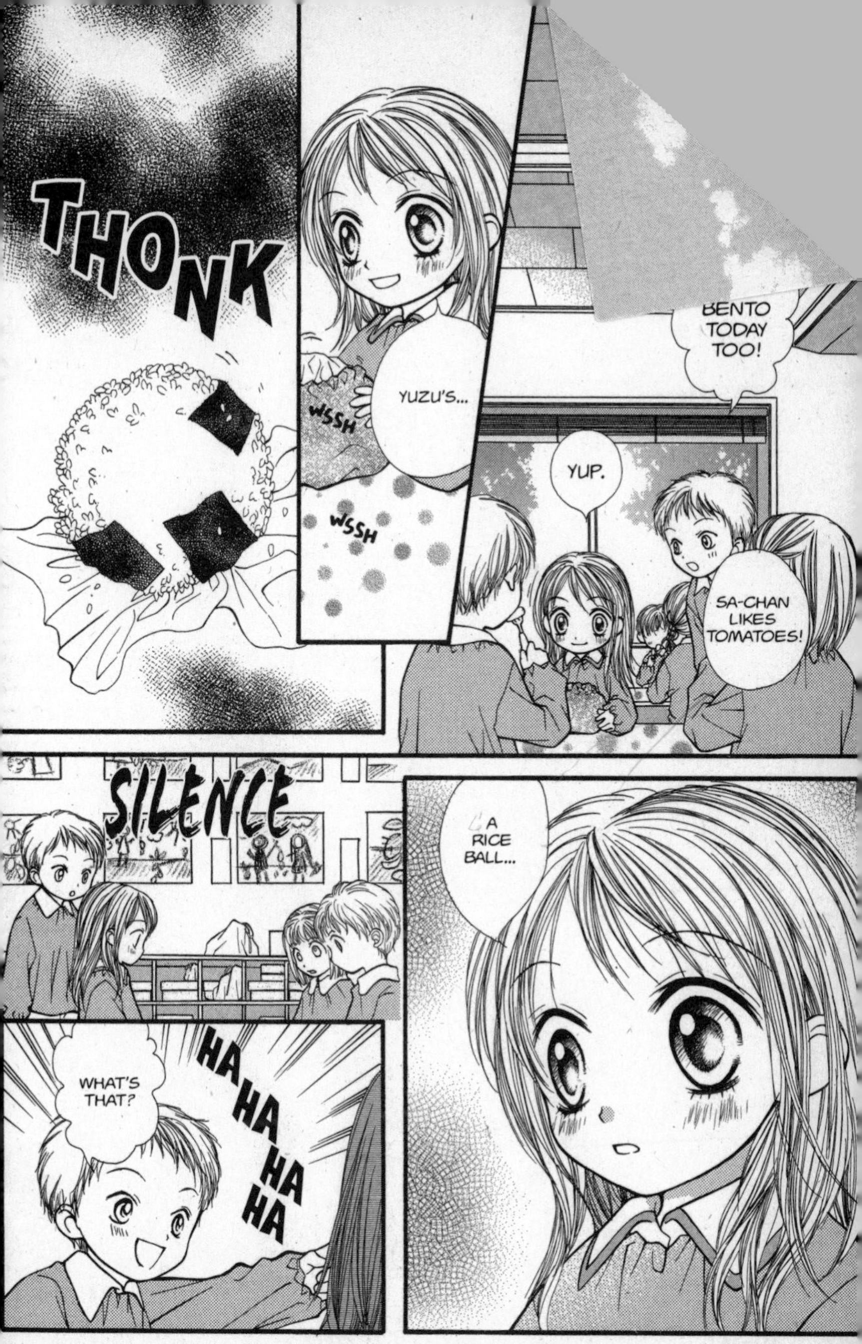
BENTO TODAY TOO!
YUP.
SA-CHAN LIKES TOMATOES!
YUZU'S...
WSSH
WSSH
THONK
A RICE BALL...
SILENCE
HA HA HA HA
WHAT'S THAT?

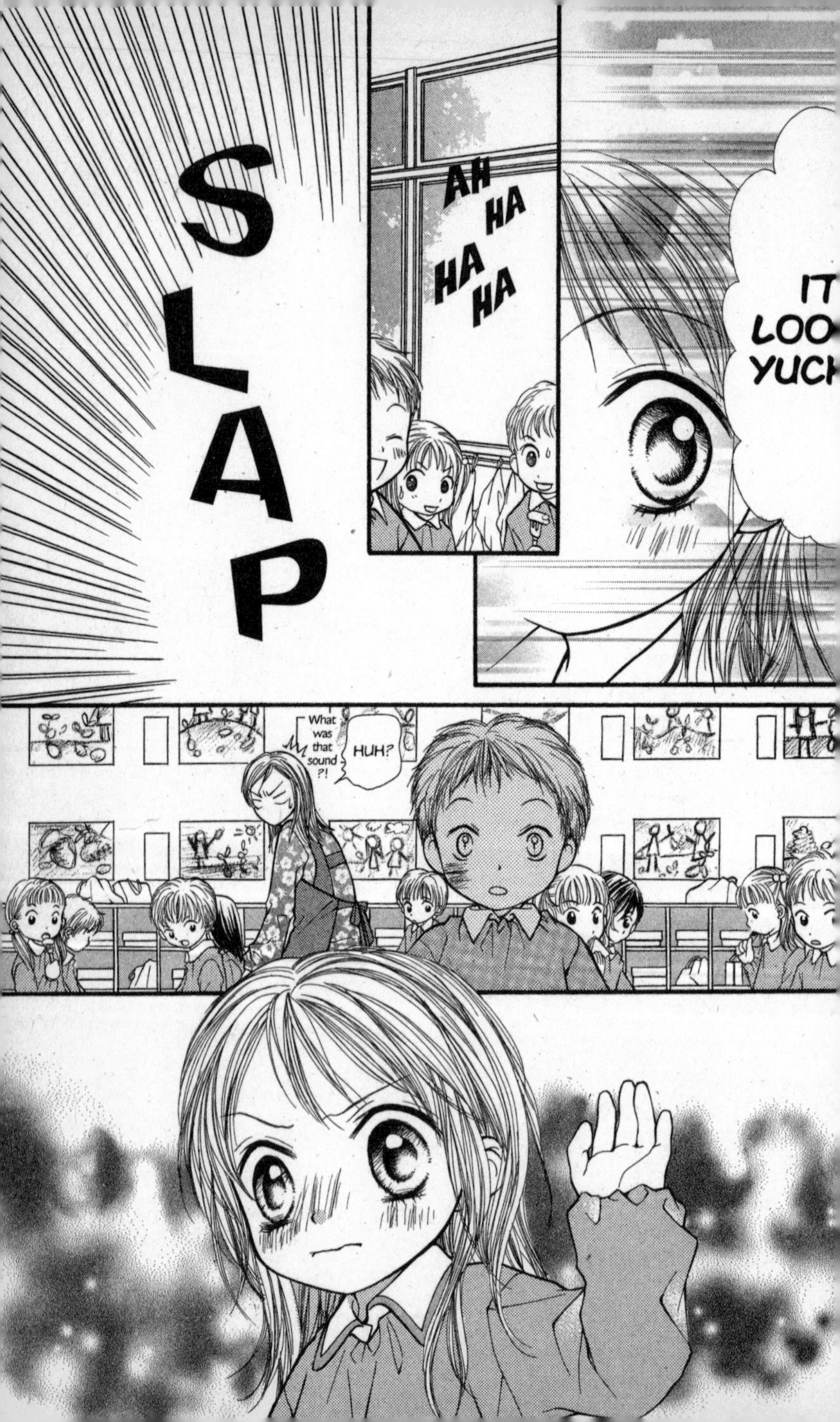
IT LOO YUCK
AH HA HA HA
SLAP
HUH?
What was that sound ?!

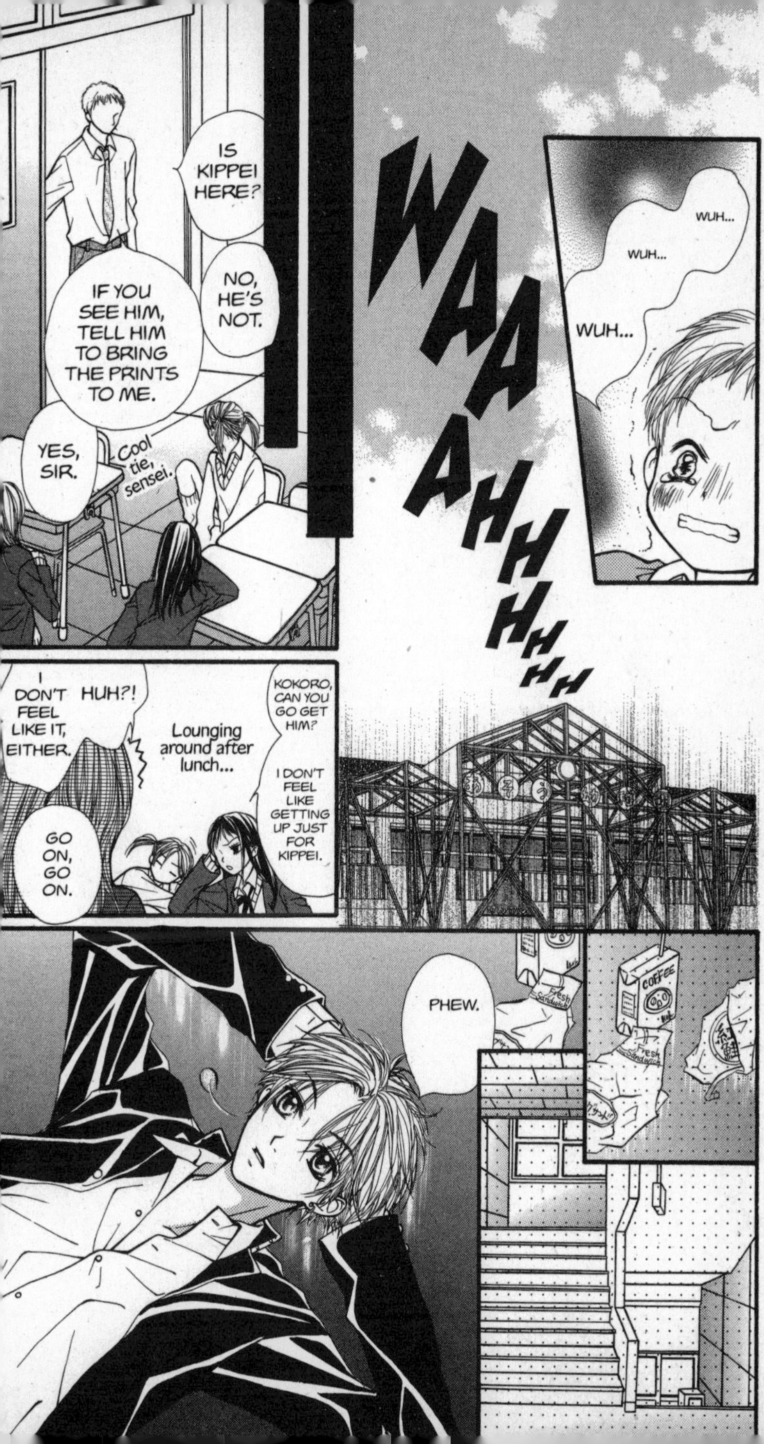
WUH...
WUH...
WUH...
WAAAHHHHHH
IS KIPPEI HERE?
NO, HE'S NOT.
IF YOU SEE HIM, TELL HIM TO BRING THE PRINTS TO ME.
YES, SIR.
Cool tie, sensei.
KOKORO, CAN YOU GO GET HIM?
I DON'T FEEL LIKE GETTING UP JUST FOR KIPPEI.
HUH?!
I DON'T FEEL LIKE IT, EITHER.
Lounging around after lunch...
GO ON, GO ON.
COFFEE
Fresh Sandwich
PHEW.

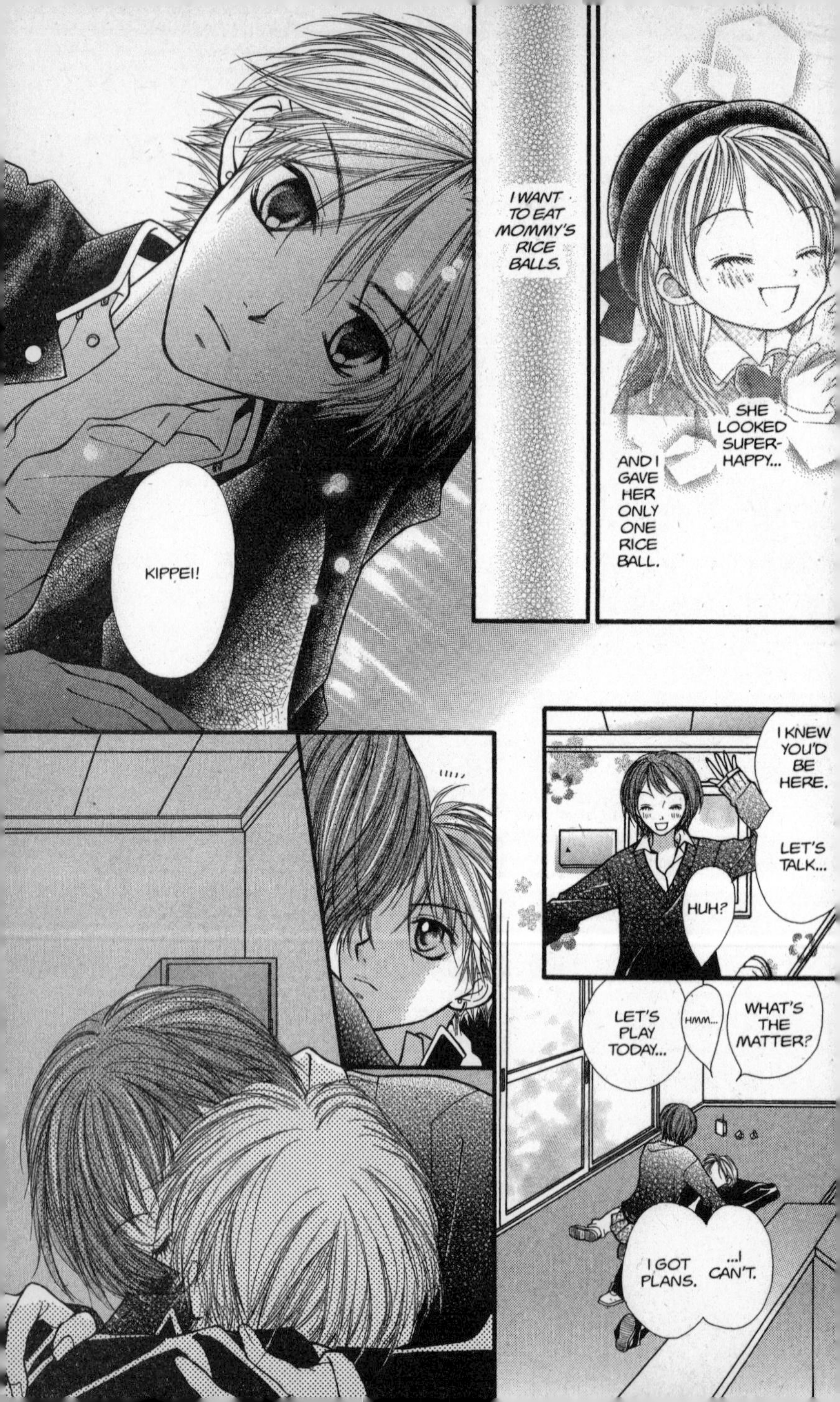

SHE LOOKED SUPER-HAPPY...
AND I GAVE HER ONLY ONE RICE BALL.
I WANT TO EAT MOMMY'S RICE BALLS.
KIPPEI!
I KNEW YOU'D BE HERE.
LET'S TALK...
HUH?
WHAT'S THE MATTER?
HMM...
LET'S PLAY TODAY...
...I CAN'T.
I GOT PLANS.

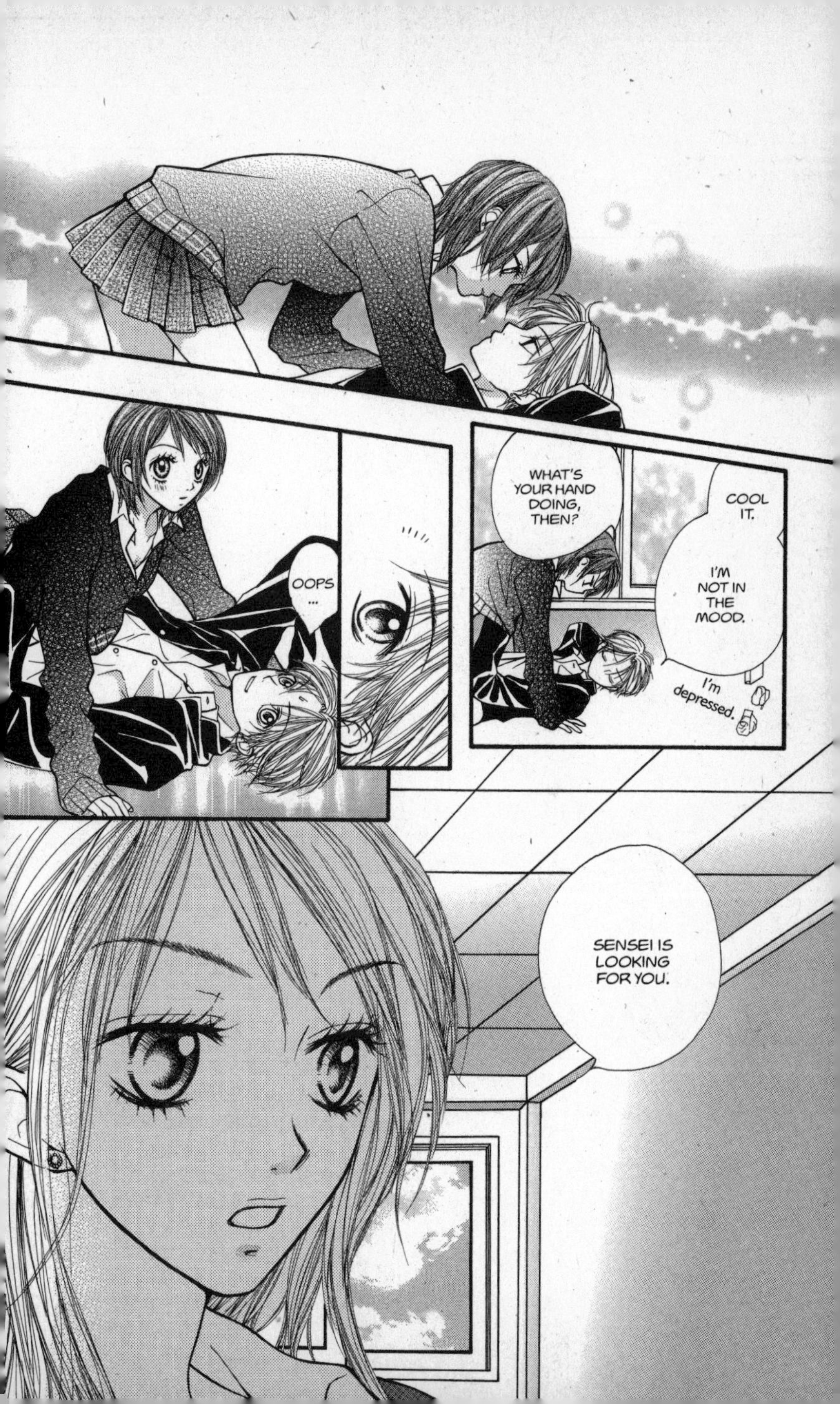
COOL IT. I'M NOT IN THE MOOD.
I'm depressed.
WHAT'S YOUR HAND DOING, THEN?
!!!
OOPS ...
SENSEI IS LOOKING FOR YOU.

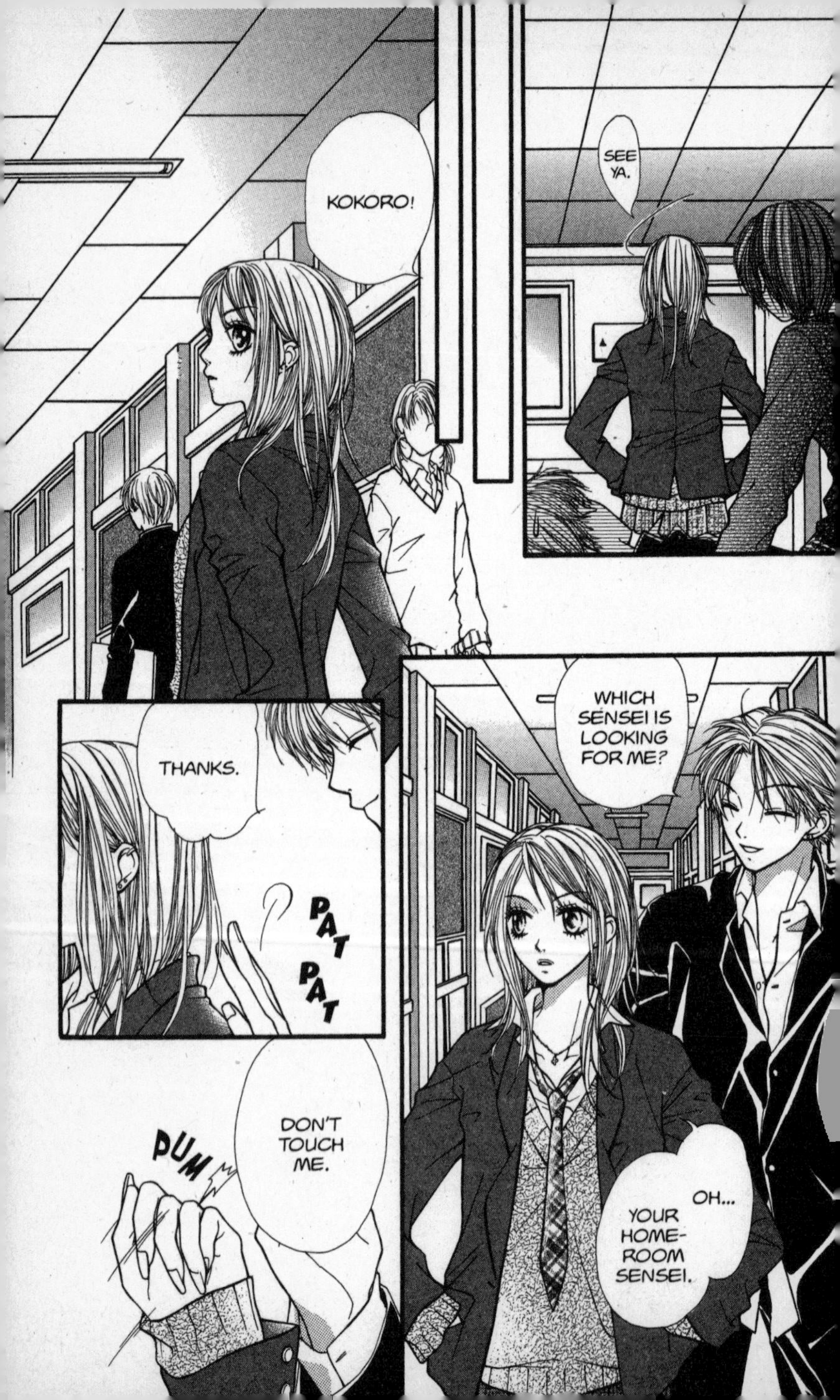
SEE YA.
KOKORO!
WHICH SENSEI IS LOOKING FOR ME?
OH... YOUR HOME-ROOM SENSEI.
THANKS.
PAT PAT
DON'T TOUCH ME.
PUM

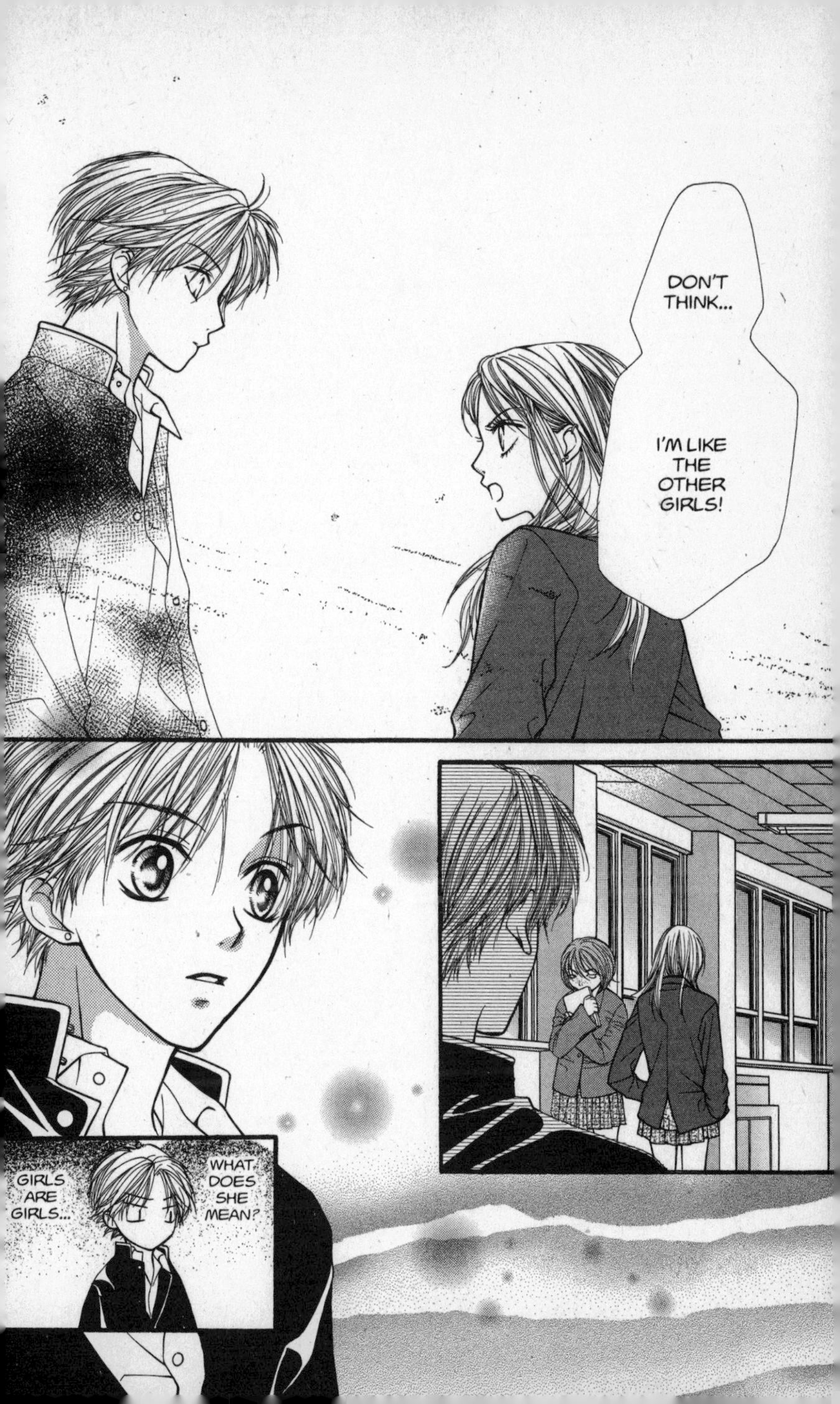
DON'T THINK...
I'M LIKE THE OTHER GIRLS!
WHAT DOES SHE MEAN?
GIRLS ARE GIRLS...

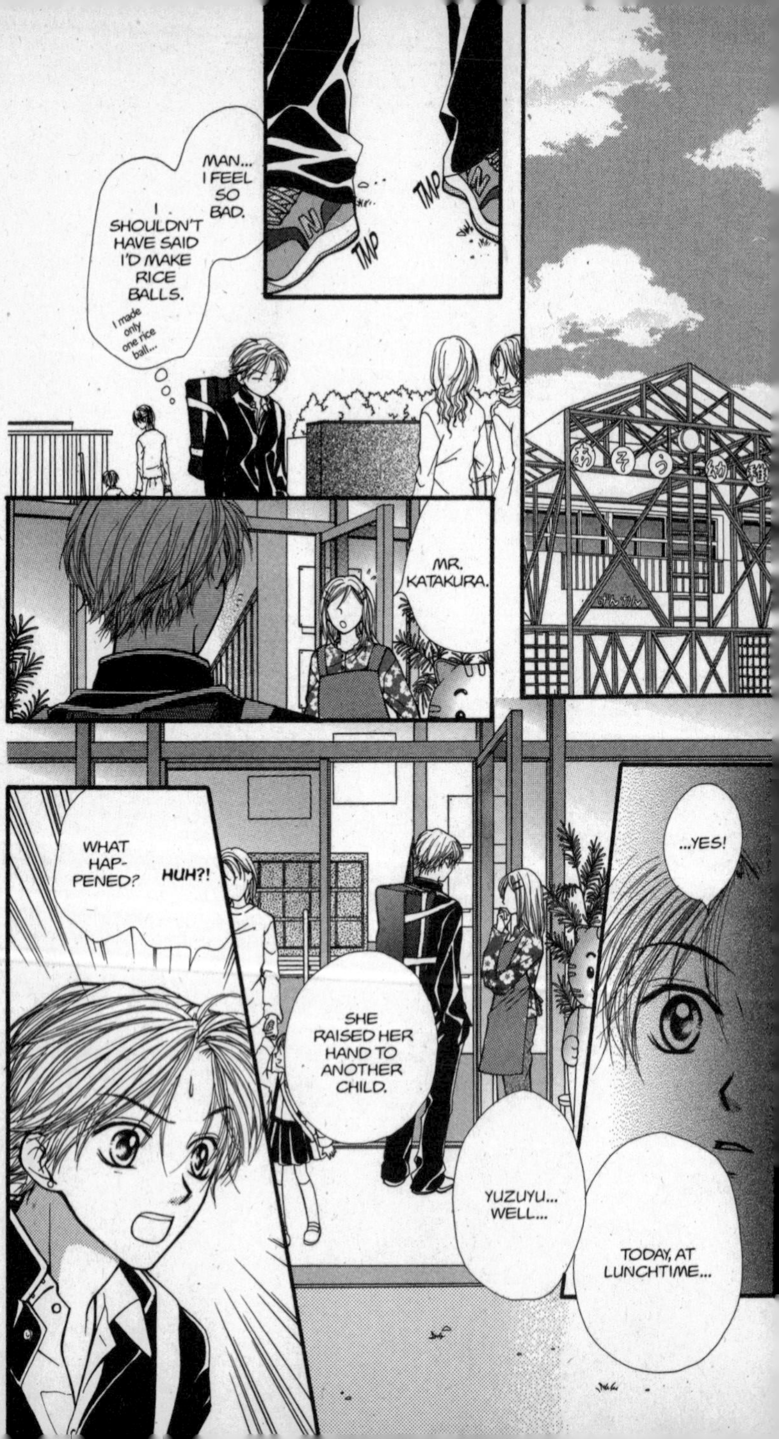
TMP
TMP
MAN... I FEEL SO BAD.
I SHOULDN'T HAVE SAID I'D MAKE RICE BALLS.
I made only one rice ball...
MR. KATAKURA.
...YES!
TODAY, AT LUNCHTIME...
YUZUYU... WELL...
SHE RAISED HER HAND TO ANOTHER CHILD.
HUH?!
WHAT HAP-PENED?

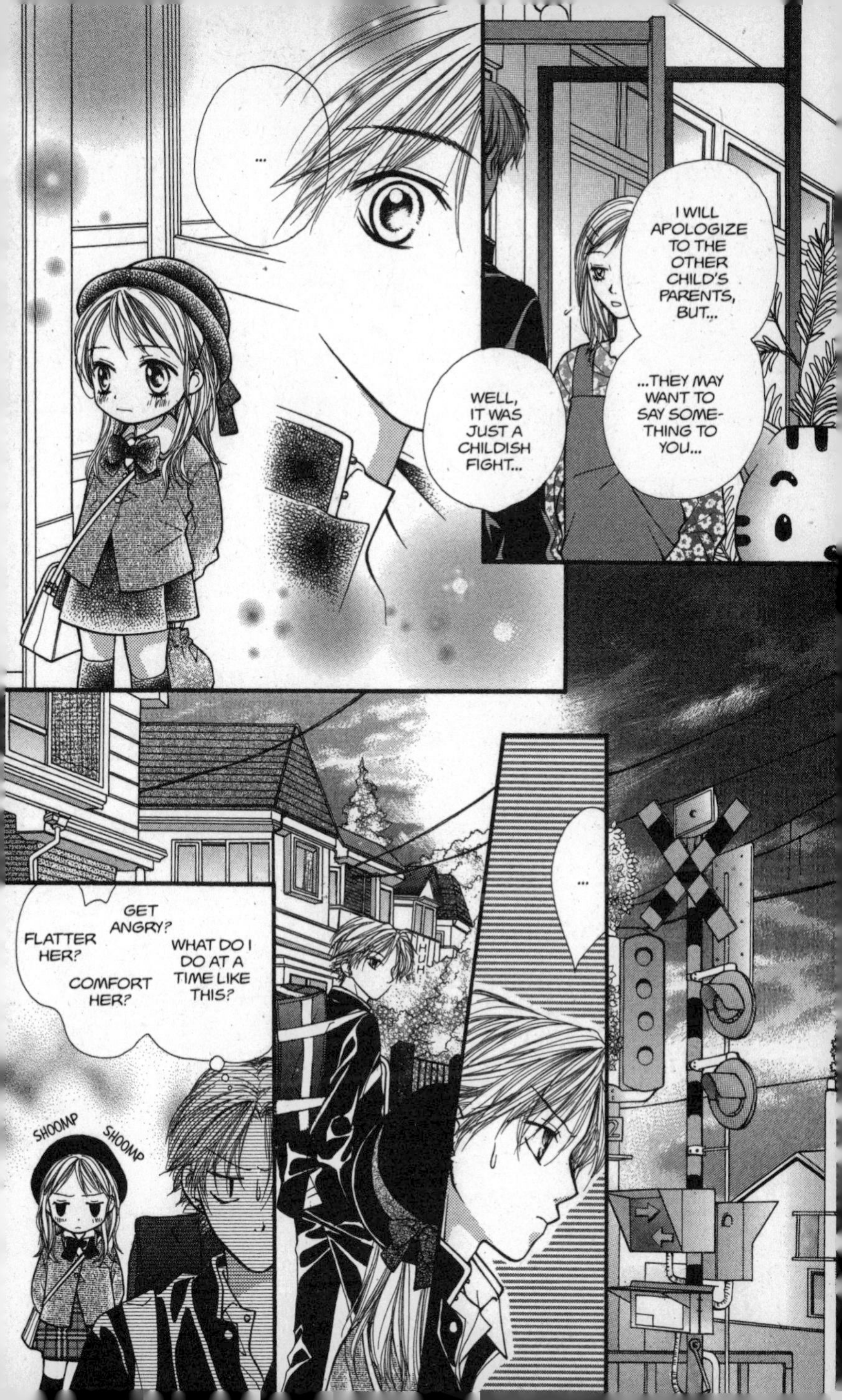
I WILL APOLOGIZE TO THE OTHER CHILD'S PARENTS, BUT...
...THEY MAY WANT TO SAY SOME-THING TO YOU...
WELL, IT WAS JUST A CHILDISH FIGHT...
...
...
HUH
GET ANGRY?
FLATTER HER?
COMFORT HER?
WHAT DO I DO AT A TIME LIKE THIS?
SHOOMP
SHOOMP

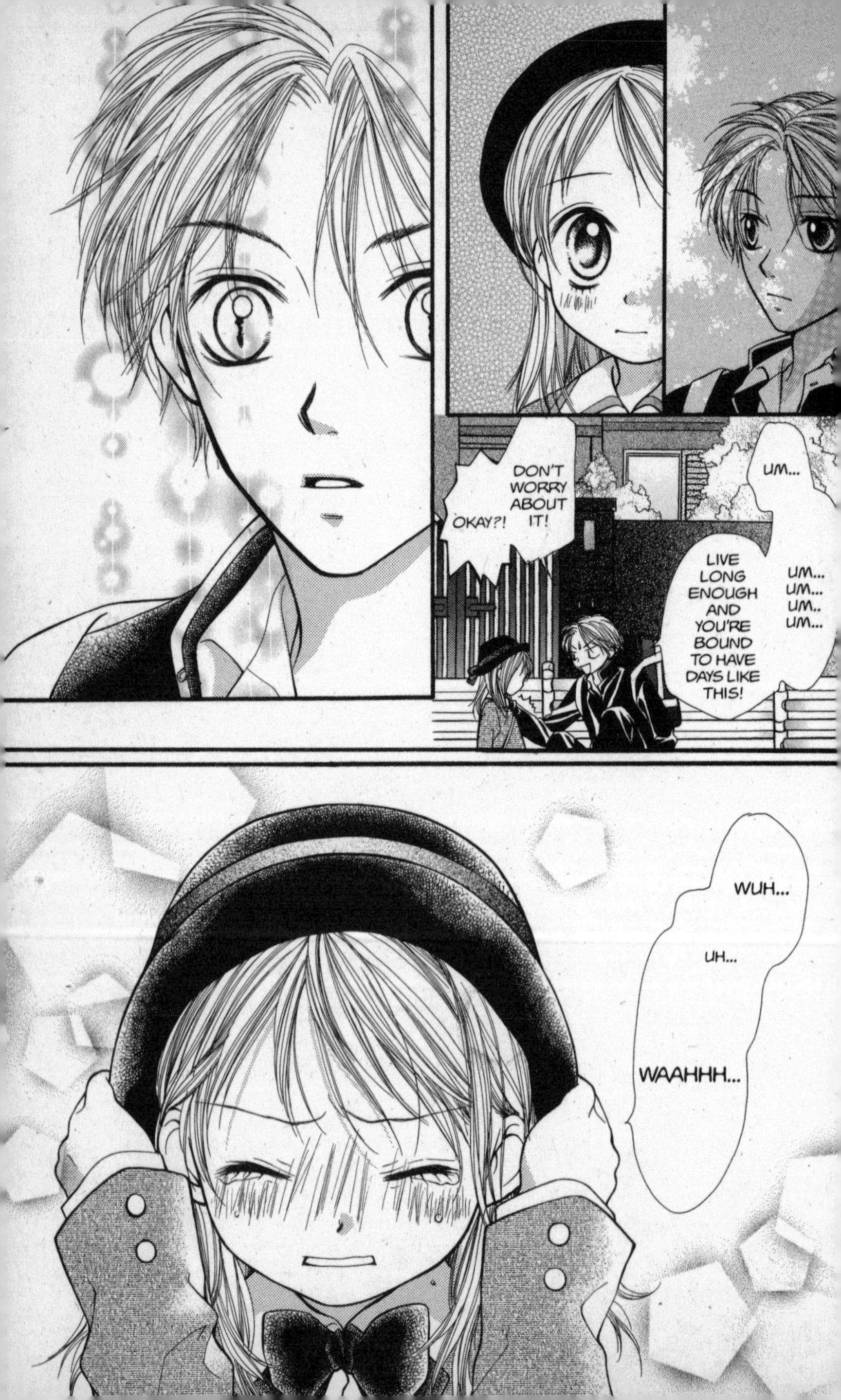
UM...
UM... UM... UM.. UM...
LIVE LONG ENOUGH AND YOU'RE BOUND TO HAVE DAYS LIKE THIS!
DON'T WORRY ABOUT IT! OKAY?!
WUH...
UH...
WAAHHH...

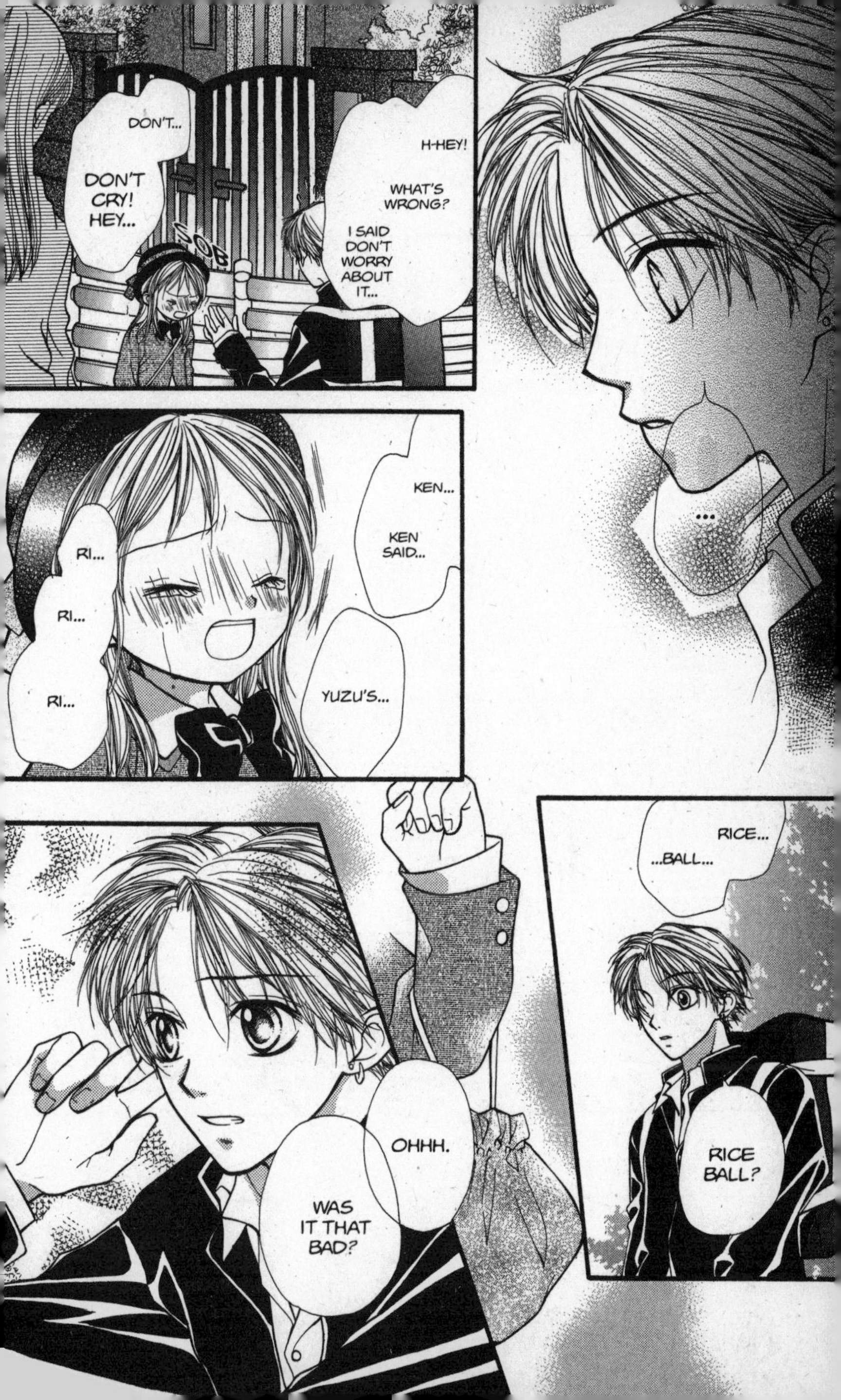

...
H-HEY!
WHAT'S WRONG?
I SAID DON'T WORRY ABOUT IT...
DON'T...
DON'T CRY! HEY...
SOB
KEN...
KEN SAID...
YUZU'S...
RI...
RI...
RI...
RICE...
...BALL...
RICE BALL?
OHHH.
WAS IT THAT BAD?

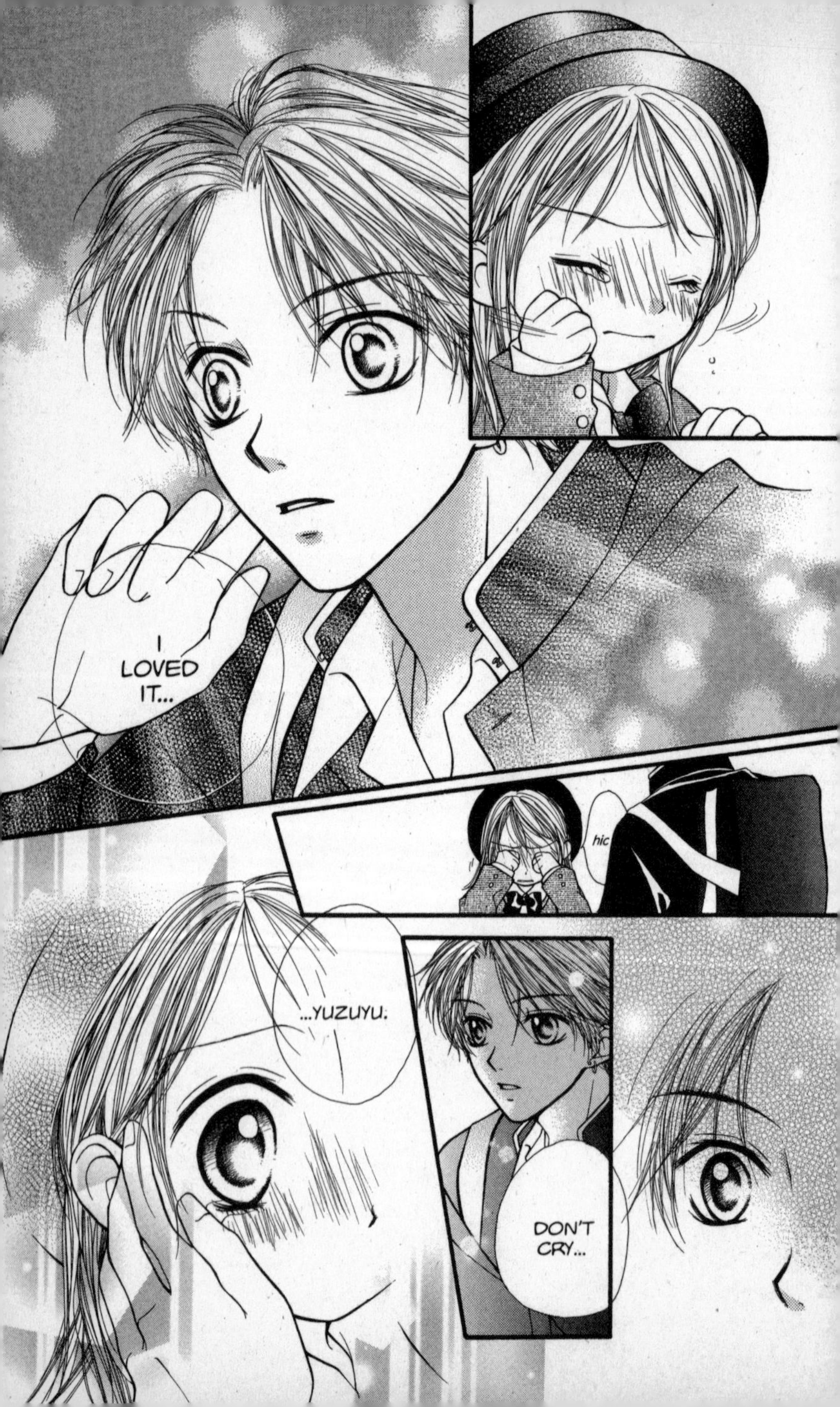
I LOVED IT...
hic
DON'T CRY...
...YUZUYU.

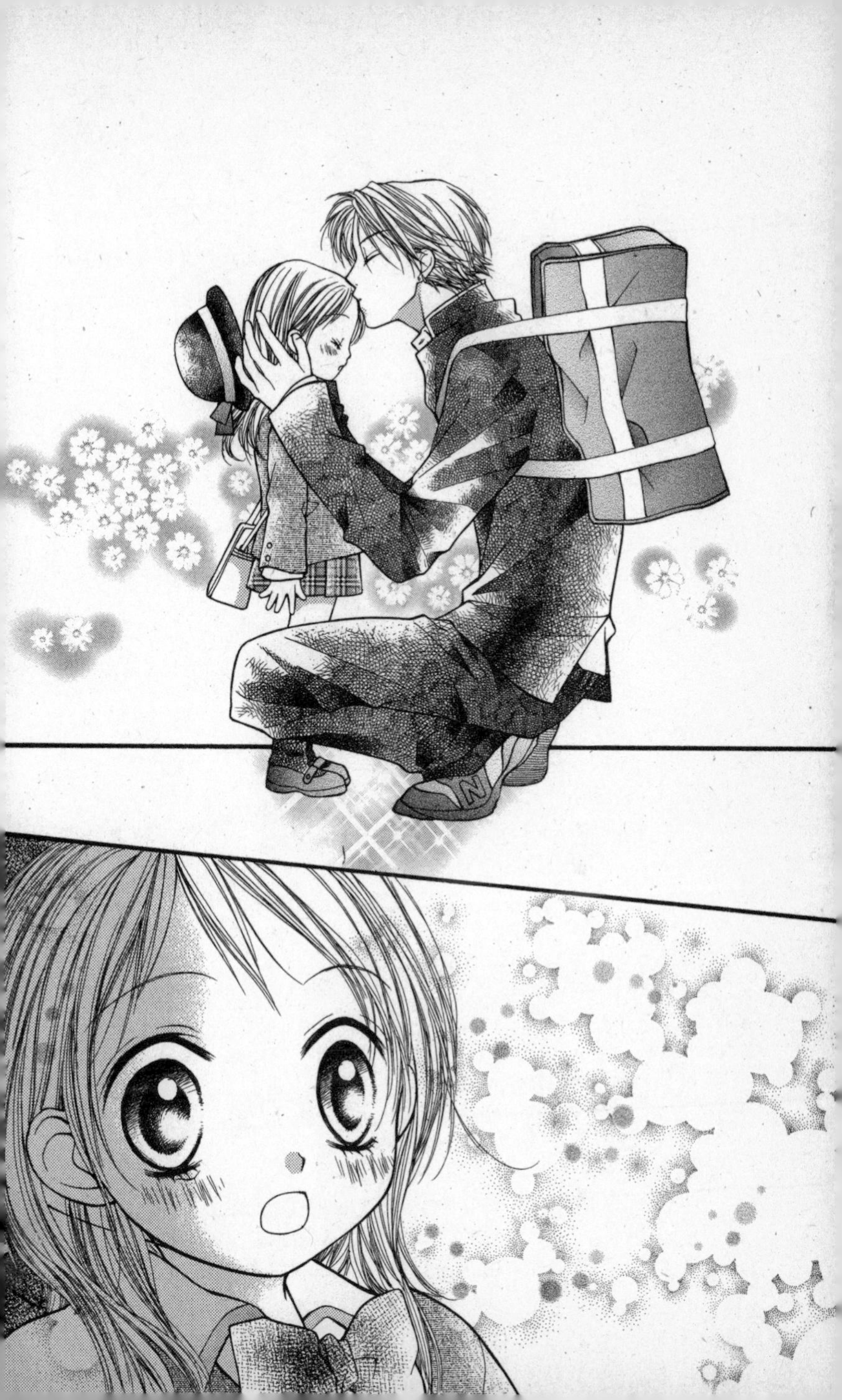

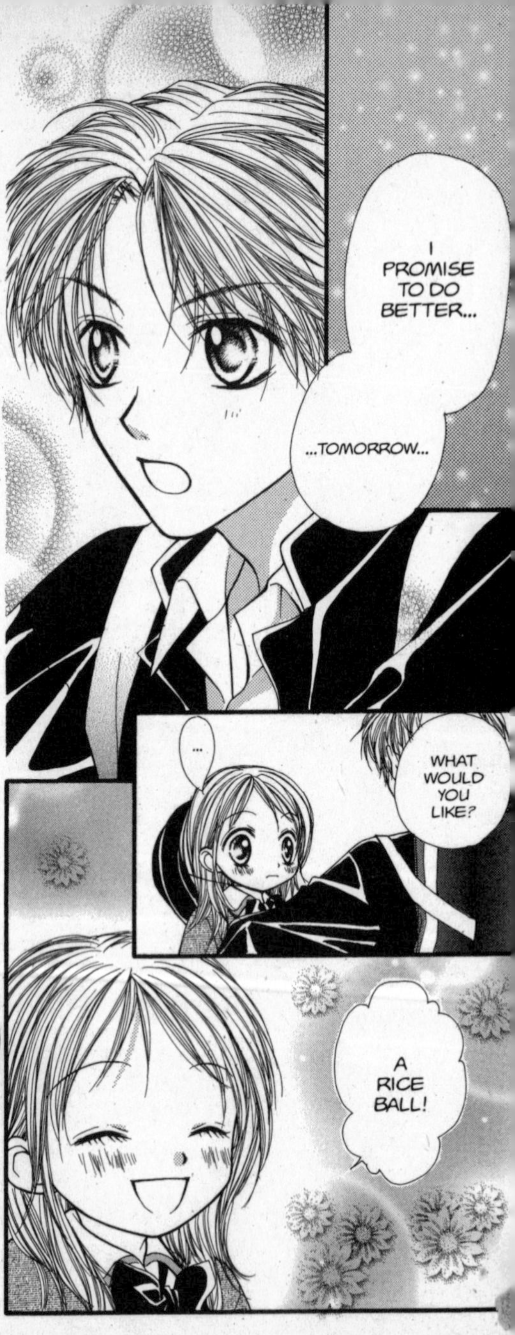
I PROMISE TO DO BETTER...
...TOMORROW...
WHAT WOULD YOU LIKE?
...
A RICE BALL!

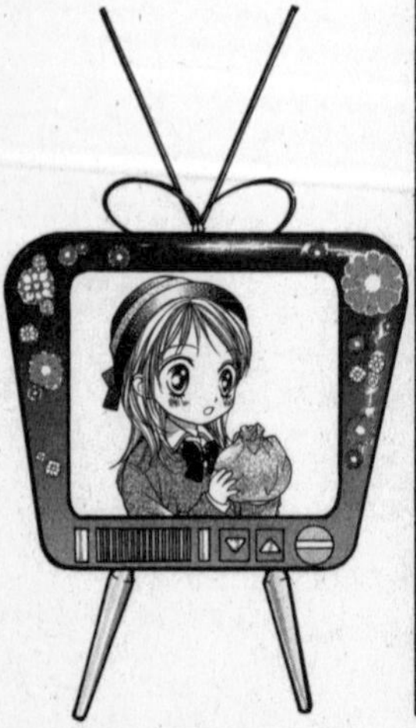

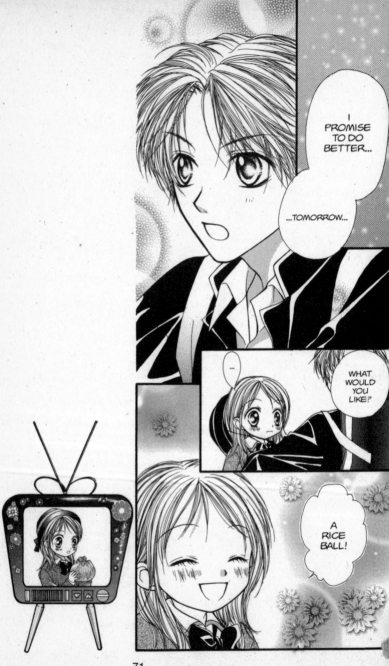

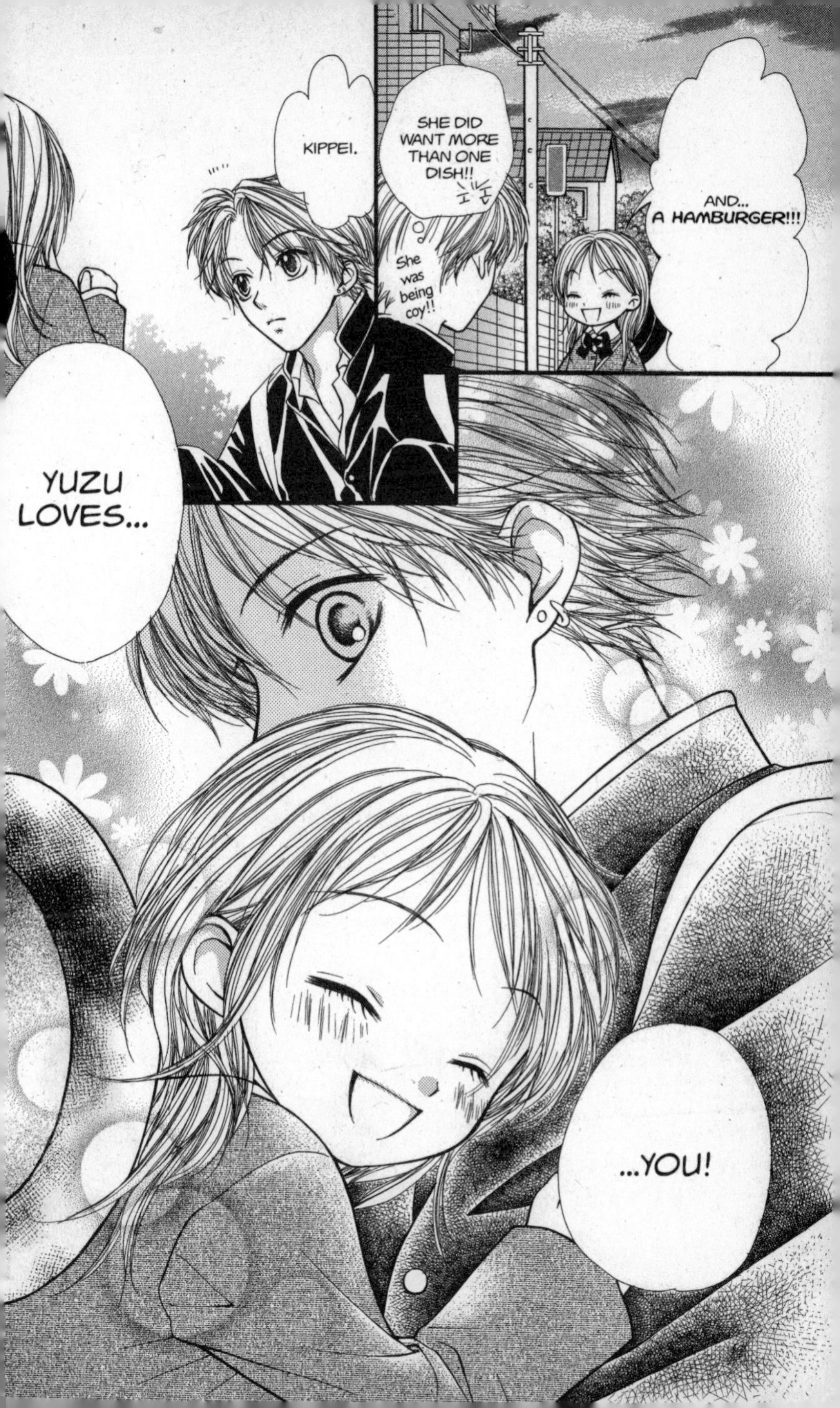
AND... A HAMBURGER!!!
SHE DID WANT MORE THAN ONE DISH!!
She was being coy!!
KIPPEI.
YUZU LOVES...
...YOU!

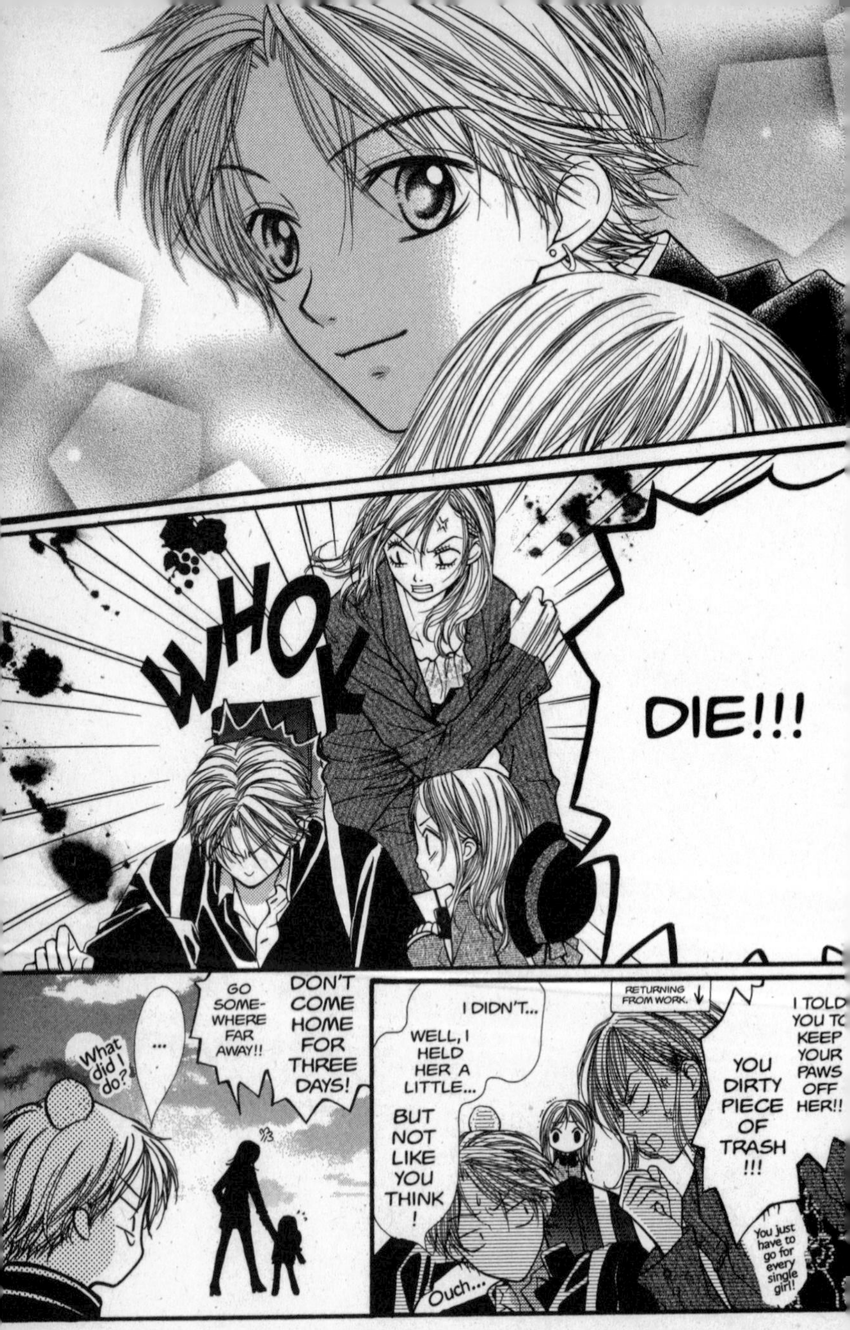
DIE!!!
WHOK
RETURNING FROM WORK.
I TOLD YOU TO KEEP YOUR PAWS OFF HER!!
YOU DIRTY PIECE OF TRASH!!!
I DIDN'T...
WELL, I HELD HER A LITTLE...
BUT NOT LIKE YOU THINK!
You just have to go for every single girl!!
Ouch...
DON'T COME HOME FOR THREE DAYS!
GO SOME-WHERE FAR AWAY!!
...
What did I do?

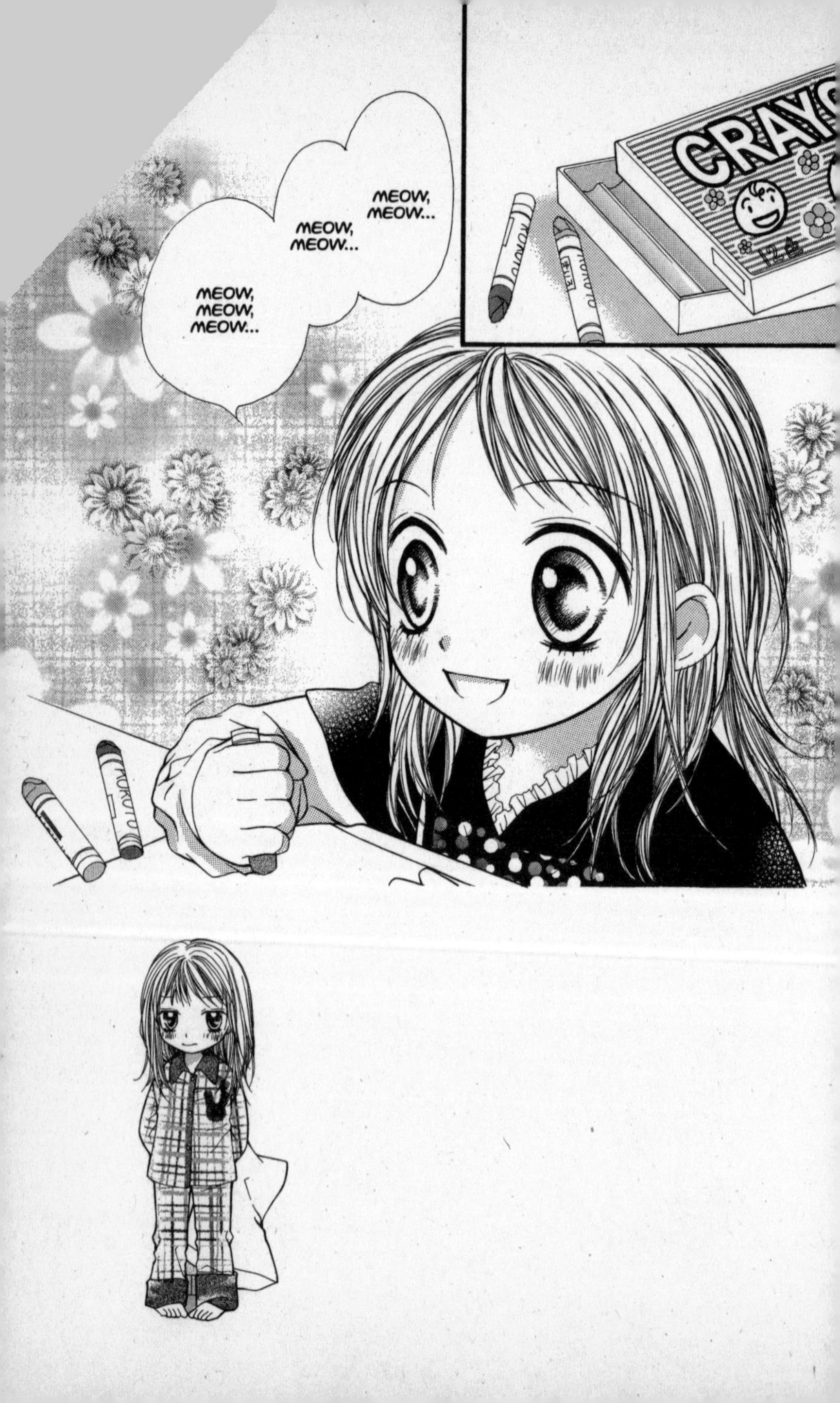
MEOW, MEOW...
MEOW, MEOW...
MEOW, MEOW, MEOW...

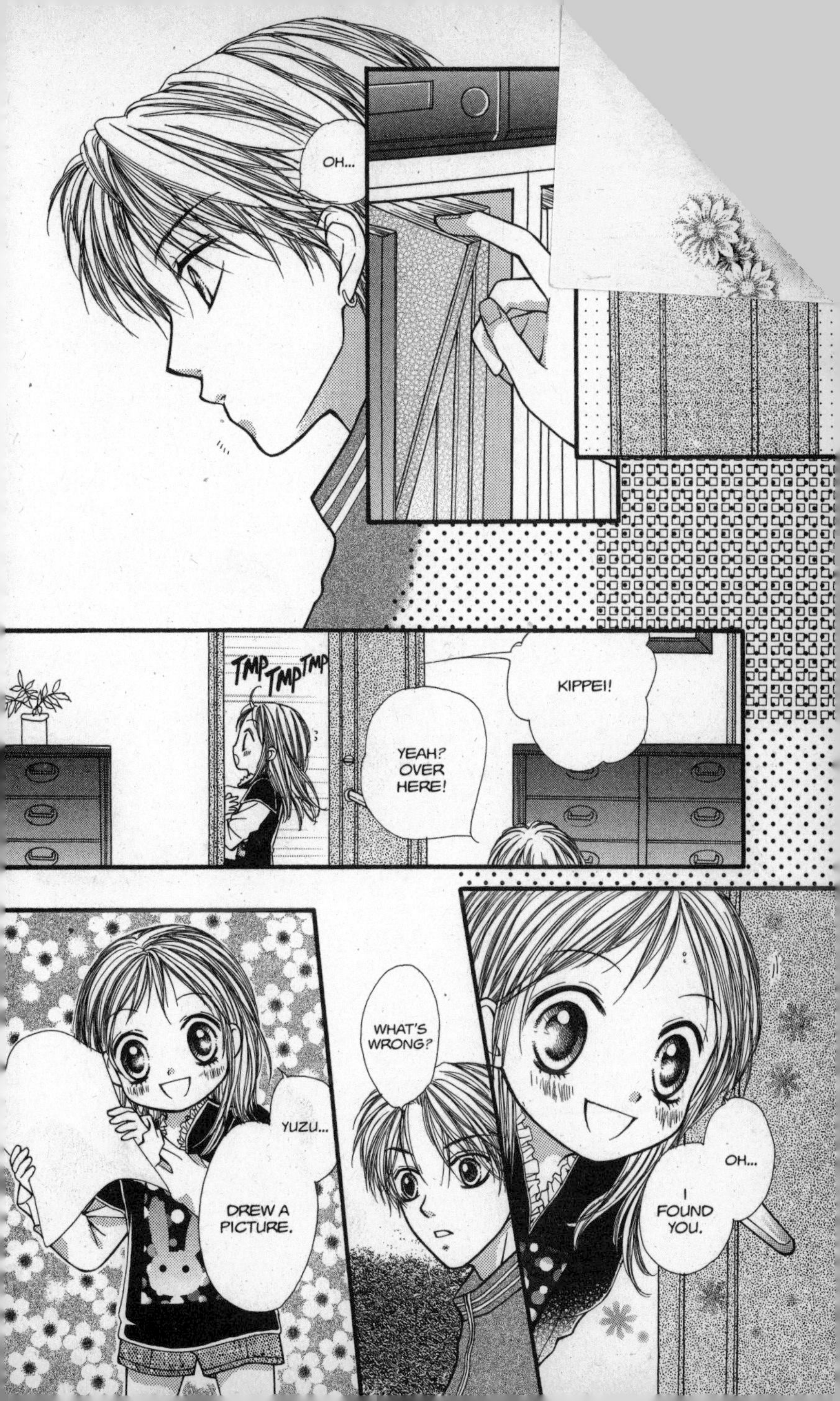
OH...
KIPPEI!
TMP TMP TMP
YEAH? OVER HERE!
OH... I FOUND YOU.
WHAT'S WRONG?
YUZU...
DREW A PICTURE.

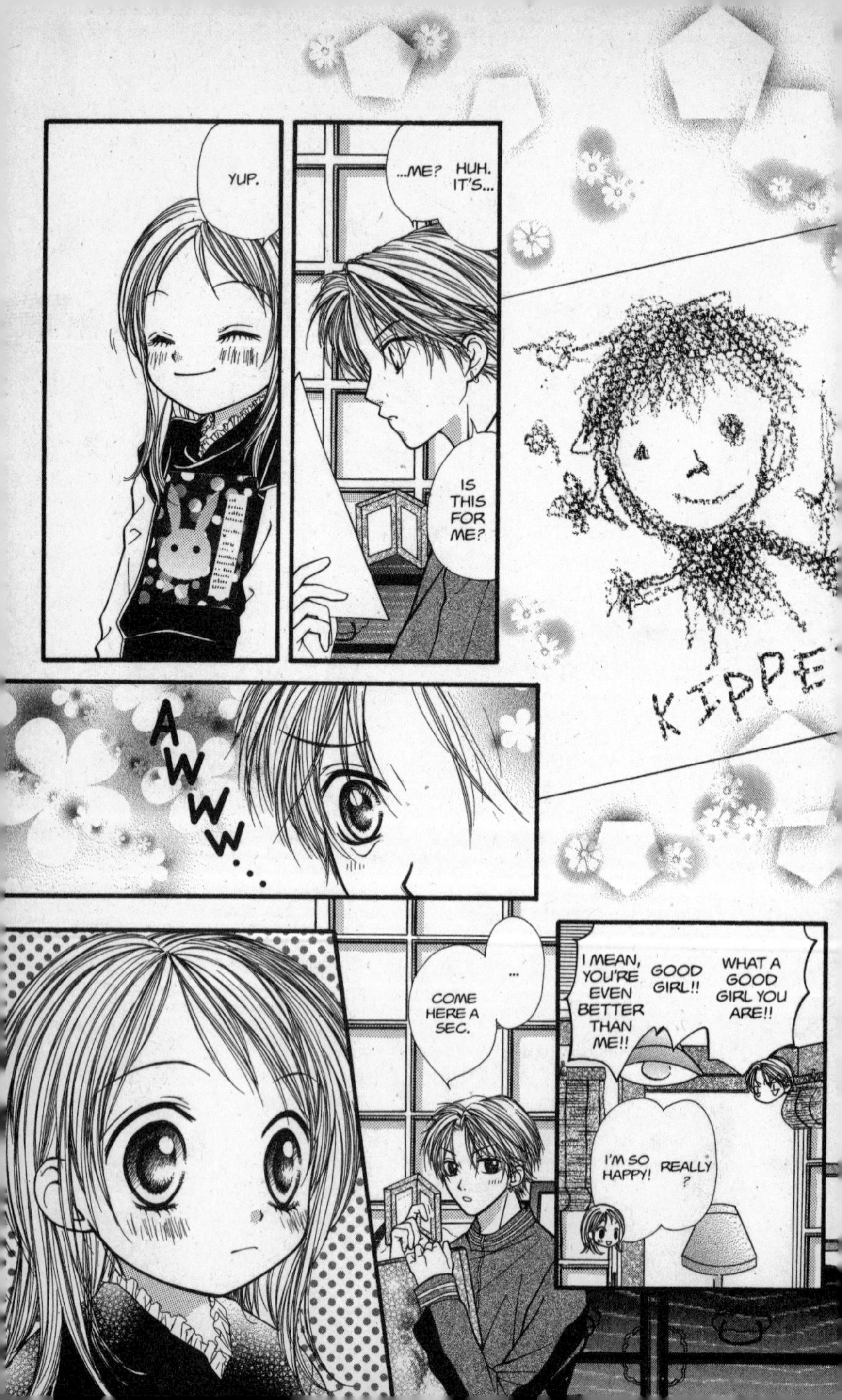

...ME? HUH. IT'S...
IS THIS FOR ME?
YUP.
KIPPE
AWWW...
WHAT A GOOD GIRL YOU ARE!!
GOOD GIRL!!
I MEAN, YOU'RE EVEN BETTER THAN ME!!
REALLY?
I'M SO HAPPY!
...
COME HERE A SEC.

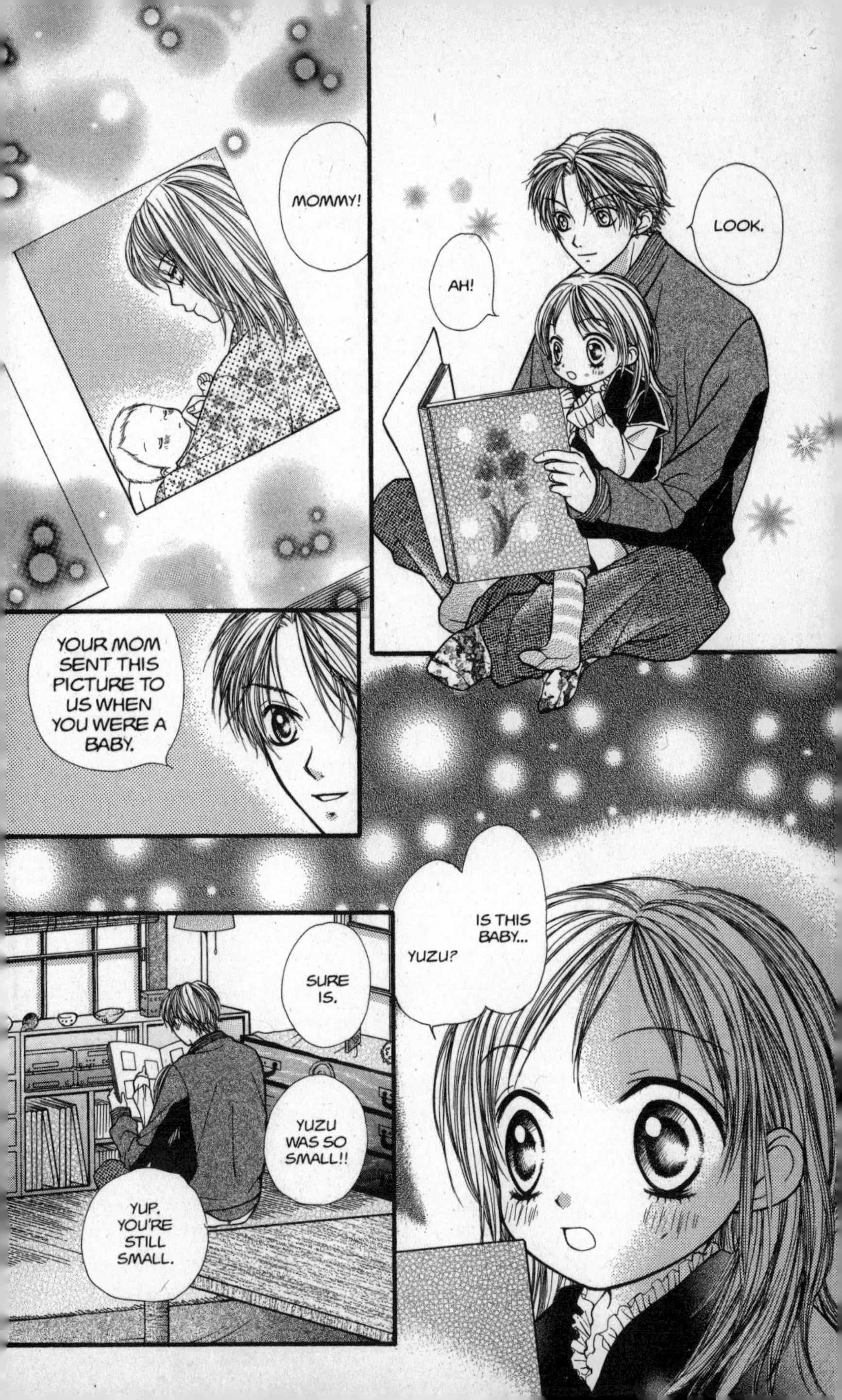

LOOK.
AH!
MOMMY!
IS THIS BABY... YUZU?
YOUR MOM SENT THIS PICTURE TO US WHEN YOU WERE A BABY.
SURE IS.
YUZU WAS SO SMALL!!
YUP. YOU'RE STILL SMALL.

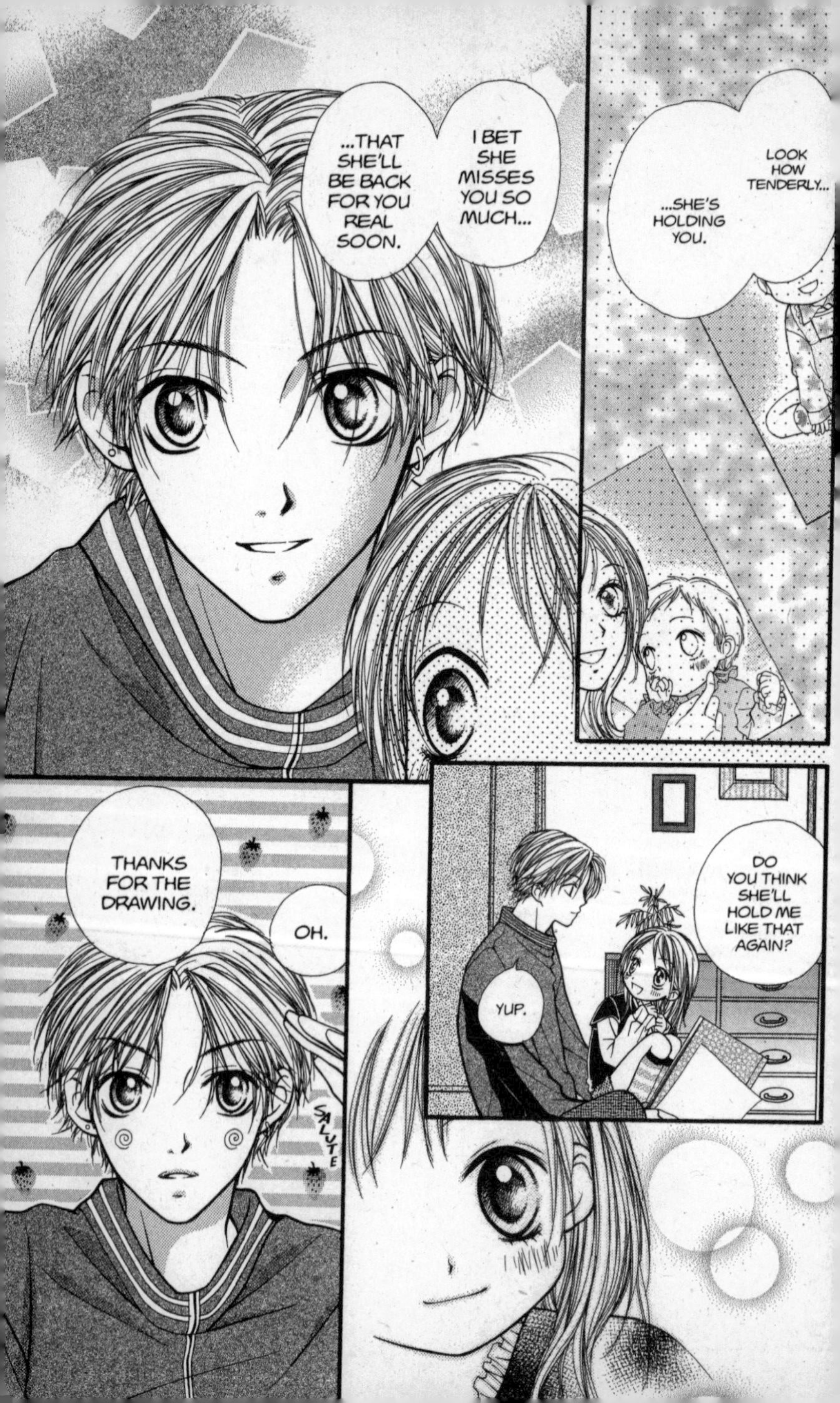
LOOK HOW TENDERLY...
...SHE'S HOLDING YOU.
I BET SHE MISSES YOU SO MUCH...
...THAT SHE'LL BE BACK FOR YOU REAL SOON.
DO YOU THINK SHE'LL HOLD ME LIKE THAT AGAIN?
YUP.
OH.
THANKS FOR THE DRAWING.
SALUTE

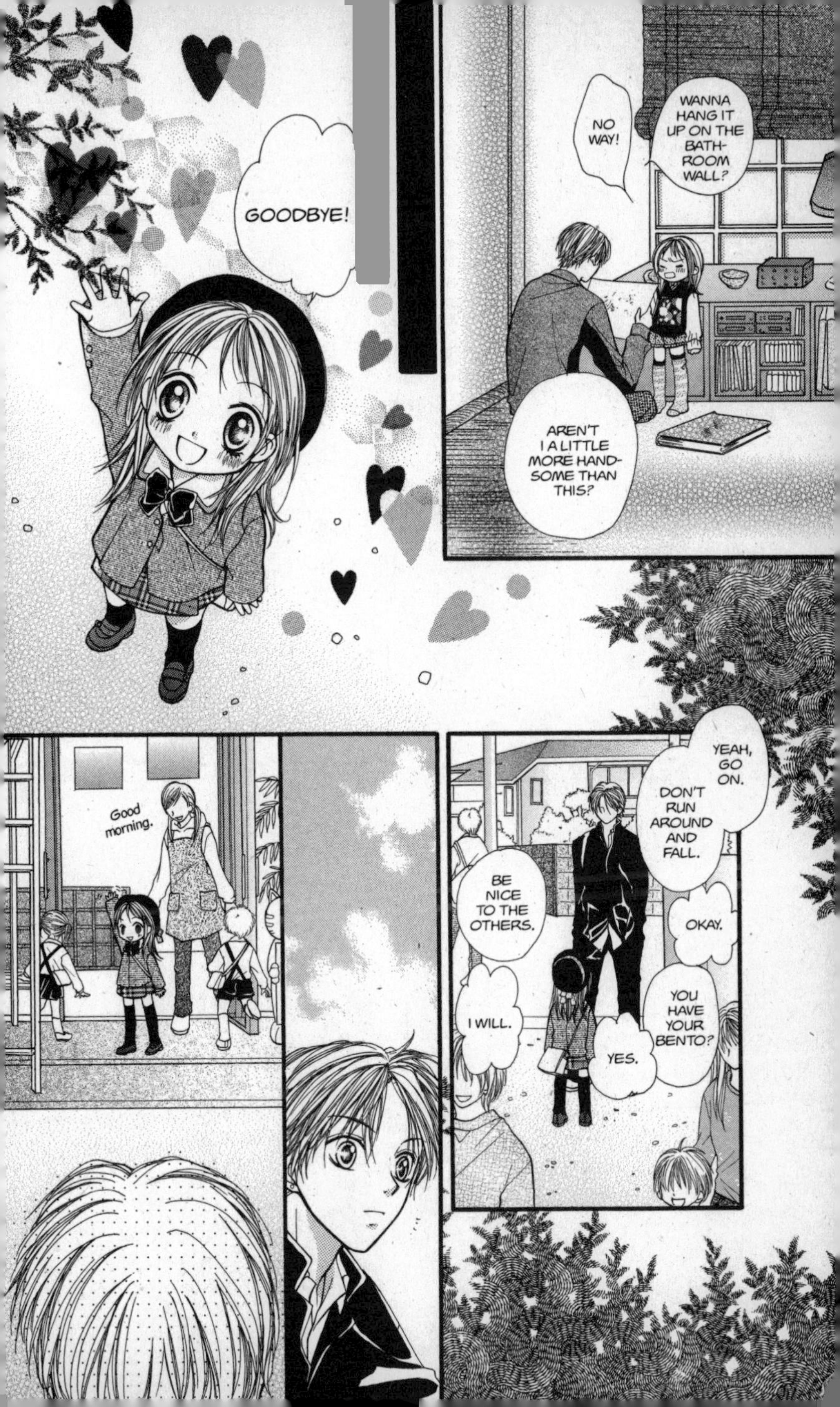

WANNA HANG IT UP ON THE BATHROOM WALL?
NO WAY!
AREN'T I A LITTLE MORE HANDSOME THAN THIS?
GOODBYE!
YEAH, GO ON.
DON'T RUN AROUND AND FALL.
OKAY.
BE NICE TO THE OTHERS.
YOU HAVE YOUR BENTO?
I WILL.
YES.
Good morning.

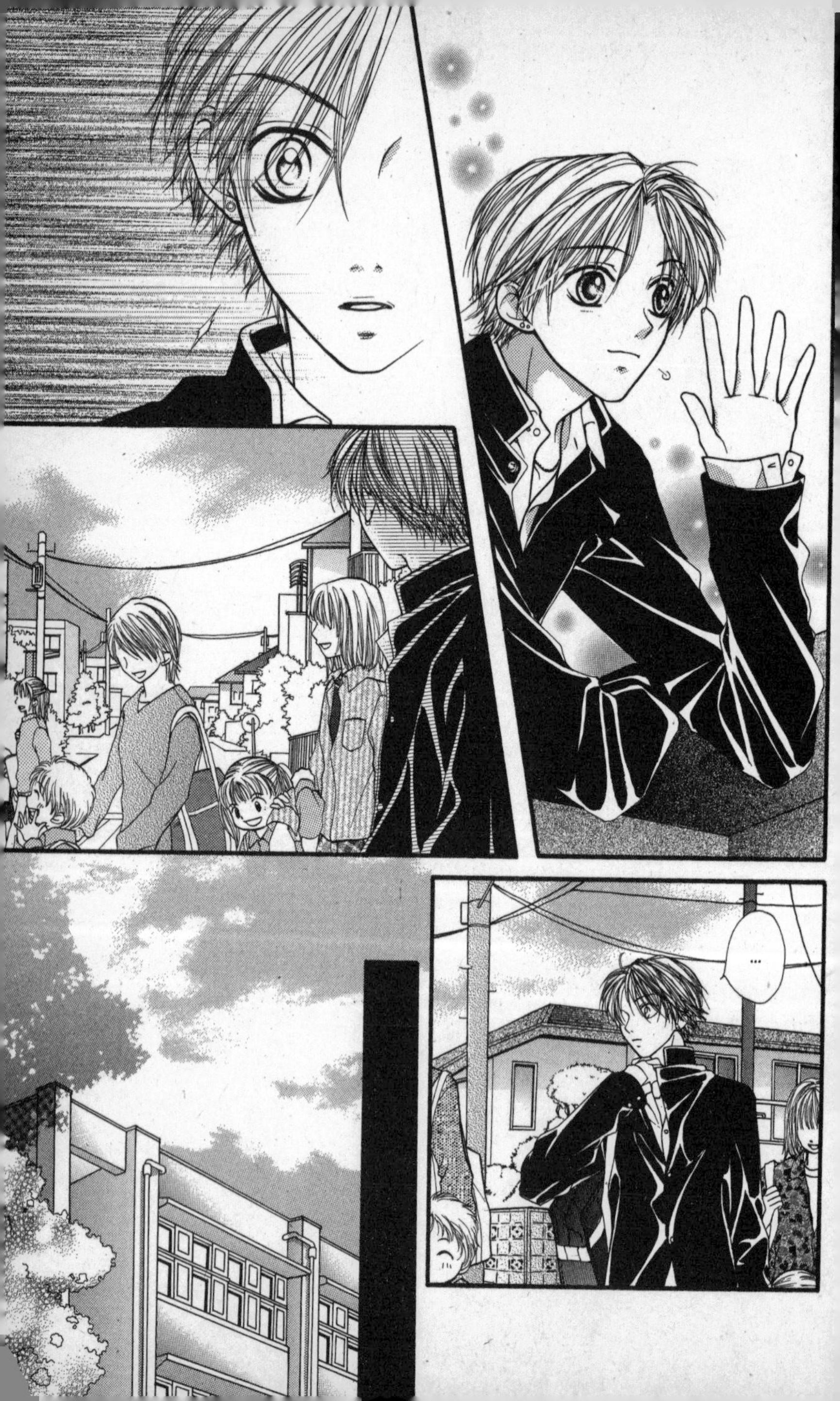
...

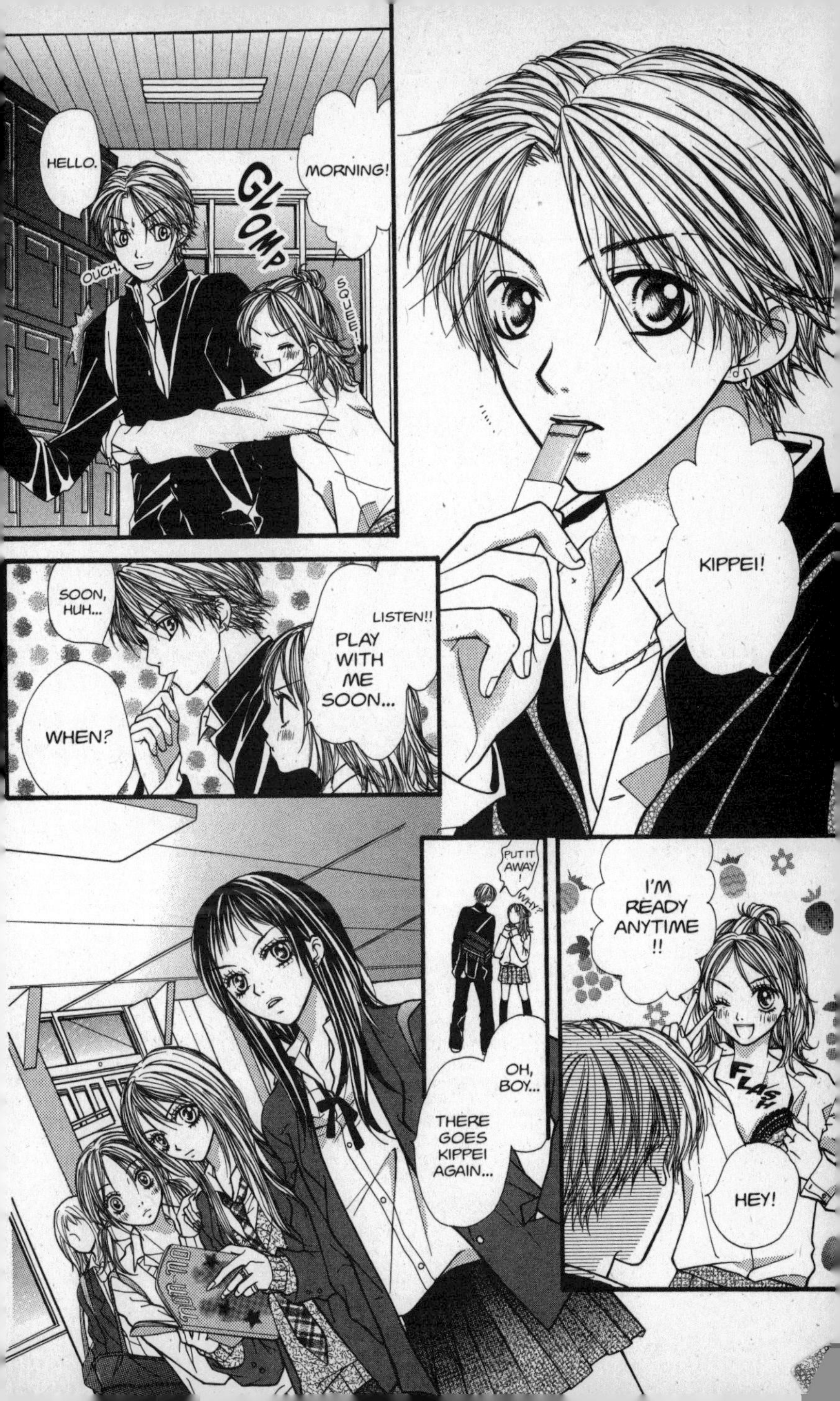
KIPPEI!
MORNING!
GLOMP
SQUEE!
HELLO.
OUCH.
LISTEN!!
PLAY WITH ME SOON...
SOON, HUH...
WHEN?
I'M READY ANYTIME!!
FLASH
HEY!
PUT IT AWAY!
WHY?
OH, BOY...
THERE GOES KIPPEI AGAIN...

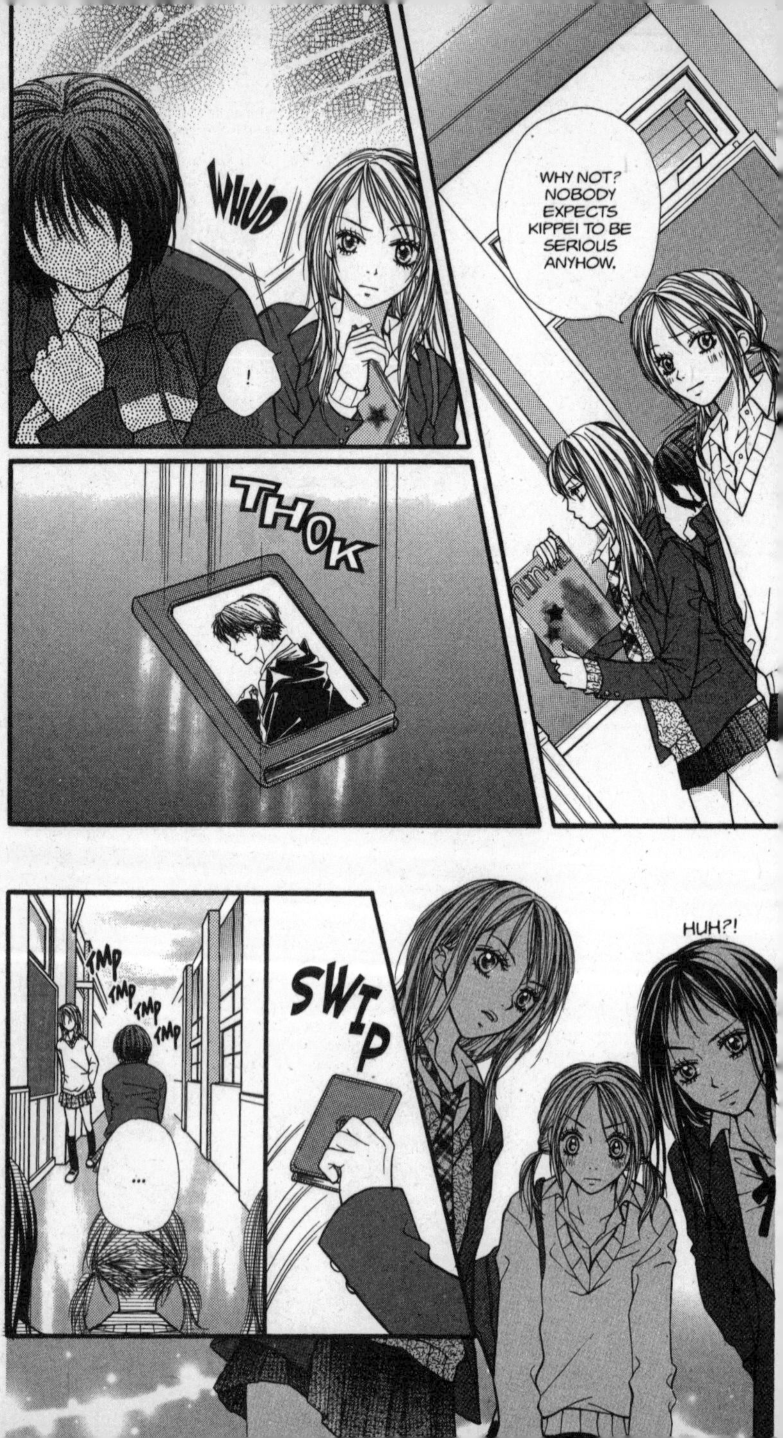
WHY NOT? NOBODY EXPECTS KIPPEI TO BE SERIOUS ANYHOW.
WHUD
!
THOK
HUH?!
SWIP
TMP TMP TMP TMP
...

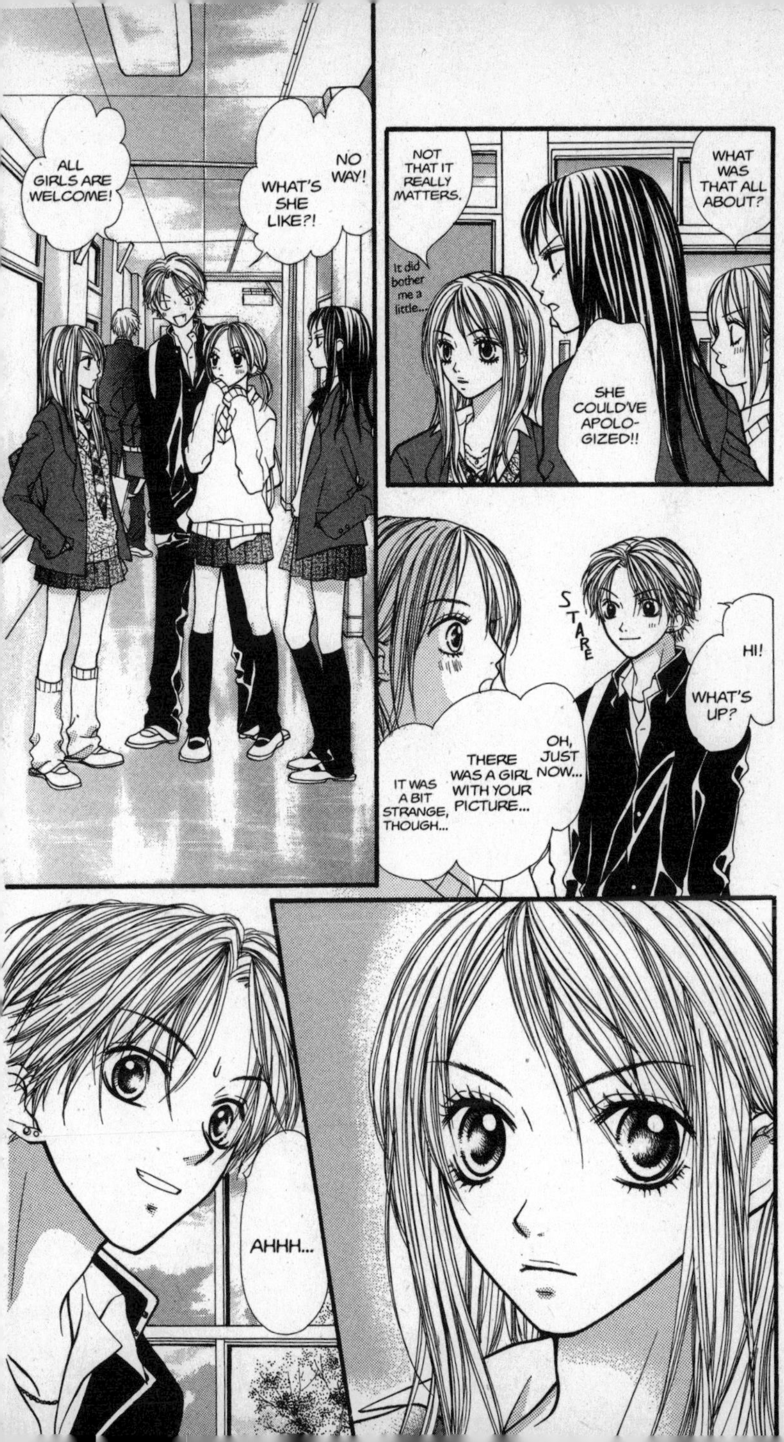
WHAT WAS THAT ALL ABOUT?
NOT THAT IT REALLY MATTERS.
It did bother me a little...
SHE COULD'VE APOLO-GIZED!!
STARE
HI!
WHAT'S UP?
OH, JUST NOW...
THERE WAS A GIRL WITH YOUR PICTURE...
IT WAS A BIT STRANGE, THOUGH...
NO WAY!
WHAT'S SHE LIKE?!
ALL GIRLS ARE WELCOME!
AHHH...

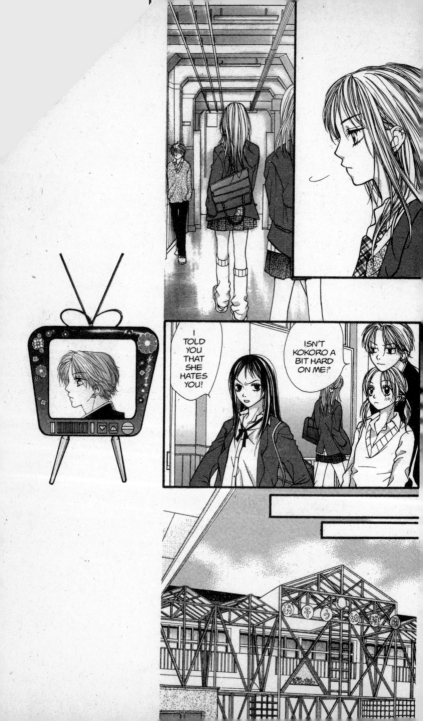

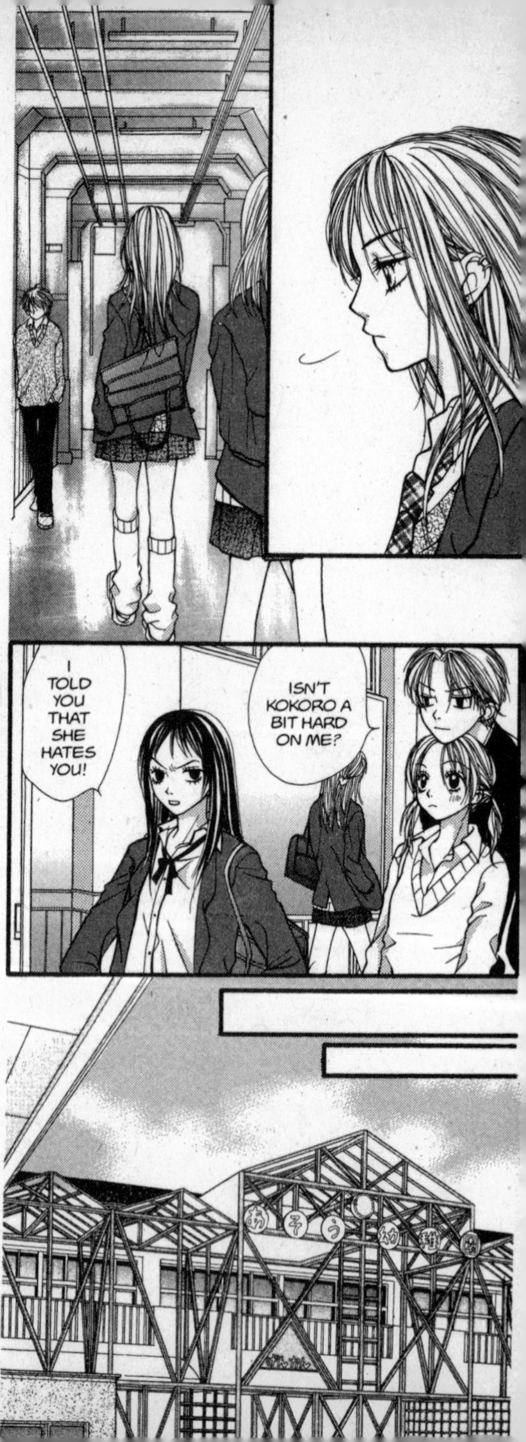
ISN'T KOKORO A BIT HARD ON ME?
I TOLD YOU THAT SHE HATES YOU!

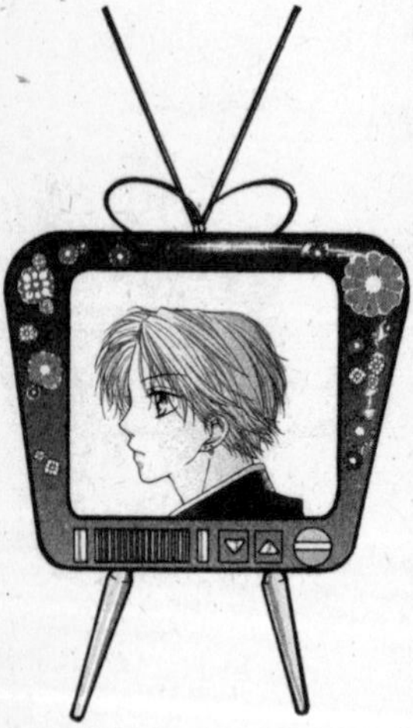

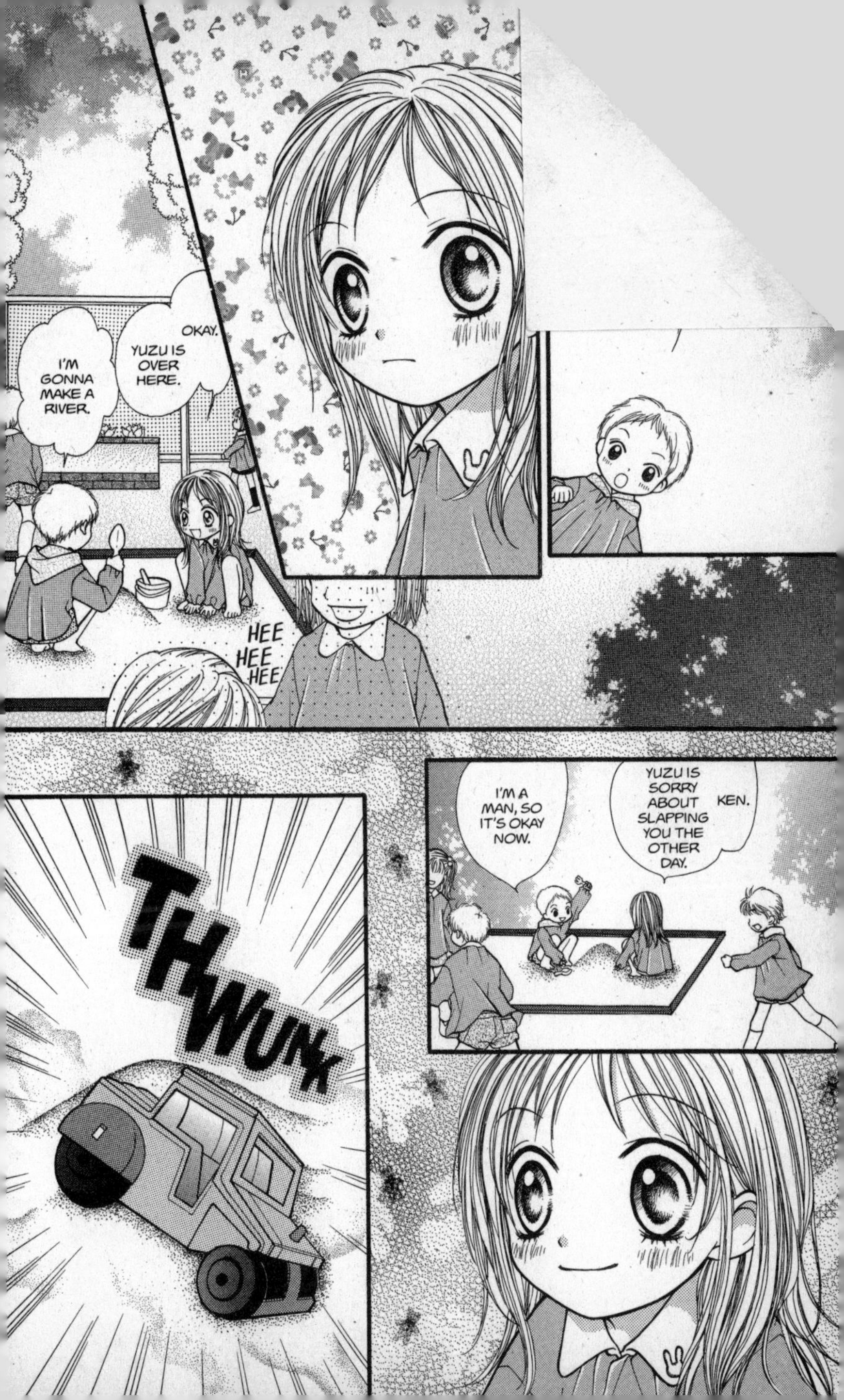
OKAY.
YUZU IS OVER HERE.
I'M GONNA MAKE A RIVER.
HEE HEE HEE
YUZU IS SORRY ABOUT SLAPPING YOU THE OTHER DAY.
KEN.
I'M A MAN, SO IT'S OKAY NOW.
THWUNK

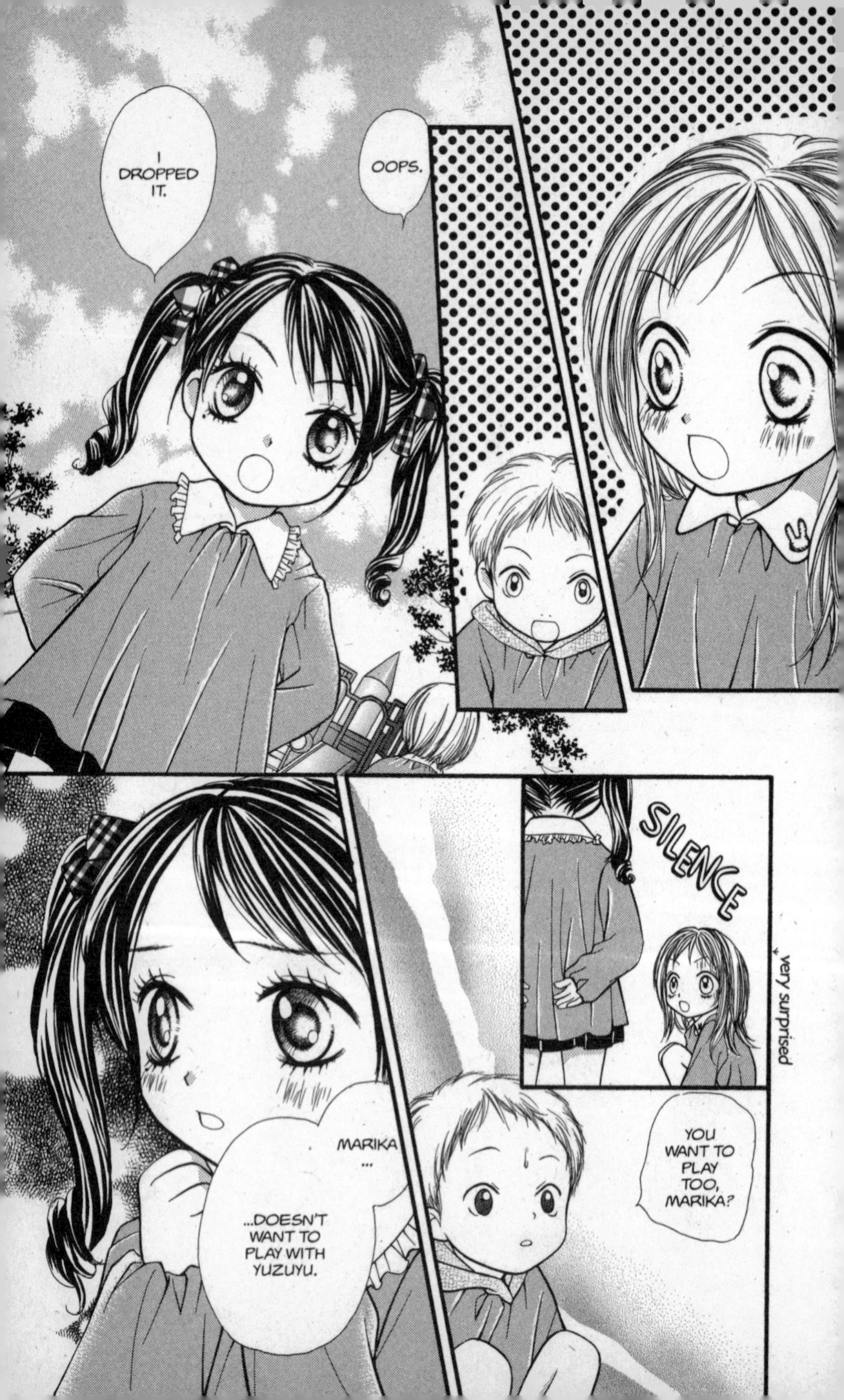
OOPS.
I DROPPED IT.
SILENCE
very surprised
YOU WANT TO PLAY TOO, MARIKA?
MARIKA ...
...DOESN'T WANT TO PLAY WITH YUZUYU.

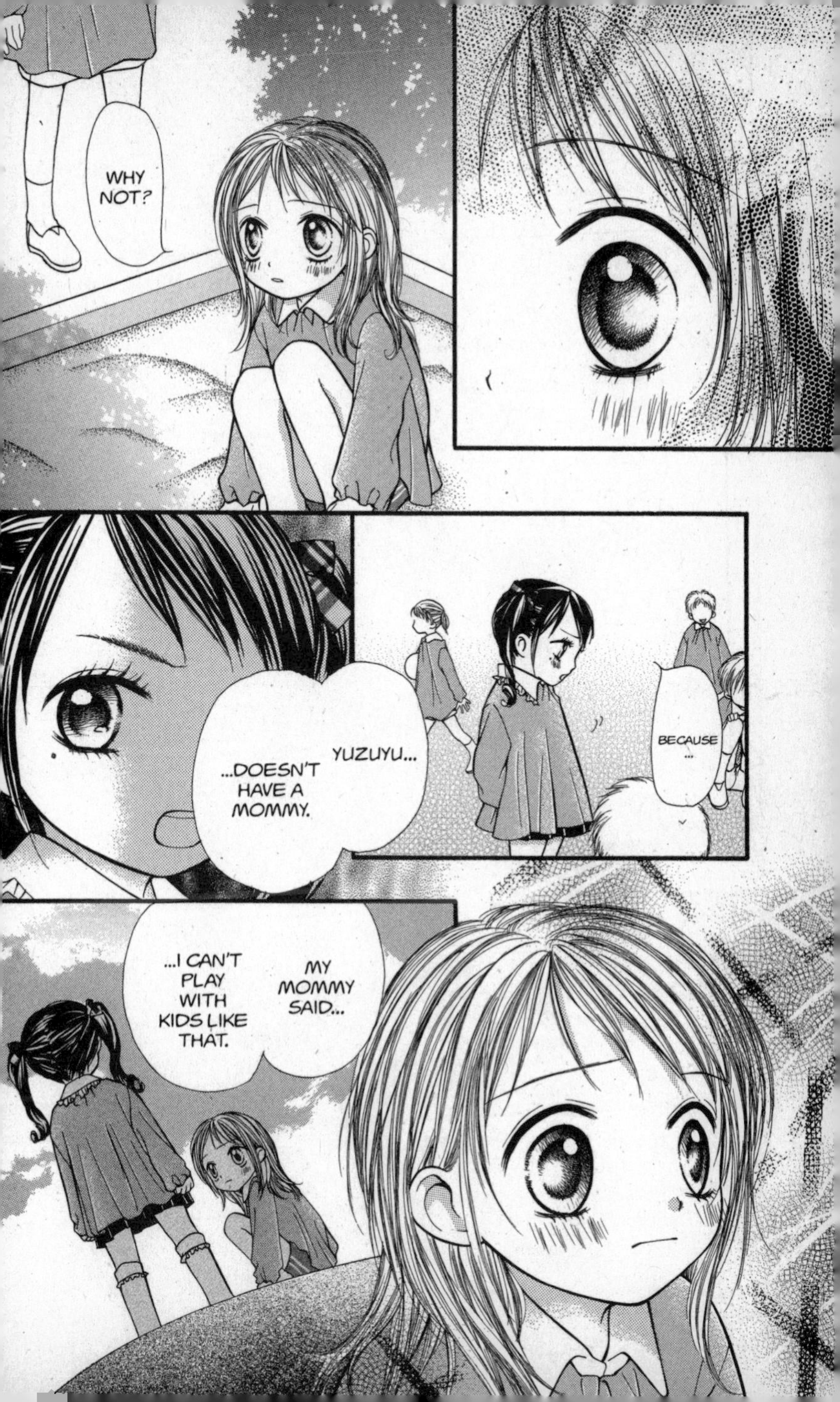
WHY NOT?
BECAUSE ...
YUZUYU... ...DOESN'T HAVE A MOMMY.
MY MOMMY SAID... ...I CAN'T PLAY WITH KIDS LIKE THAT.

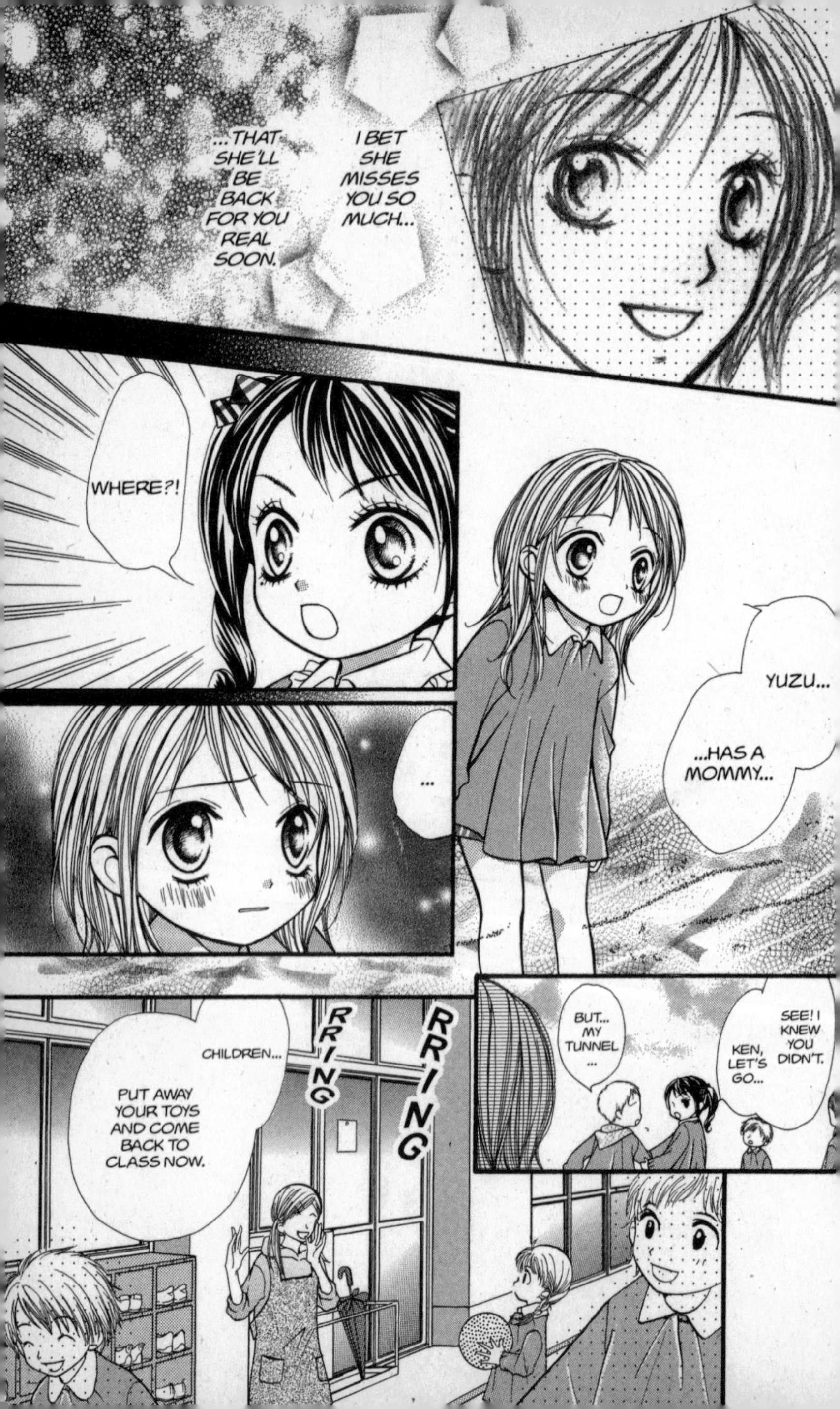
I BET SHE MISSES YOU SO MUCH...
...THAT SHE'LL BE BACK FOR YOU REAL SOON.
YUZU...
...HAS A MOMMY...
WHERE?!
...
SEE! I KNEW YOU DIDN'T.
KEN, LET'S GO...
BUT... MY TUNNEL ...
RRING
RRING
CHILDREN...
PUT AWAY YOUR TOYS AND COME BACK TO CLASS NOW.

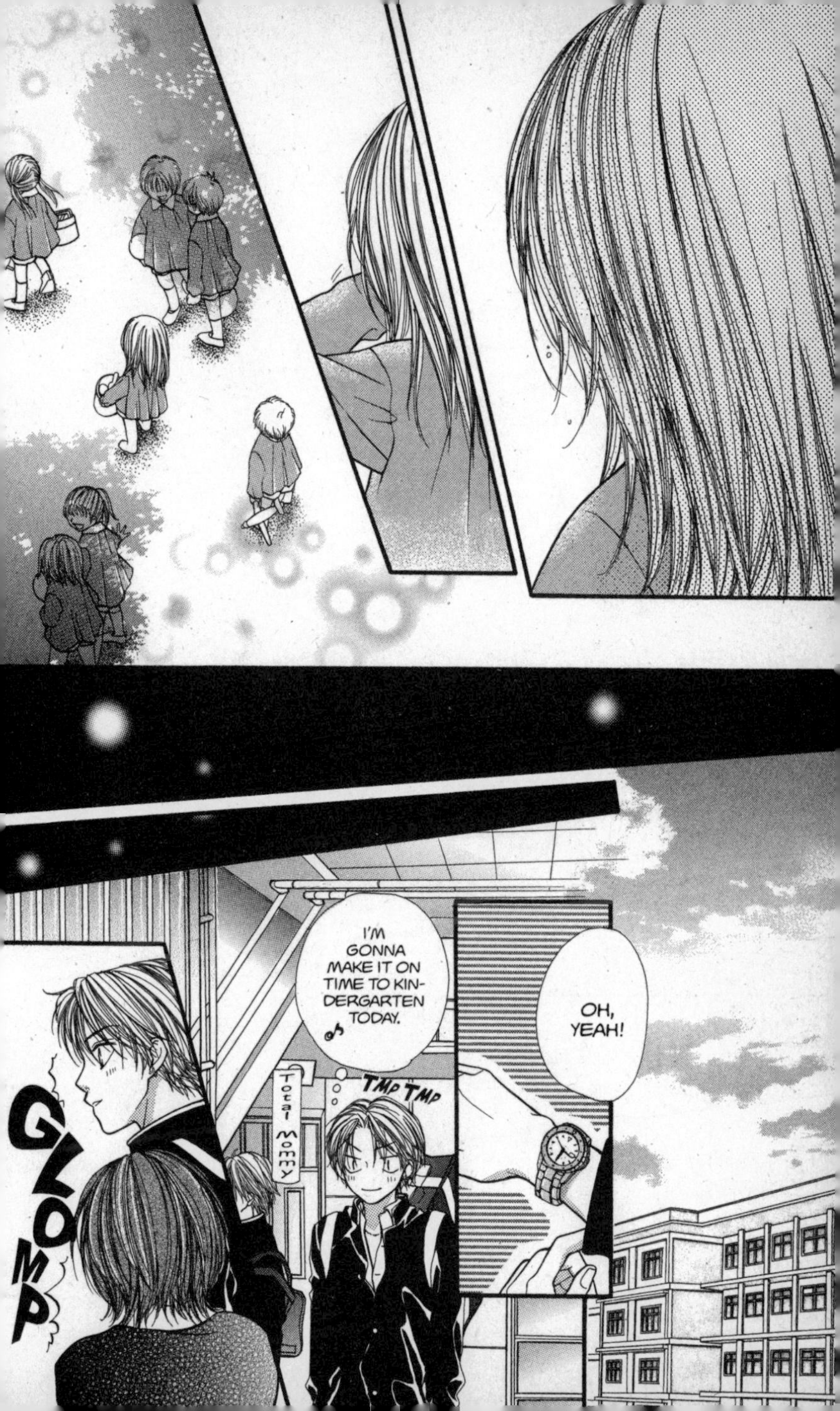
OH, YEAH!
I'M GONNA MAKE IT ON TIME TO KINDERGARTEN TODAY.
TMP TMP
Total Mommy
GLOMP

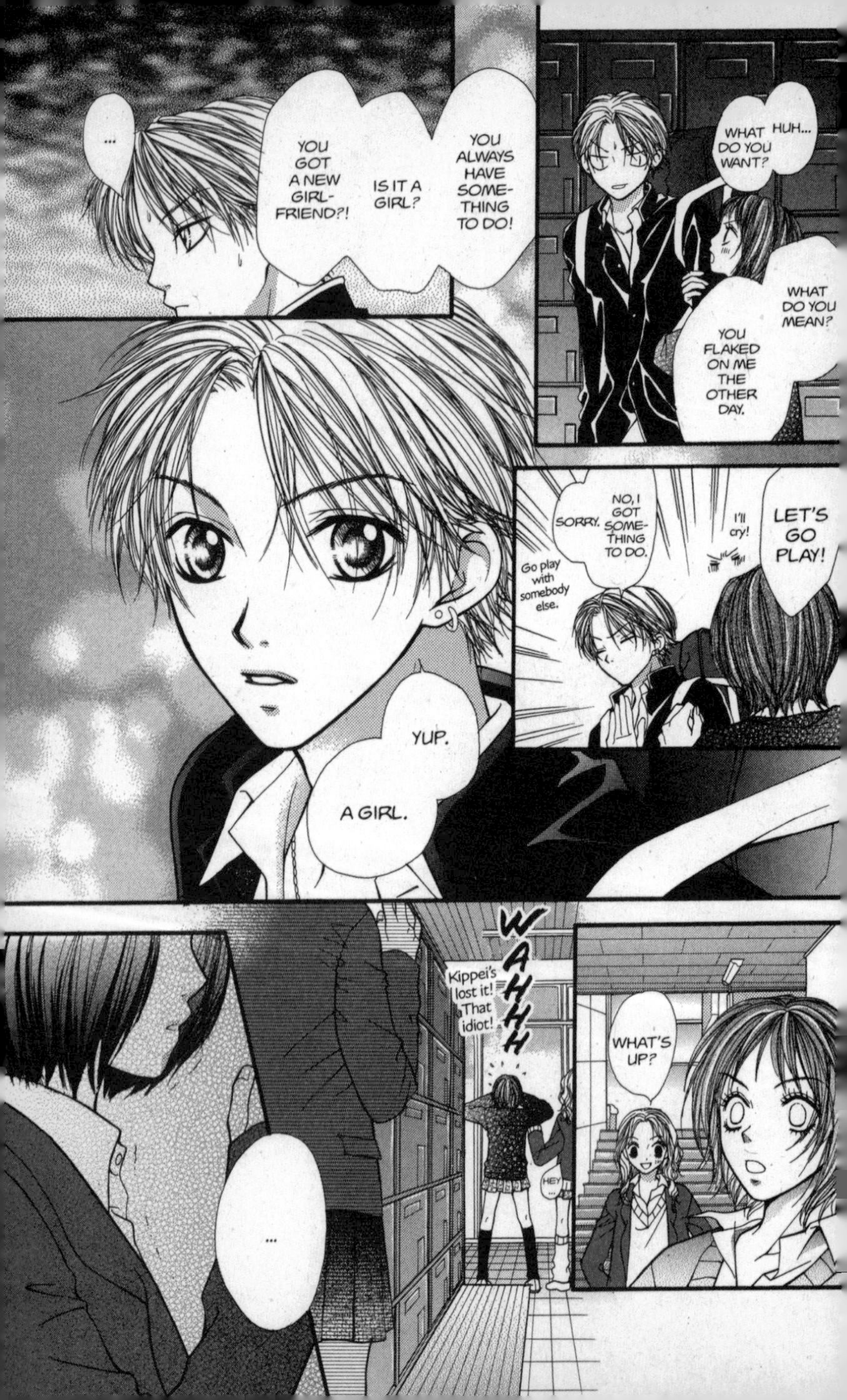
HUH...
WHAT DO YOU WANT?
WHAT DO YOU MEAN?
YOU FLAKED ON ME THE OTHER DAY.
LET'S GO PLAY!
I'll cry!
NO, I GOT SOMETHING TO DO.
SORRY.
Go play with somebody else.
YOU ALWAYS HAVE SOMETHING TO DO!
IS IT A GIRL?
YOU GOT A NEW GIRLFRIEND?!
...
YUP.
A GIRL.
WHAT'S UP?
WAHHH
Kippei's lost it! That idiot!
HEY...
...

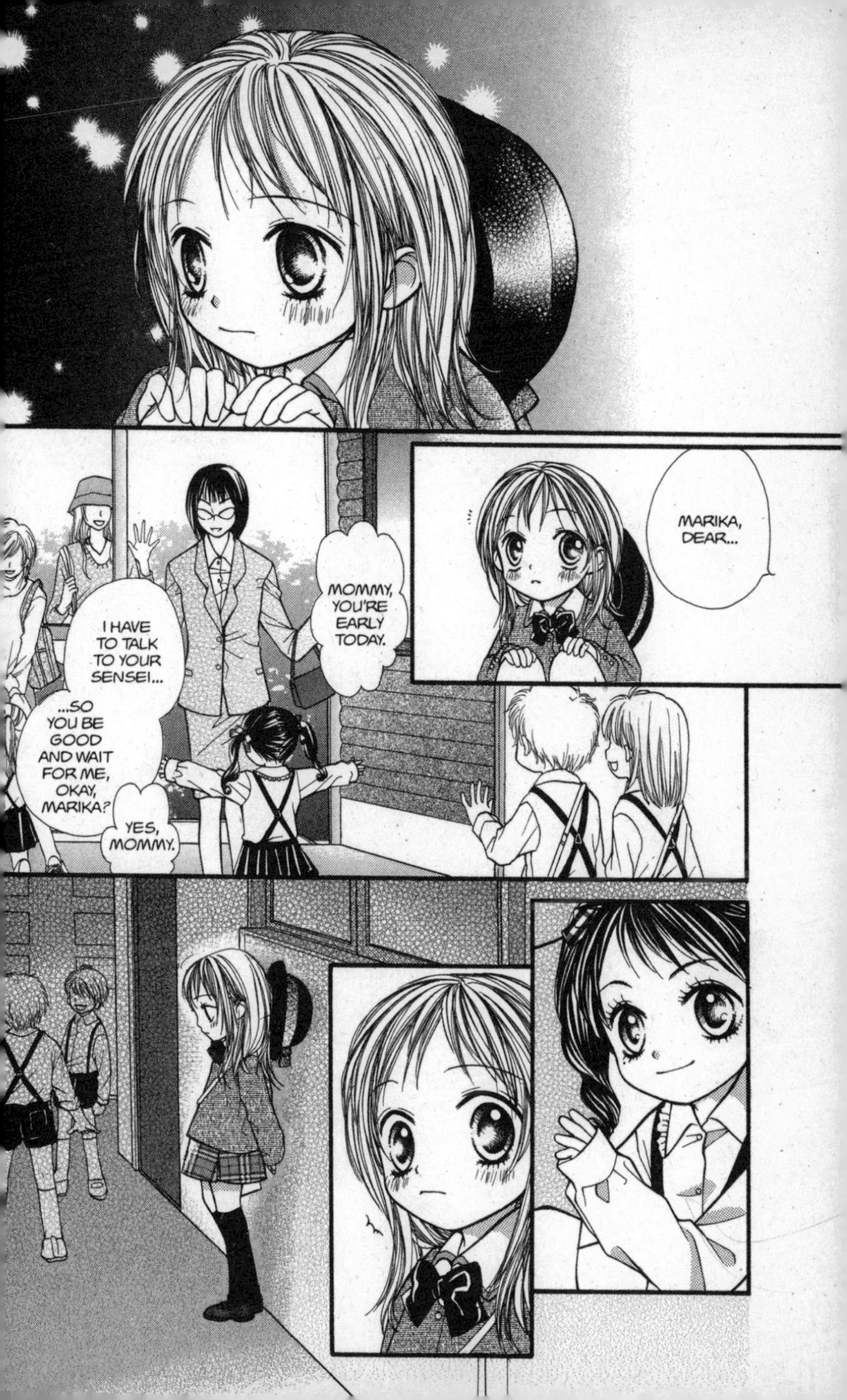
MARIKA, DEAR...
MOMMY, YOU'RE EARLY TODAY.
I HAVE TO TALK TO YOUR SENSEI...
...SO YOU BE GOOD AND WAIT FOR ME, OKAY, MARIKA?
YES, MOMMY.

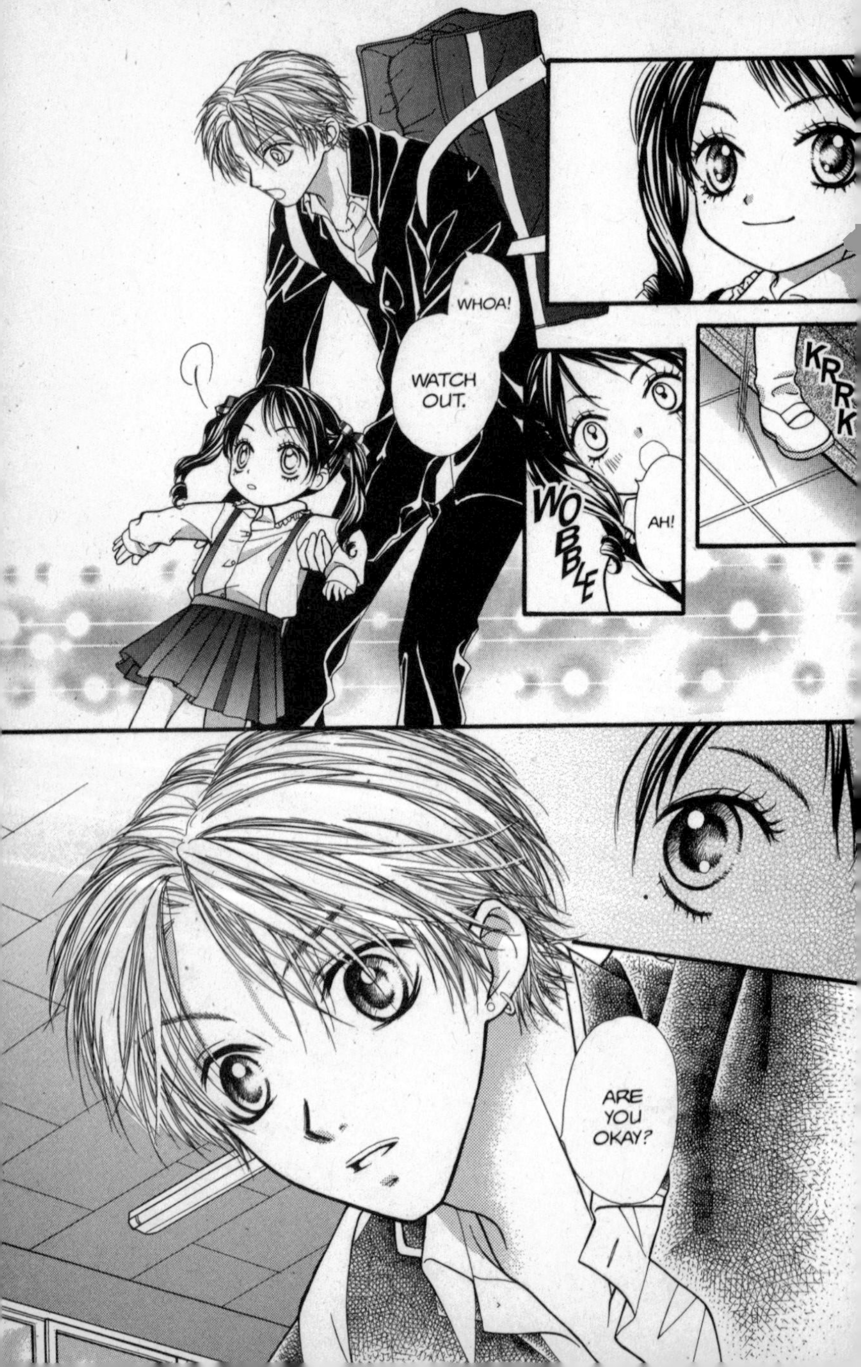
KRRK
WOBBLE
AH!
WHOA!
WATCH OUT.
ARE YOU OKAY?

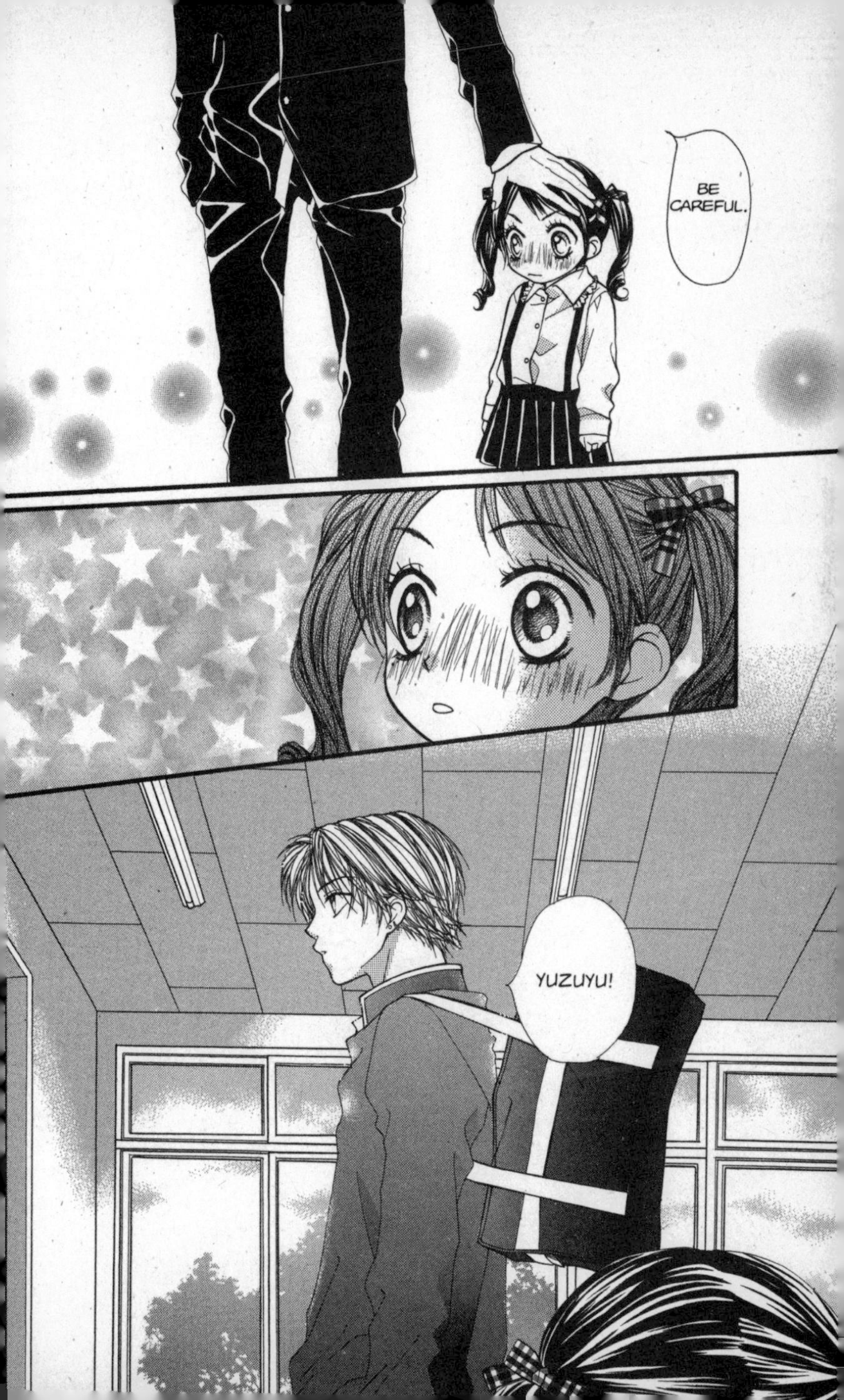
BE CAREFUL.
YUZUYU!

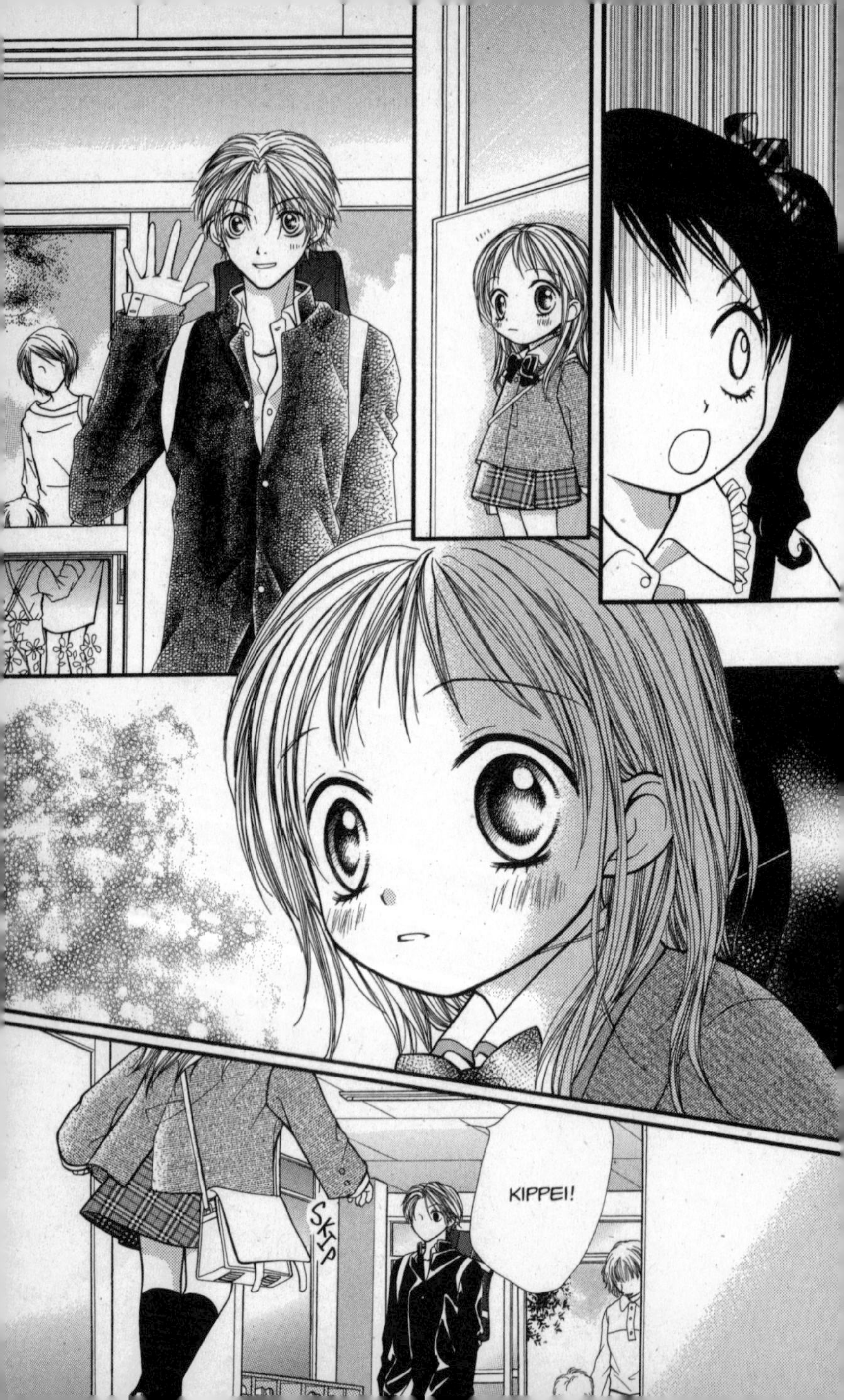
KIPPEI!
SKIP

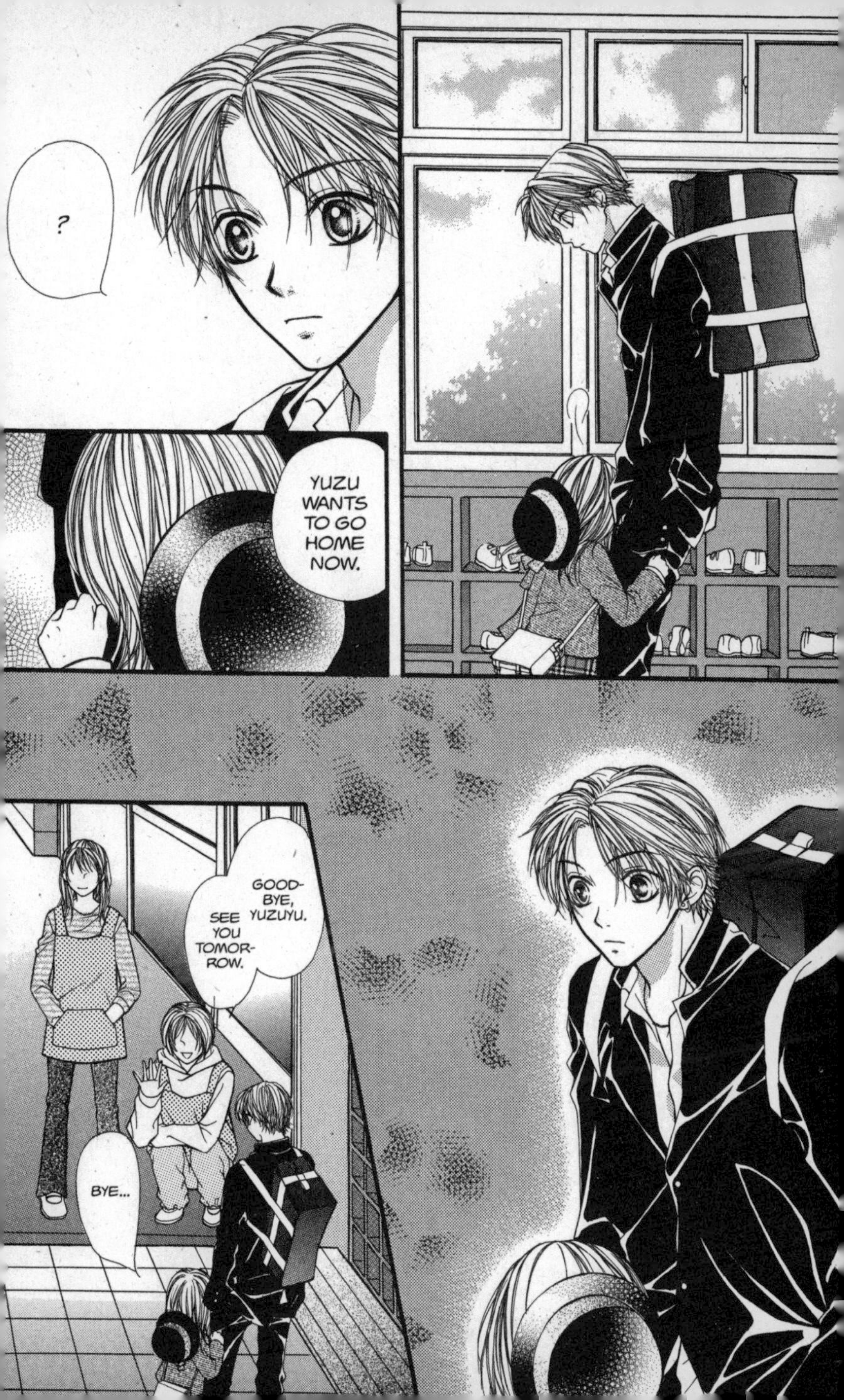
?
YUZU WANTS TO GO HOME NOW.
GOOD-BYE, YUZUYU. SEE YOU TOMORROW.
BYE...

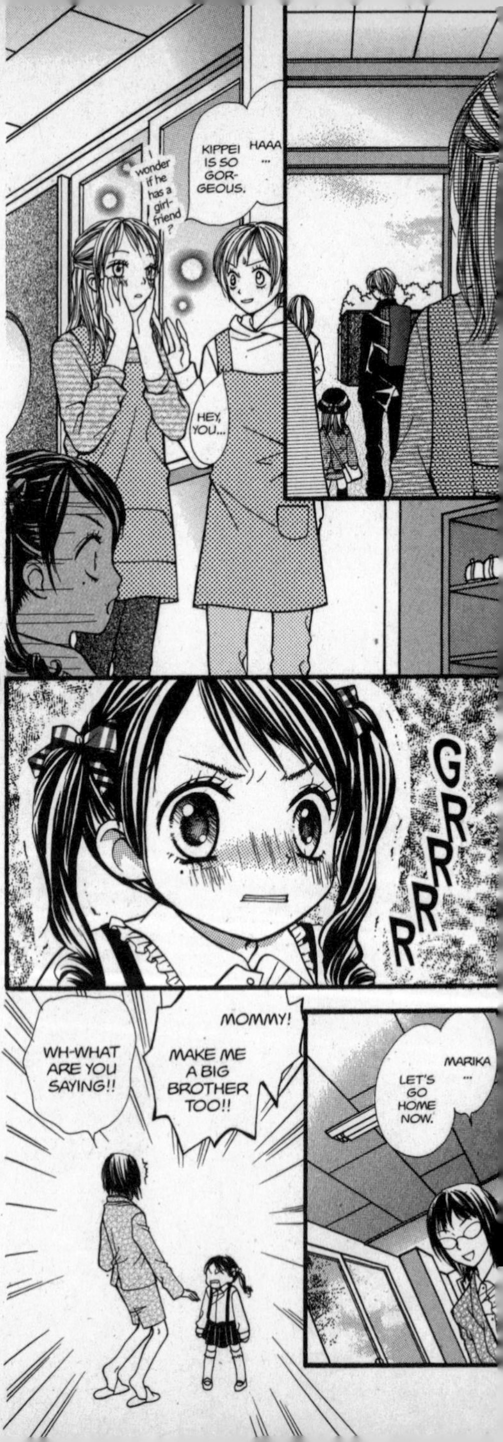
HAAA ...
KIPPEI IS SO GORGEOUS.
I wonder if he has a girlfriend?
HEY, YOU...
GRRRRR
MARIKA ...
LET'S GO HOME NOW.
MOMMY!
MAKE ME A BIG BROTHER TOO!!
WH-WHAT ARE YOU SAYING!!

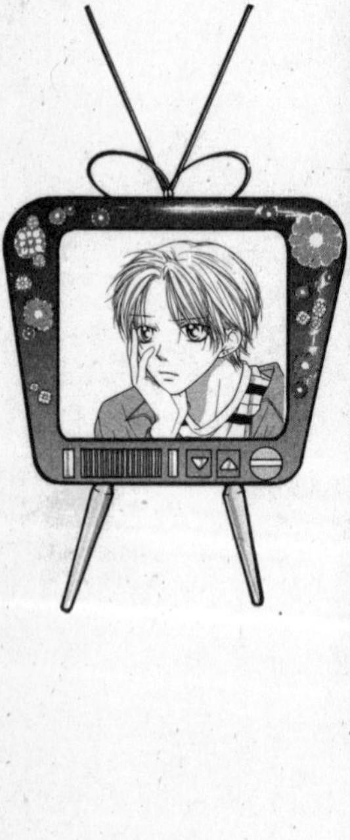

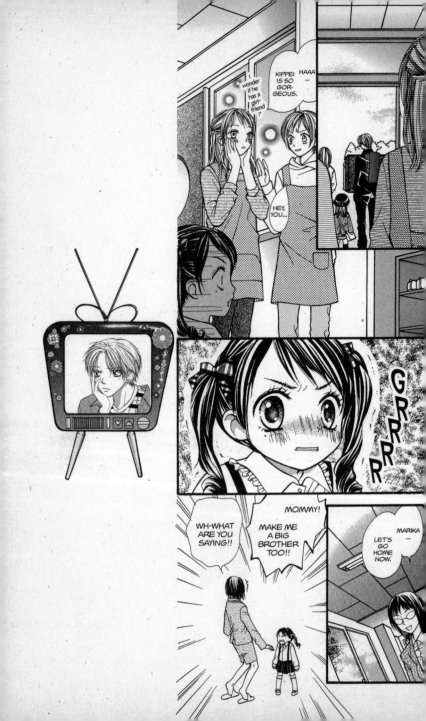

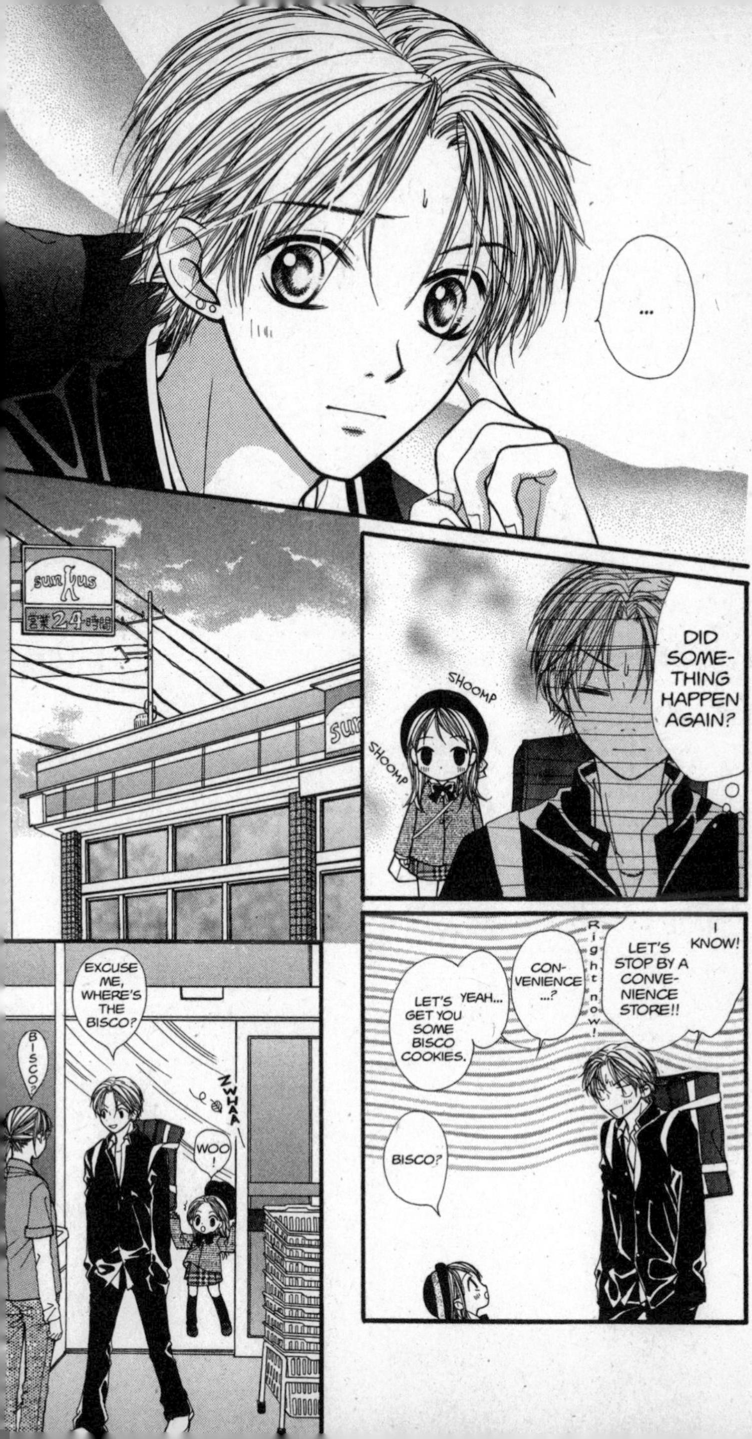
...
DID SOMETHING HAPPEN AGAIN?
SHOOMP
SHOOMP
sunkus
営業24時間
I KNOW!
LET'S STOP BY A CONVENIENCE STORE!!
Right now!
CONVENIENCE ...?
YEAH...
LET'S GET YOU SOME BISCO COOKIES.
BISCO?
EXCUSE ME, WHERE'S THE BISCO?
BISCO?
ZWHAA
WOO!

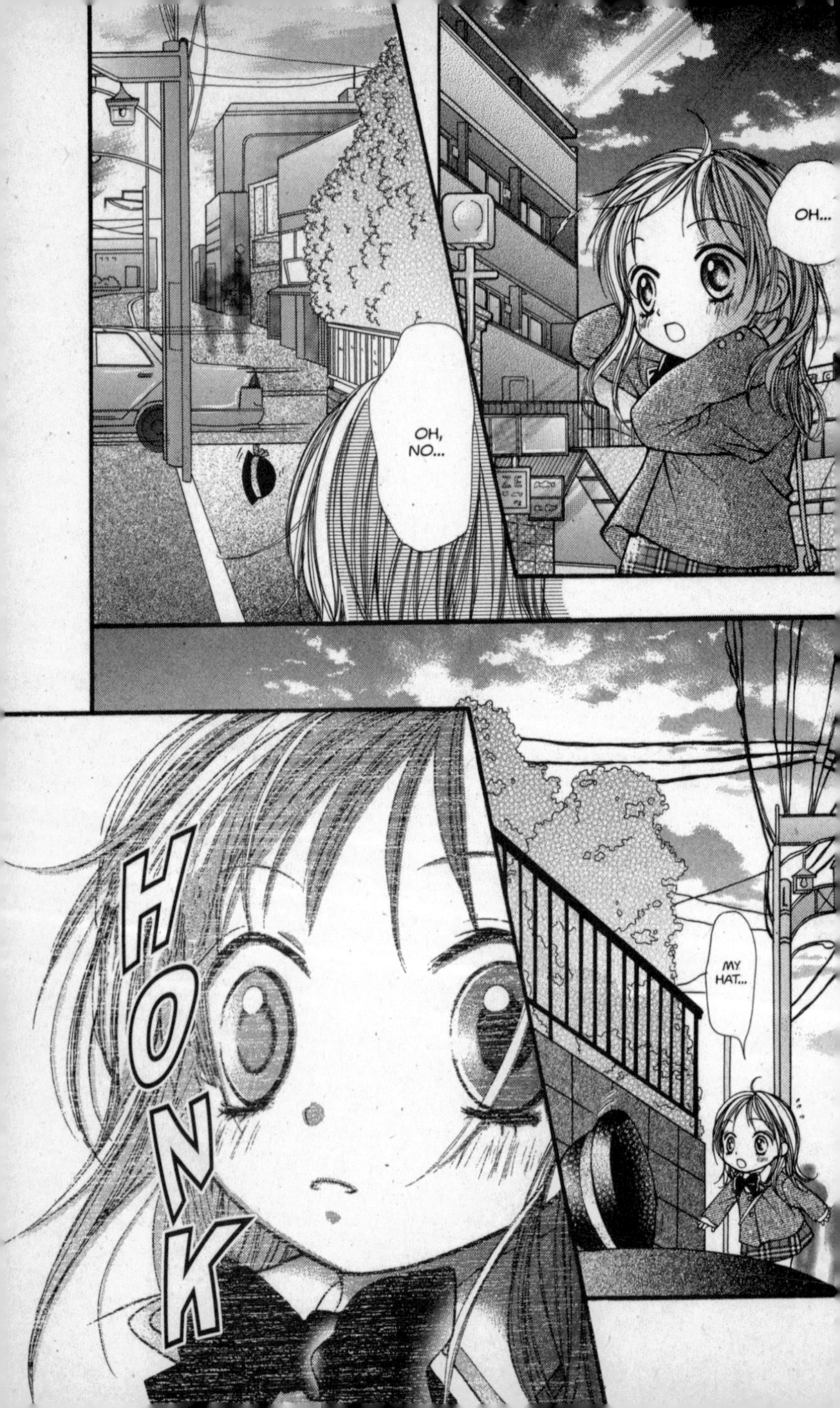
OH...
OH, NO...
MY HAT...
HONK

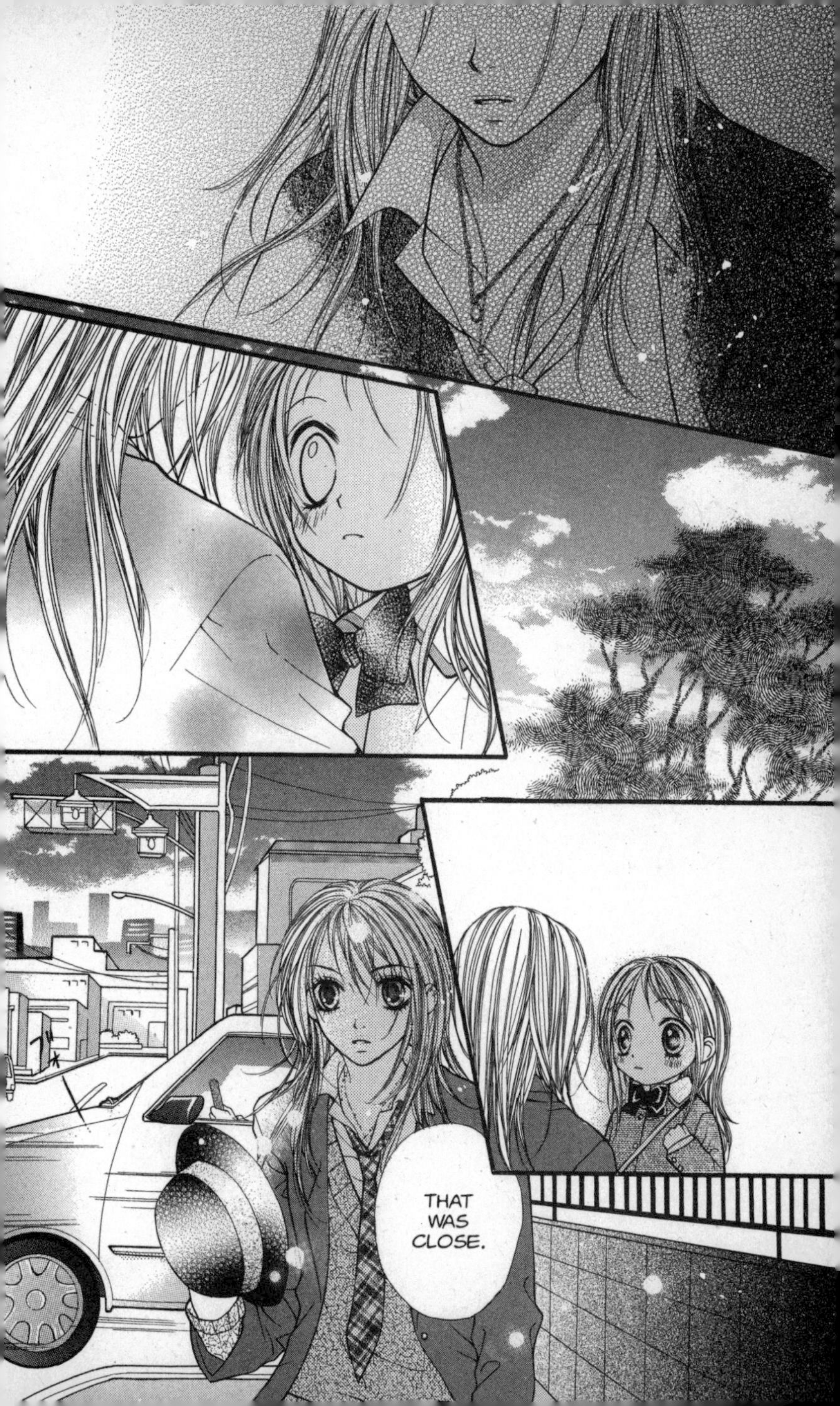
THAT WAS CLOSE.

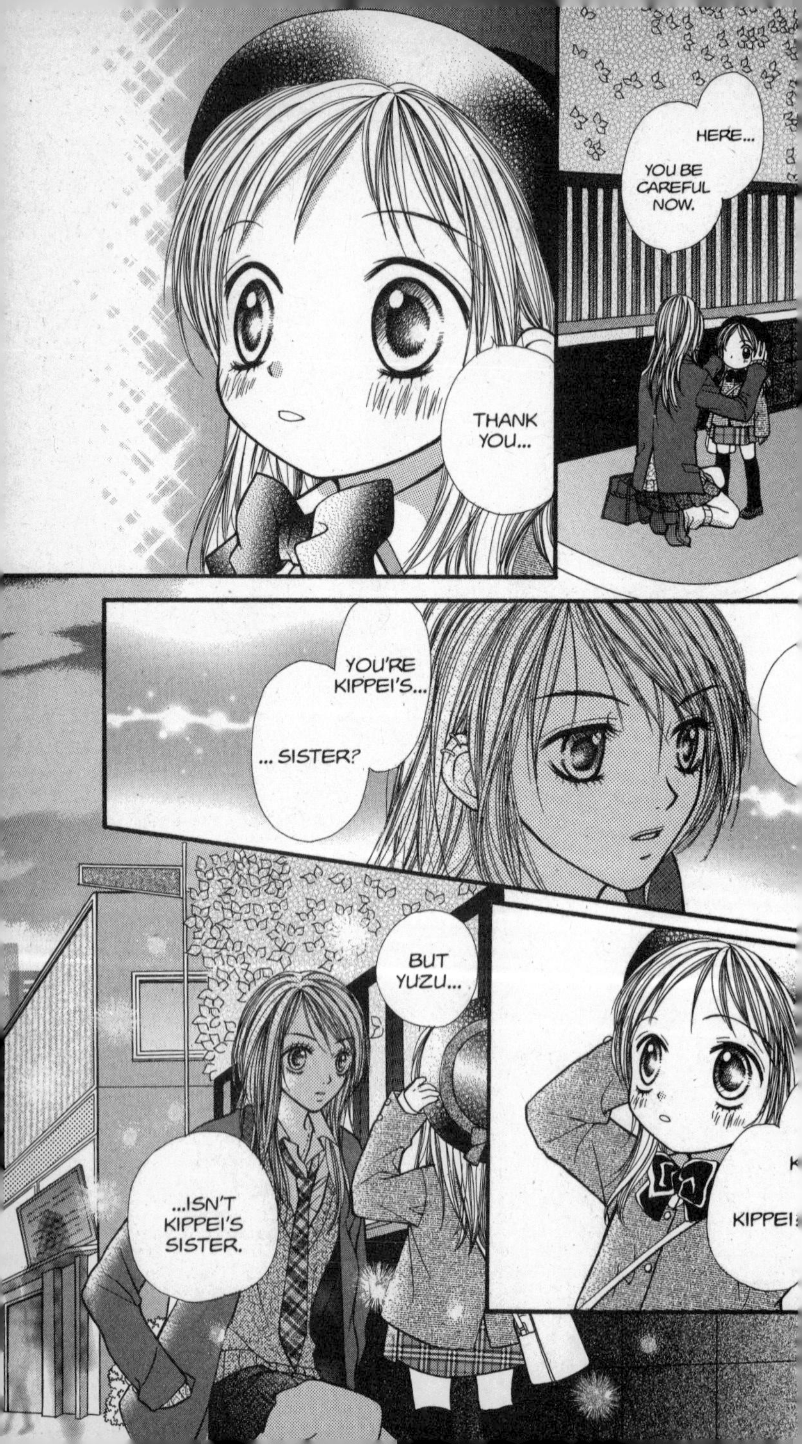
HERE...
YOU BE CAREFUL NOW.
THANK YOU...
YOU'RE KIPPEI'S...
... SISTER?
BUT YUZU...
...ISN'T KIPPEI'S SISTER.

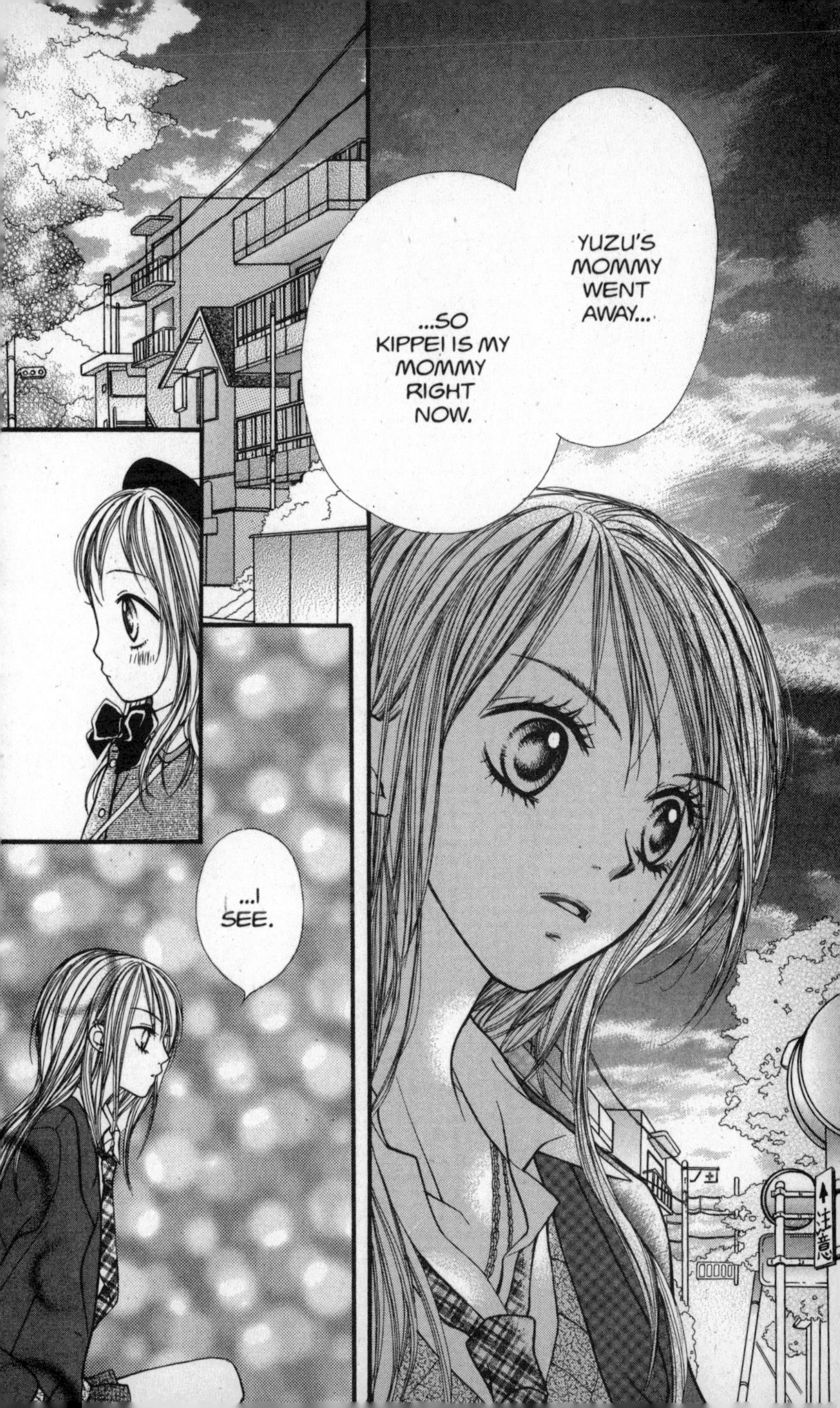
YUZU'S MOMMY WENT AWAY...
...SO KIPPEI IS MY MOMMY RIGHT NOW.
...I SEE.

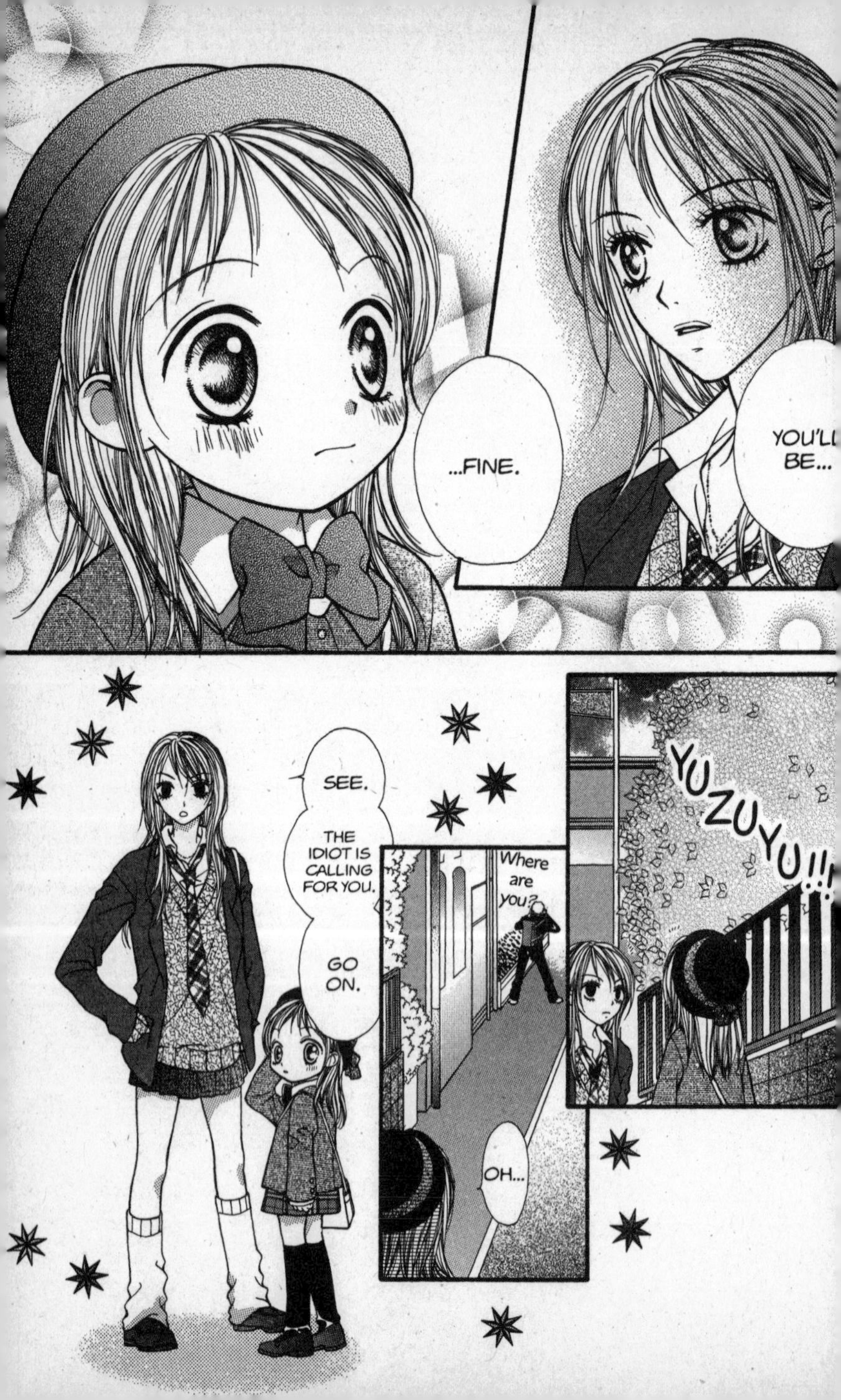
YOU'LL BE...
...FINE.
YUZUYU!!!
Where are you?
OH...
SEE.
THE IDIOT IS CALLING FOR YOU.
GO ON.

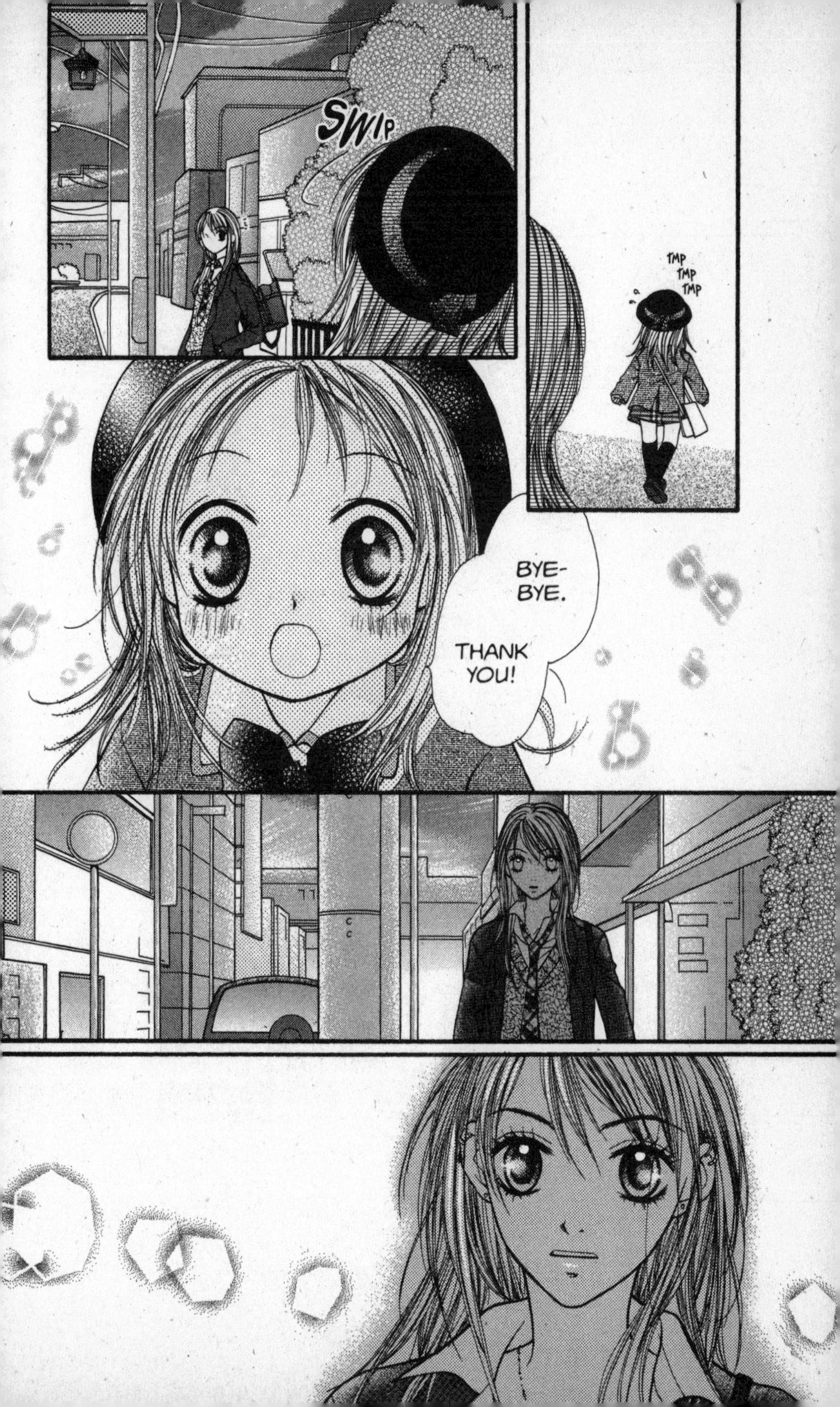
TMP
TMP
TMP
SWIP
BYE-BYE.
THANK YOU!

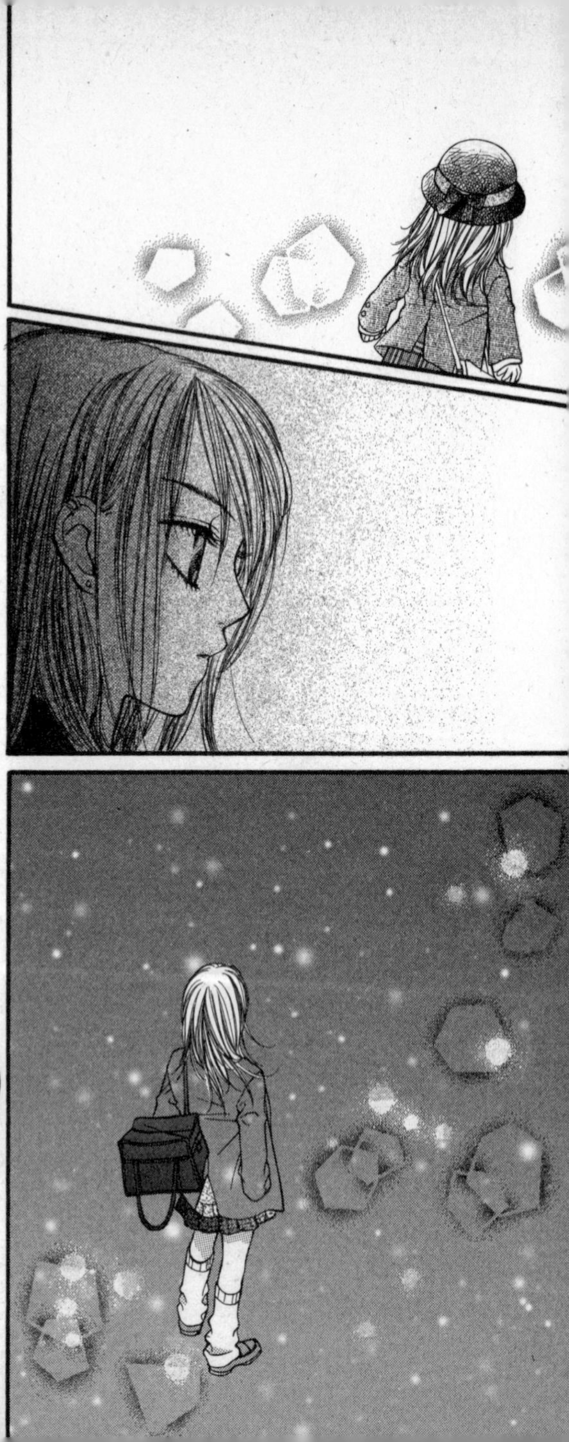

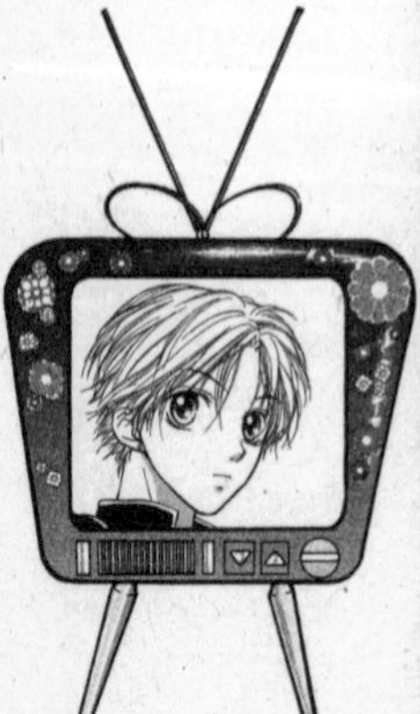

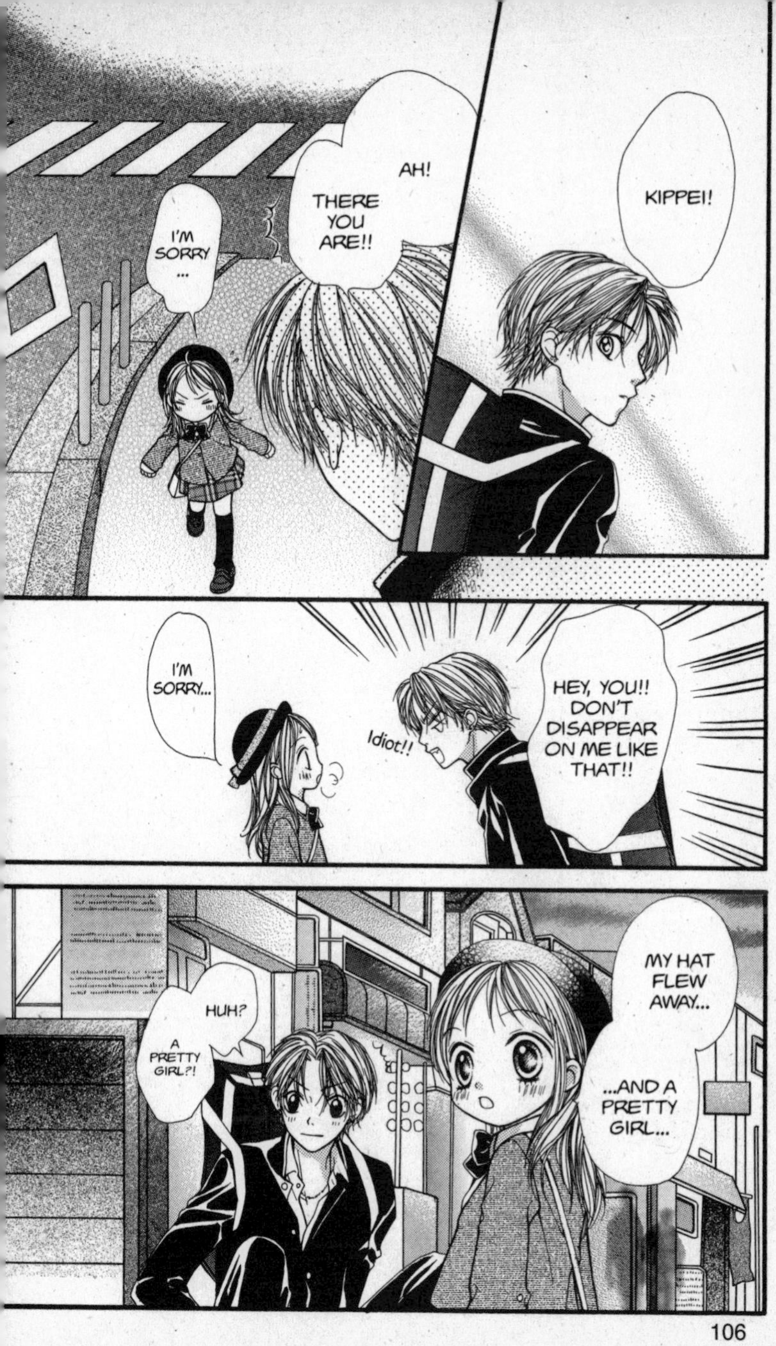
KIPPEI!
AH!
THERE YOU ARE!!
I'M SORRY ...
HEY, YOU!! DON'T DISAPPEAR ON ME LIKE THAT!!
Idiot!!
I'M SORRY...
MY HAT FLEW AWAY...
...AND A PRETTY GIRL...
HUH?
A PRETTY GIRL?!

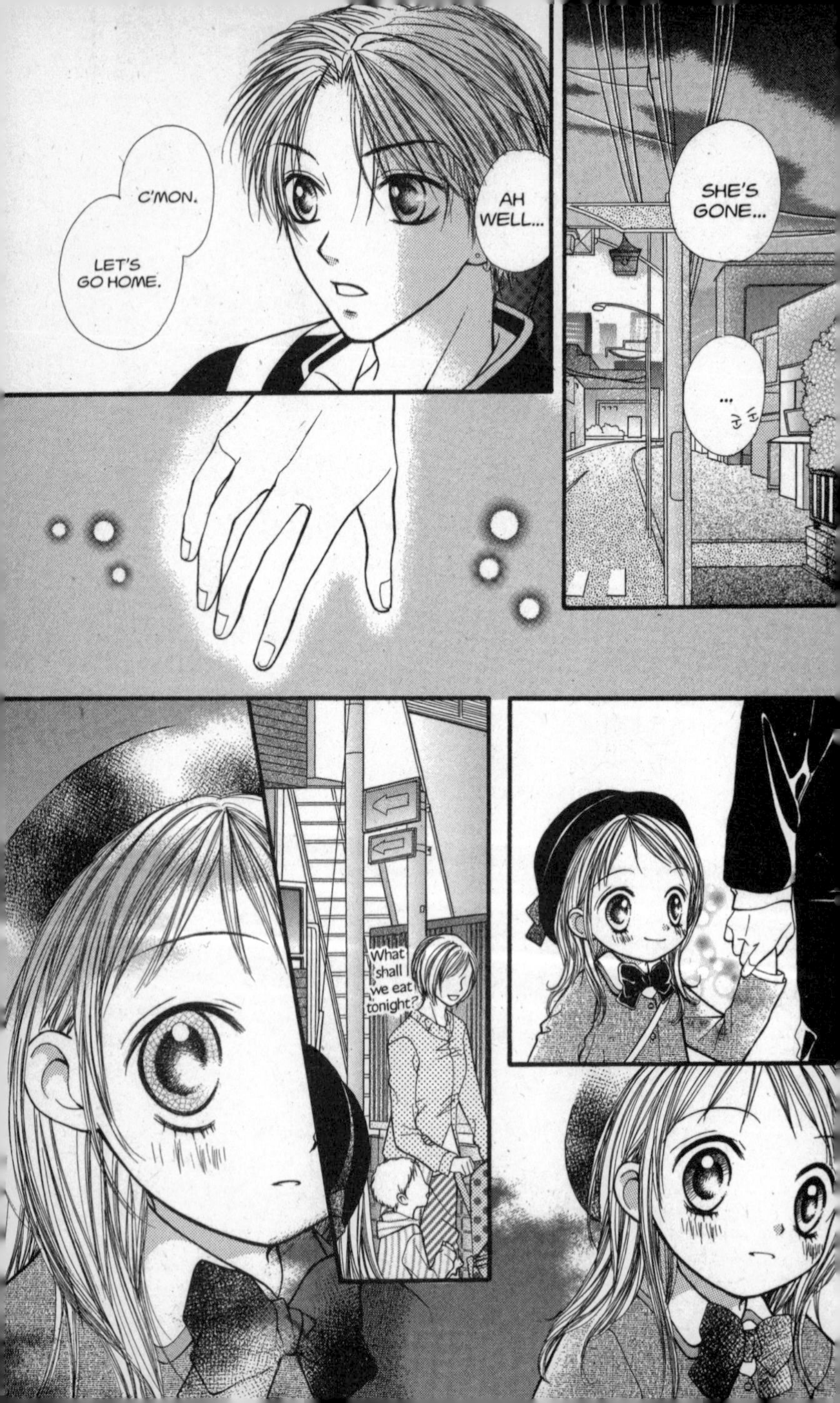
SHE'S GONE...
...
AH WELL...
C'MON.
LET'S GO HOME.
What shall we eat tonight?

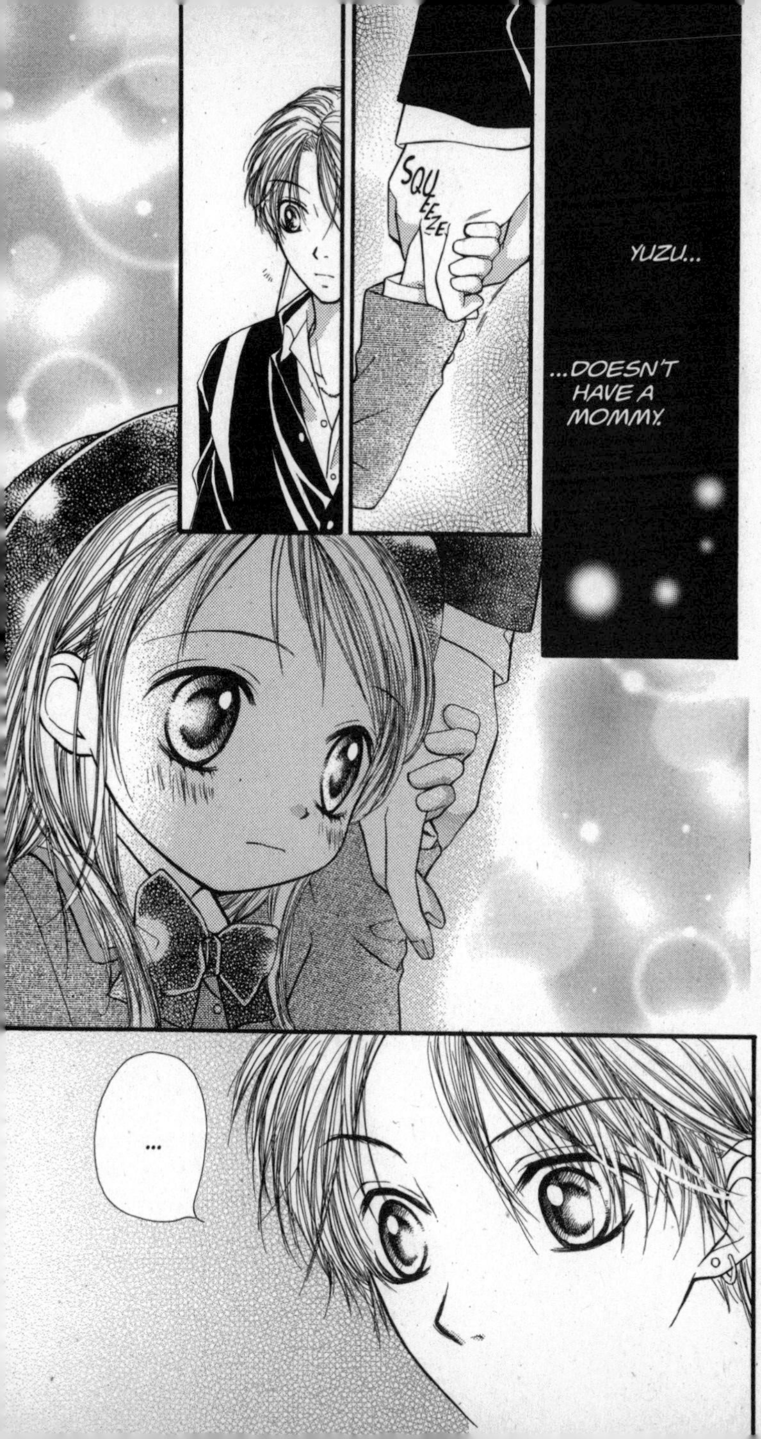
YUZU...
...DOESN'T HAVE A MOMMY.
SQUEEZE
...

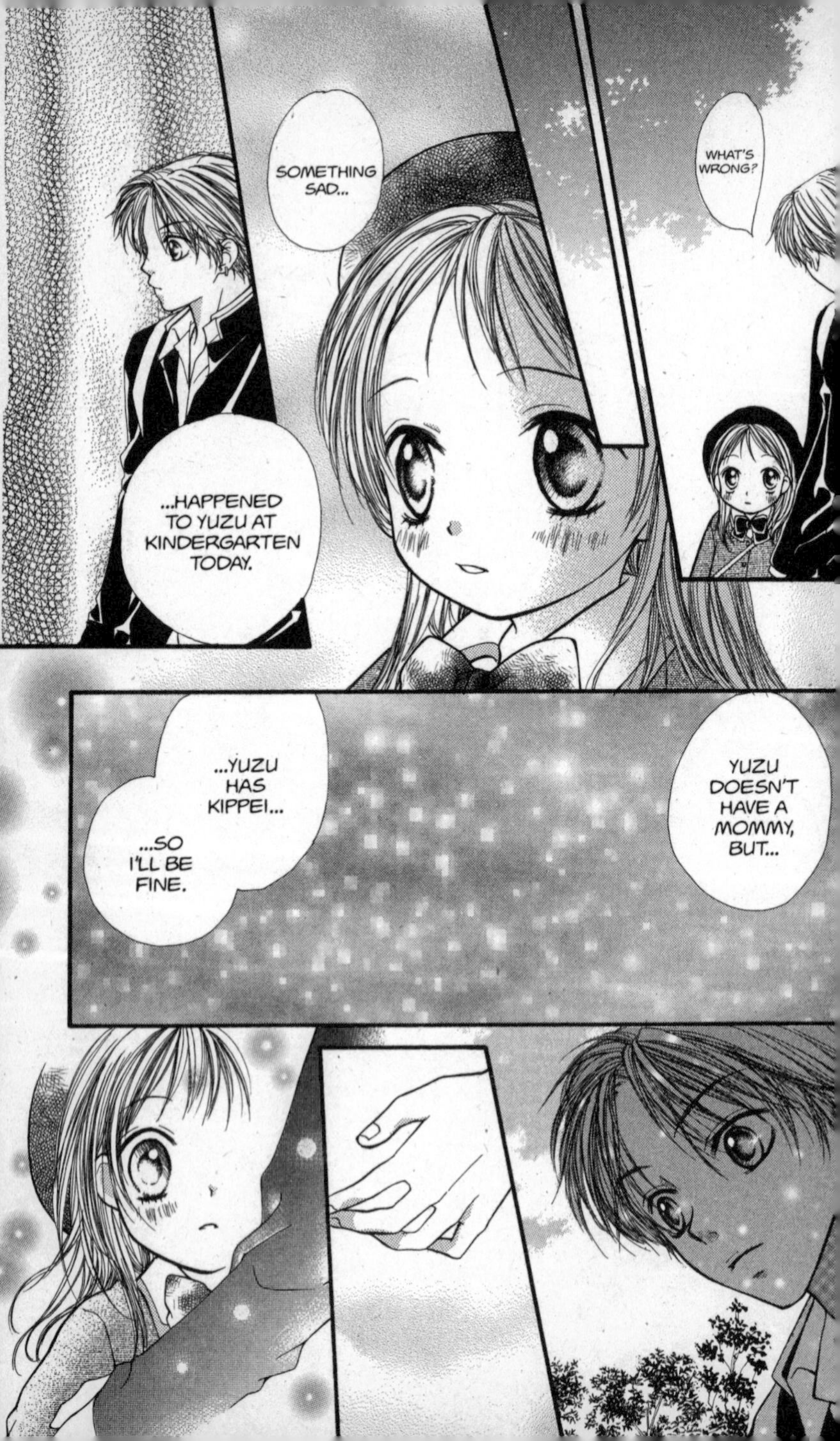
WHAT'S WRONG?
SOMETHING SAD...
...HAPPENED TO YUZU AT KINDERGARTEN TODAY.
YUZU DOESN'T HAVE A MOMMY, BUT...
...YUZU HAS KIPPEI...
...SO I'LL BE FINE.

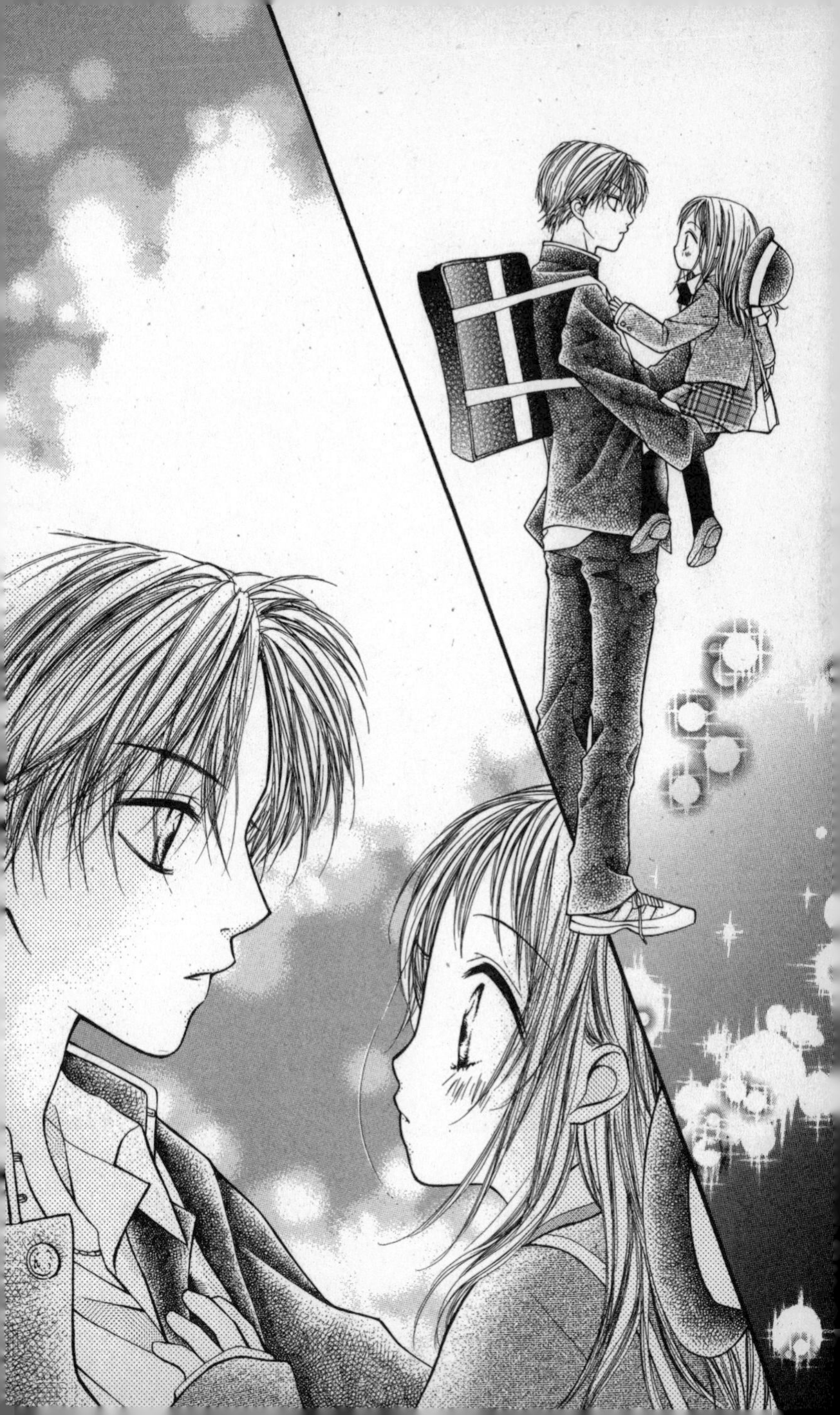

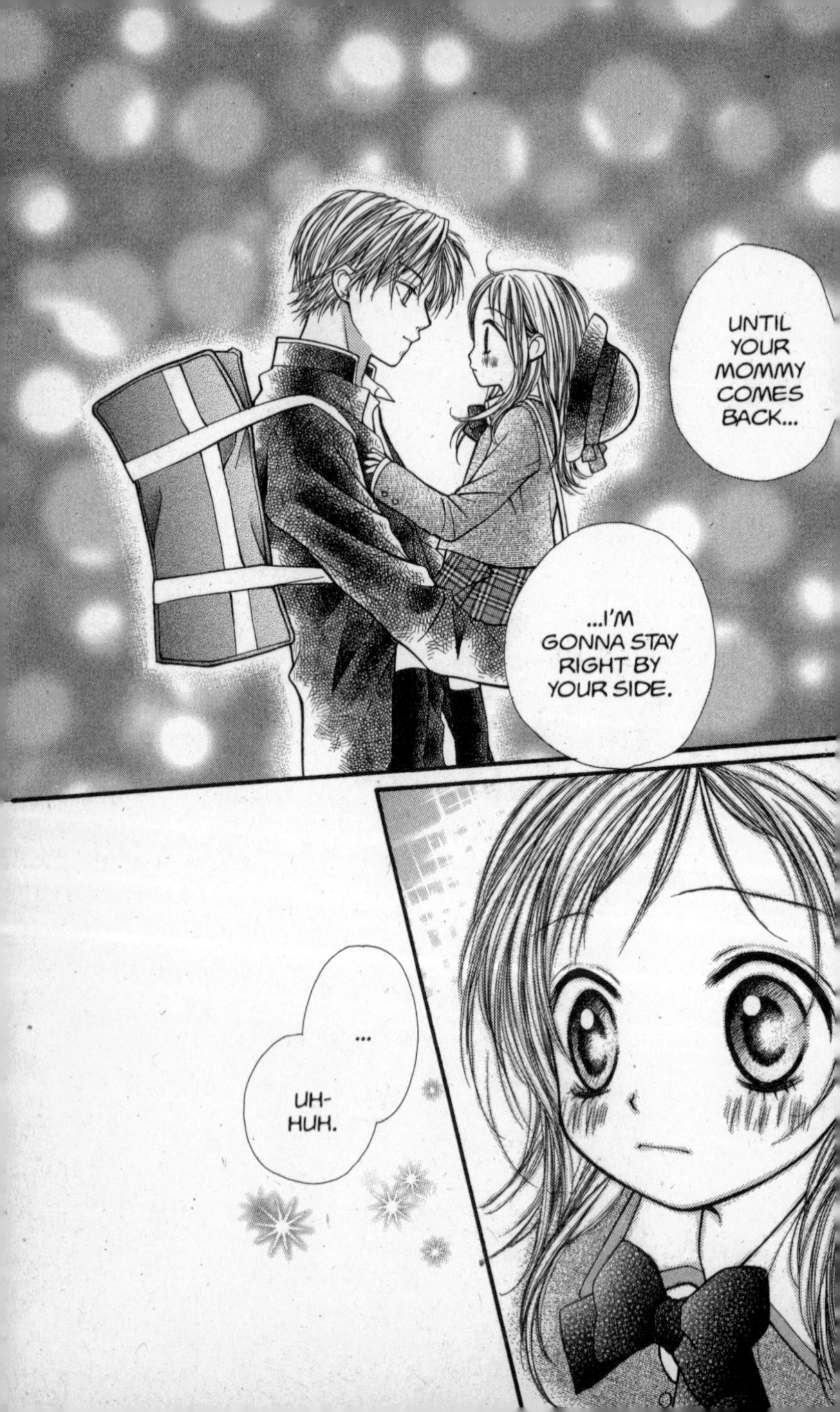
UNTIL YOUR MOMMY COMES BACK...
...I'M GONNA STAY RIGHT BY YOUR SIDE.
... UH-HUH.

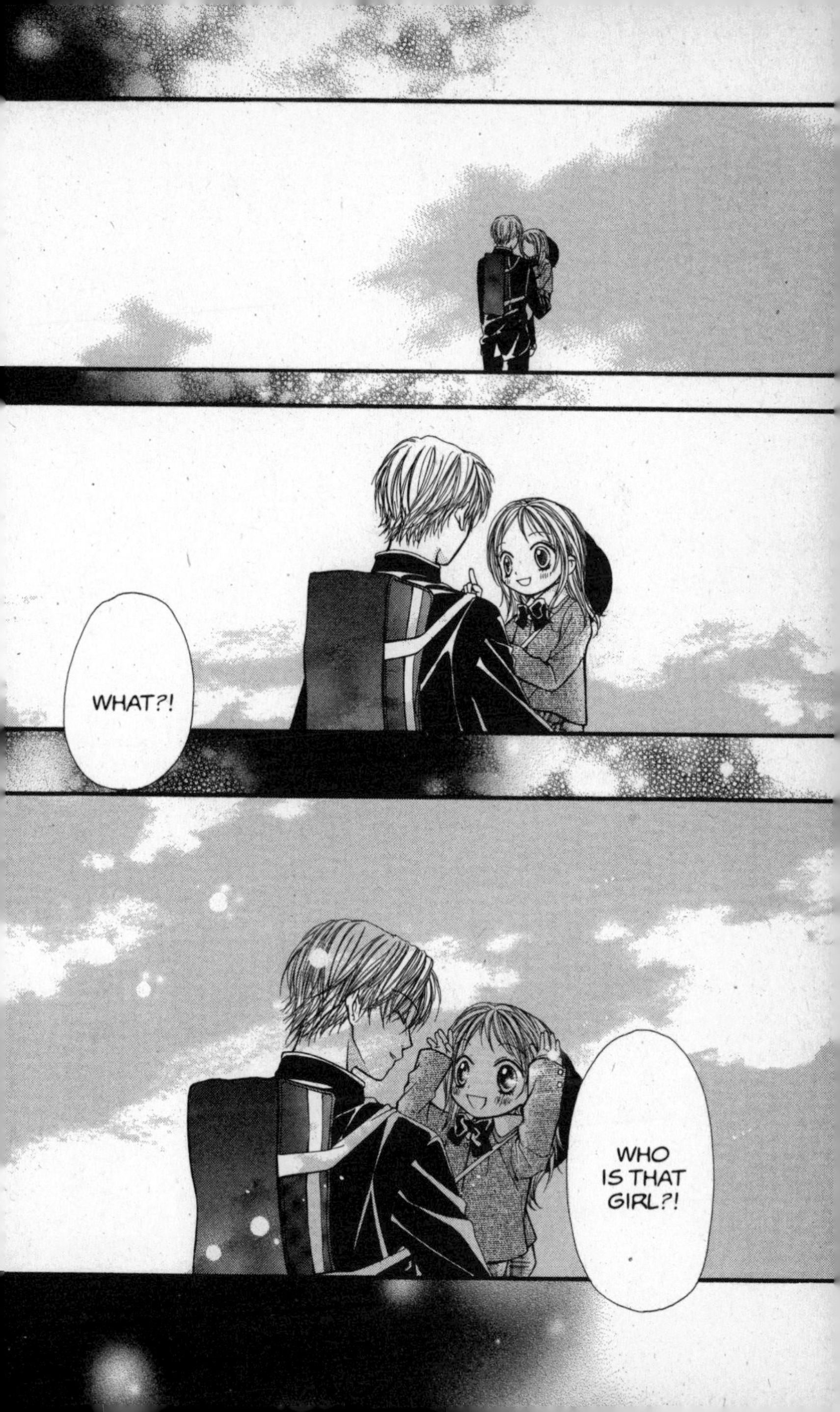
WHAT?!
WHO IS THAT GIRL?!

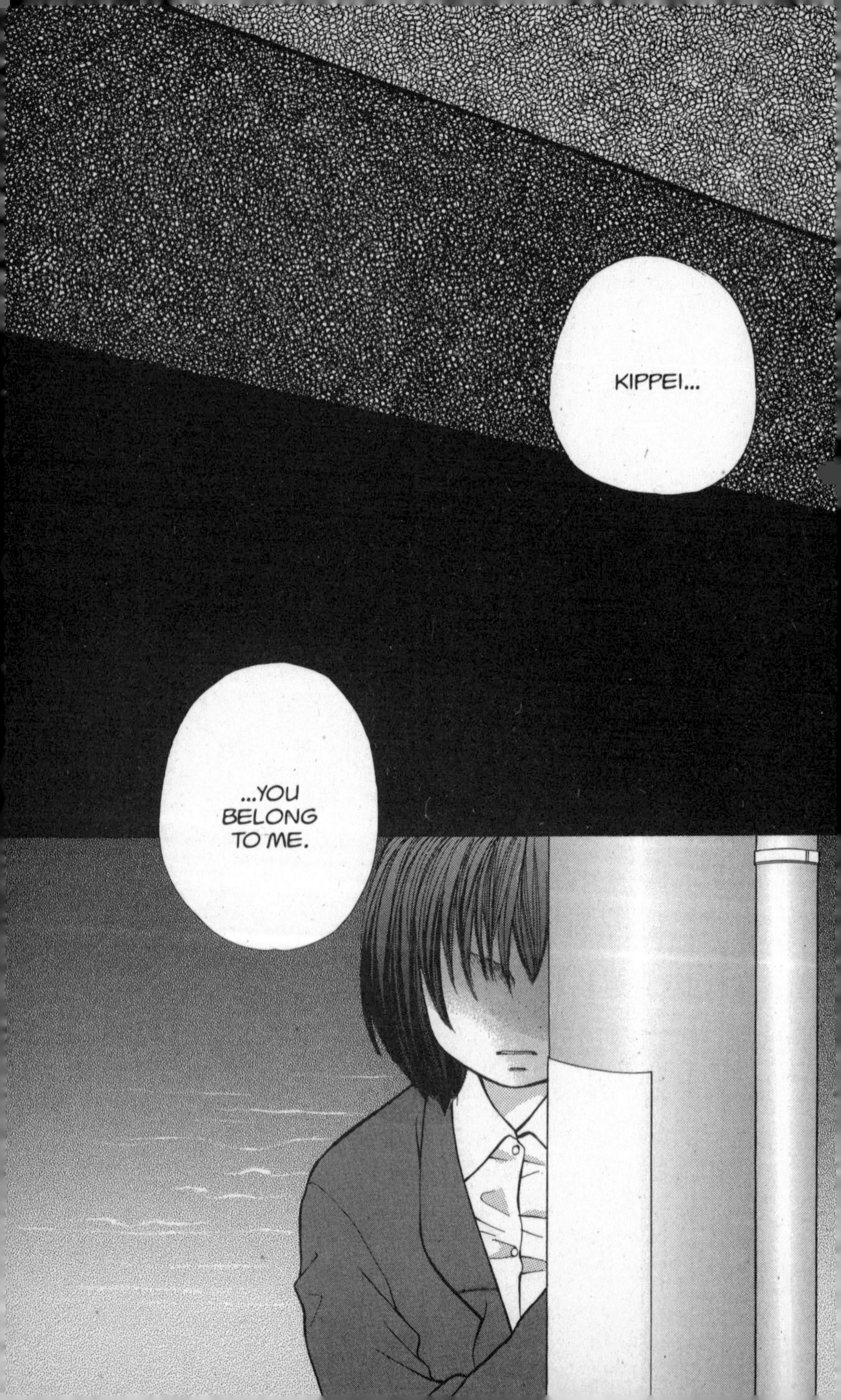
KIPPEI...
...YOU BELONG TO ME.

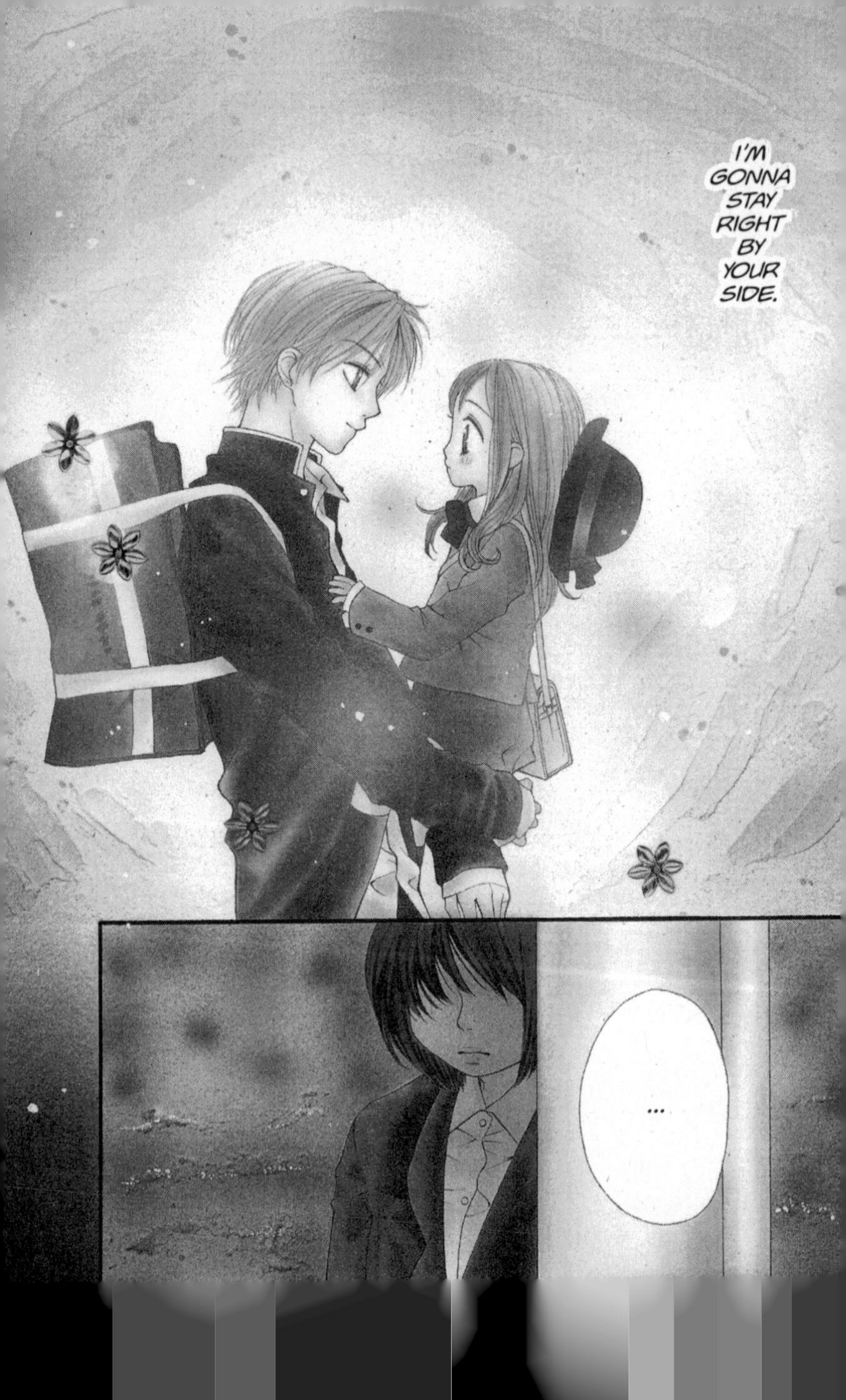
I'M GONNA STAY RIGHT BY YOUR SIDE.
...

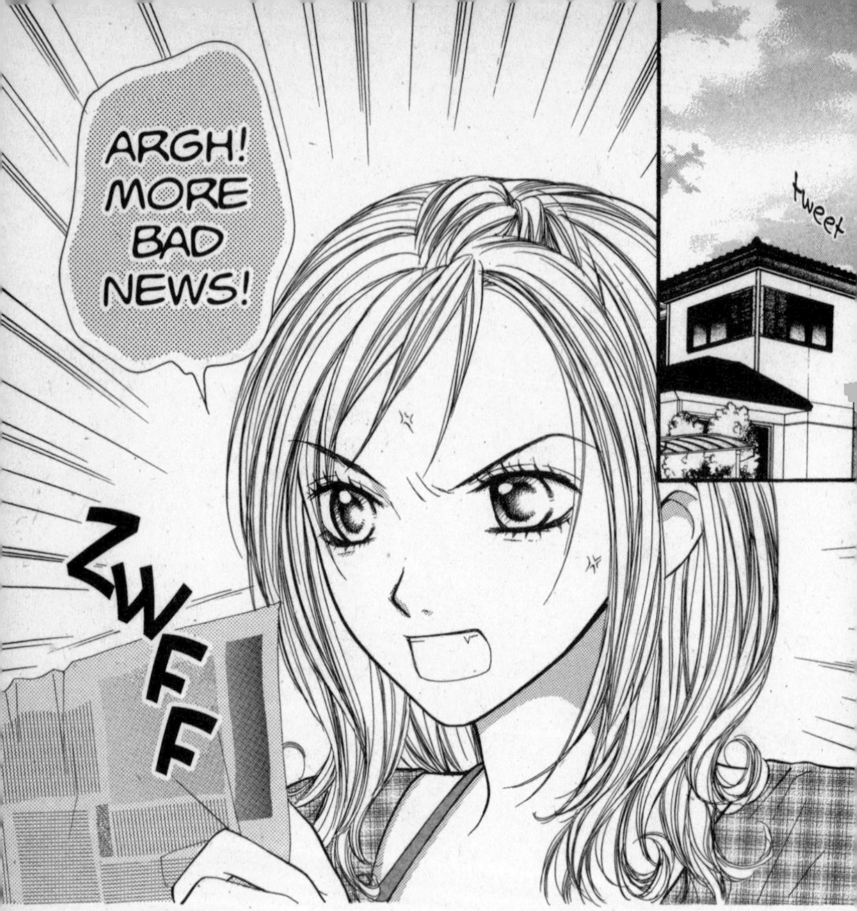
tweet
ARGH! MORE BAD NEWS!
ZWFF

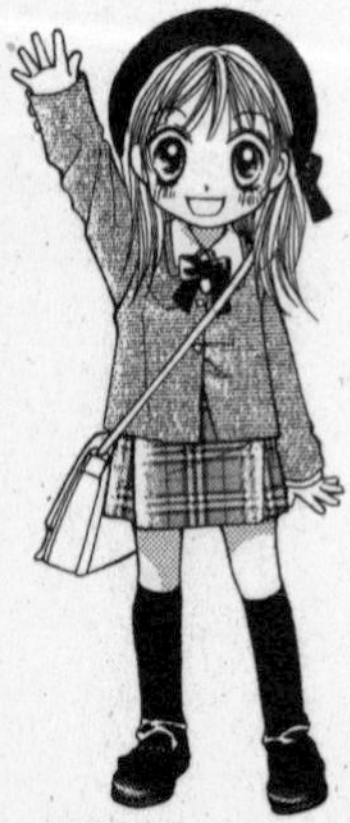

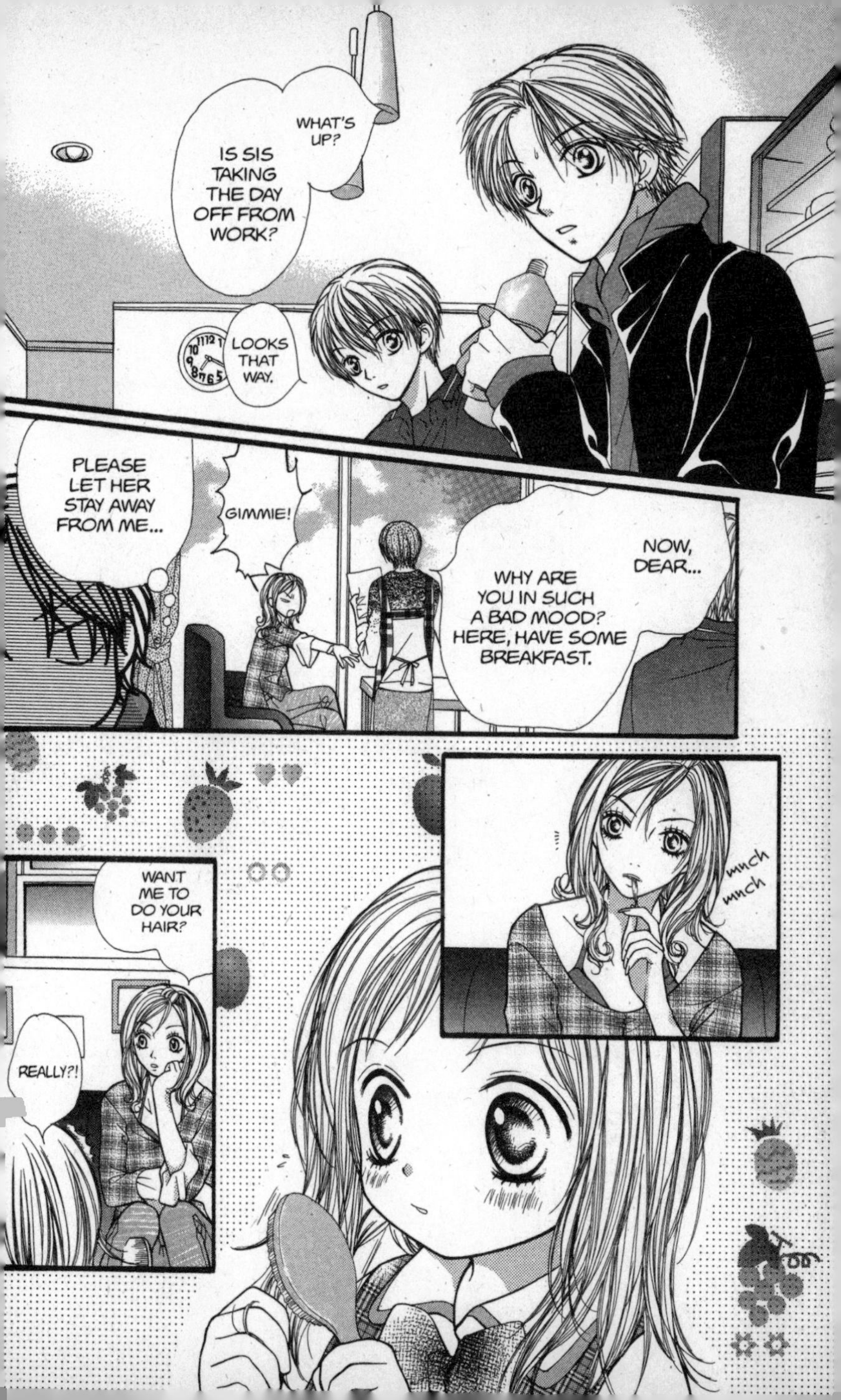
WHAT'S UP?
IS SIS TAKING THE DAY OFF FROM WORK?
LOOKS THAT WAY.
NOW, DEAR...
WHY ARE YOU IN SUCH A BAD MOOD? HERE, HAVE SOME BREAKFAST.
GIMMIE!
PLEASE LET HER STAY AWAY FROM ME...
mnch mnch
WANT ME TO DO YOUR HAIR?
REALLY?!

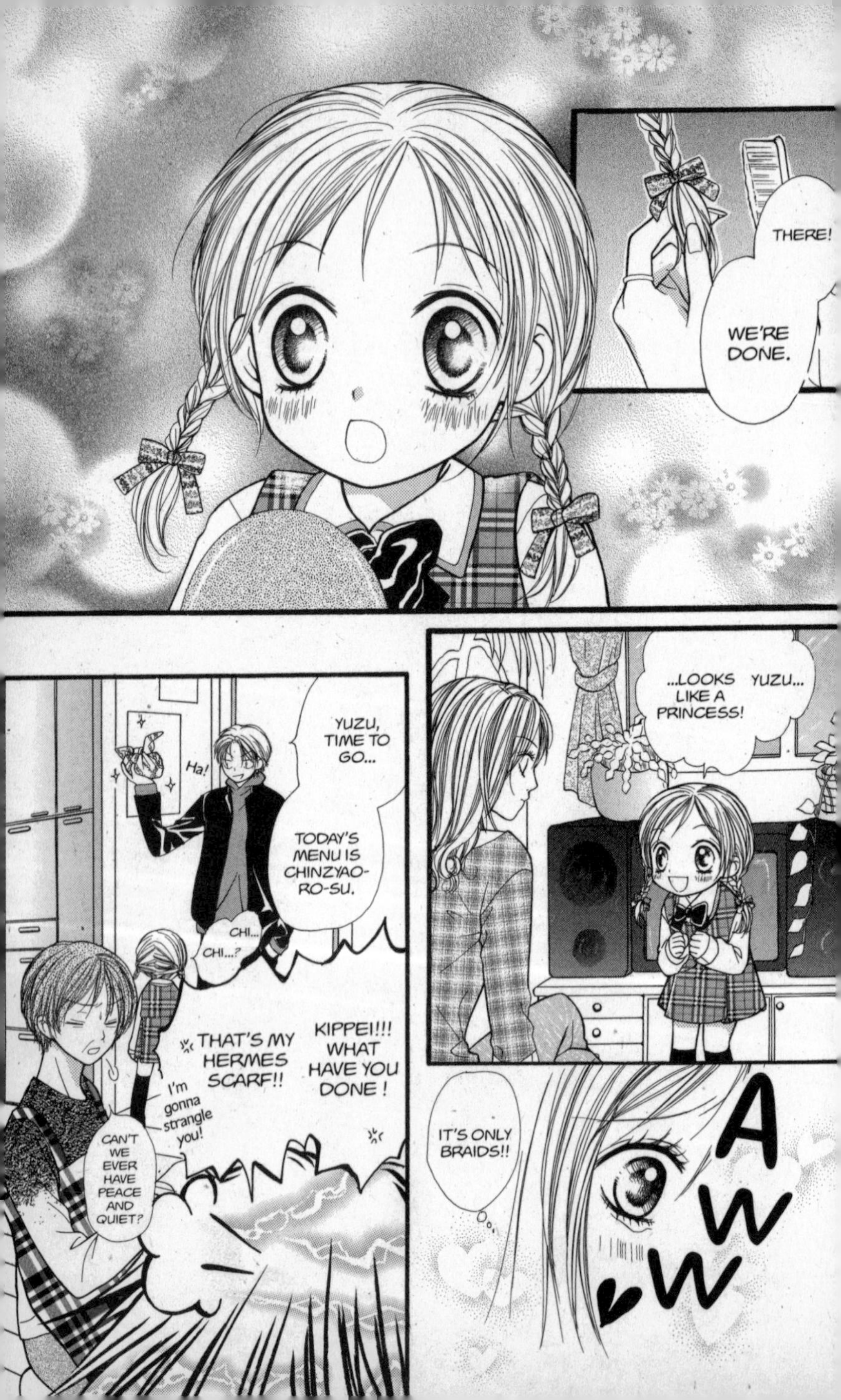
THERE!
WE'RE DONE.
YUZU...
...LOOKS LIKE A PRINCESS!
AWW
IT'S ONLY BRAIDS!!
YUZU, TIME TO GO...
Ha!
TODAY'S MENU IS CHINZYAO-RO-SU.
CHI... CHI...?
KIPPEI!!!! WHAT HAVE YOU DONE!
THAT'S MY HERMES SCARF!!
I'm gonna strangle you!
CAN'T WE EVER HAVE PEACE AND QUIET?

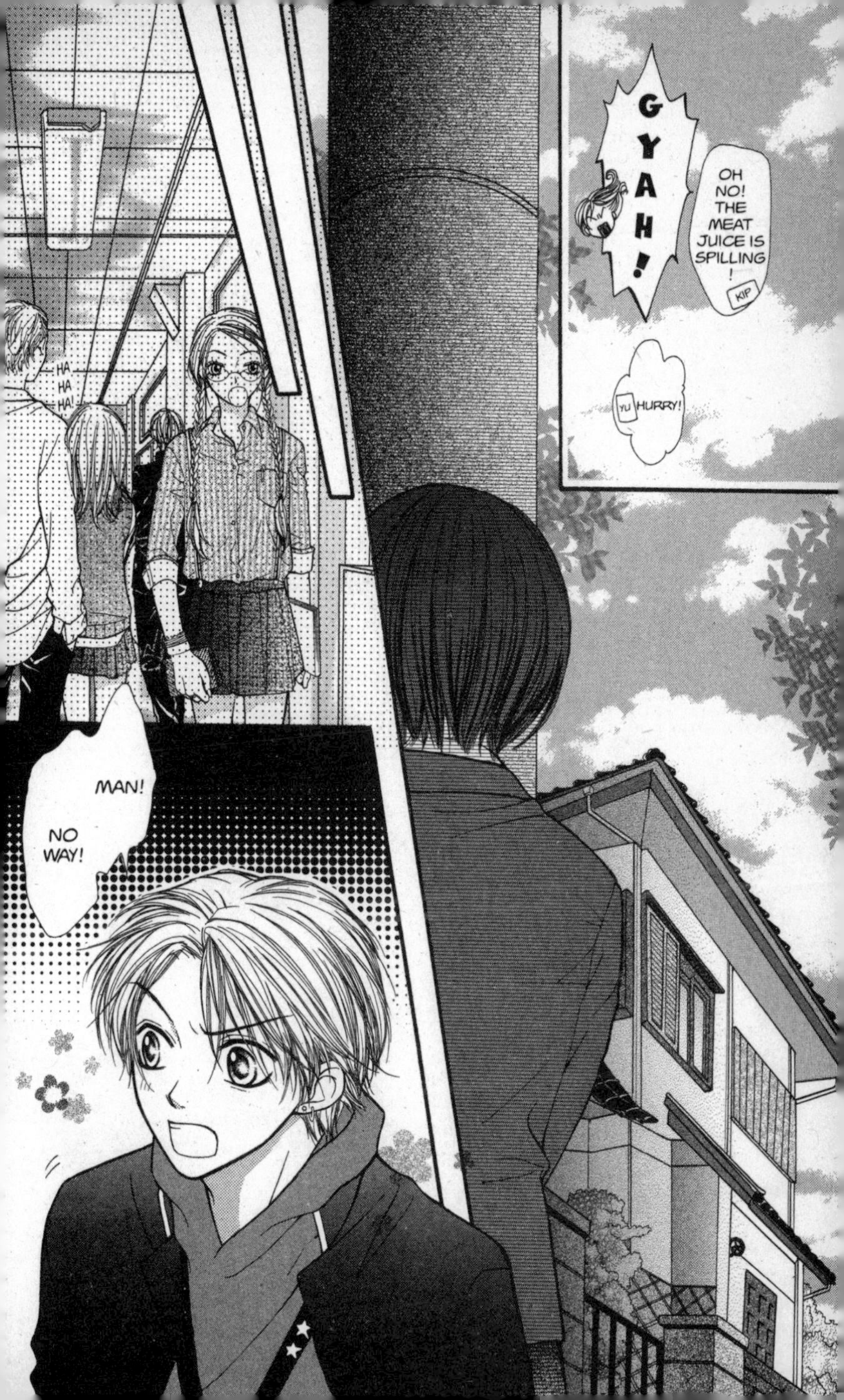
GYAH!
OH NO! THE MEAT JUICE IS SPILLING!
KIP
YU
HURRY!
HA HA HA!
MAN!
NO WAY!

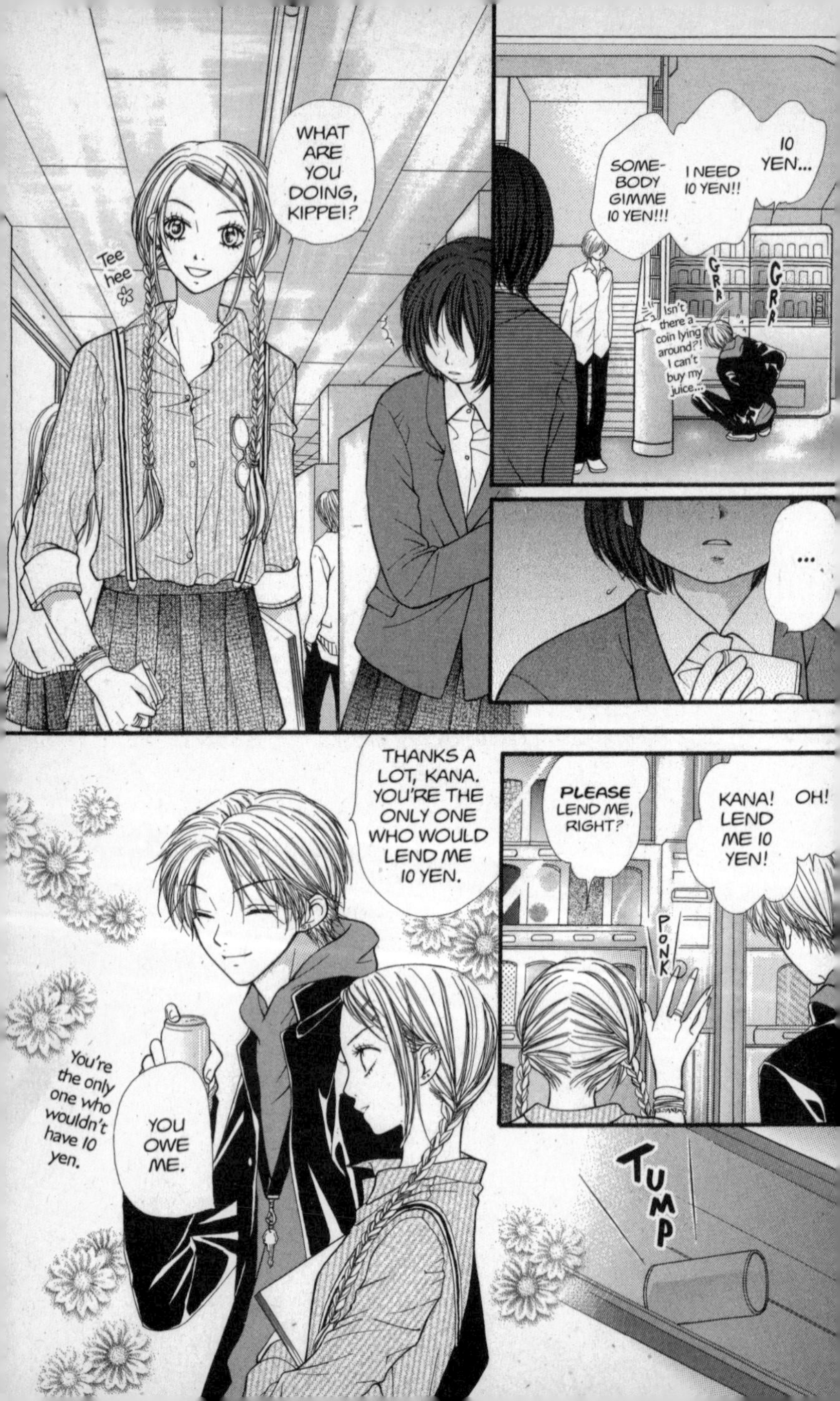
10 YEN...
I NEED 10 YEN!!
SOMEBODY GIMME 10 YEN!!!
GRR
GRR
Isn't there a coin lying around?! I can't buy my juice...
...
WHAT ARE YOU DOING, KIPPEI?
Tee hee
OH!
KANA! LEND ME 10 YEN!
PLEASE LEND ME, RIGHT?
PONK
TUMP
THANKS A LOT, KANA. YOU'RE THE ONLY ONE WHO WOULD LEND ME 10 YEN.
YOU OWE ME.
You're the only one who wouldn't have 10 yen.

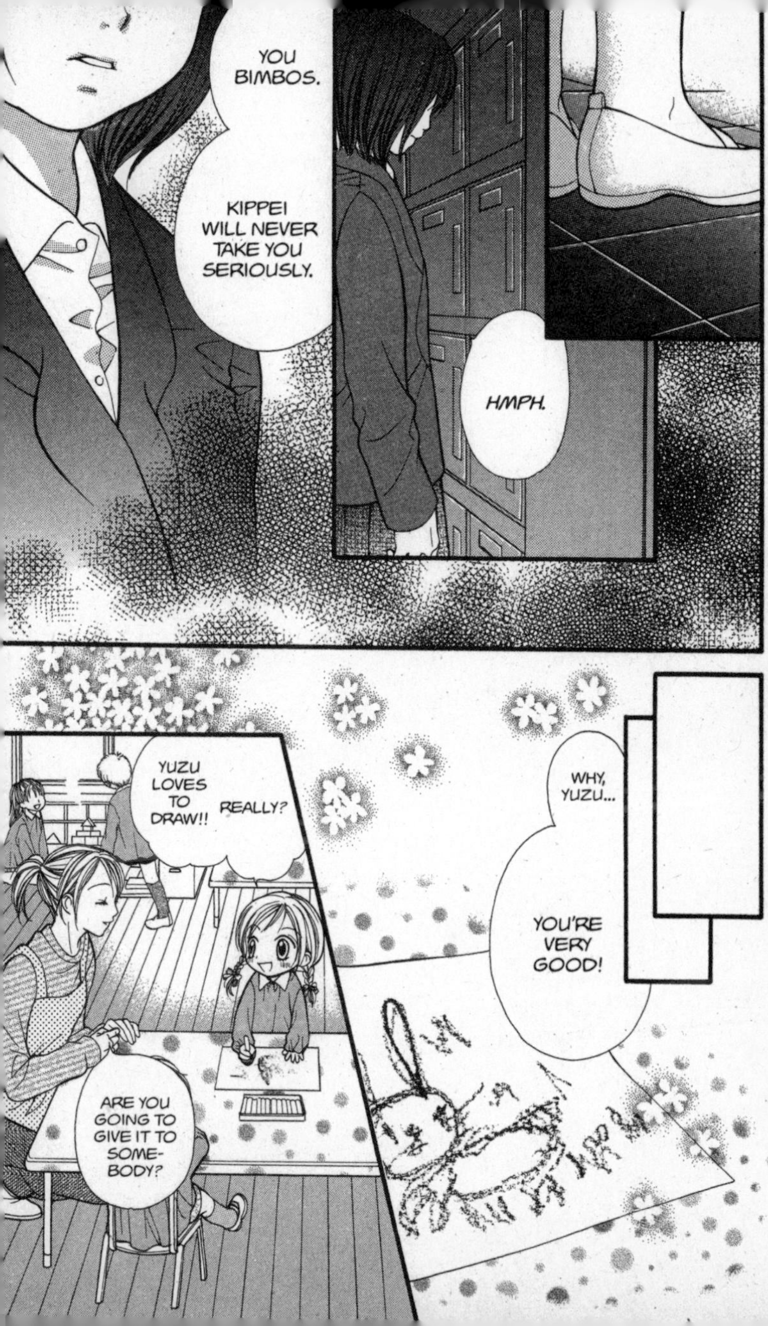
HMPH.
YOU BIMBOS.
KIPPEI WILL NEVER TAKE YOU SERIOUSLY.
WHY, YUZU...
YOU'RE VERY GOOD!
YUZU LOVES TO DRAW!!
REALLY?
ARE YOU GOING TO GIVE IT TO SOMEBODY?

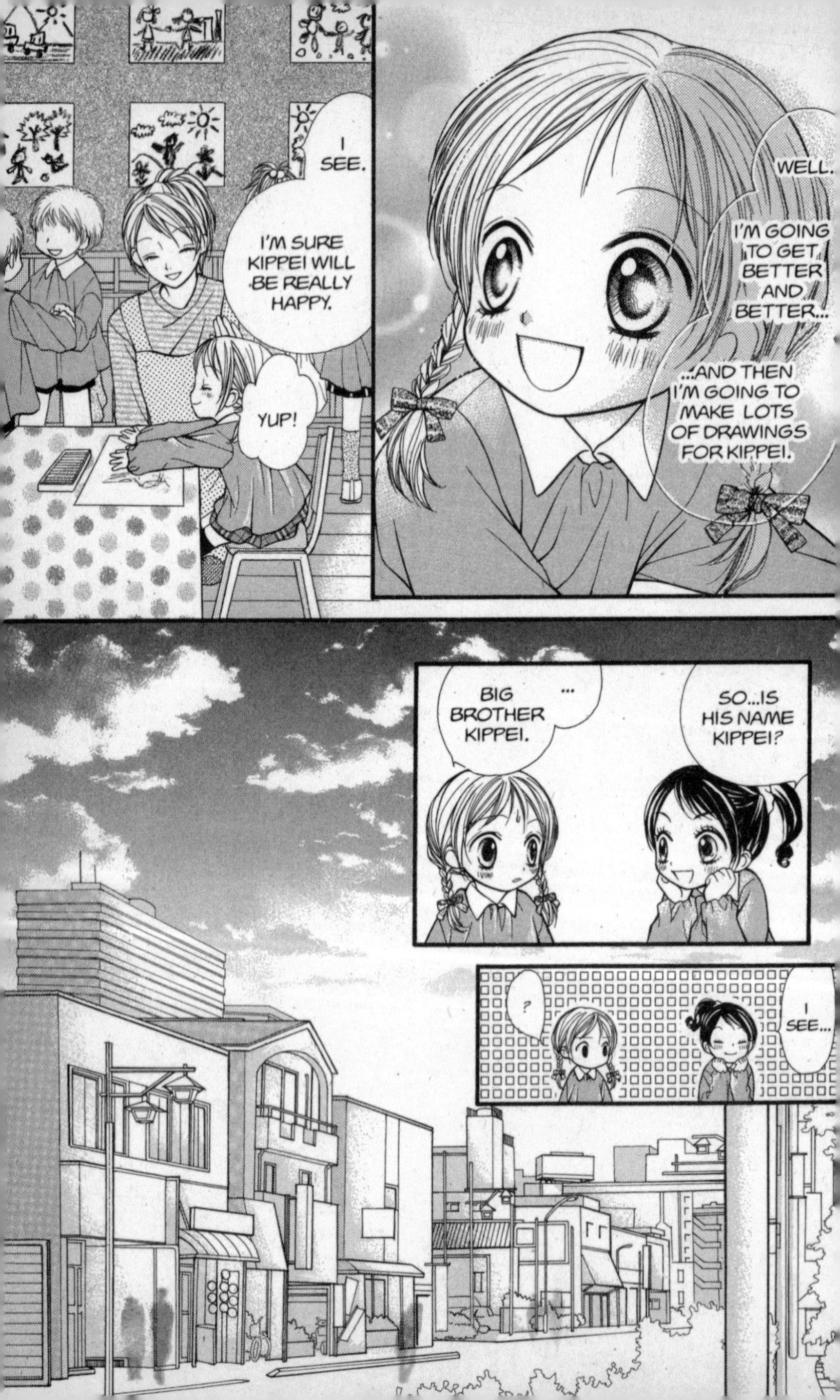
WELL...
I'M GOING TO GET BETTER AND BETTER...
...AND THEN I'M GOING TO MAKE LOTS OF DRAWINGS FOR KIPPEI.
I SEE.
I'M SURE KIPPEI WILL BE REALLY HAPPY.
YUP!
SO...IS HIS NAME KIPPEI?
...
BIG BROTHER KIPPEI.
I SEE...
?

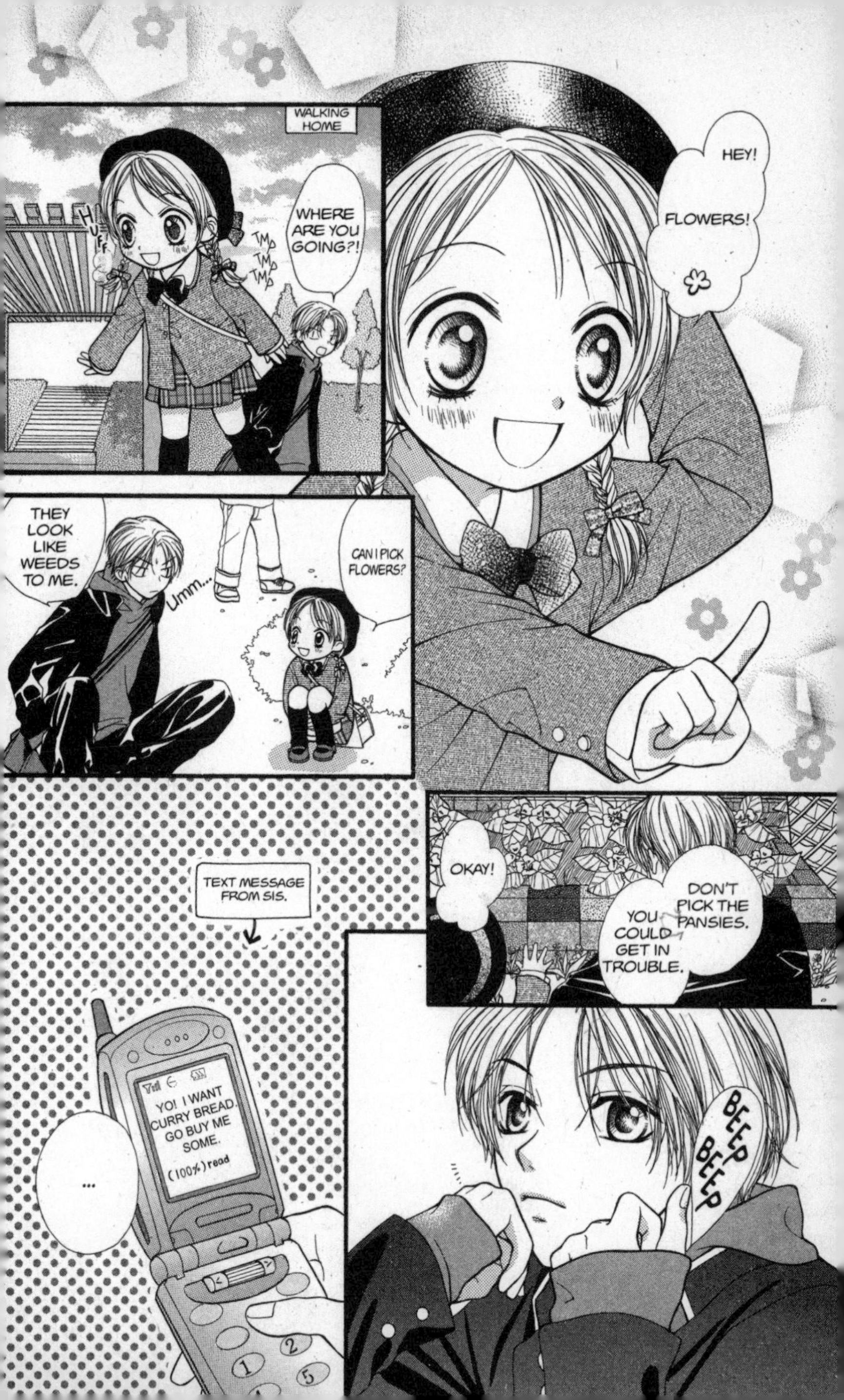
HEY!
FLOWERS!
WALKING HOME
WHERE ARE YOU GOING?!
TMP TMP TMP
HUFF
CAN I PICK FLOWERS?
Umm...
THEY LOOK LIKE WEEDS TO ME.
DON'T PICK THE PANSIES.
YOU COULD GET IN TROUBLE.
OKAY!
BEEP BEEP
TEXT MESSAGE FROM SIS.
YO! I WANT CURRY BREAD. GO BUY ME SOME.
(100%) read
...

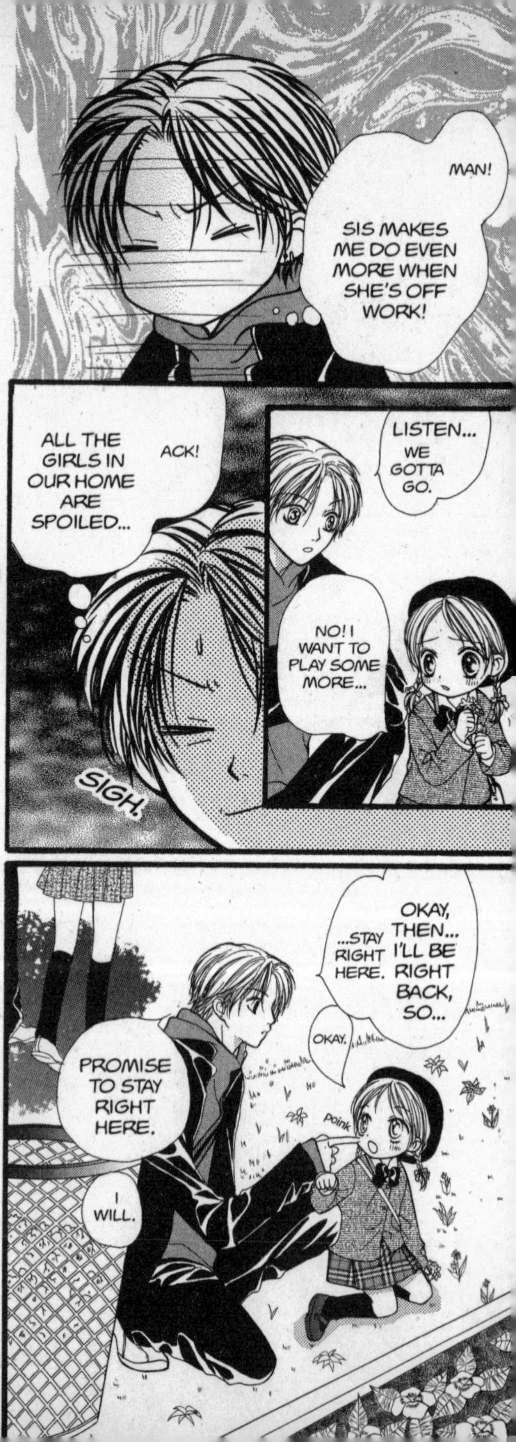
MAN!
SIS MAKES ME DO EVEN MORE WHEN SHE'S OFF WORK!
LISTEN...
WE GOTTA GO.
NO! I WANT TO PLAY SOME MORE...
ACK!
ALL THE GIRLS IN OUR HOME ARE SPOILED...
SIGH.
OKAY, THEN... I'LL BE RIGHT BACK, SO...
...STAY RIGHT HERE.
OKAY.
PROMISE TO STAY RIGHT HERE.
poink
I WILL.

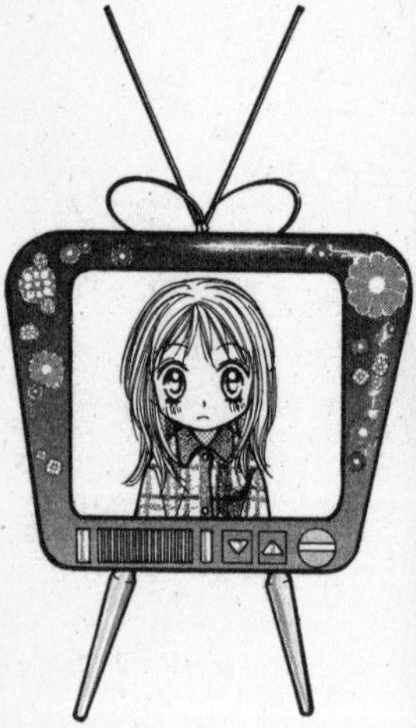

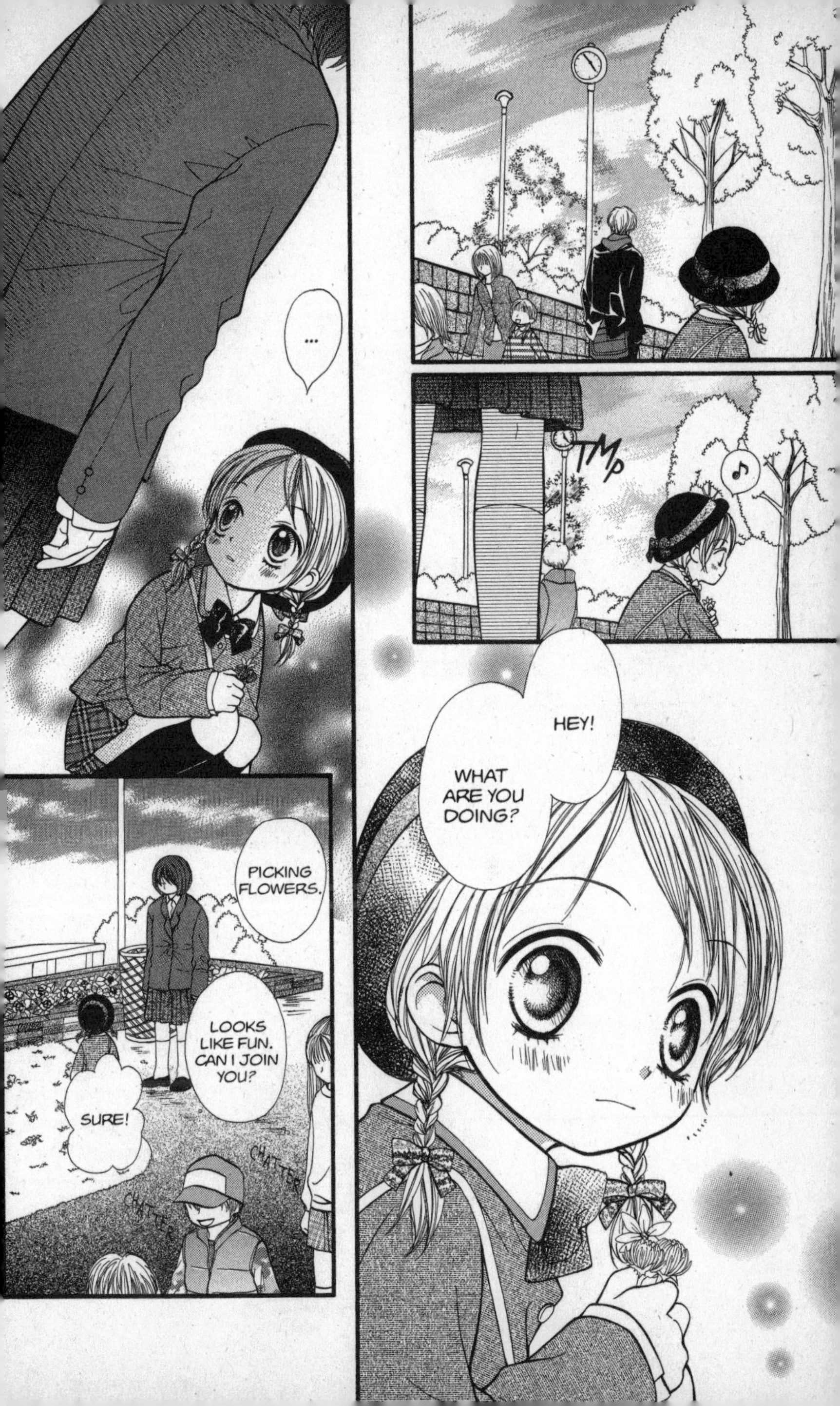
TMP
♪
HEY!
WHAT ARE YOU DOING?
...
PICKING FLOWERS.
LOOKS LIKE FUN. CAN I JOIN YOU?
SURE!
CHATTER
CHATTER

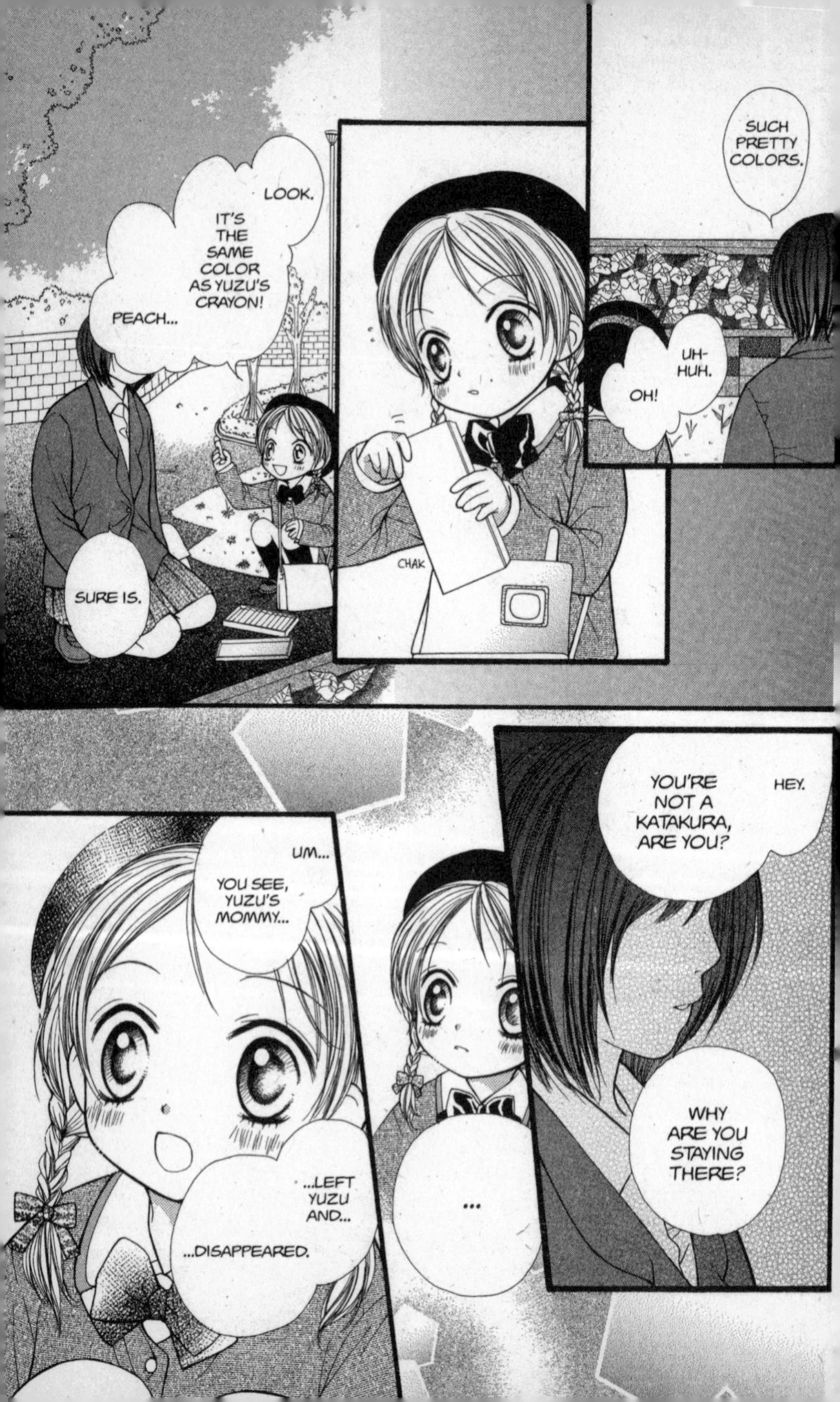
SUCH PRETTY COLORS.
UH-HUH.
OH!
CHAK
LOOK.
IT'S THE SAME COLOR AS YUZU'S CRAYON!
PEACH...
SURE IS.
HEY.
YOU'RE NOT A KATAKURA, ARE YOU?
WHY ARE YOU STAYING THERE?
...
UM...
YOU SEE, YUZU'S MOMMY...
...LEFT YUZU AND...
...DISAPPEARED.

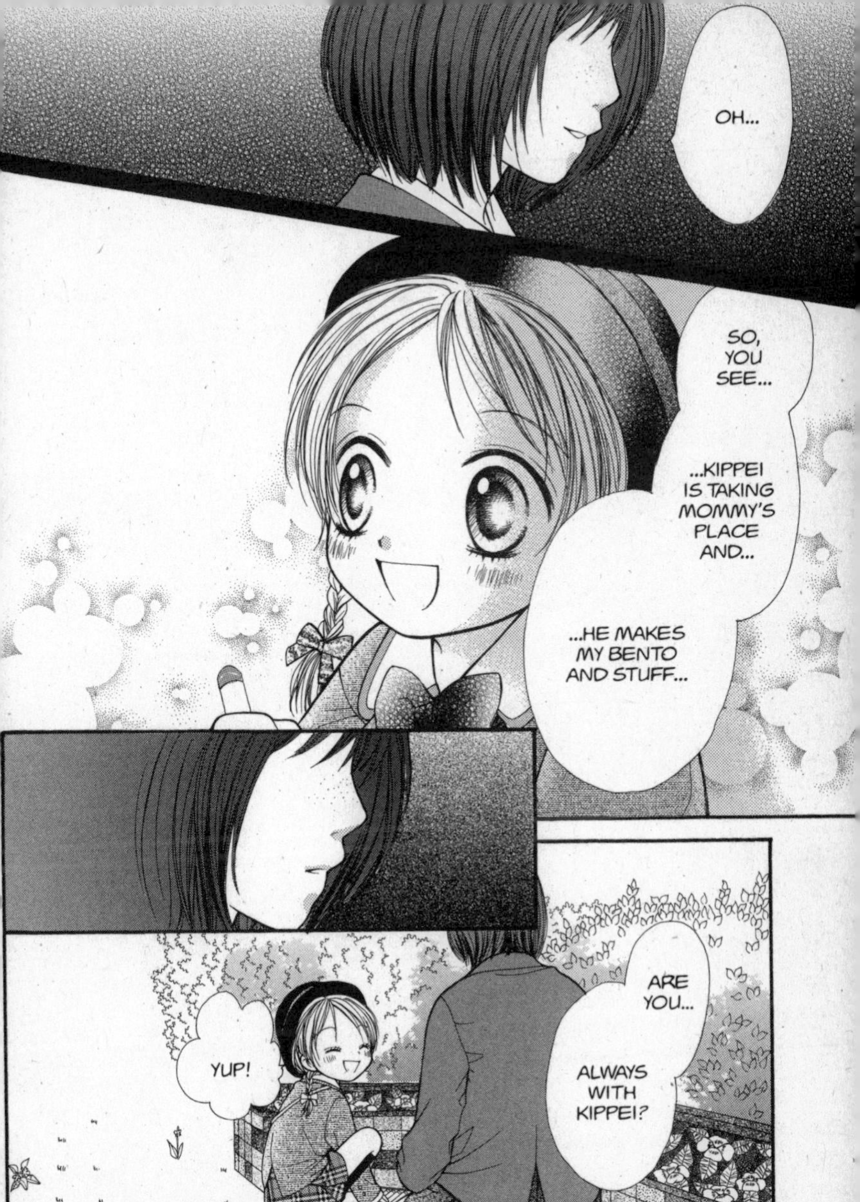
OH...
SO, YOU SEE...
...KIPPEI IS TAKING MOMMY'S PLACE AND...
...HE MAKES MY BENTO AND STUFF...
ARE YOU...
ALWAYS WITH KIPPEI?
YUP!

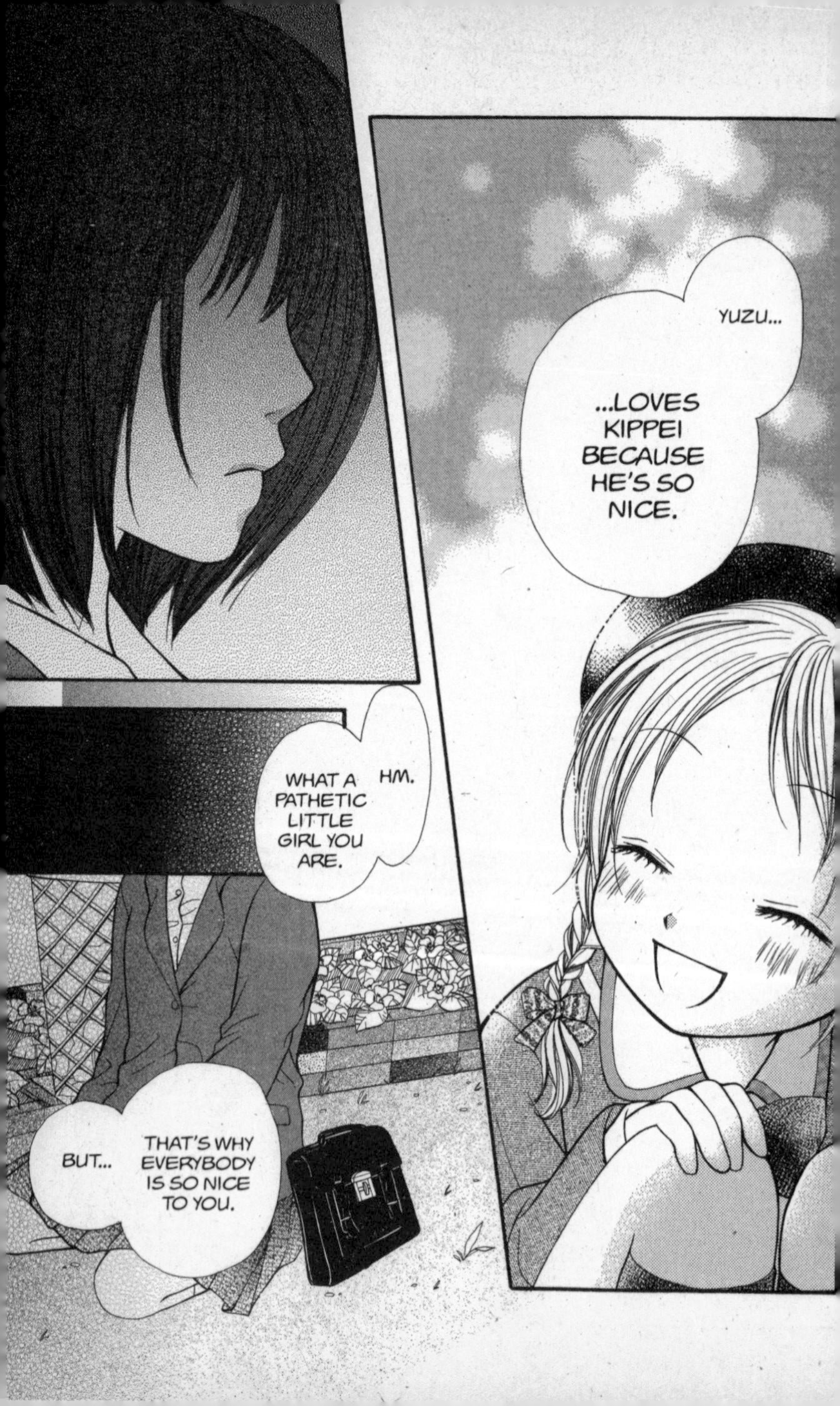
YUZU...
...LOVES KIPPEI BECAUSE HE'S SO NICE.
HM.
WHAT A PATHETIC LITTLE GIRL YOU ARE.
BUT...
THAT'S WHY EVERYBODY IS SO NICE TO YOU.

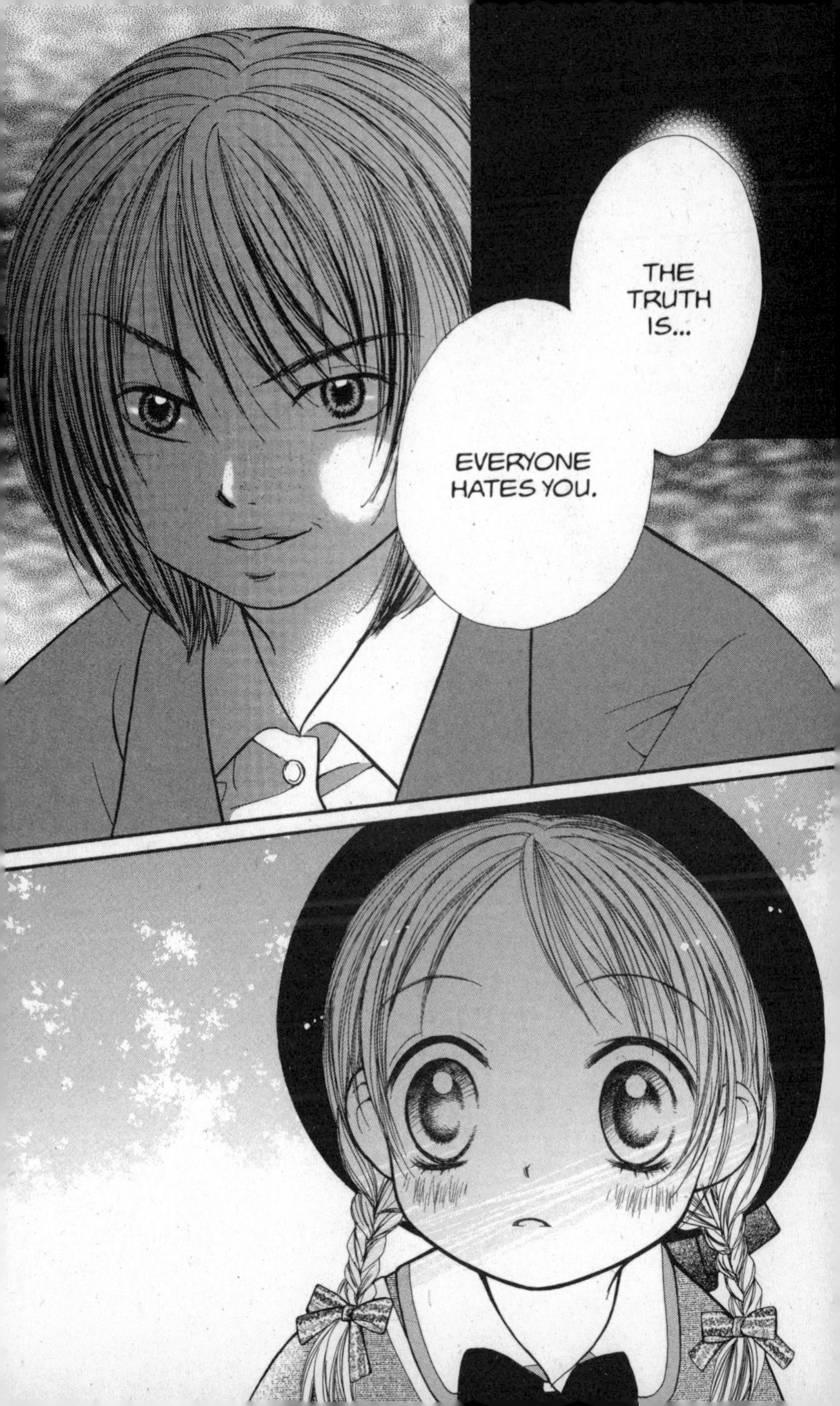
THE TRUTH IS...
EVERYONE HATES YOU.

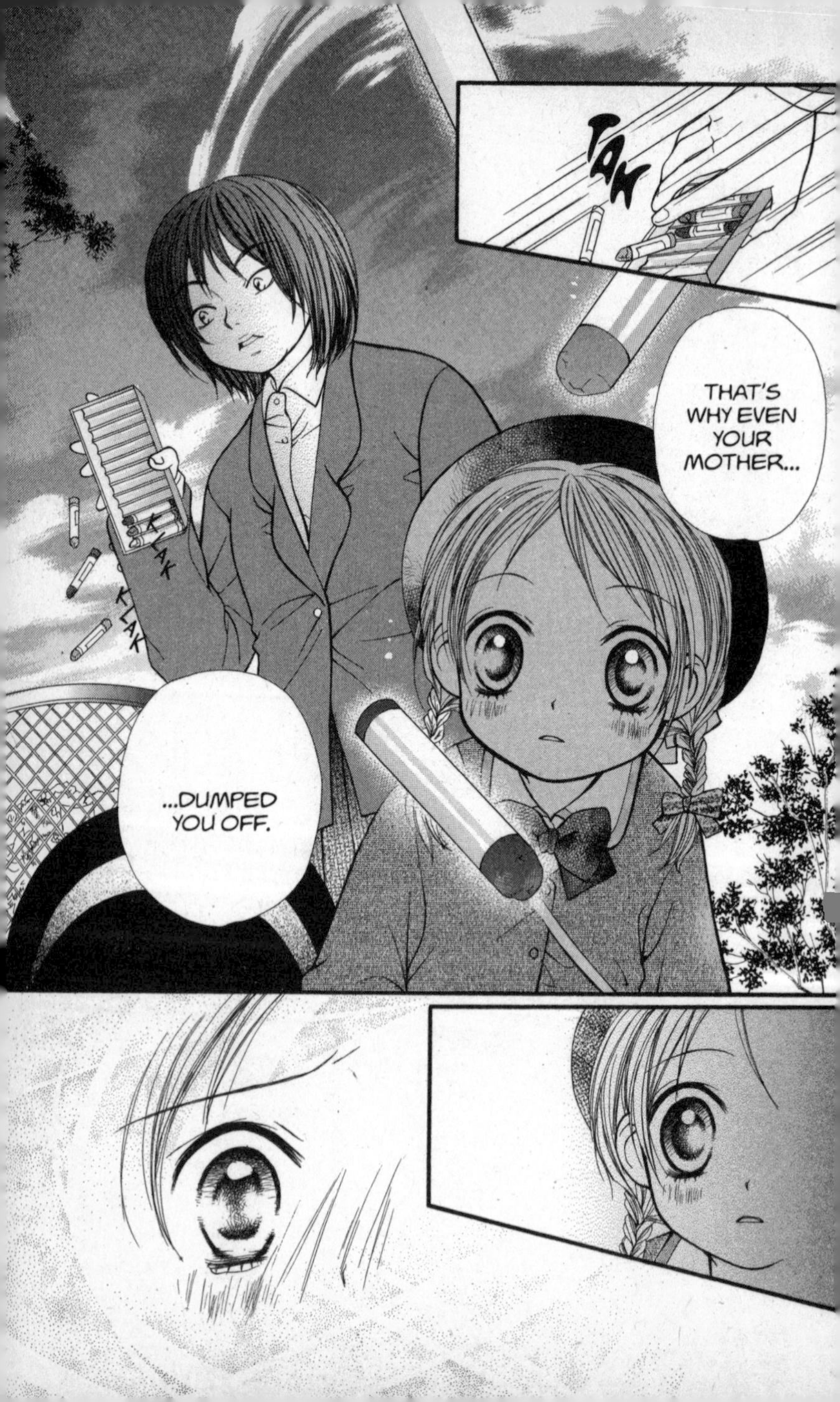
TAK
THAT'S WHY EVEN YOUR MOTHER...
KLAK
KLAK
...DUMPED YOU OFF.

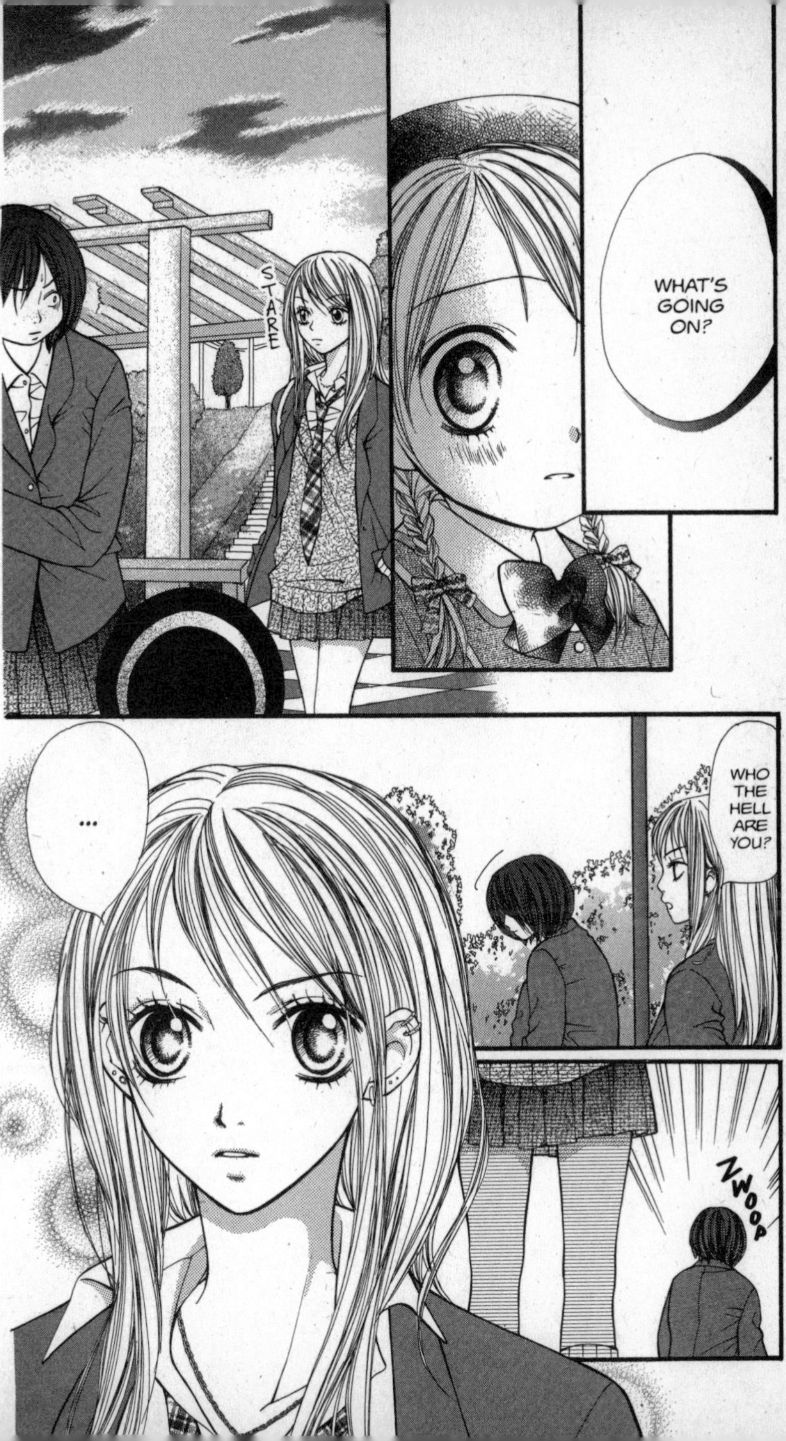
WHAT'S GOING ON?
STARE
WHO THE HELL ARE YOU?
ZWOOP
...

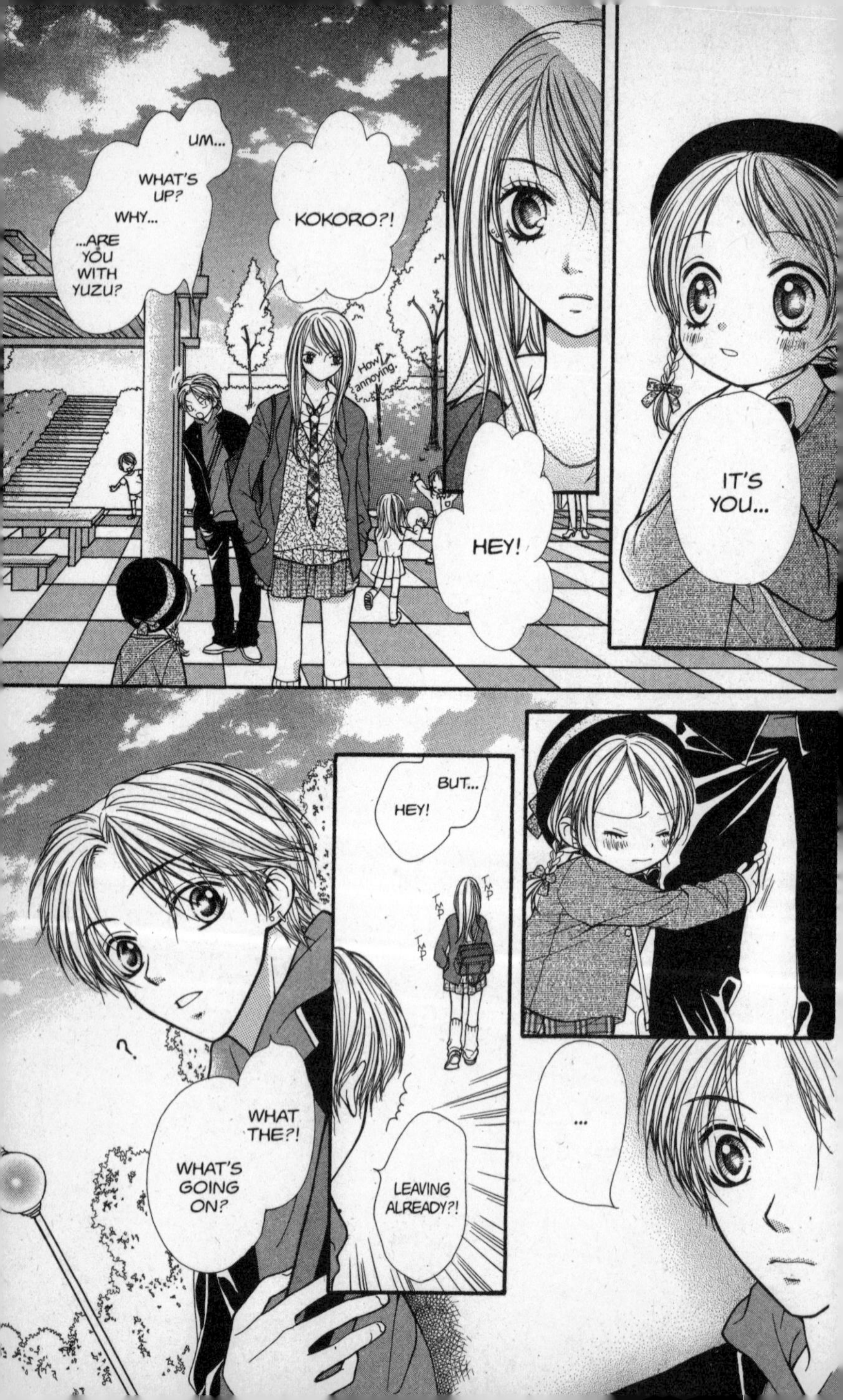
IT'S YOU...
HEY!
KOKORO?!
How annoying.
UM... WHAT'S UP? WHY... ...ARE YOU WITH YUZU?
...
BUT... HEY!
TMP TMP TMP
LEAVING ALREADY?!
WHAT THE?! WHAT'S GOING ON?
?

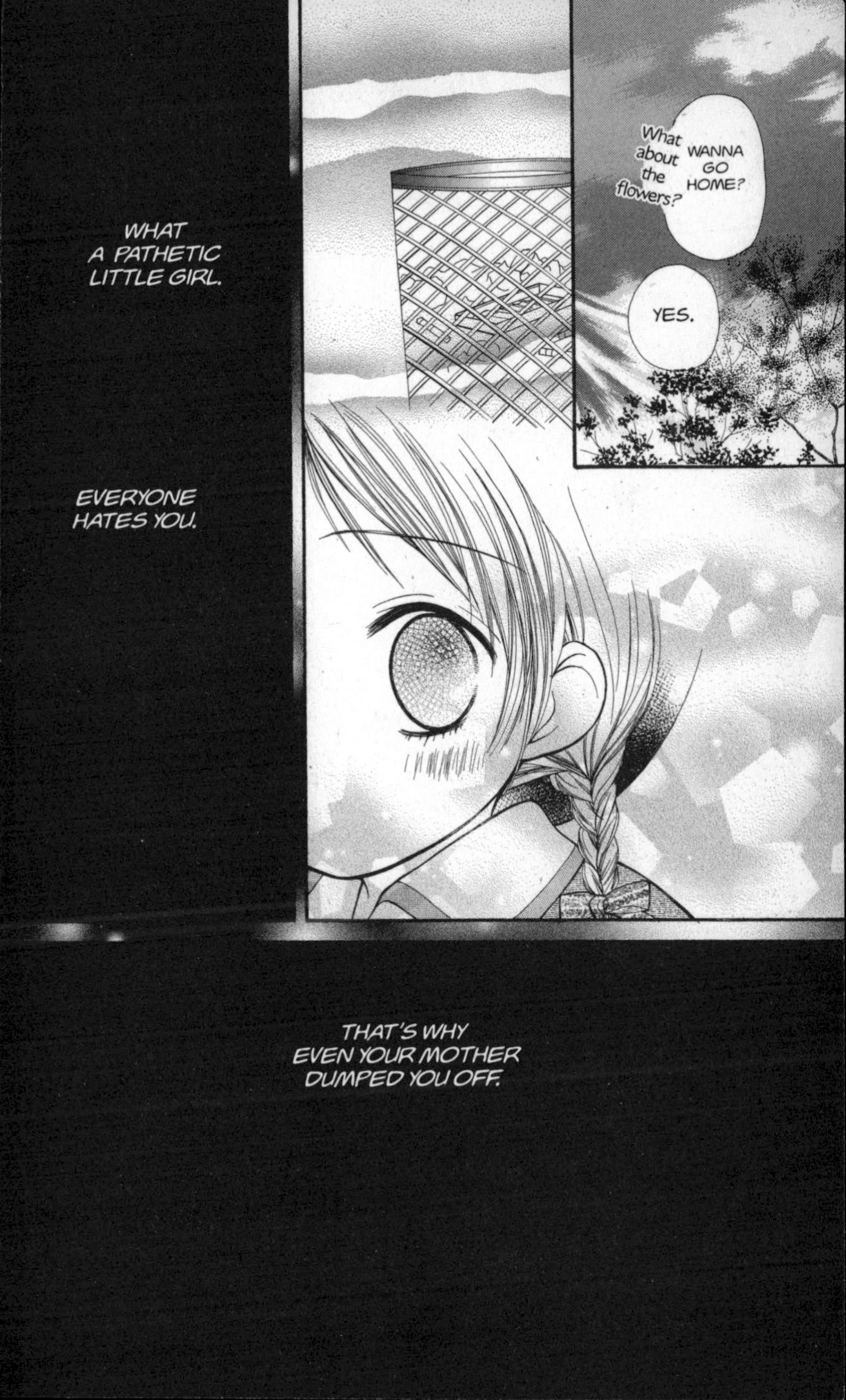
WANNA GO HOME?
What about the flowers?
YES.
WHAT A PATHETIC LITTLE GIRL.
EVERYONE HATES YOU.
THAT'S WHY EVEN YOUR MOTHER DUMPED YOU OFF.

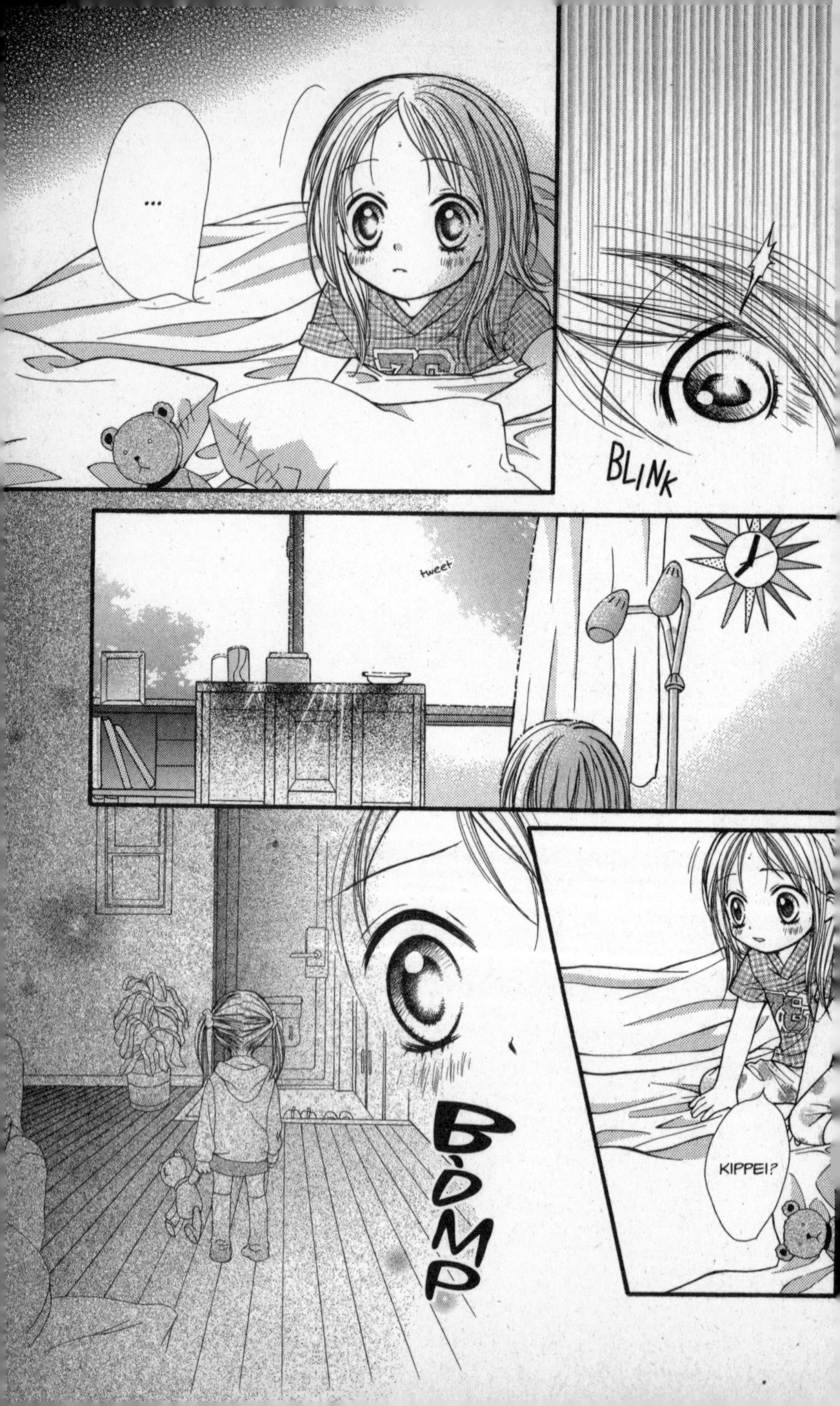
BLINK
...
tweet
KIPPEI?
BOMP

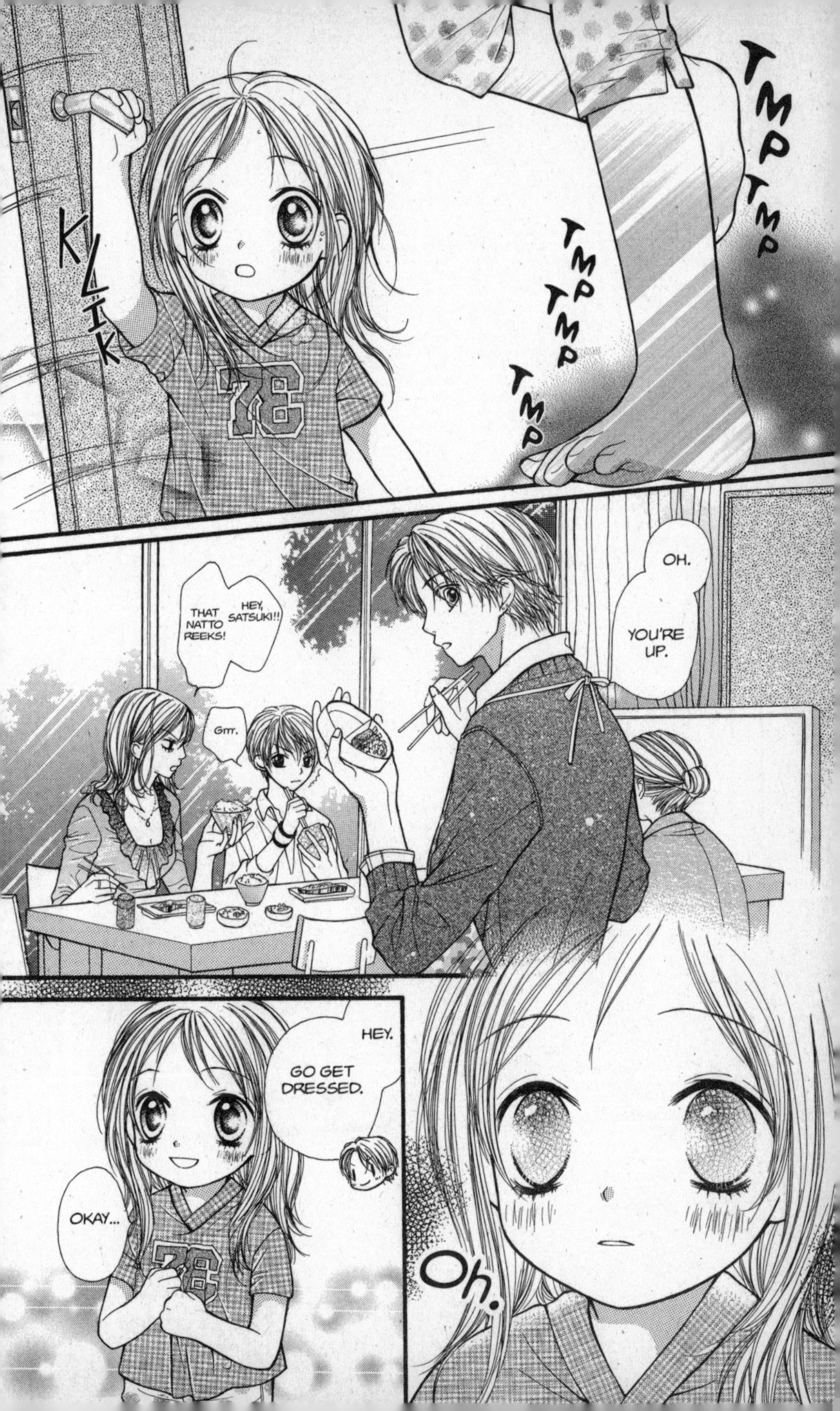
TMP TMP
TMP TMP TMP TMP
KLIK
OH.
YOU'RE UP.
HEY, SATSUKI!!
THAT NATTO REEKS!
Grrr.
Oh.
HEY.
GO GET DRESSED.
OKAY...

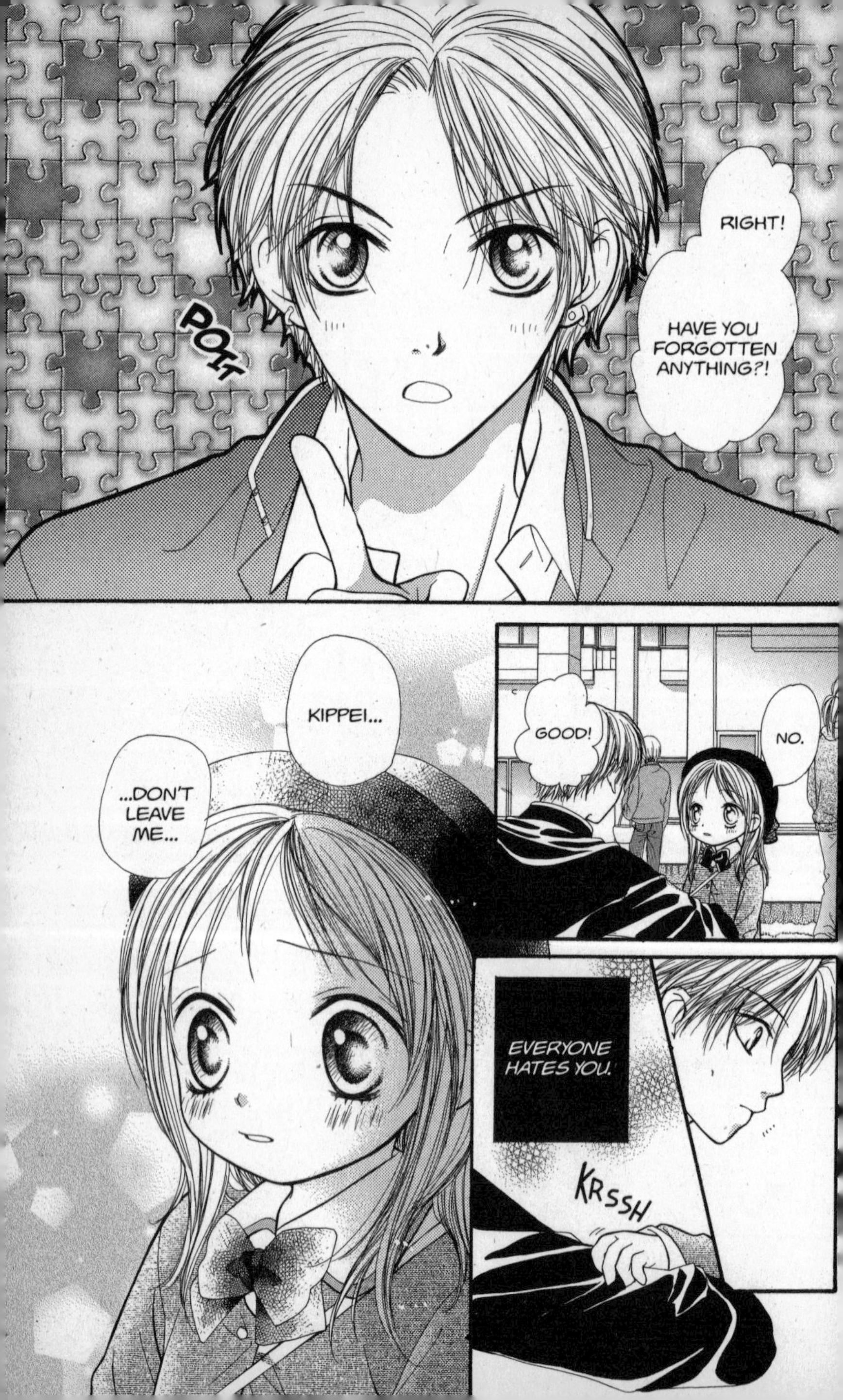
RIGHT!
HAVE YOU FORGOTTEN ANYTHING?!
POIT
NO.
GOOD!
EVERYONE HATES YOU.
...
KRSSH
KIPPEI...
...DON'T LEAVE ME...

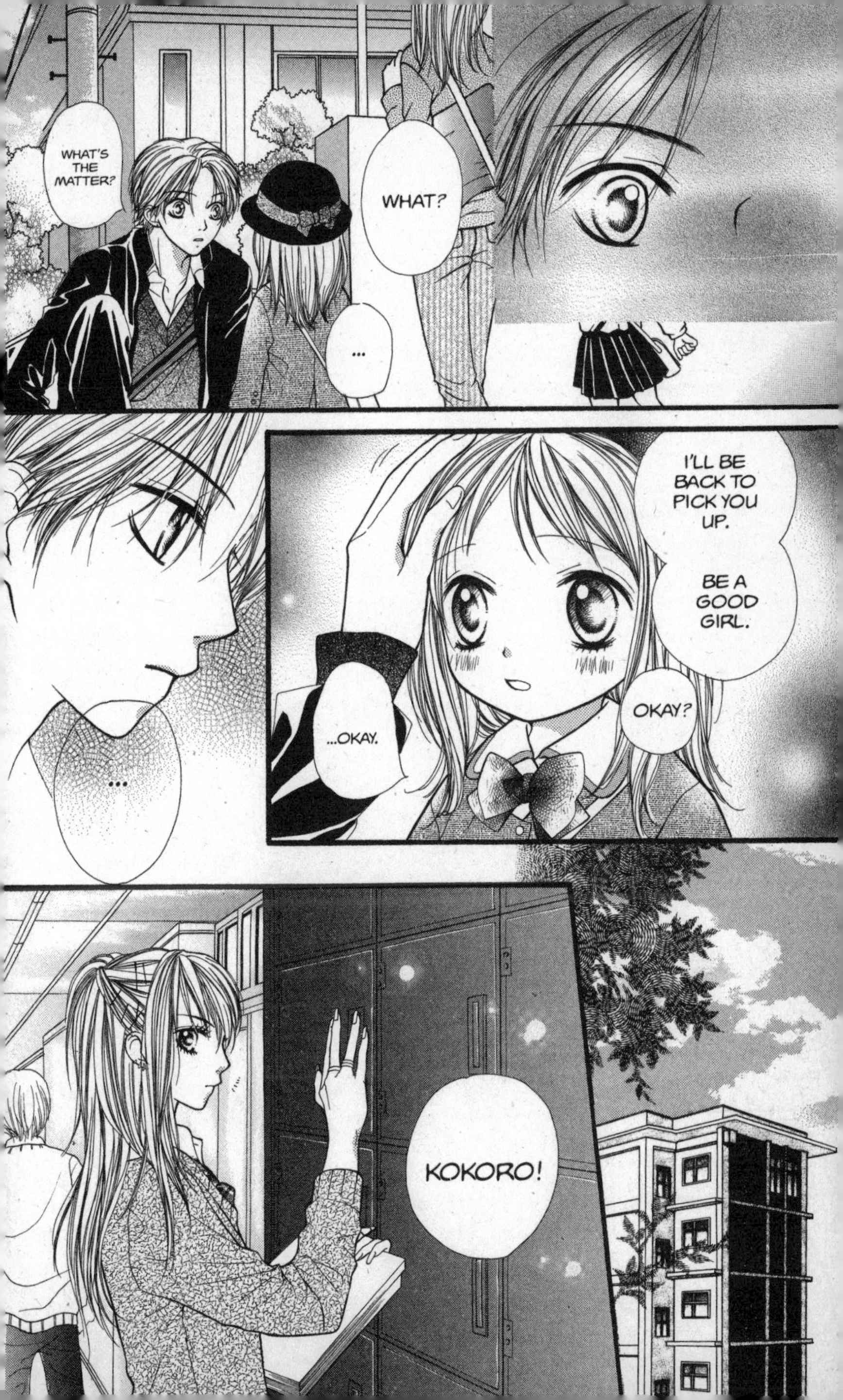
WHAT?
WHAT'S THE MATTER?
...
I'LL BE BACK TO PICK YOU UP.
BE A GOOD GIRL.
OKAY?
...OKAY.
...
KOKORO!

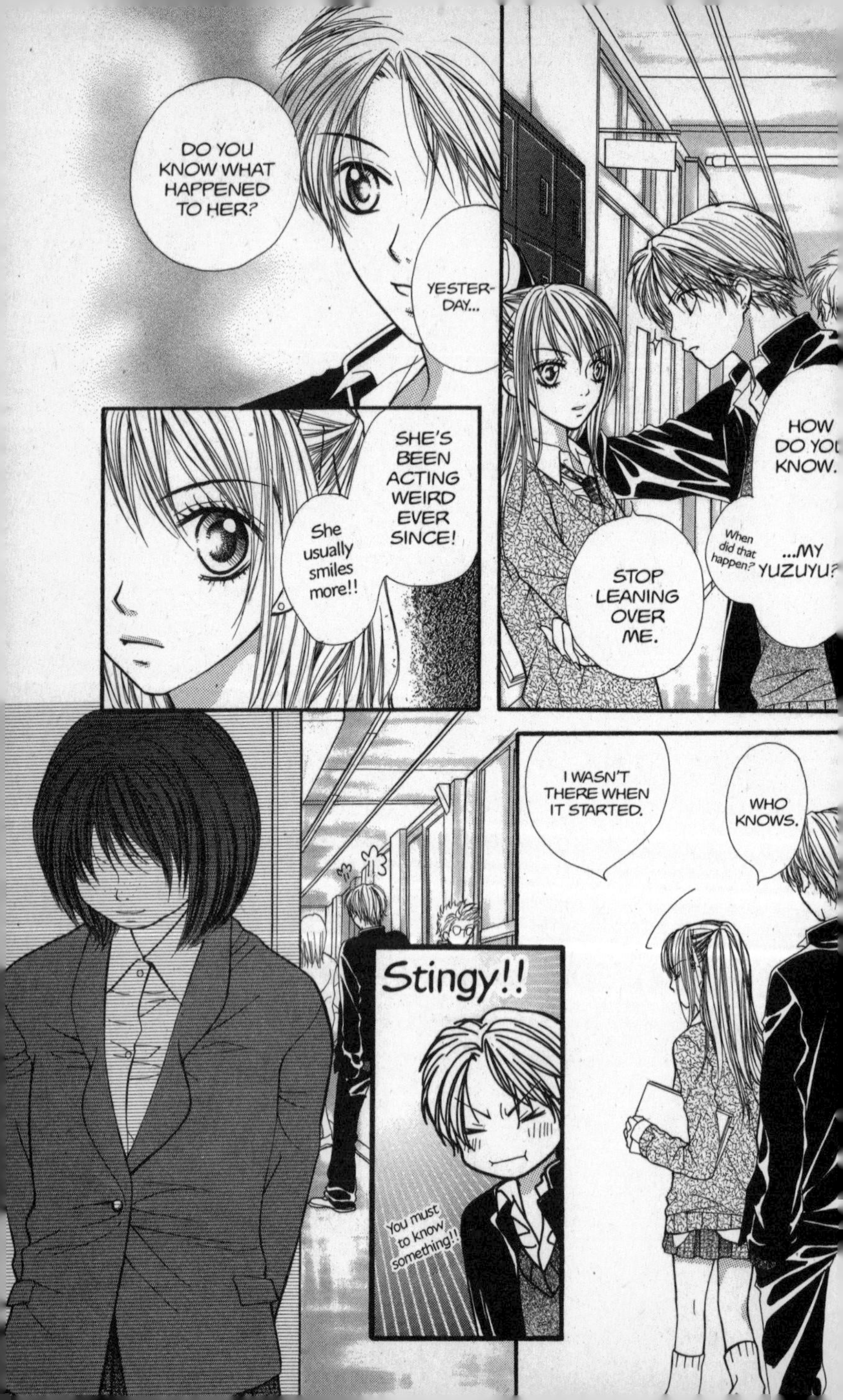
HOW DO YOU KNOW...
...MY YUZUYU?
When did that happen?
STOP LEANING OVER ME.
DO YOU KNOW WHAT HAPPENED TO HER?
YESTER-DAY...
SHE'S BEEN ACTING WEIRD EVER SINCE!
She usually smiles more!!
WHO KNOWS.
I WASN'T THERE WHEN IT STARTED.
Stingy!!
You must to know something!!

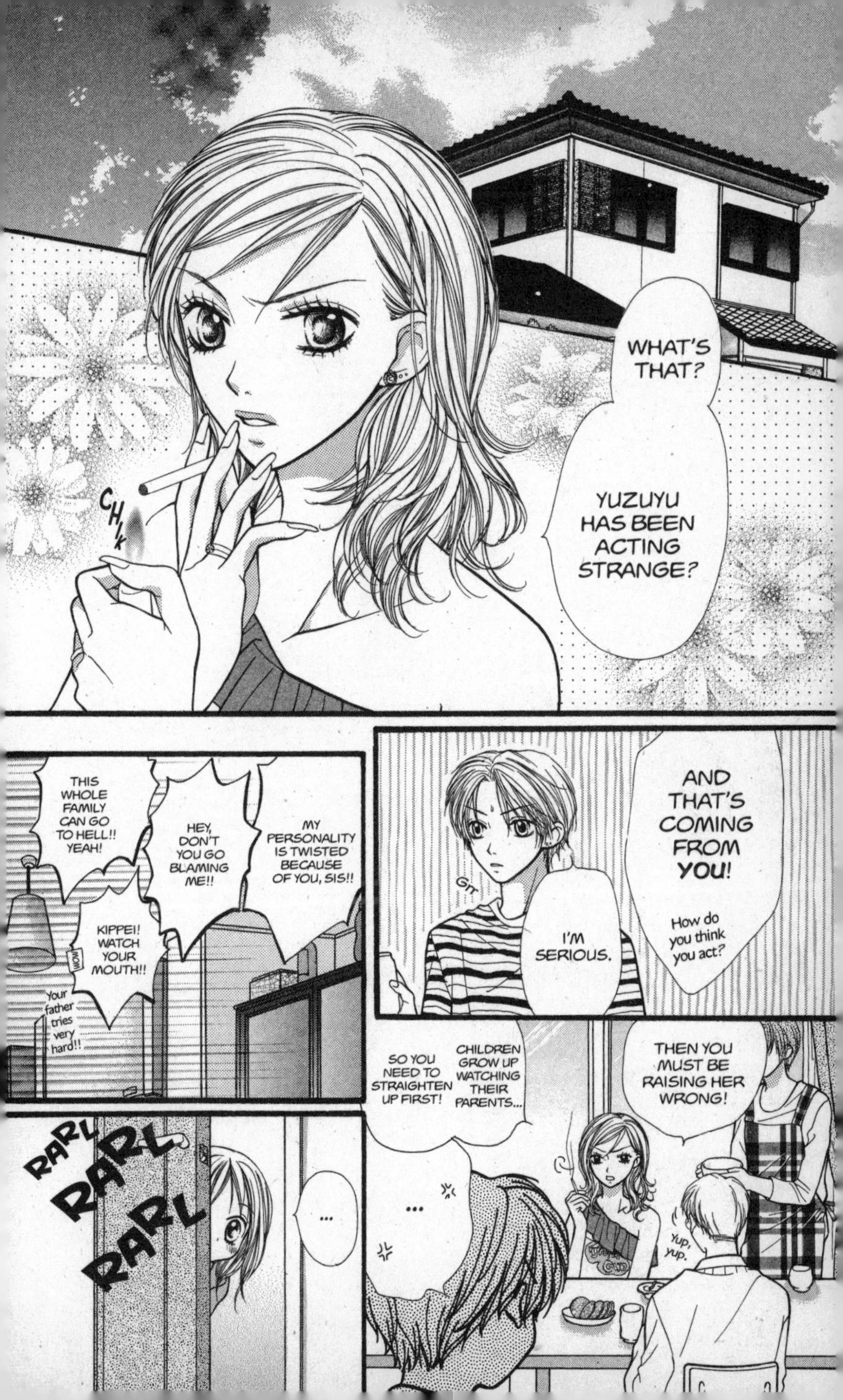
WHAT'S THAT?
YUZUYU HAS BEEN ACTING STRANGE?
CHIK
AND THAT'S COMING FROM YOU!
How do you think you act?
I'M SERIOUS.
THEN YOU MUST BE RAISING HER WRONG!
CHILDREN GROW UP WATCHING THEIR PARENTS...
SO YOU NEED TO STRAIGHTEN UP FIRST!
Yup, yup.
...
MY PERSONALITY IS TWISTED BECAUSE OF YOU, SIS!!
HEY, DON'T YOU GO BLAMING ME!!
THIS WHOLE FAMILY CAN GO TO HELL!! YEAH!
KIPPEI! WATCH YOUR MOUTH!!
Your father tries very hard!!
...
RARL RARL RARL RARL

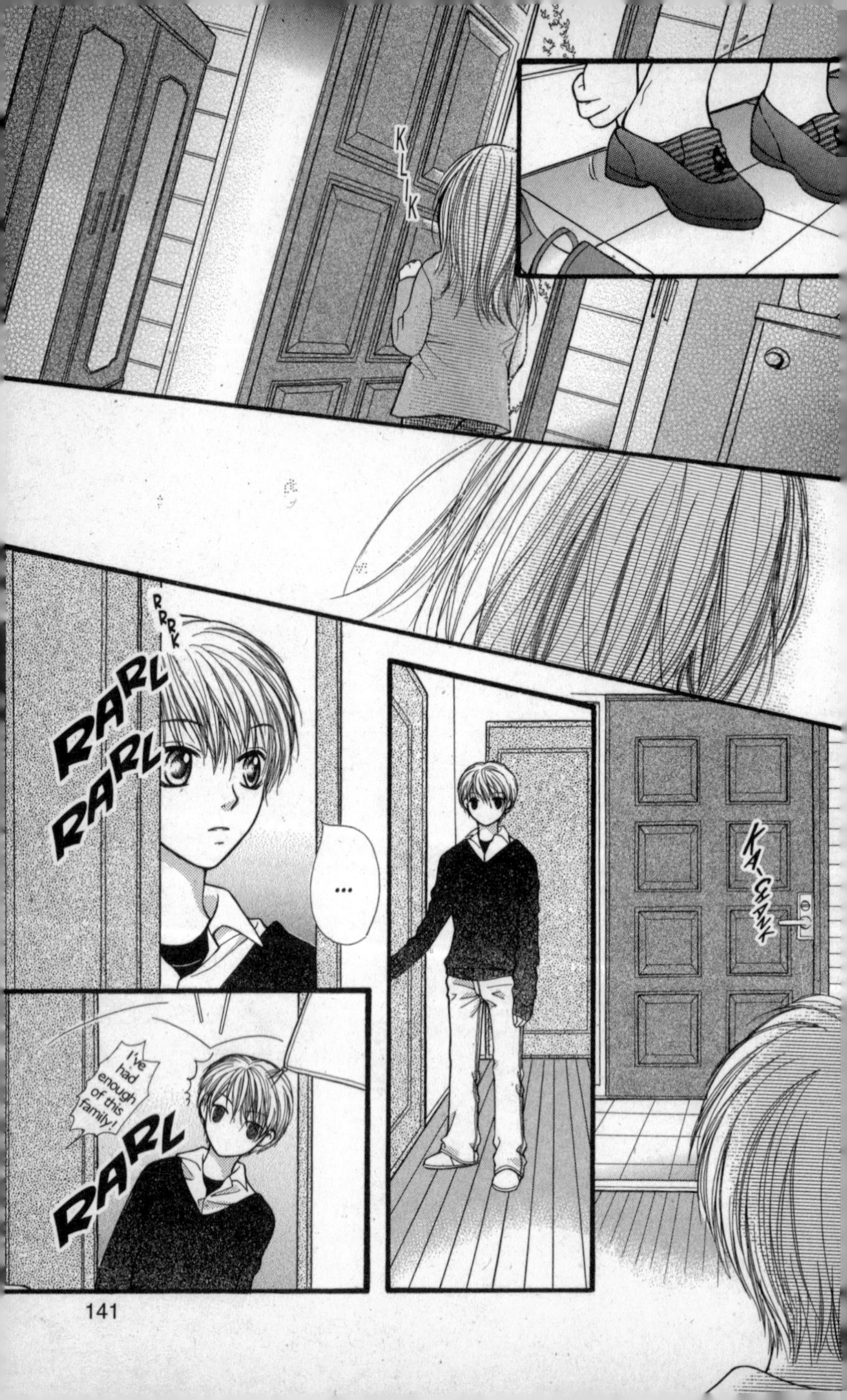
KLIK
KA-CHANK
RRRK
RARL RARL
...
I've had enough of this family!
RARL

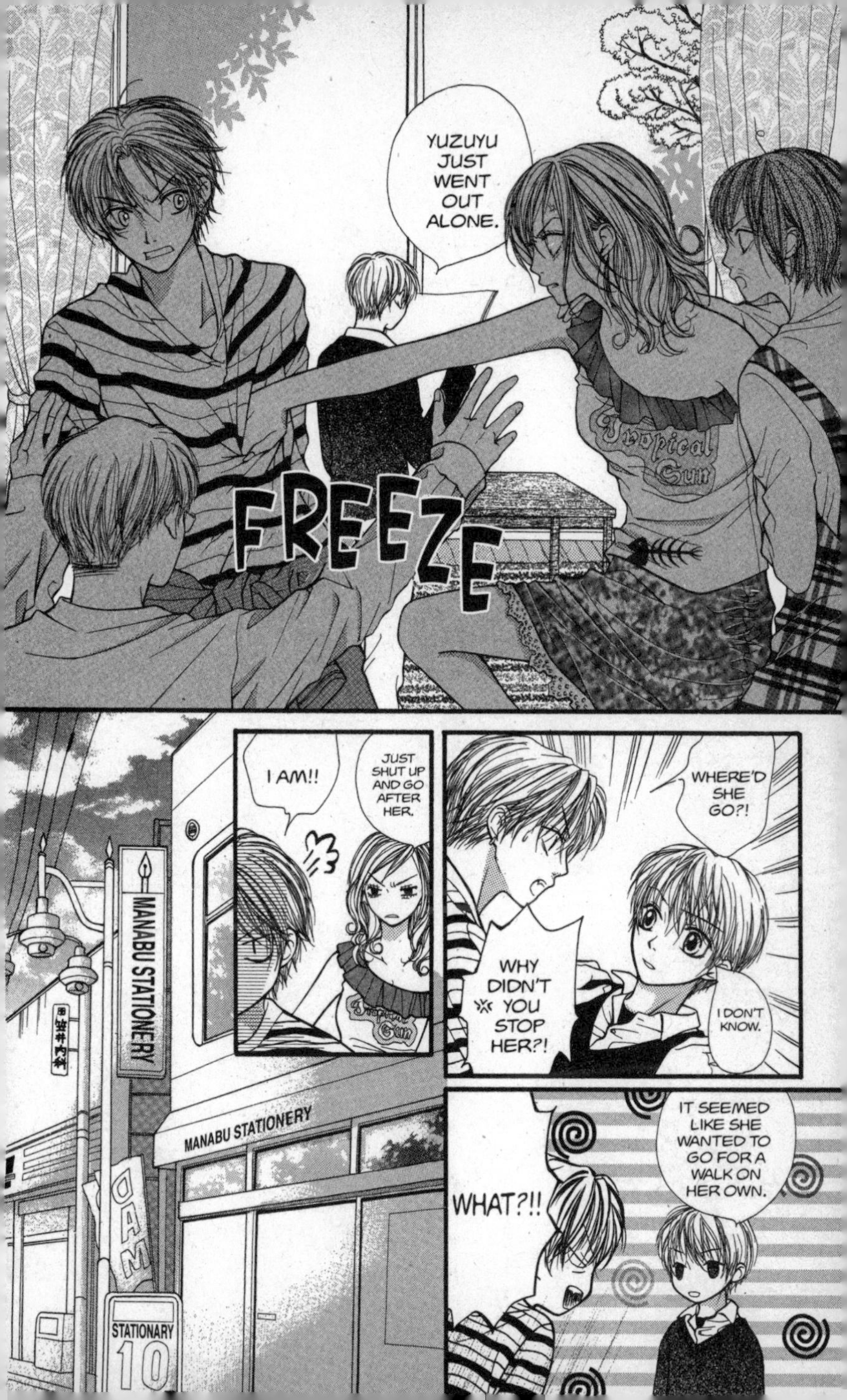

YUZUYU JUST WENT OUT ALONE.
FREEZE
WHERE'D SHE GO?!
WHY DIDN'T YOU STOP HER?!
I DON'T KNOW.
JUST SHUT UP AND GO AFTER HER.
I AM!!
IT SEEMED LIKE SHE WANTED TO GO FOR A WALK ON HER OWN.
WHAT?!!
MANABU STATIONERY
笠井内科
MANABU STATIONERY
DAM
STATIONARY
10

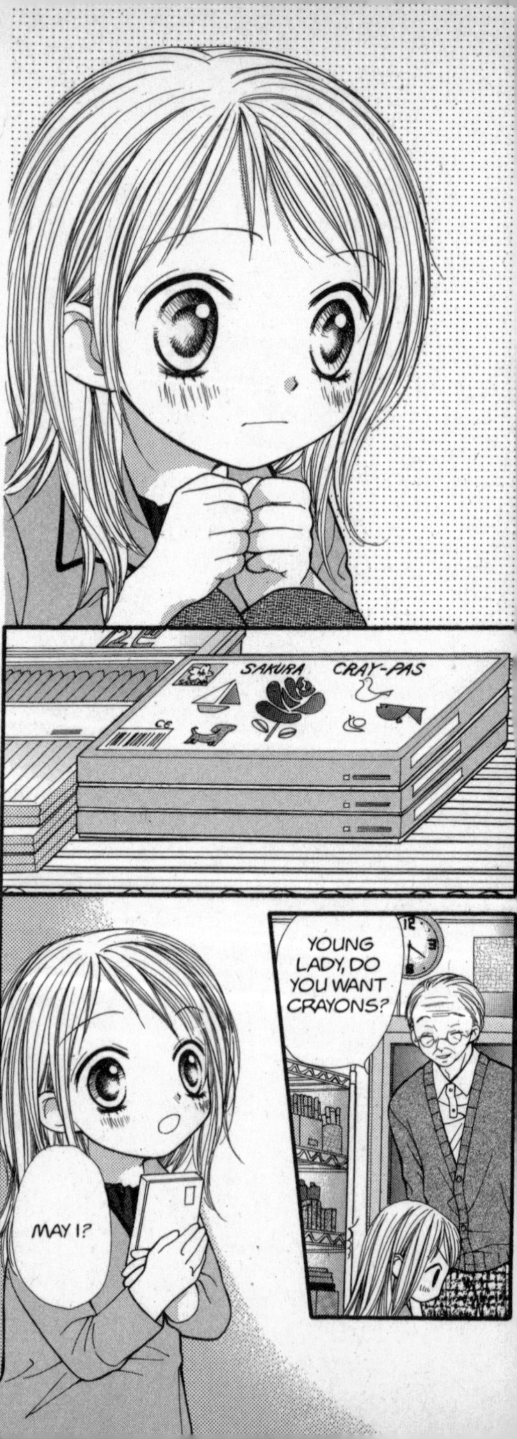
SAKURA CRAY-PAS
YOUNG LADY, DO YOU WANT CRAYONS?
MAY I?

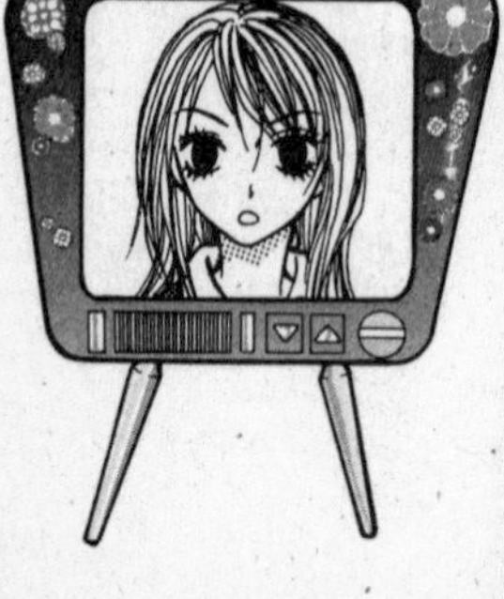

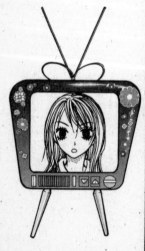

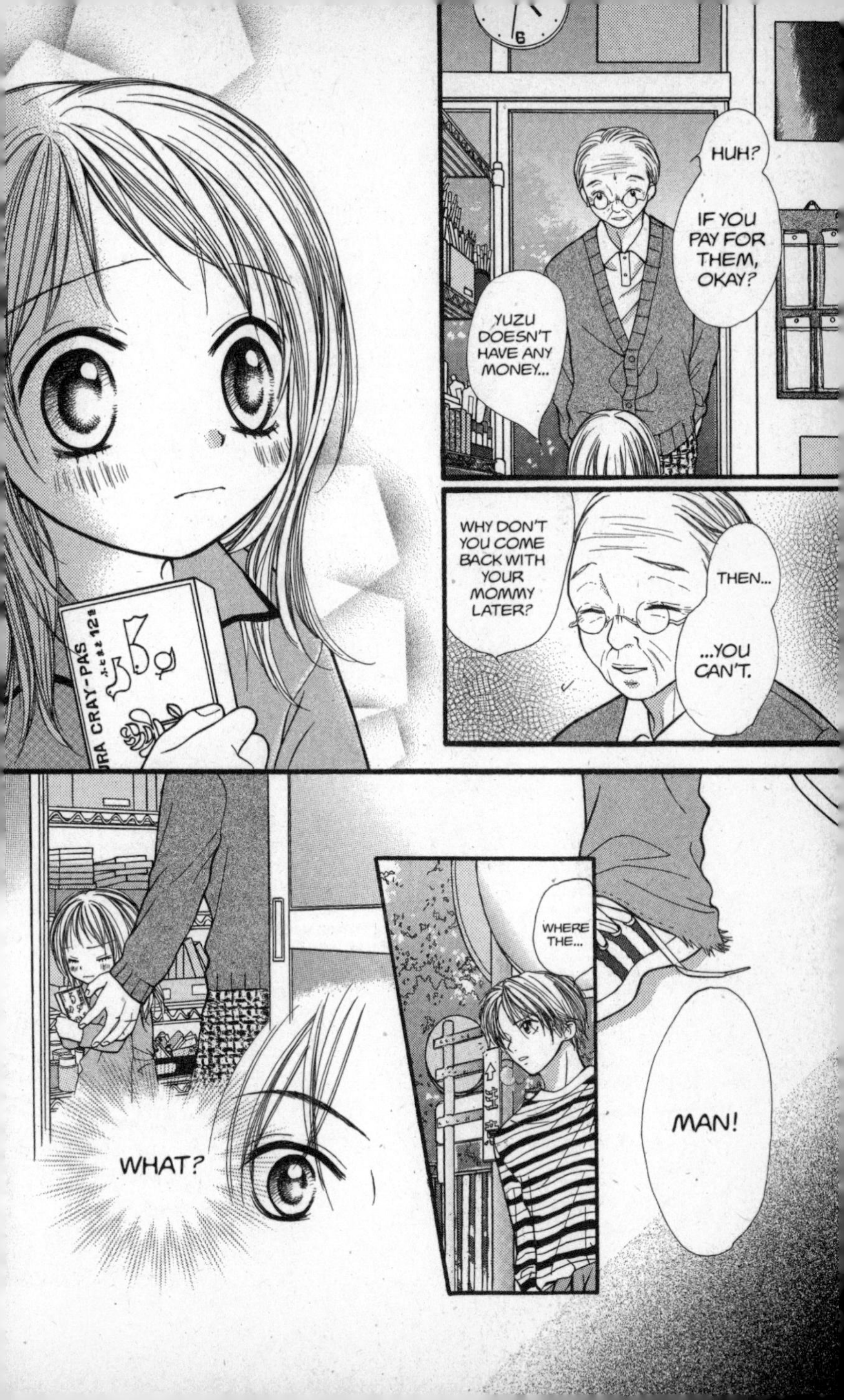
HUH?
IF YOU PAY FOR THEM, OKAY?
YUZU DOESN'T HAVE ANY MONEY...
THEN...
...YOU CAN'T.
WHY DON'T YOU COME BACK WITH YOUR MOMMY LATER?
WHERE THE...
MAN!
WHAT?

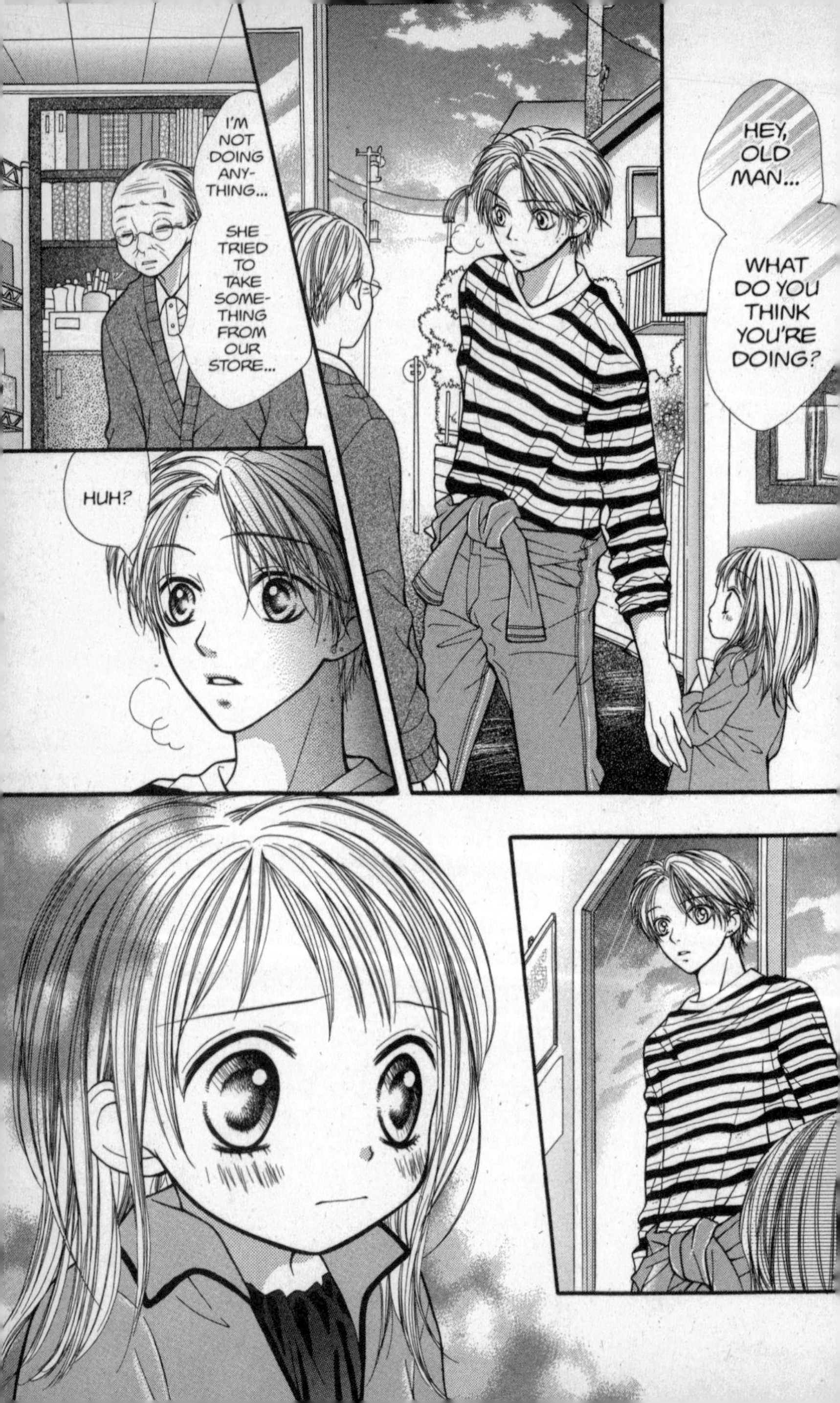
HEY, OLD MAN...
WHAT DO YOU THINK YOU'RE DOING?
I'M NOT DOING ANYTHING...
SHE TRIED TO TAKE SOMETHING FROM OUR STORE...
HUH?

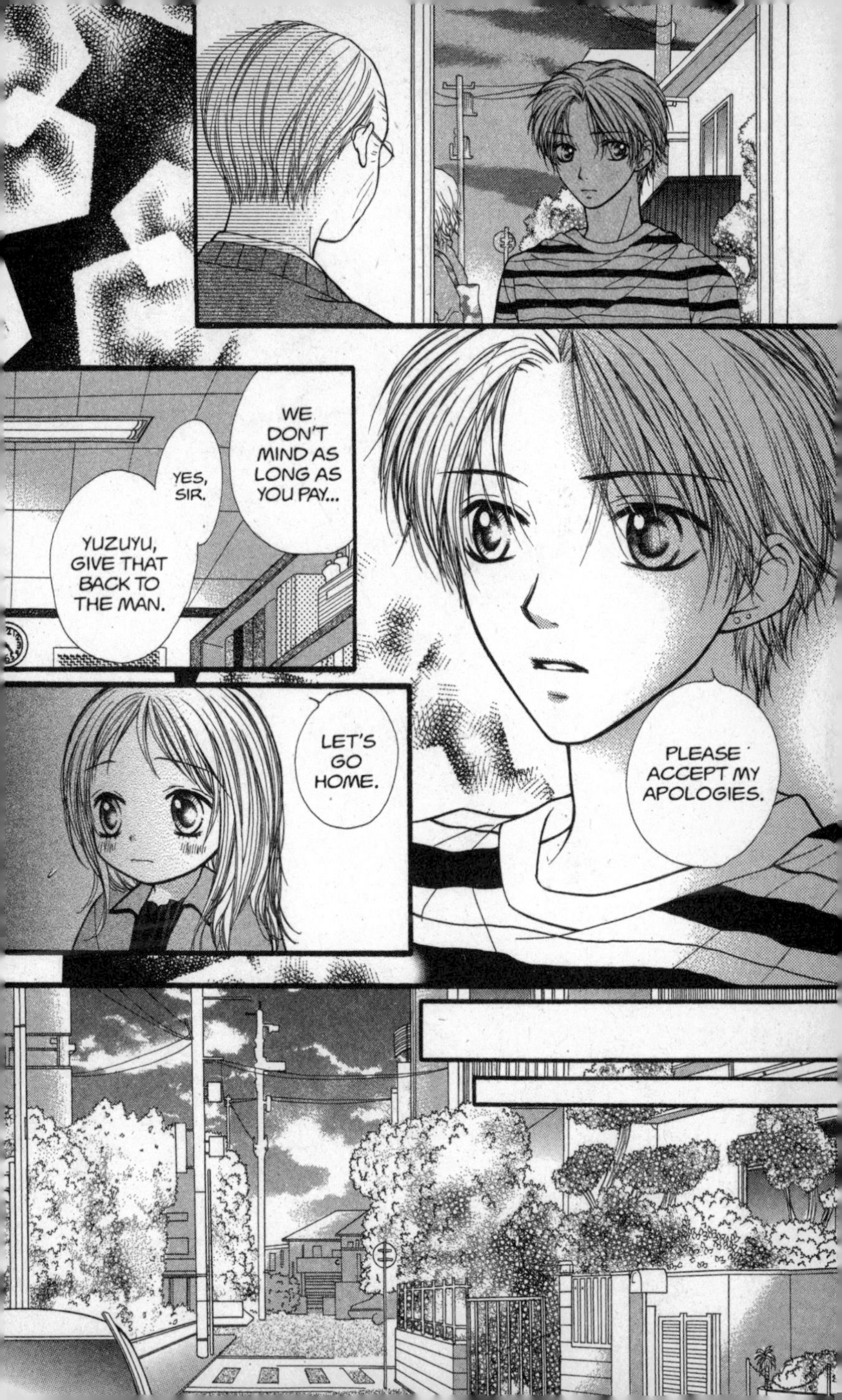
PLEASE ACCEPT MY APOLOGIES.
WE DON'T MIND AS LONG AS YOU PAY...
YES, SIR.
YUZUYU, GIVE THAT BACK TO THE MAN.
LET'S GO HOME.

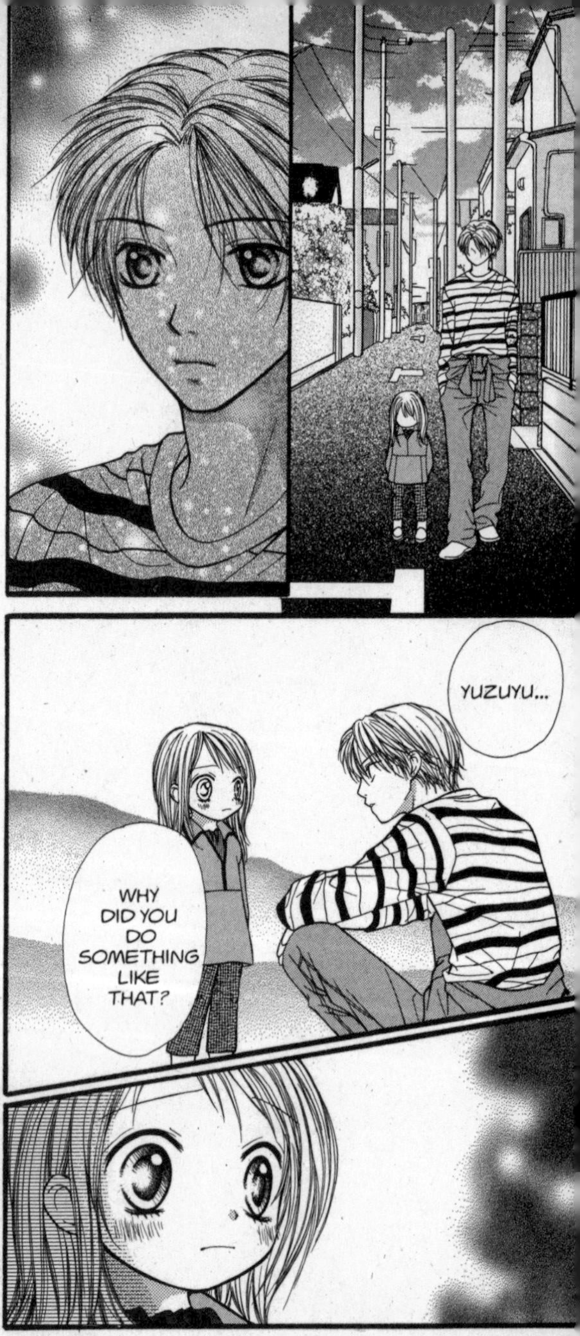
YUZUYU...
WHY DID YOU DO SOMETHING LIKE THAT?

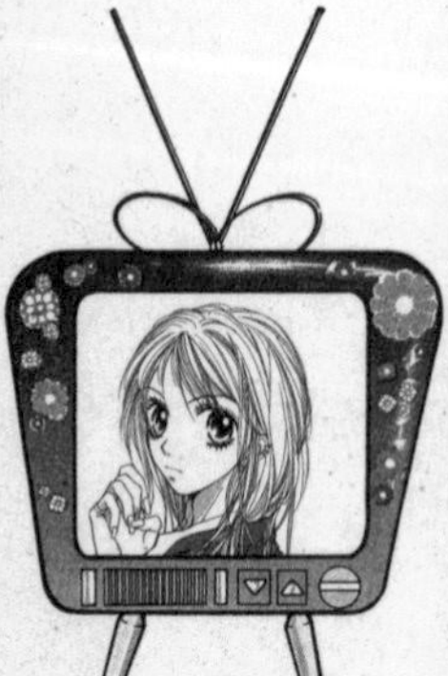

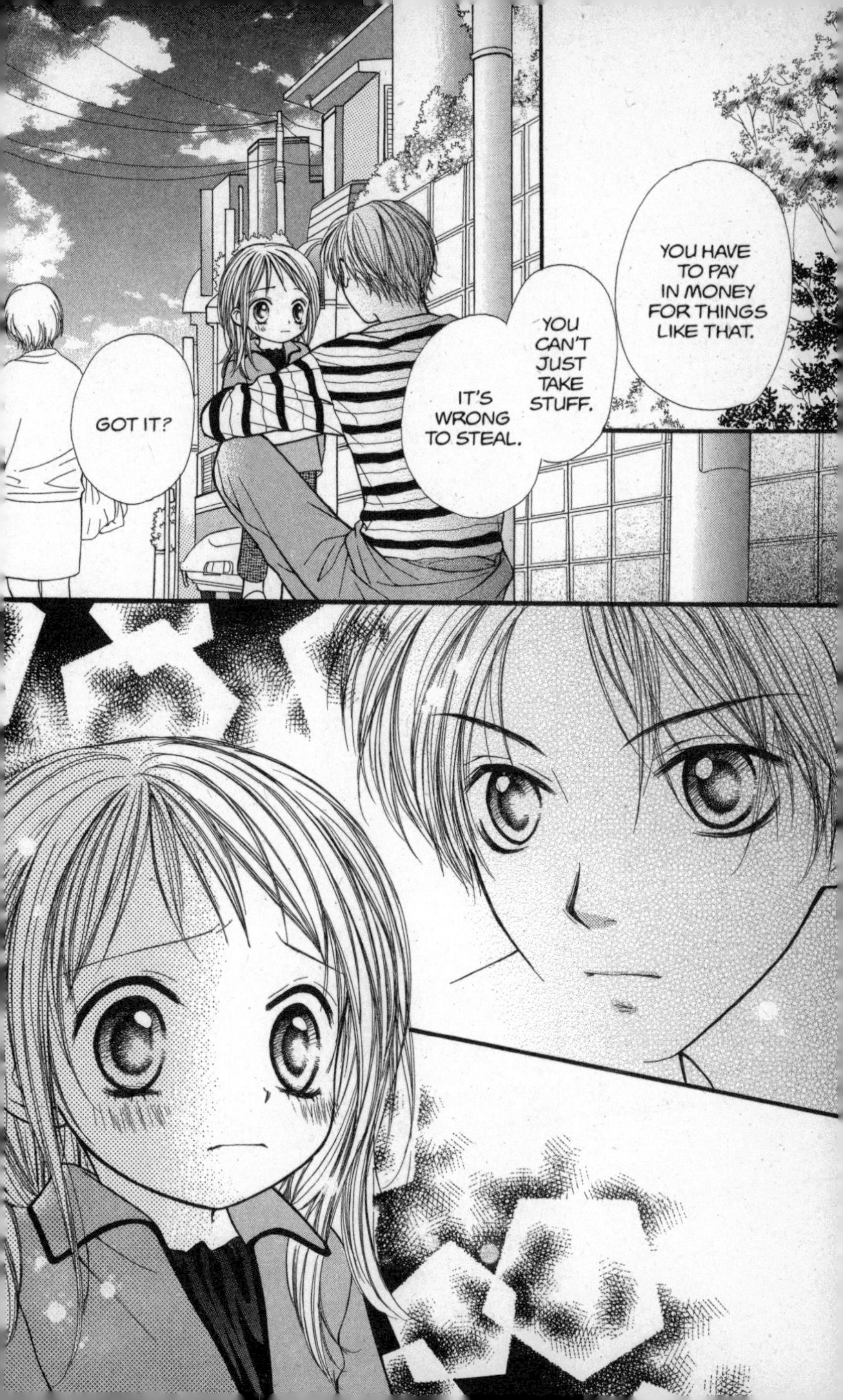
YOU HAVE TO PAY IN MONEY FOR THINGS LIKE THAT.
YOU CAN'T JUST TAKE STUFF.
IT'S WRONG TO STEAL.
GOT IT?

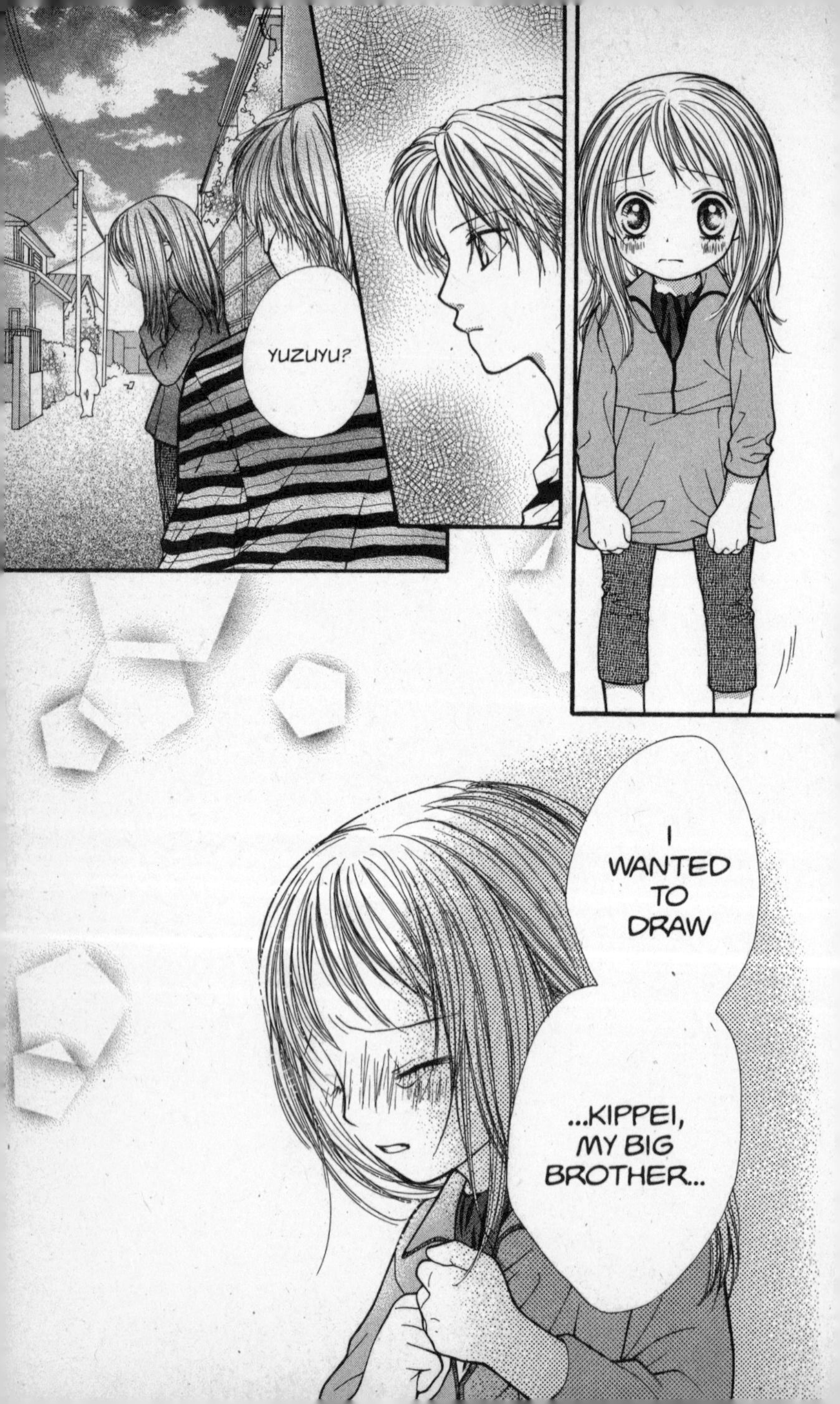
YUZUYU?
I WANTED TO DRAW
...KIPPEI, MY BIG BROTHER...

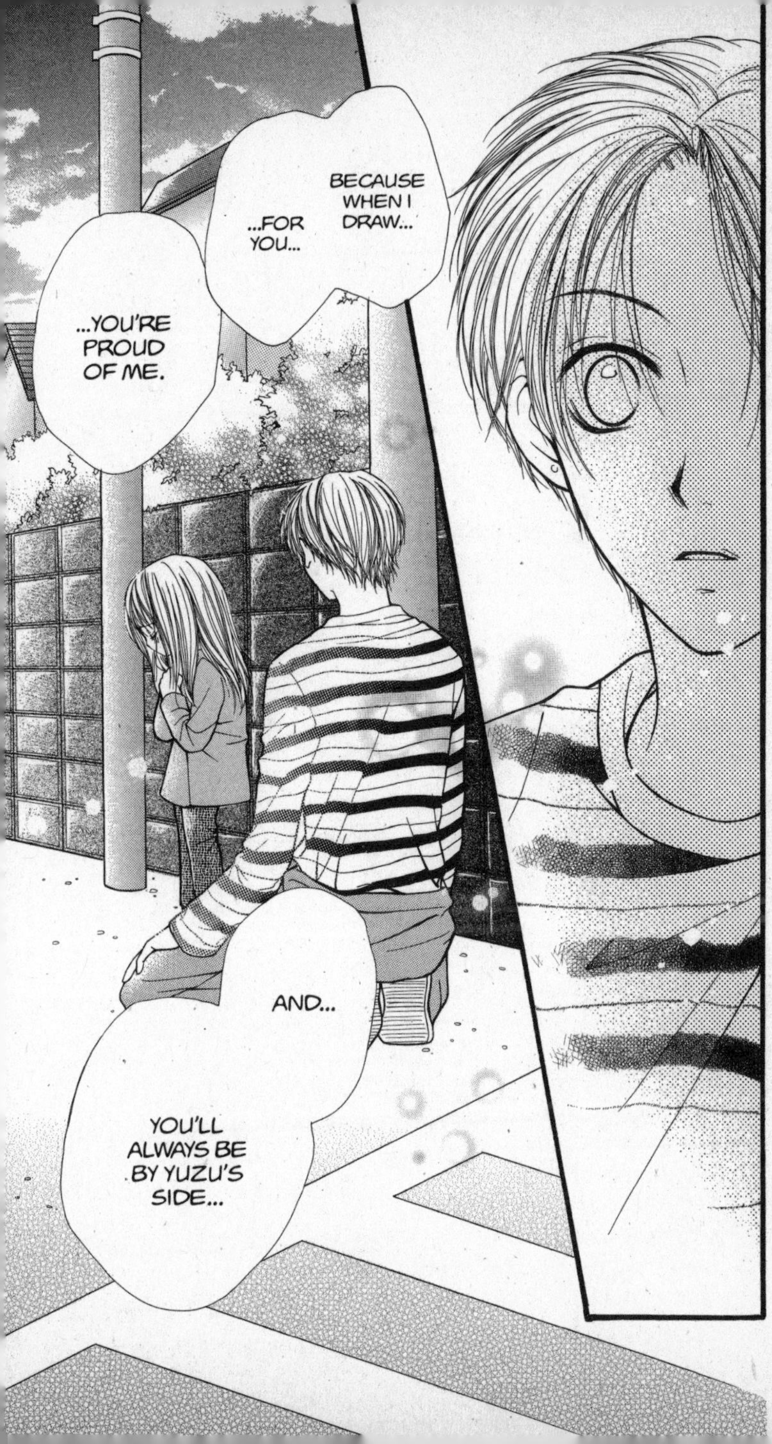
BECAUSE WHEN I DRAW... ...FOR YOU...
...YOU'RE PROUD OF ME.
AND...
YOU'LL ALWAYS BE BY YUZU'S SIDE...

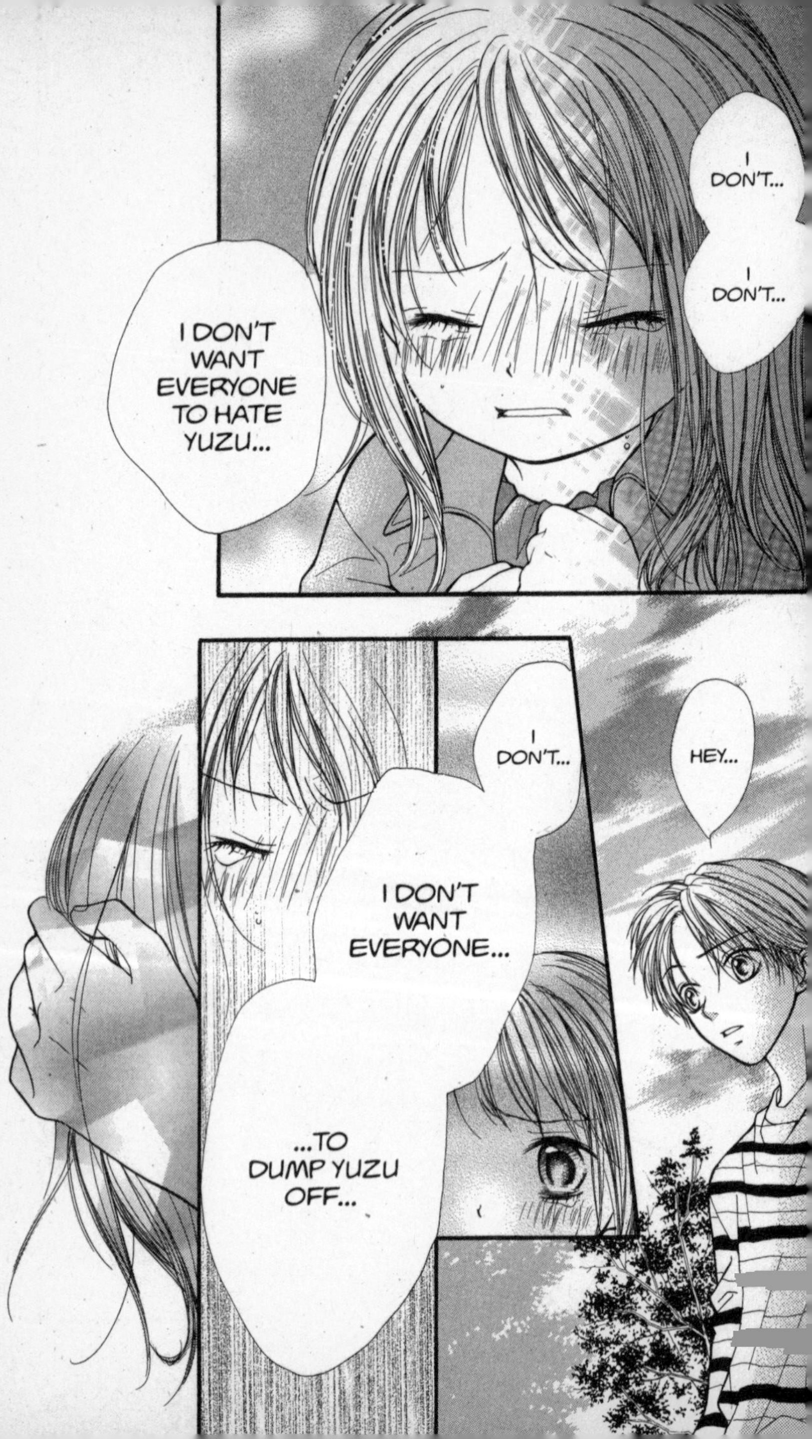
I DON'T...
I DON'T...
I DON'T WANT EVERYONE TO HATE YUZU...
HEY...
I DON'T...
I DON'T WANT EVERYONE...
...TO DUMP YUZU OFF...

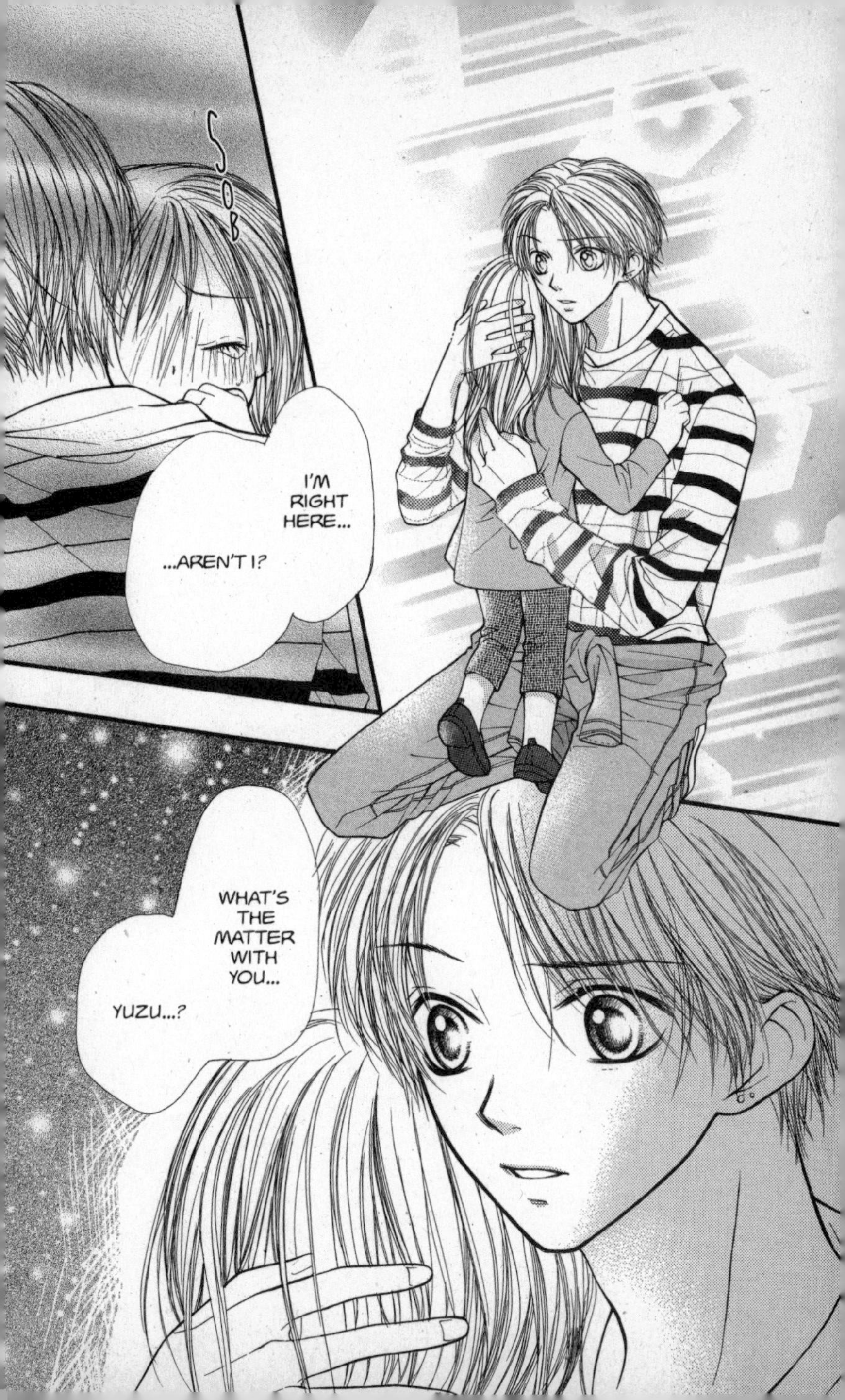
SOB
I'M RIGHT HERE... ...AREN'T I?
WHAT'S THE MATTER WITH YOU... YUZU...?

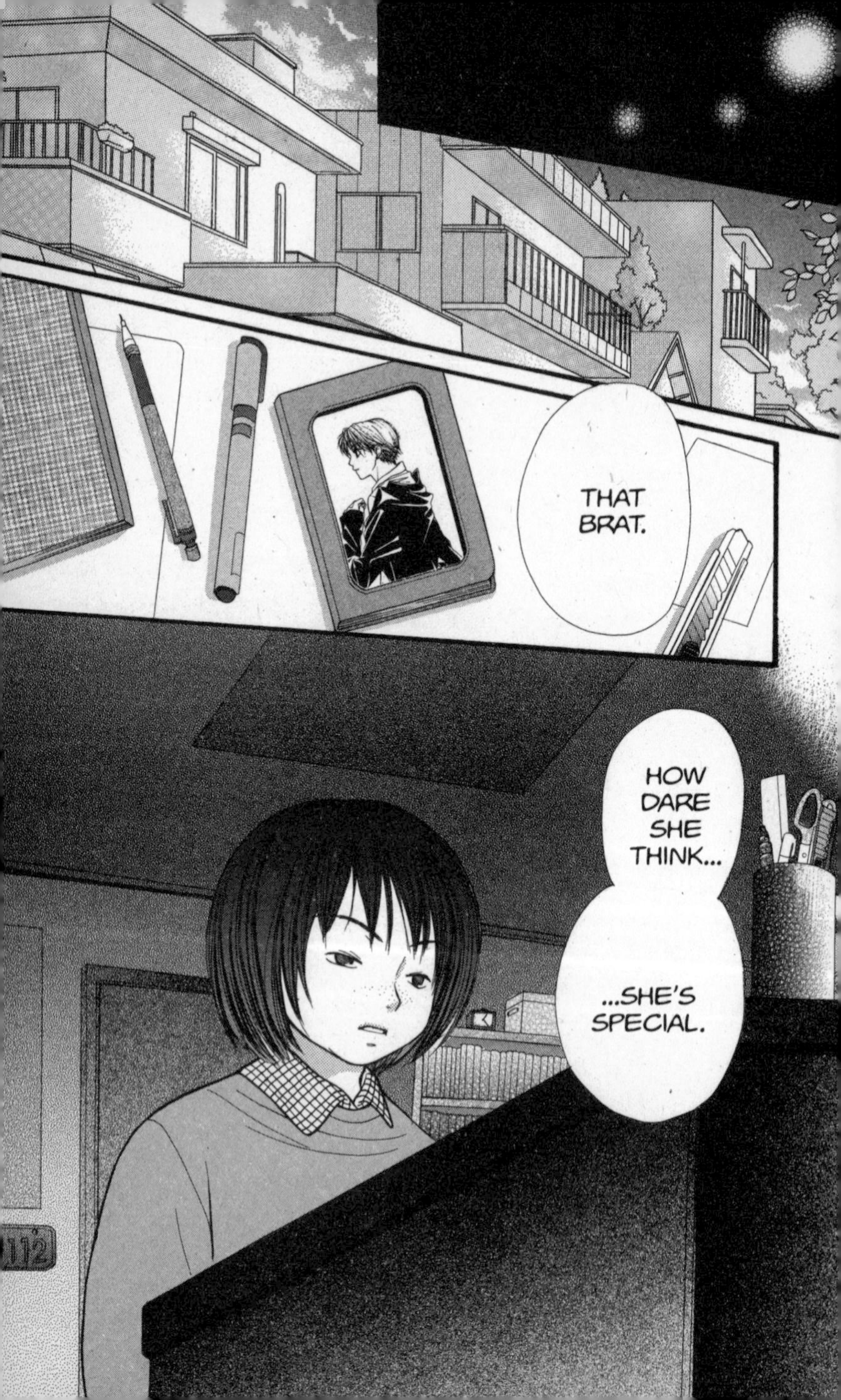
THAT BRAT.
HOW DARE SHE THINK...
...SHE'S SPECIAL.

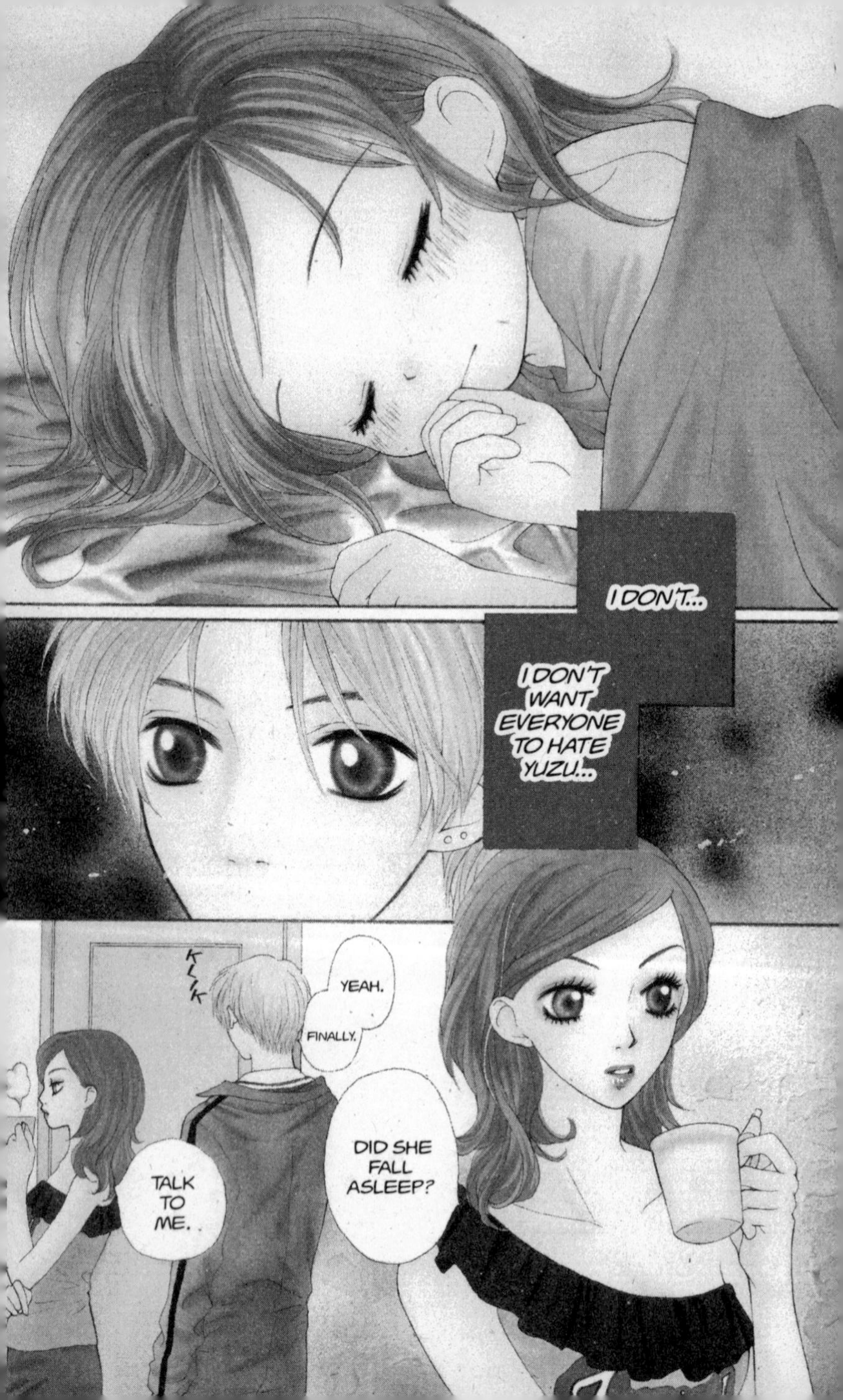
I DON'T...
I DON'T WANT EVERYONE TO HATE YUZU...
DID SHE FALL ASLEEP?
YEAH.
FINALLY.
KLIK
TALK TO ME.

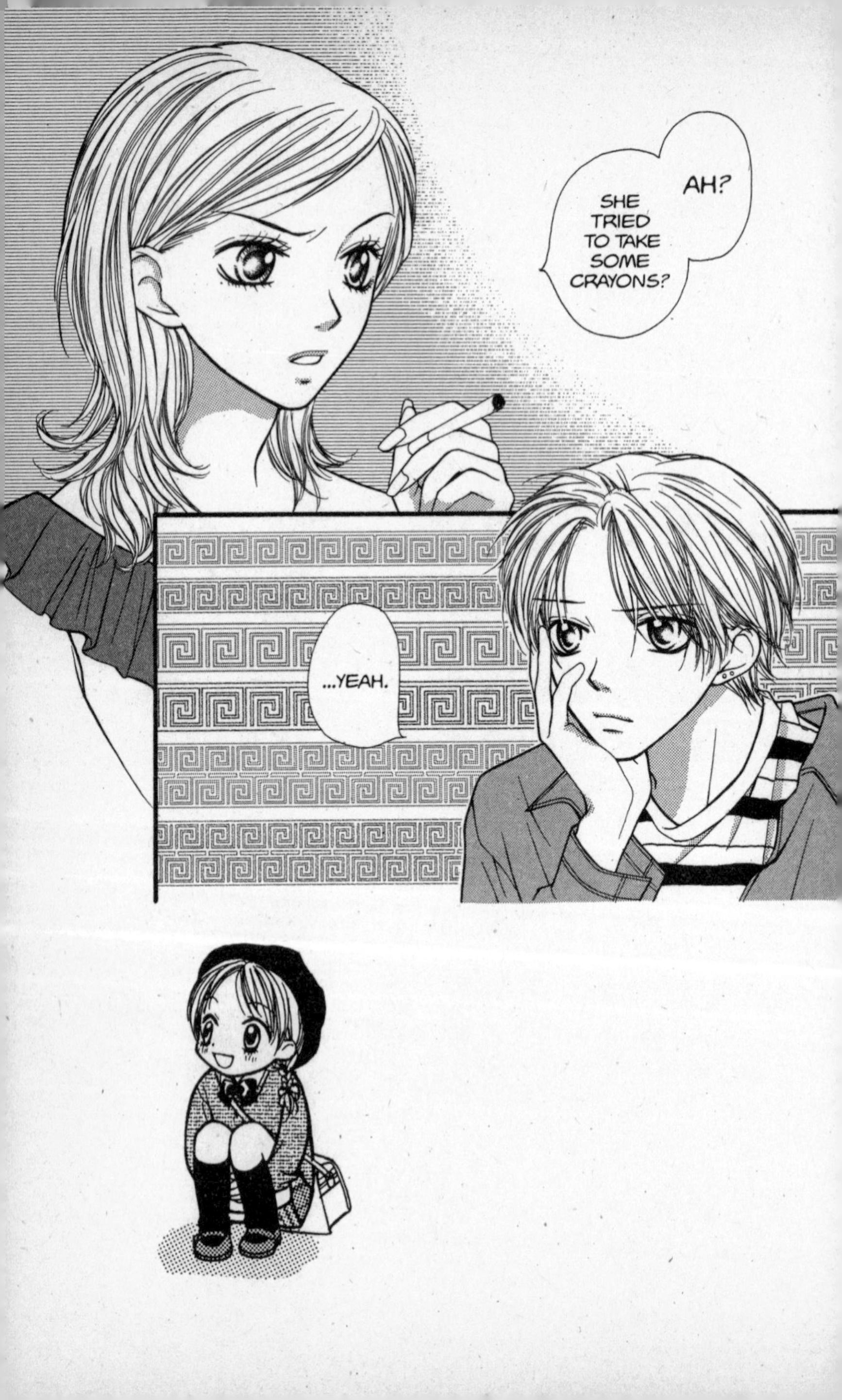
AH? SHE TRIED TO TAKE SOME CRAYONS?
...YEAH.

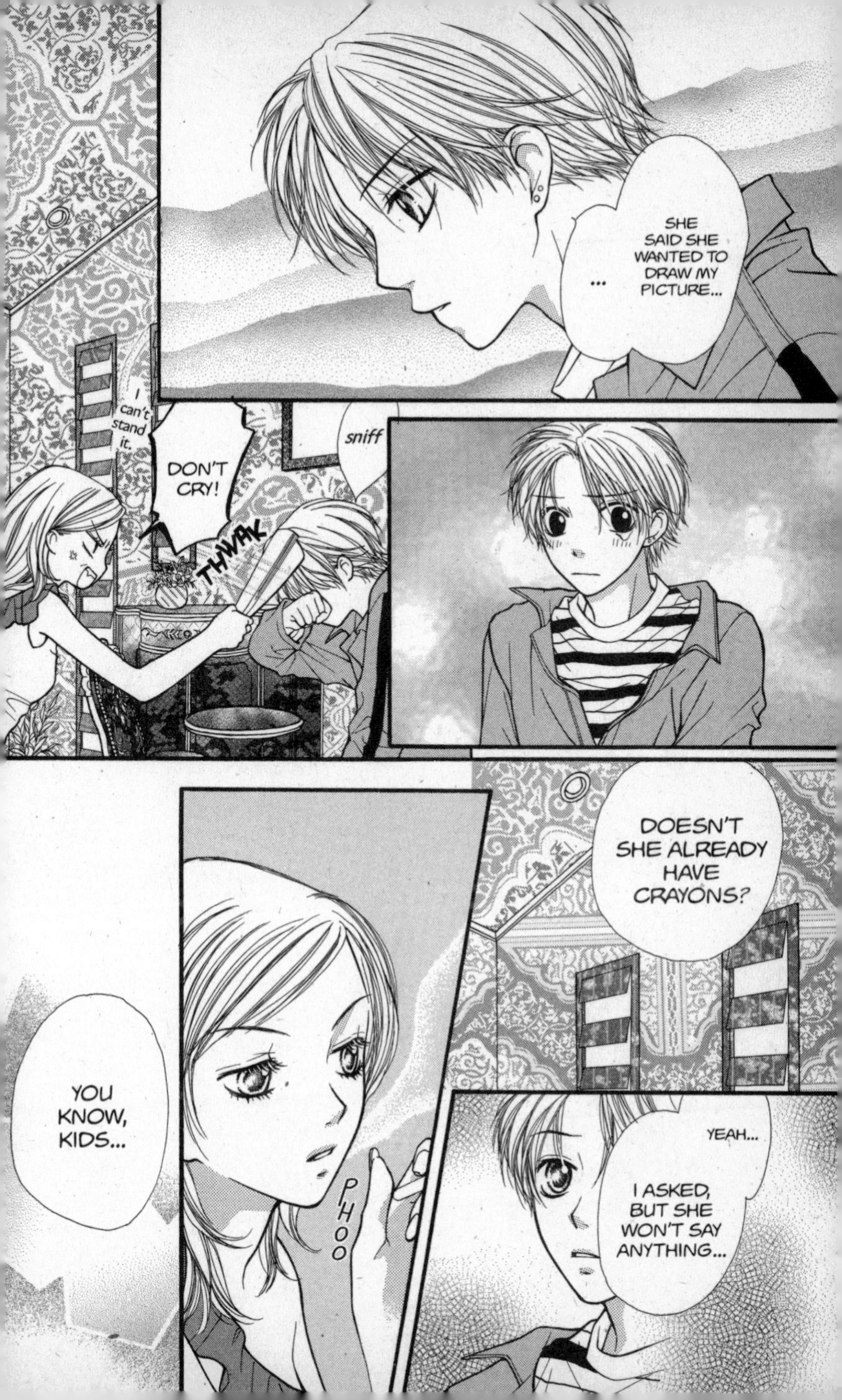
SHE SAID SHE WANTED TO DRAW MY PICTURE...
...
sniff
DON'T CRY!
I can't stand it.
THWAK
DOESN'T SHE ALREADY HAVE CRAYONS?
YEAH...
I ASKED, BUT SHE WON'T SAY ANYTHING...
PHOO
YOU KNOW, KIDS...

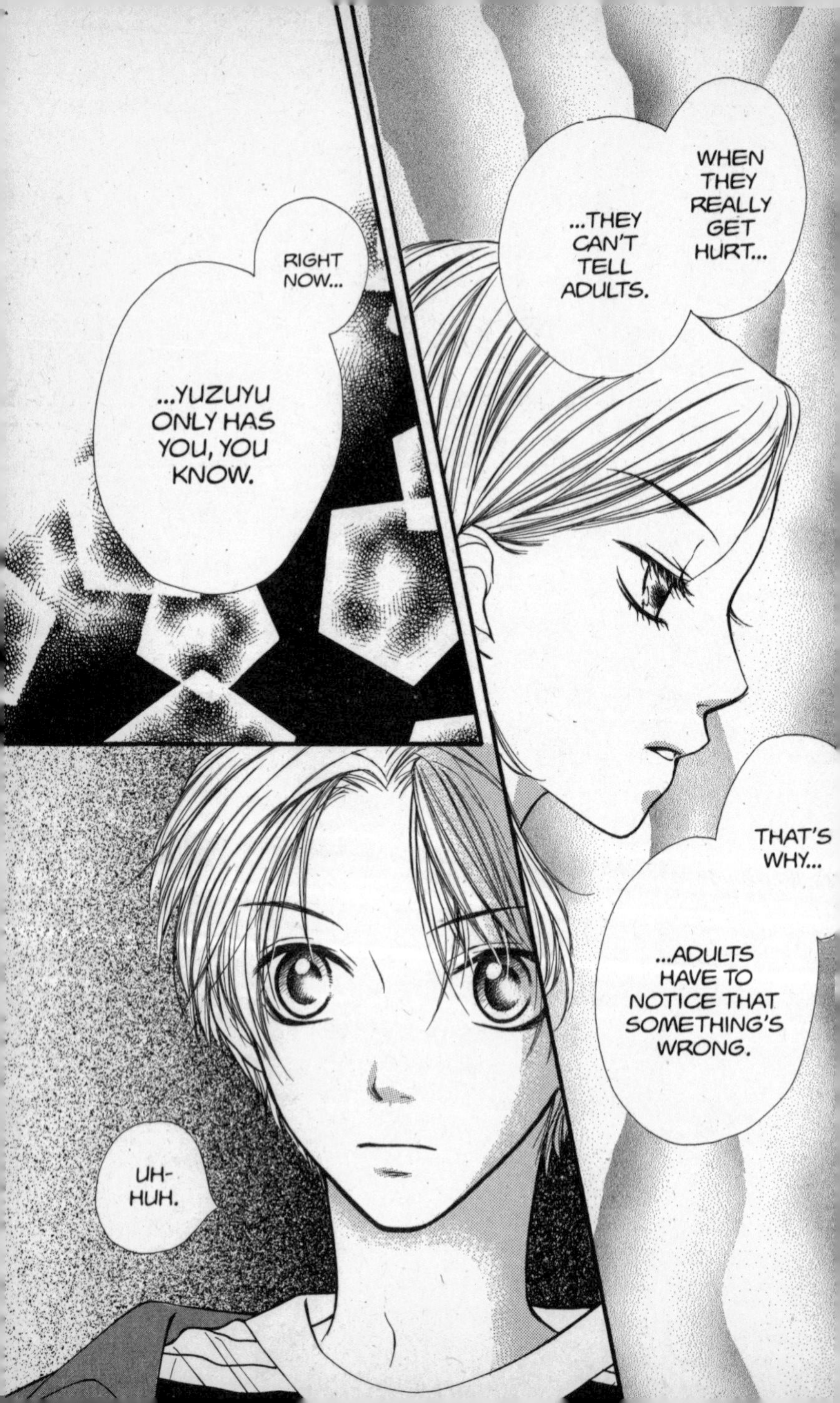
WHEN THEY REALLY GET HURT...
...THEY CAN'T TELL ADULTS.
THAT'S WHY...
...ADULTS HAVE TO NOTICE THAT SOMETHING'S WRONG.
RIGHT NOW...
...YUZUYU ONLY HAS YOU, YOU KNOW.
UH-HUH.

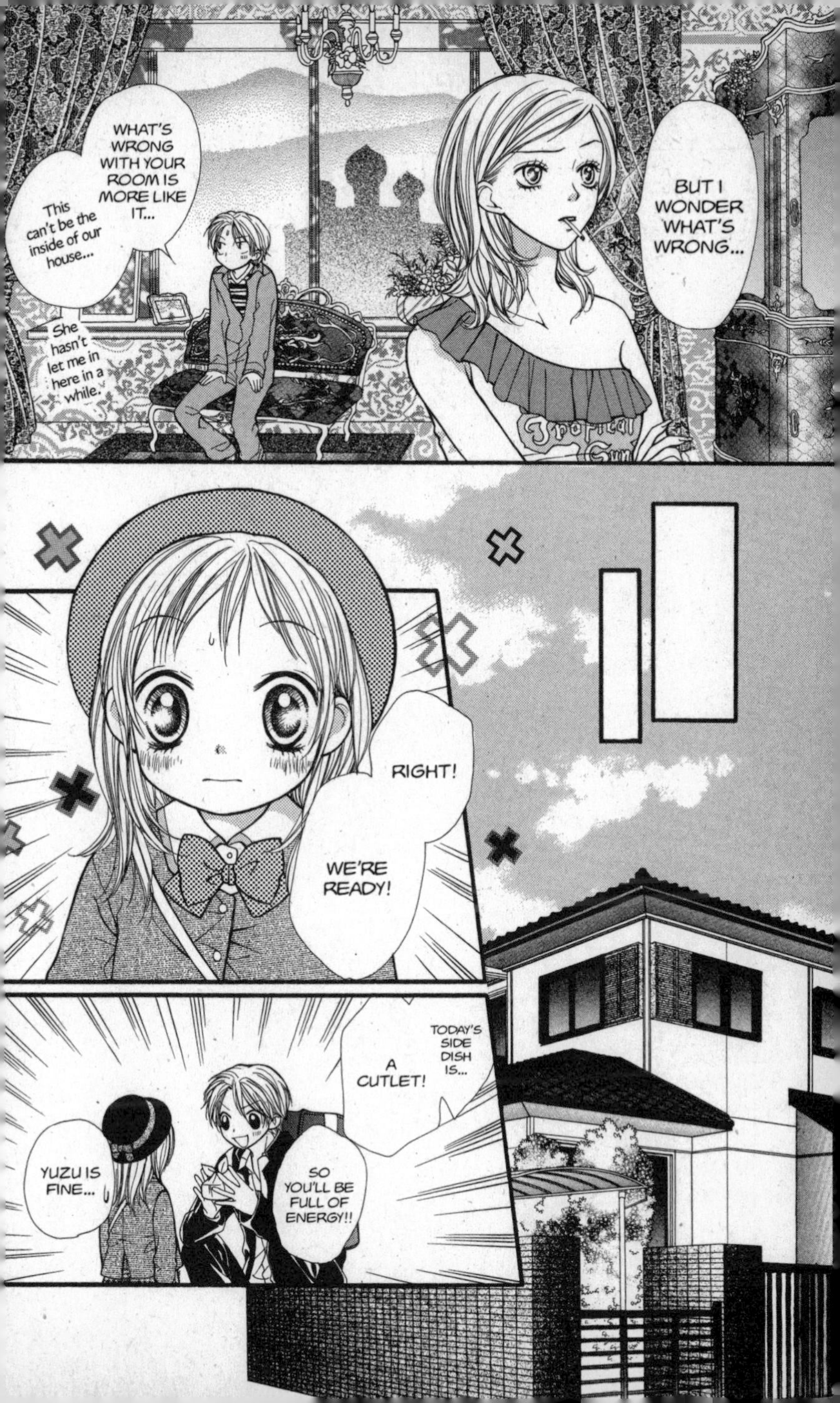
BUT I WONDER WHAT'S WRONG...
WHAT'S WRONG WITH YOUR ROOM IS MORE LIKE IT...
This can't be the inside of our house...
She hasn't let me in here in a while.
RIGHT!
WE'RE READY!
TODAY'S SIDE DISH IS...
A CUTLET!
SO YOU'LL BE FULL OF ENERGY!!
YUZU IS FINE...

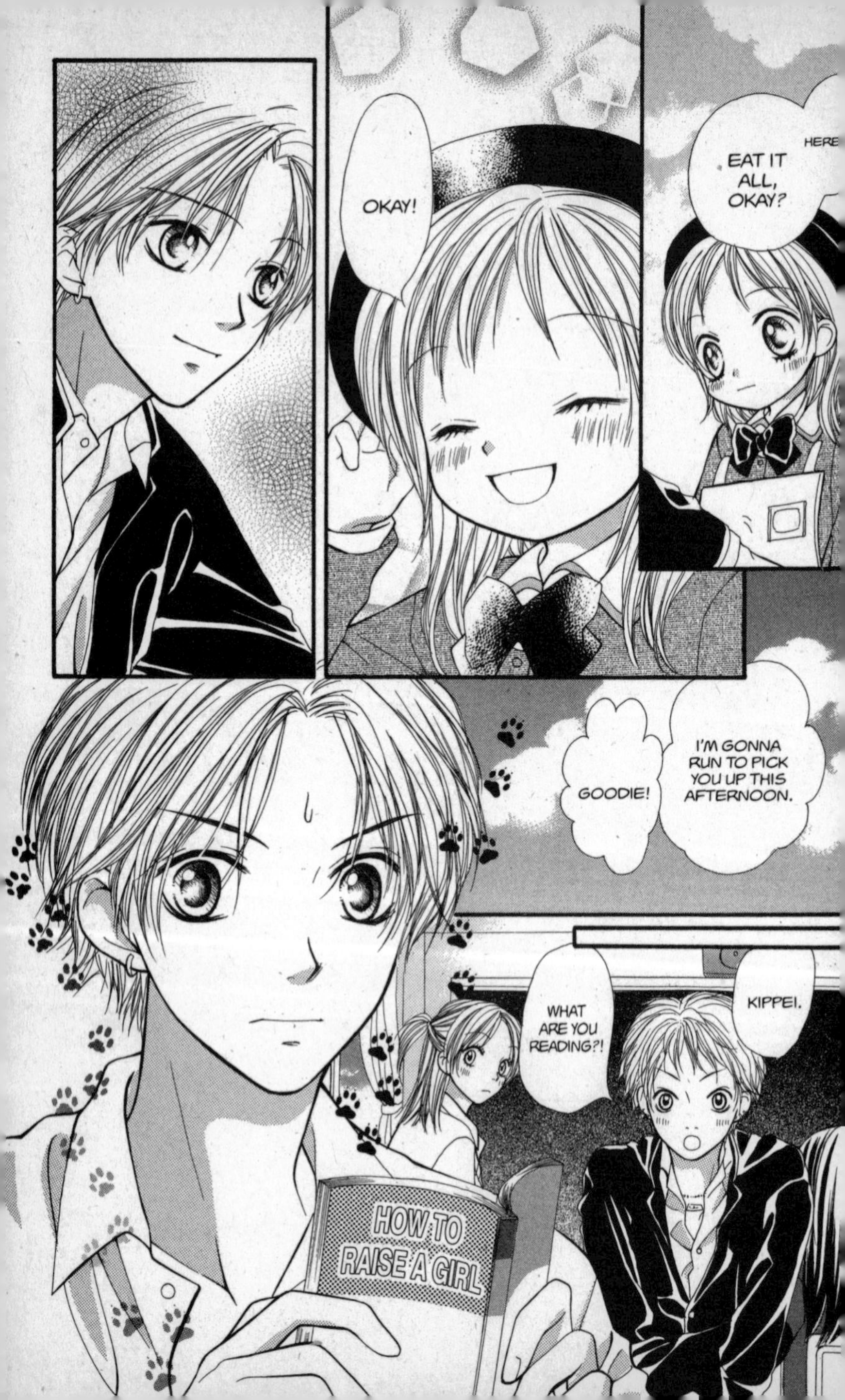
HERE
EAT IT ALL, OKAY?
OKAY!
I'M GONNA RUN TO PICK YOU UP THIS AFTERNOON.
GOODIE!
KIPPEI.
WHAT ARE YOU READING?!
HOW TO RAISE A GIRL

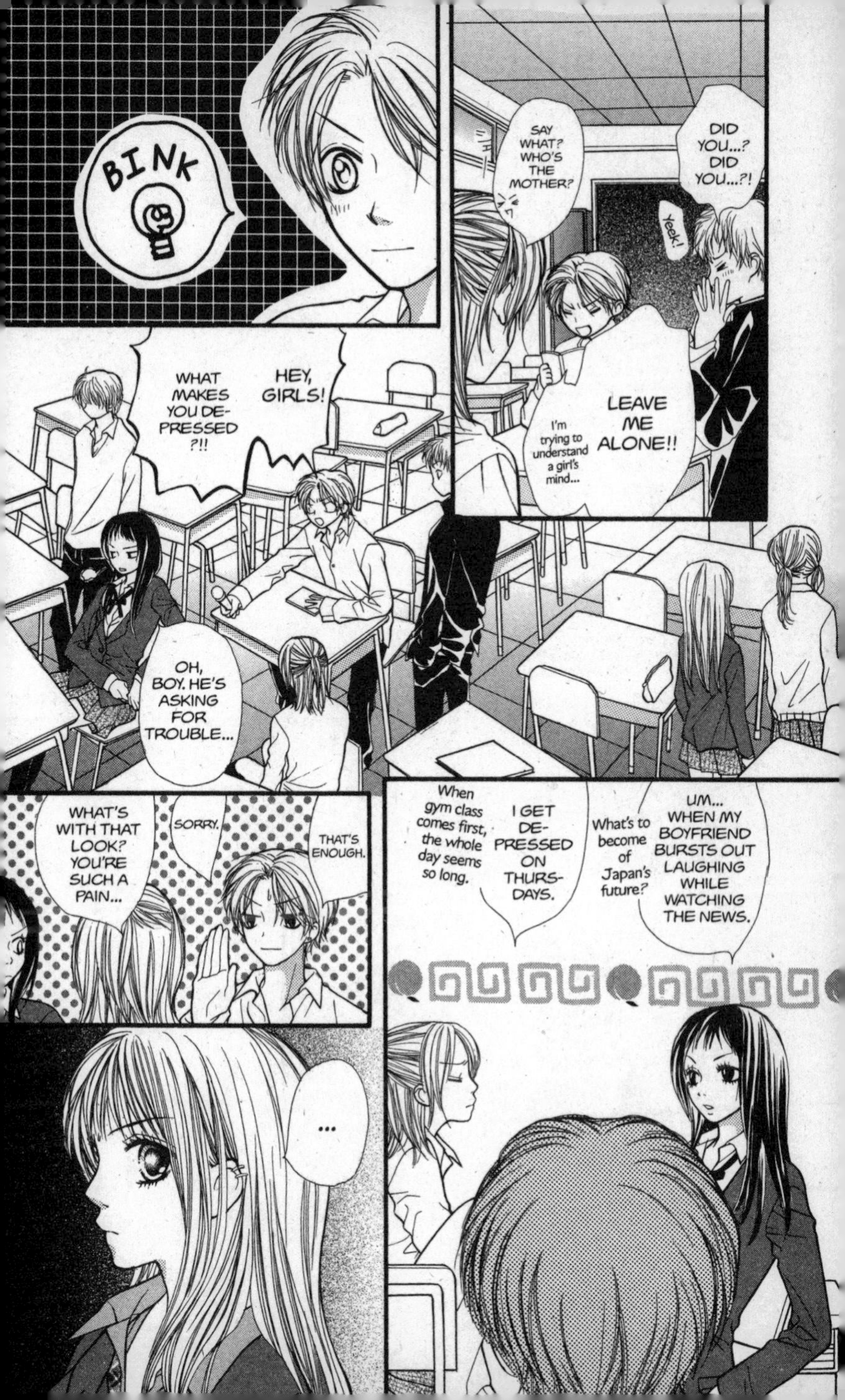

DID YOU...? DID YOU...?!
Yeek!
SAY WHAT? WHO'S THE MOTHER?
LEAVE ME ALONE!!
I'm trying to understand a girl's mind...
BINK
HEY, GIRLS!
WHAT MAKES YOU DE-PRESSED?!!
OH, BOY. HE'S ASKING FOR TROUBLE...
UM... WHEN MY BOYFRIEND BURSTS OUT LAUGHING WHILE WATCHING THE NEWS.
What's to become of Japan's future?
I GET DE-PRESSED ON THURS-DAYS.
When gym class comes first, the whole day seems so long.
THAT'S ENOUGH.
SORRY.
WHAT'S WITH THAT LOOK? YOU'RE SUCH A PAIN...
...

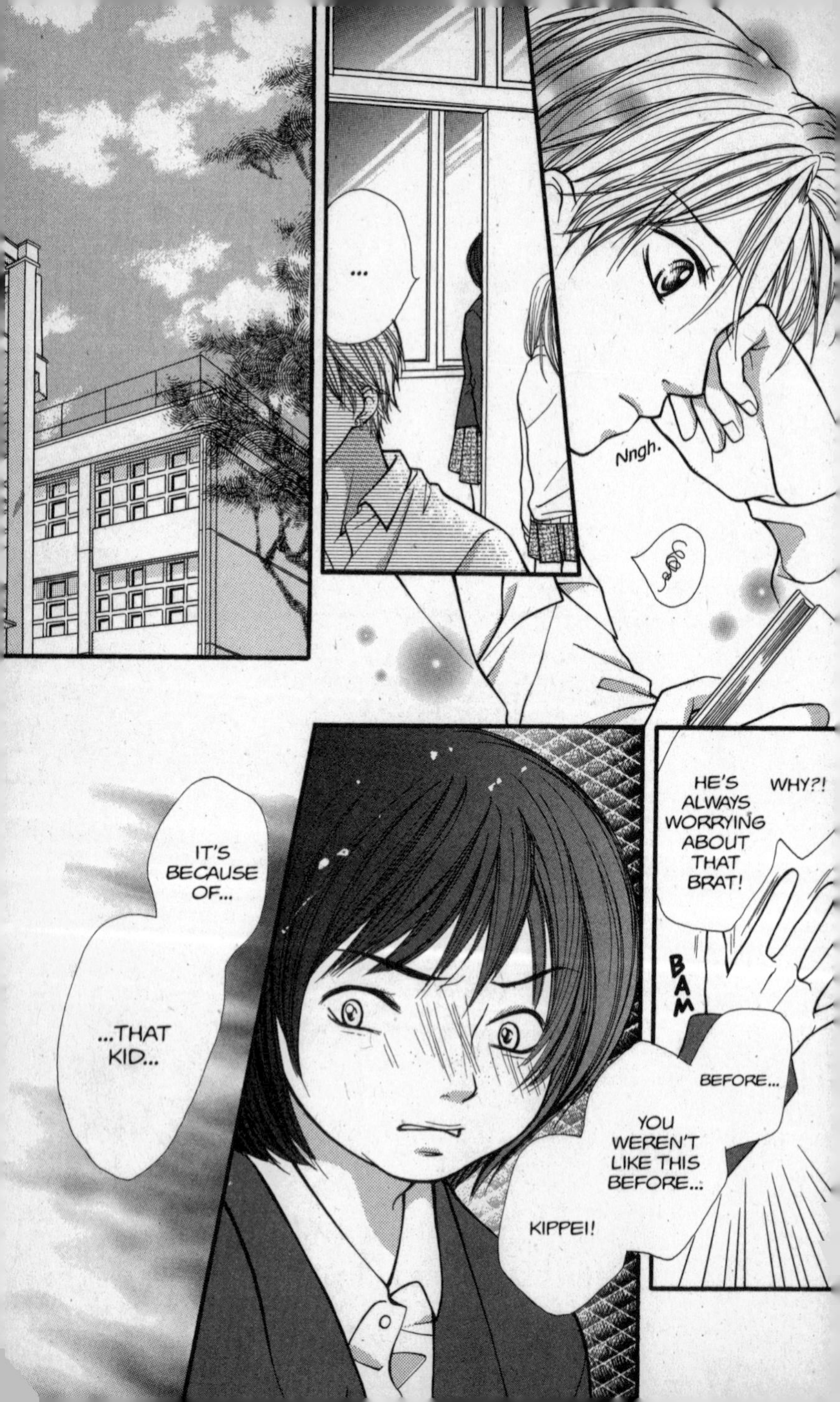
...
Nngh.
HE'S ALWAYS WORRYING ABOUT THAT BRAT!
WHY?!
BAM
BEFORE...
YOU WEREN'T LIKE THIS BEFORE...
KIPPEI!
IT'S BECAUSE OF...
...THAT KID...

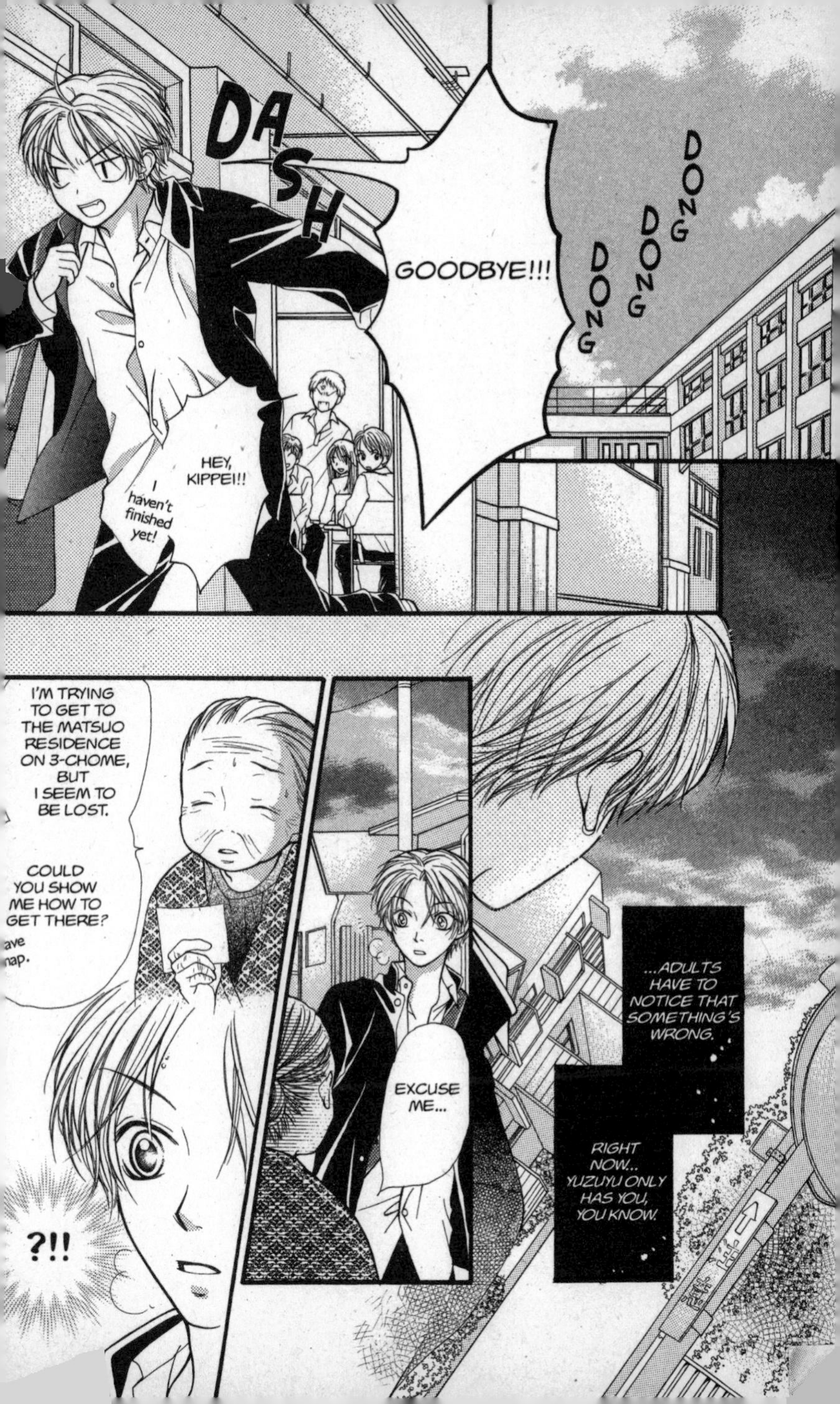
DONG DONG DONG
DASH
GOODBYE!!!
HEY, KIPPEI!!!
I haven't finished yet!
...ADULTS HAVE TO NOTICE THAT SOMETHING'S WRONG.
RIGHT NOW... YUZUYU ONLY HAS YOU, YOU KNOW.
EXCUSE ME...
I'M TRYING TO GET TO THE MATSUO RESIDENCE ON 3-CHOME, BUT I SEEM TO BE LOST.
COULD YOU SHOW ME HOW TO GET THERE?
?!!

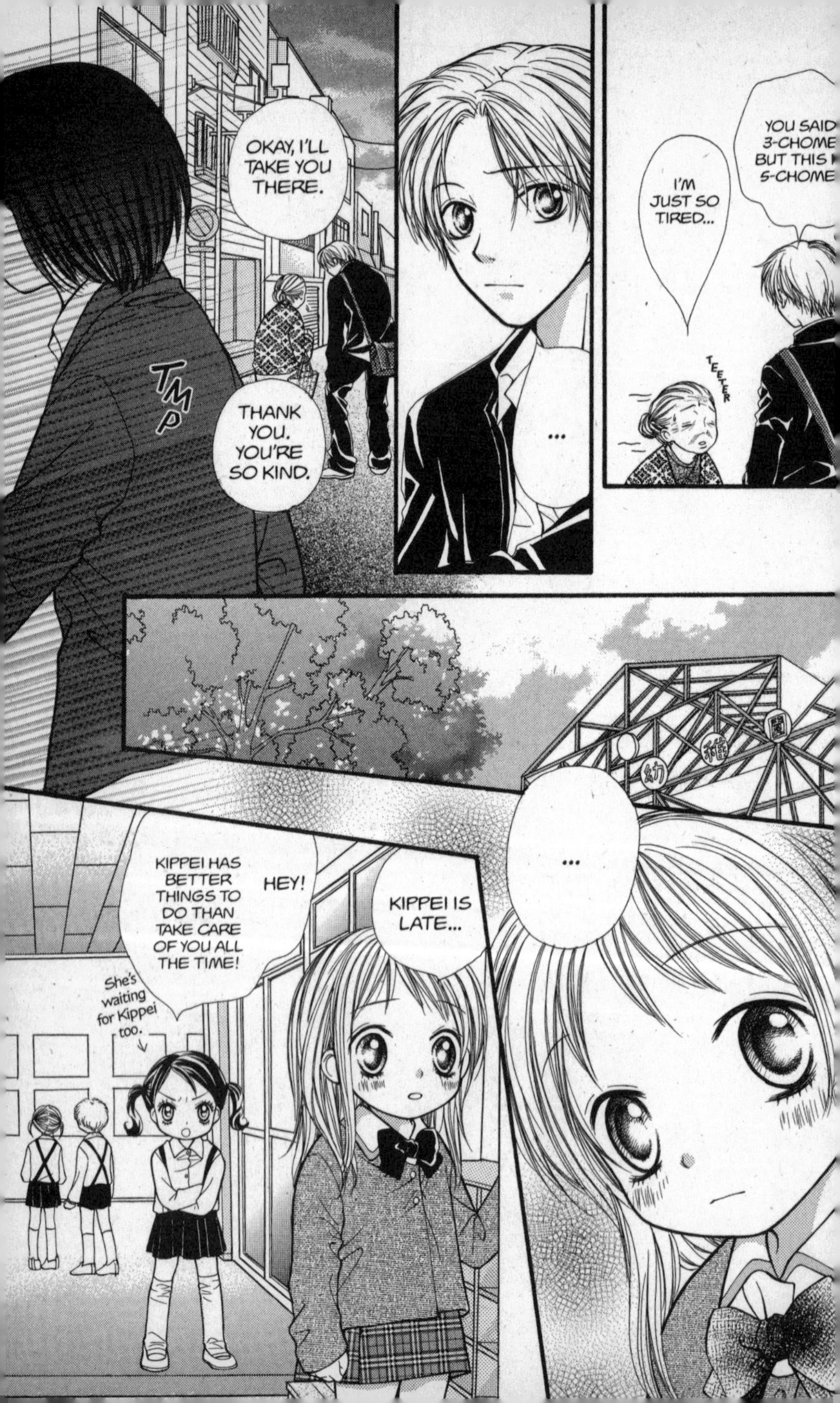
YOU SAID 3-CHOME BUT THIS
5-CHOME
I'M JUST SO TIRED...
TEETER
...
OKAY, I'LL TAKE YOU THERE.
THANK YOU. YOU'RE SO KIND.
TMP
幼稚園
...
KIPPEI IS LATE...
HEY!
KIPPEI HAS BETTER THINGS TO DO THAN TAKE CARE OF YOU ALL THE TIME!
She's waiting for Kippei too.

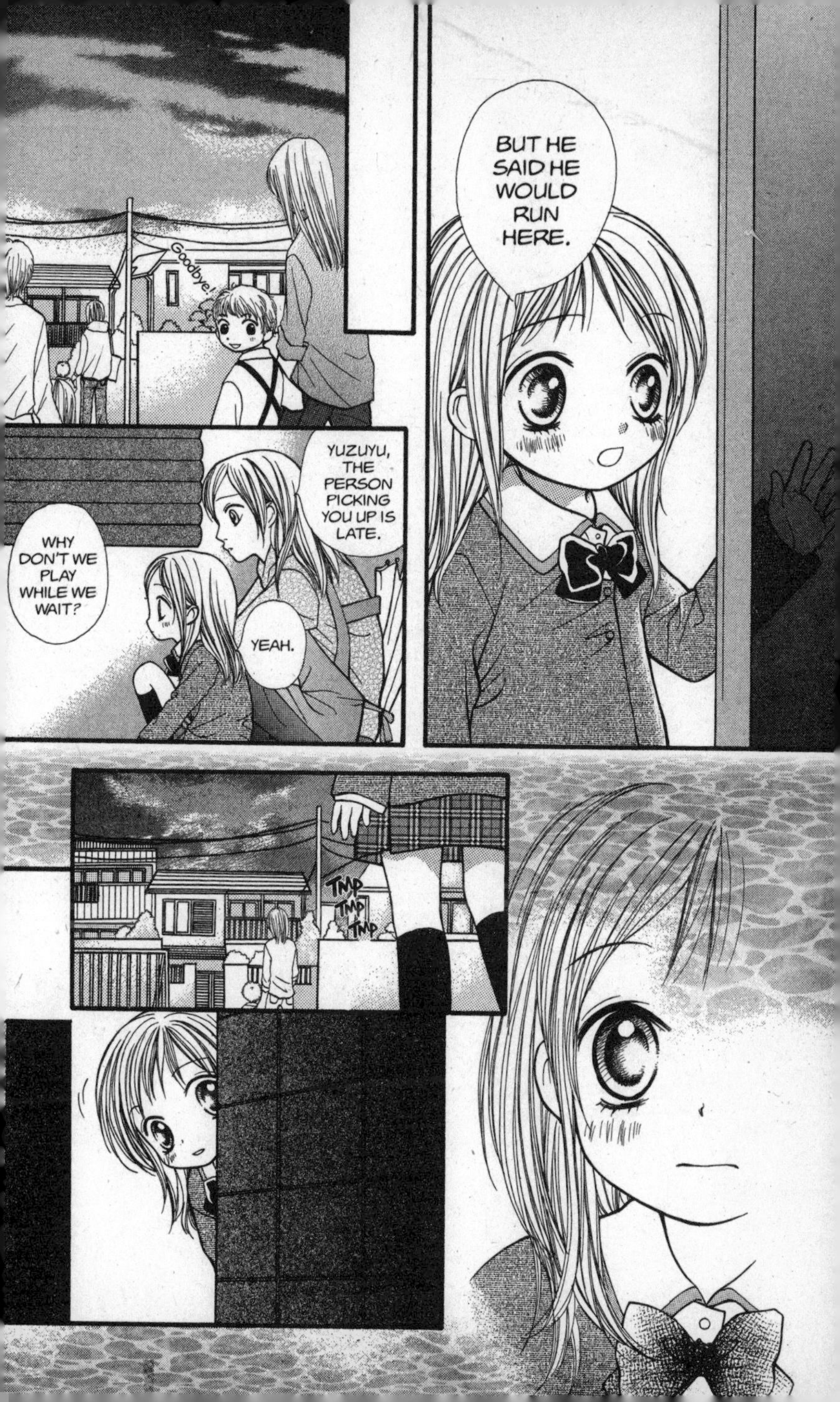
BUT HE SAID HE WOULD RUN HERE.
Goodbye!
YUZUYU, THE PERSON PICKING YOU UP IS LATE.
WHY DON'T WE PLAY WHILE WE WAIT?
YEAH.
TMP TMP TMP

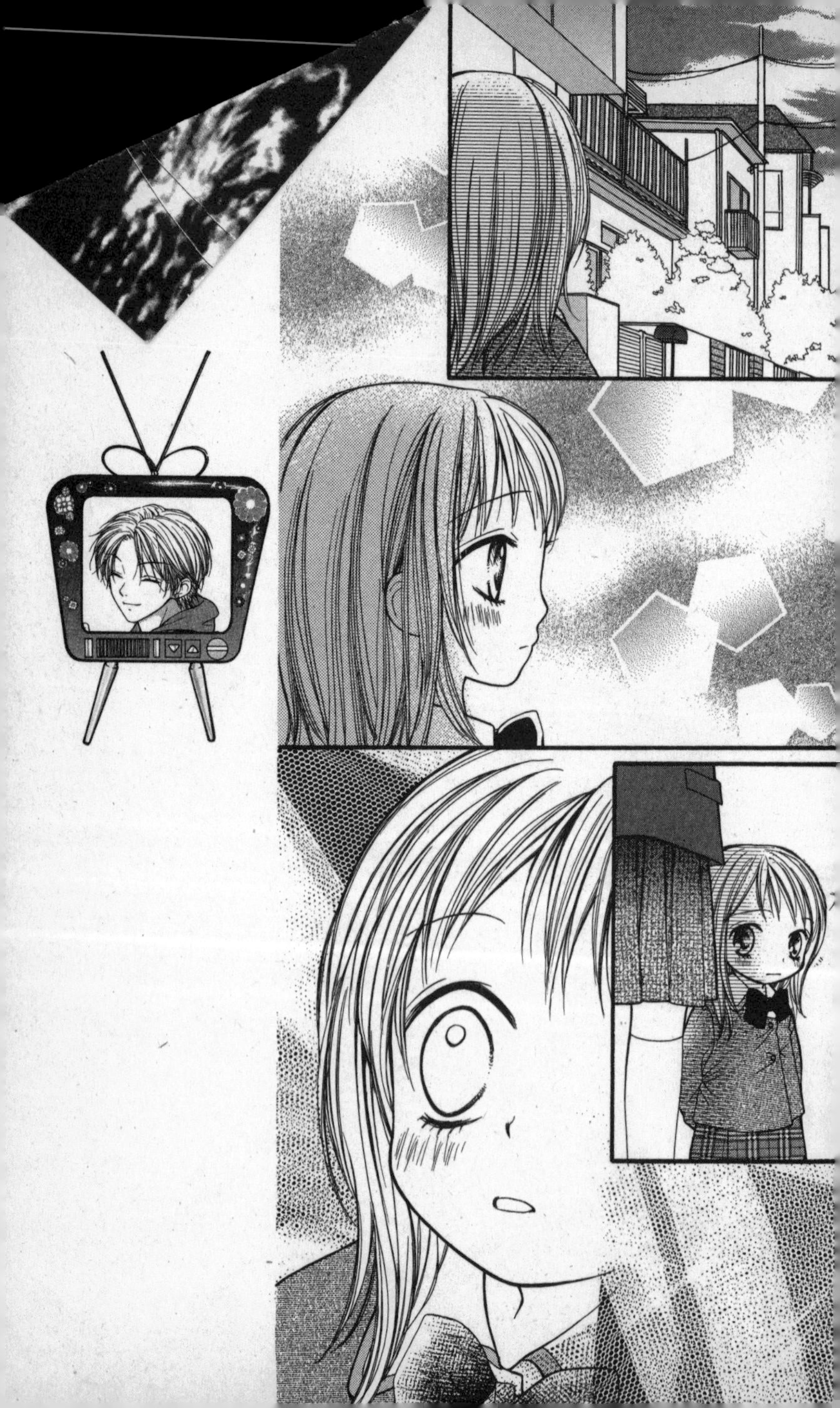

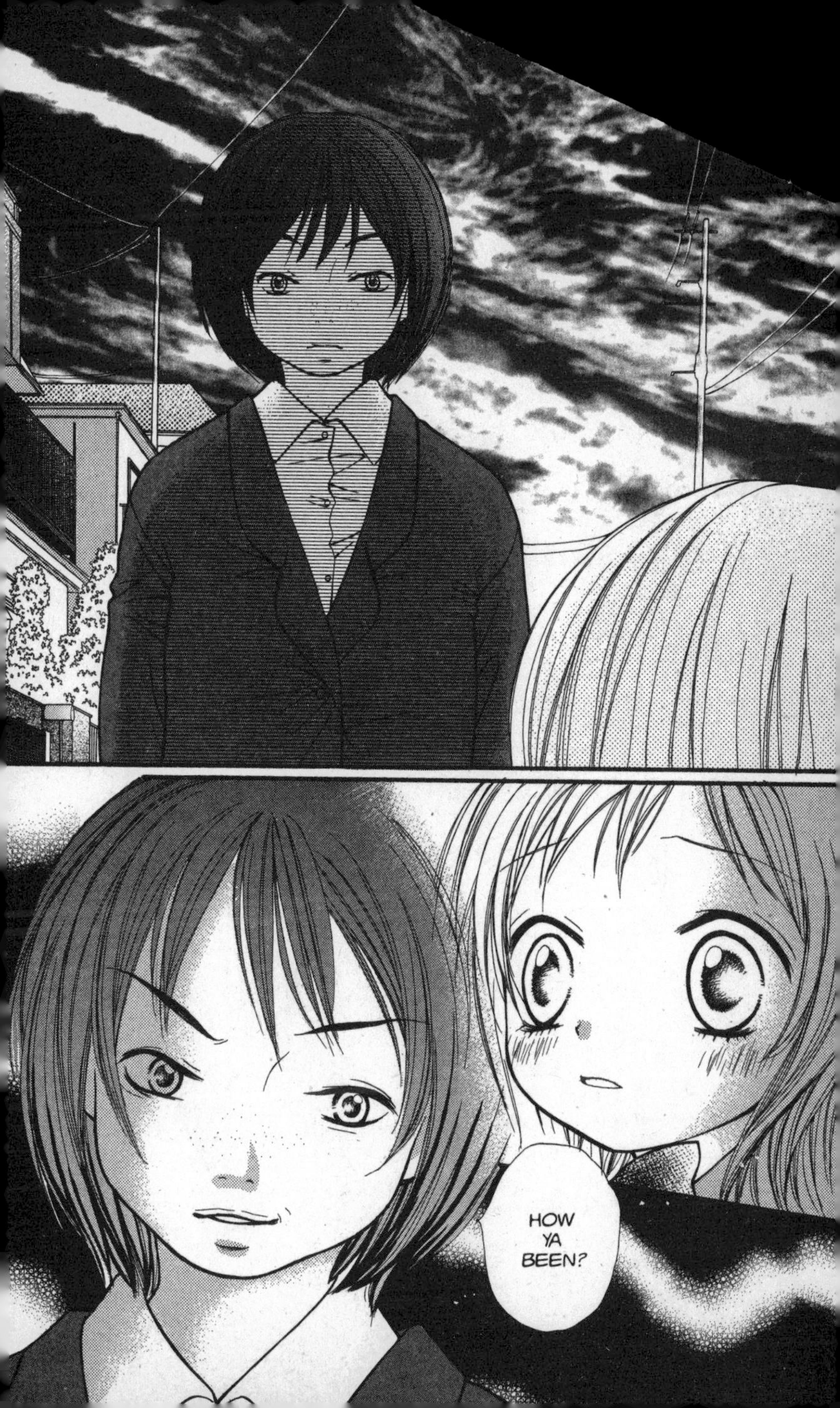
HOW YA BEEN?

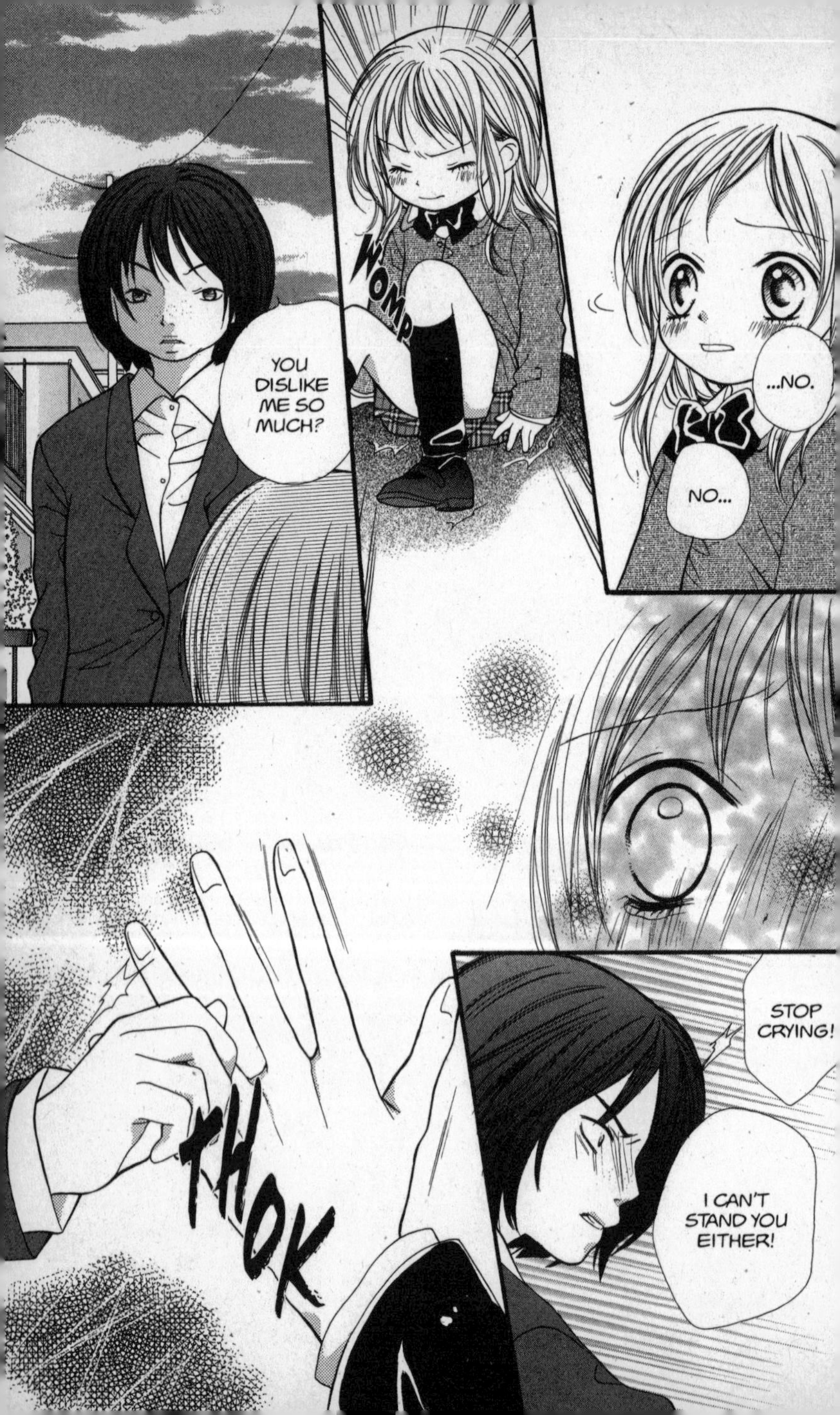
...NO.
NO...
WOMP
YOU DISLIKE ME SO MUCH?
STOP CRYING!
I CAN'T STAND YOU EITHER!
THOK

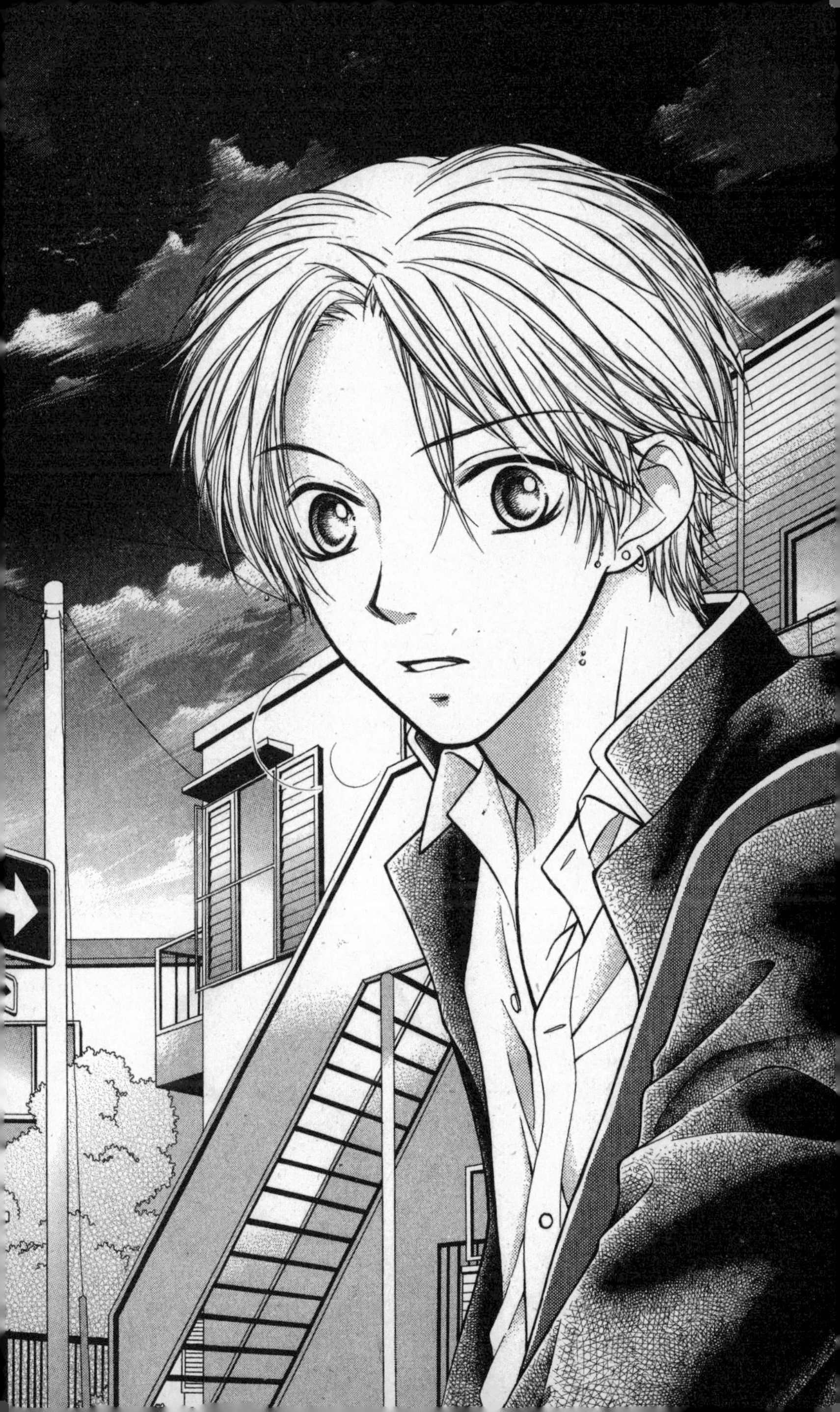

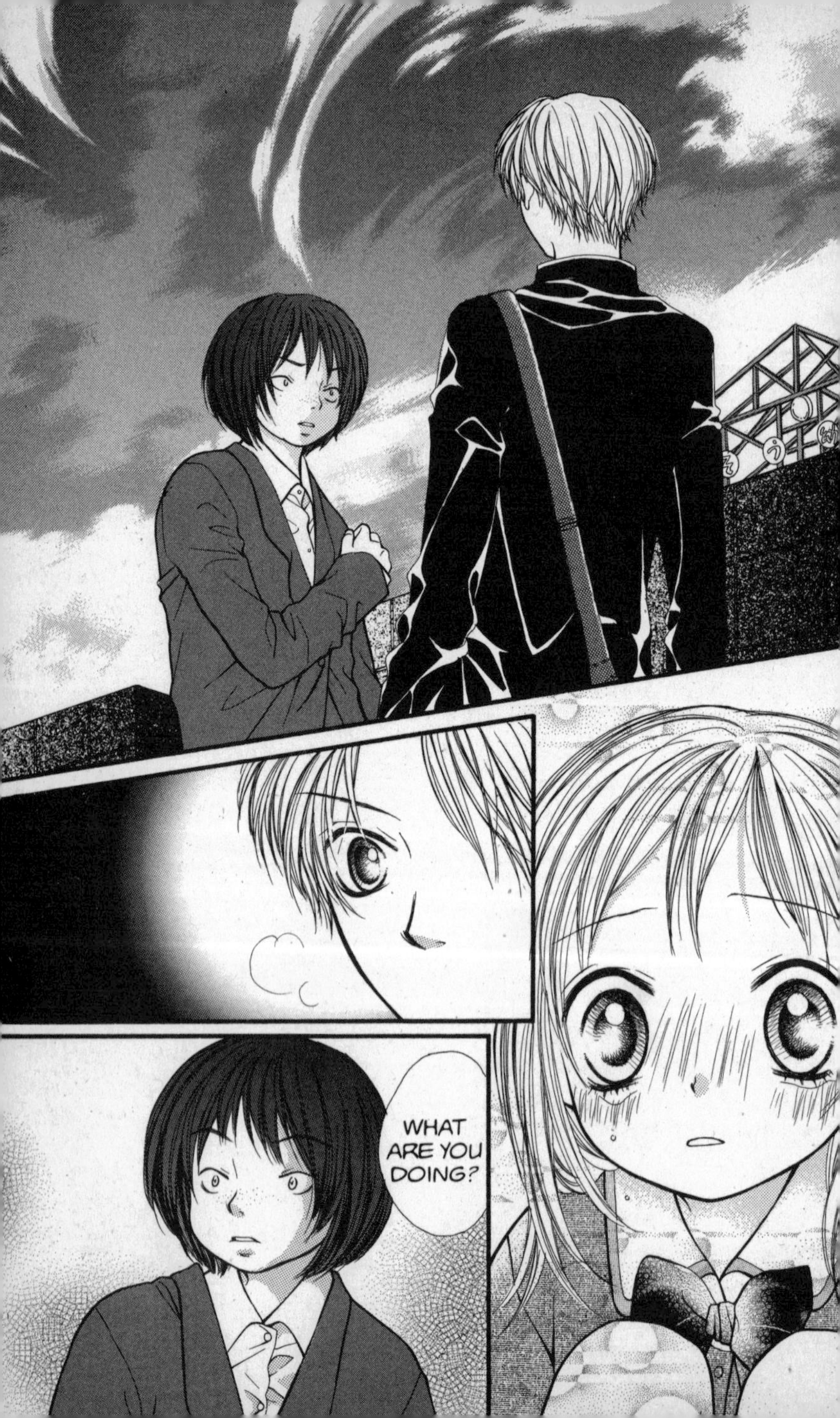
WHAT ARE YOU DOING?

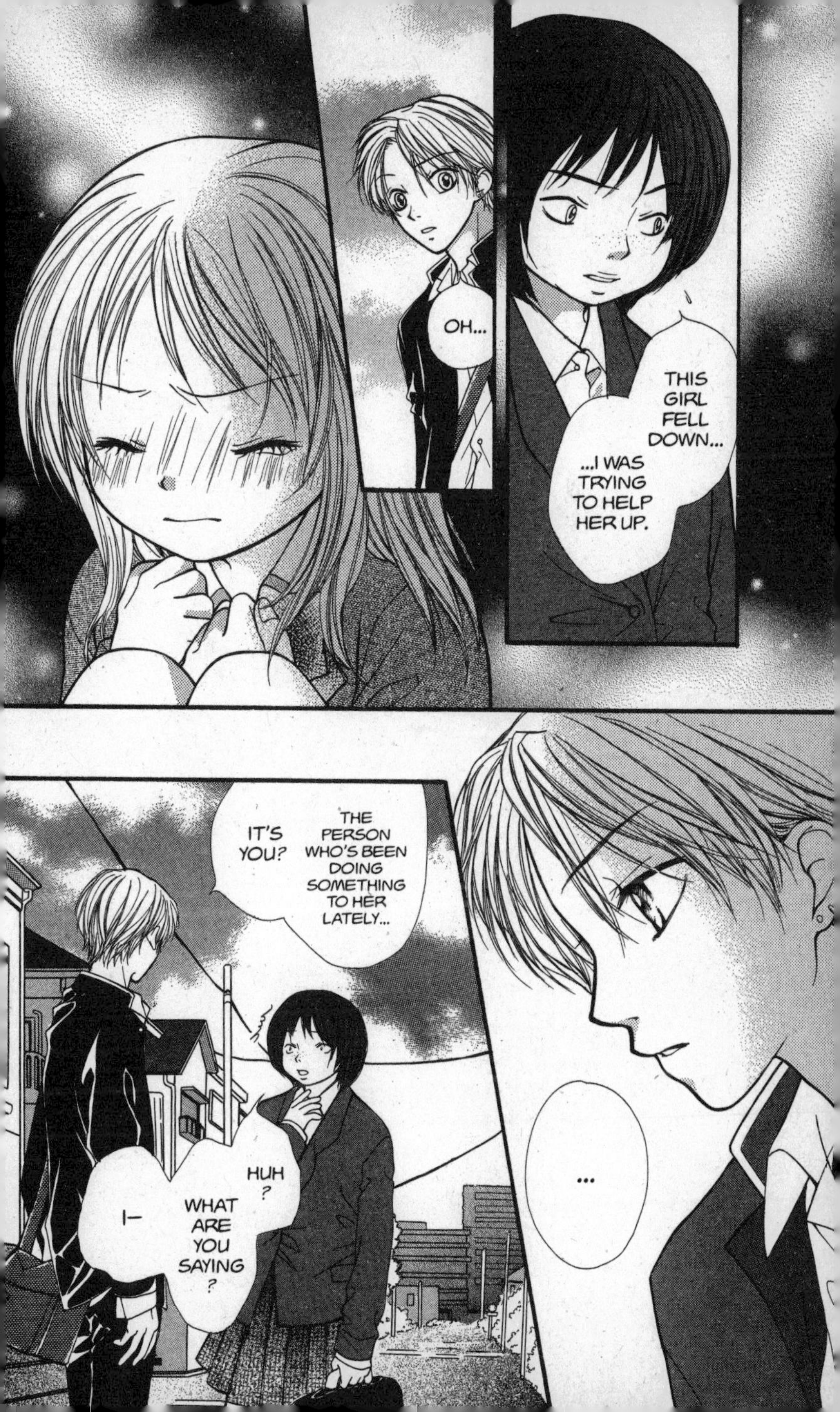
THIS GIRL FELL DOWN...
...I WAS TRYING TO HELP HER UP.
OH...
THE PERSON WHO'S BEEN DOING SOMETHING TO HER LATELY...
IT'S YOU?
...
HUH?
WHAT ARE YOU SAYING?
I—

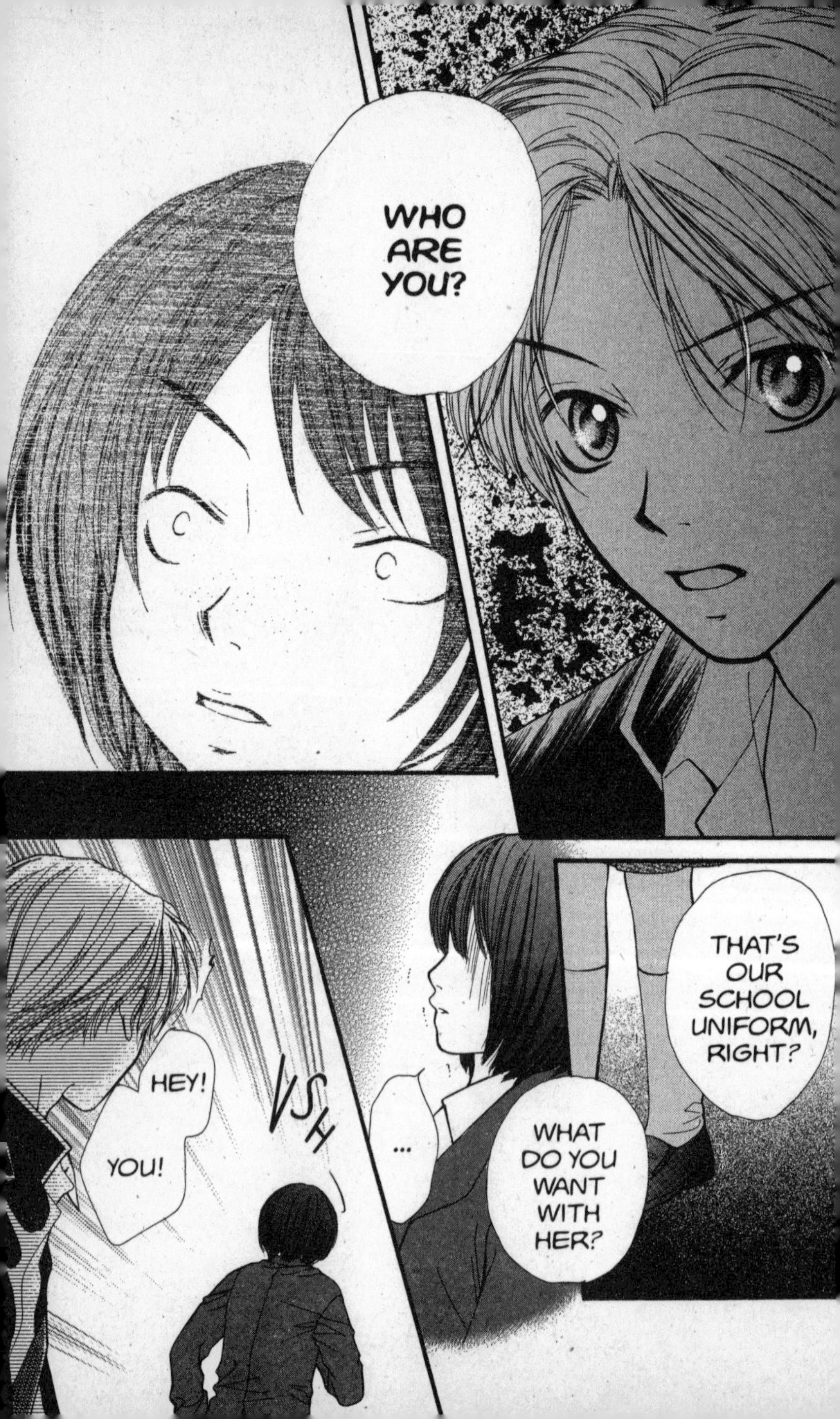
WHO ARE YOU?
THAT'S OUR SCHOOL UNIFORM, RIGHT?
WHAT DO YOU WANT WITH HER?
...
VSH
HEY!
YOU!

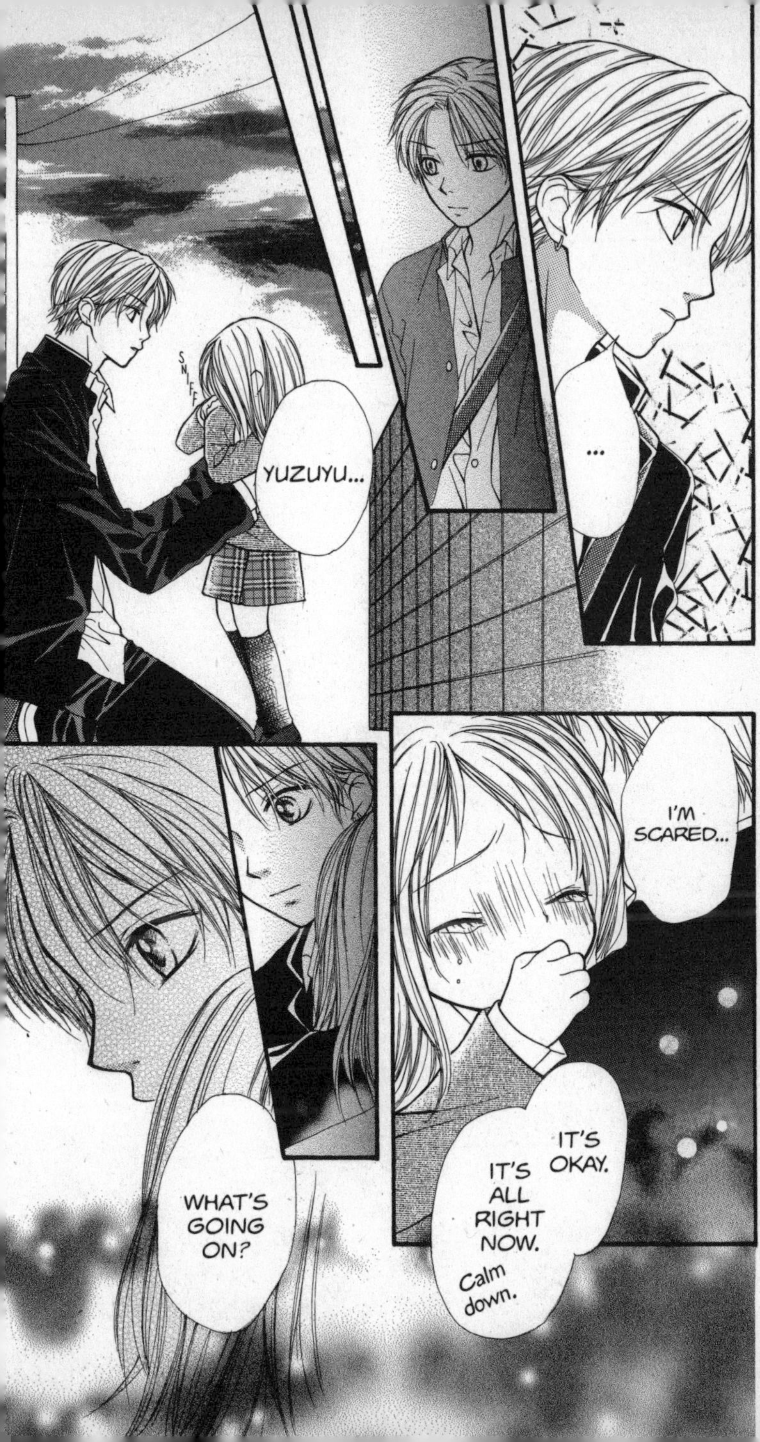
...
YUZUYU...
SNIFF
I'M SCARED...
IT'S OKAY.
IT'S ALL RIGHT NOW.
Calm down.
WHAT'S GOING ON?

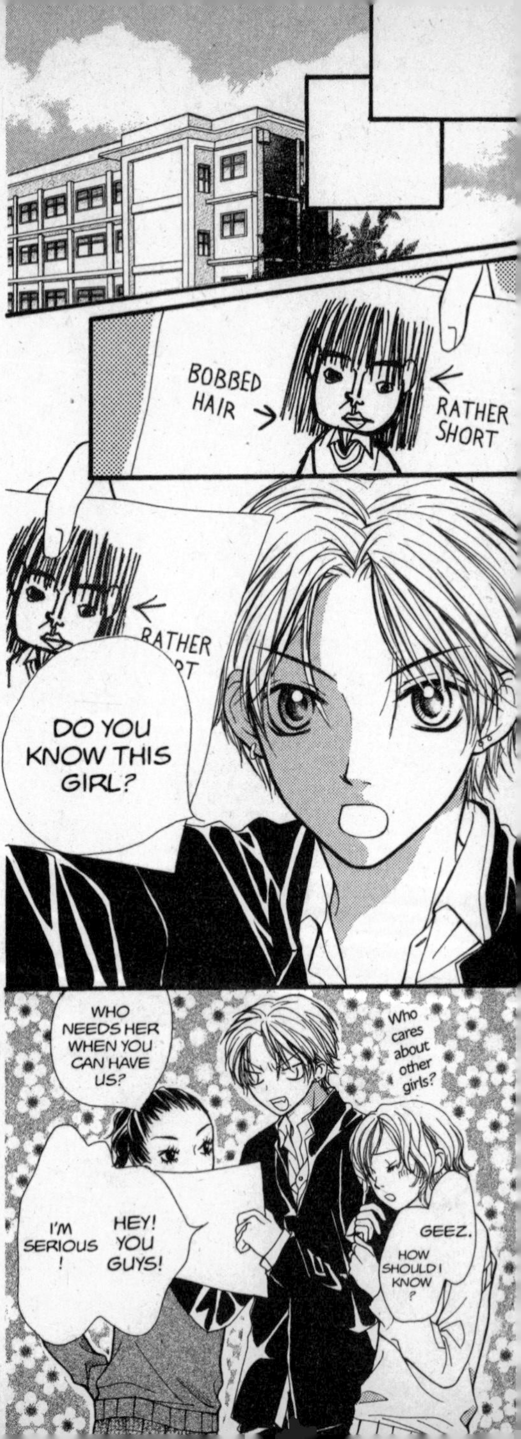
RATHER SHORT
BOBBED HAIR
RATHER
DO YOU KNOW THIS GIRL?
Who cares about other girls?
WHO NEEDS HER WHEN YOU CAN HAVE US?
GEEZ.
HOW SHOULD I KNOW?
HEY! YOU GUYS!
I'M SERIOUS!

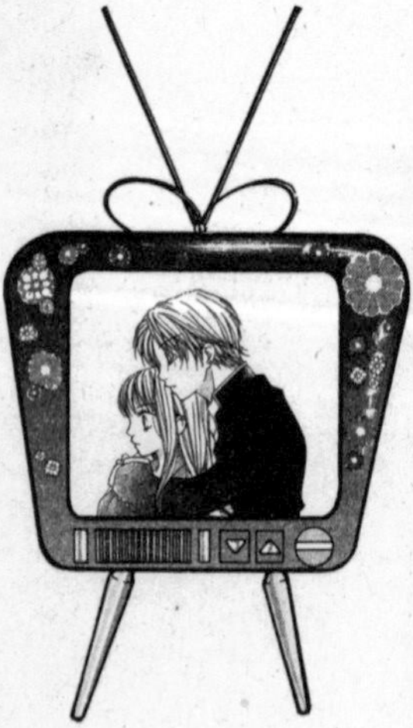

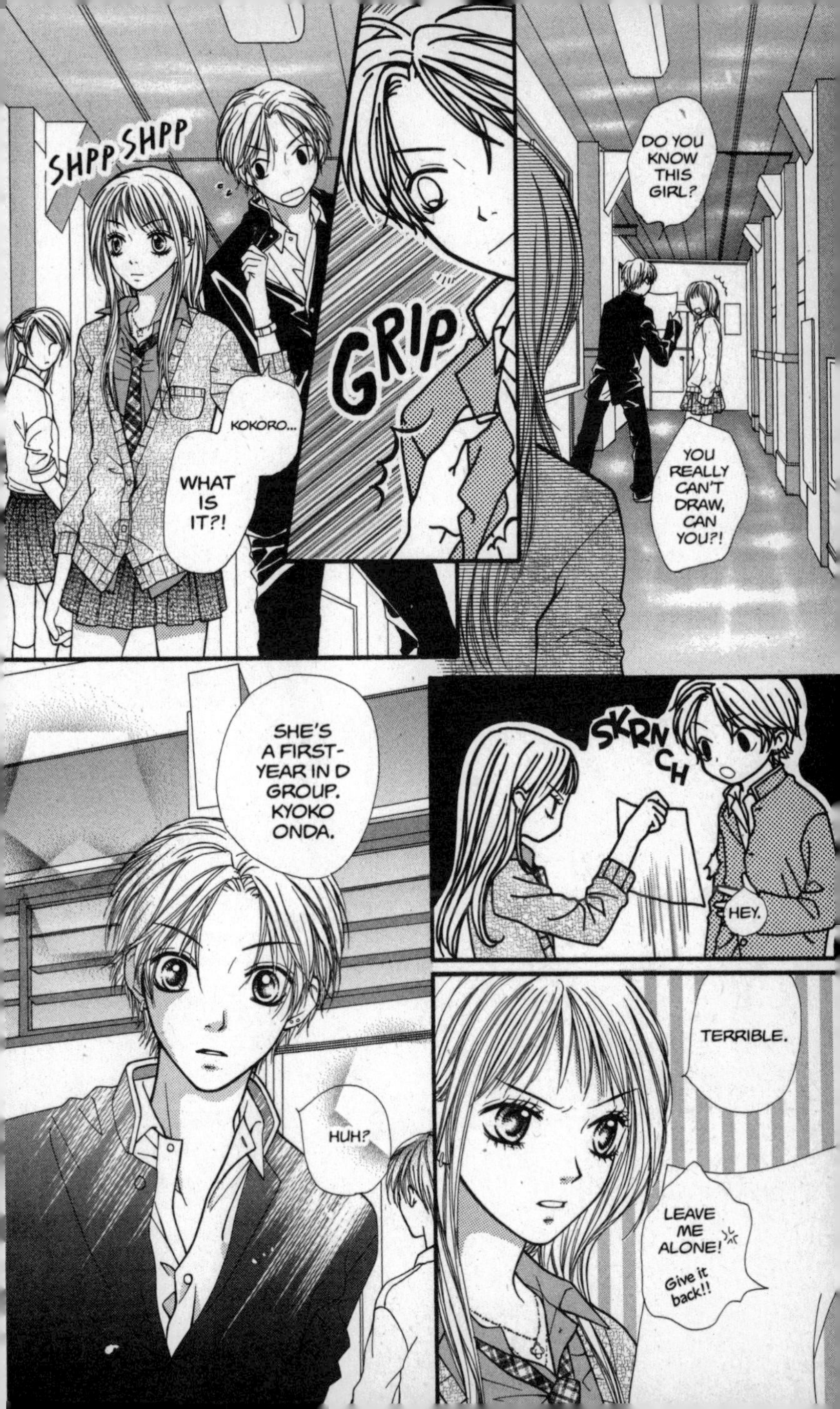
DO YOU KNOW THIS GIRL?
YOU REALLY CAN'T DRAW, CAN YOU?!
GRIP
SHPP SHPP
KOKORO...
WHAT IS IT?!
SKRNCH
HEY.
TERRIBLE.
LEAVE ME ALONE!
Give it back!!
SHE'S A FIRST-YEAR IN D GROUP. KYOKO ONDA.
HUH?

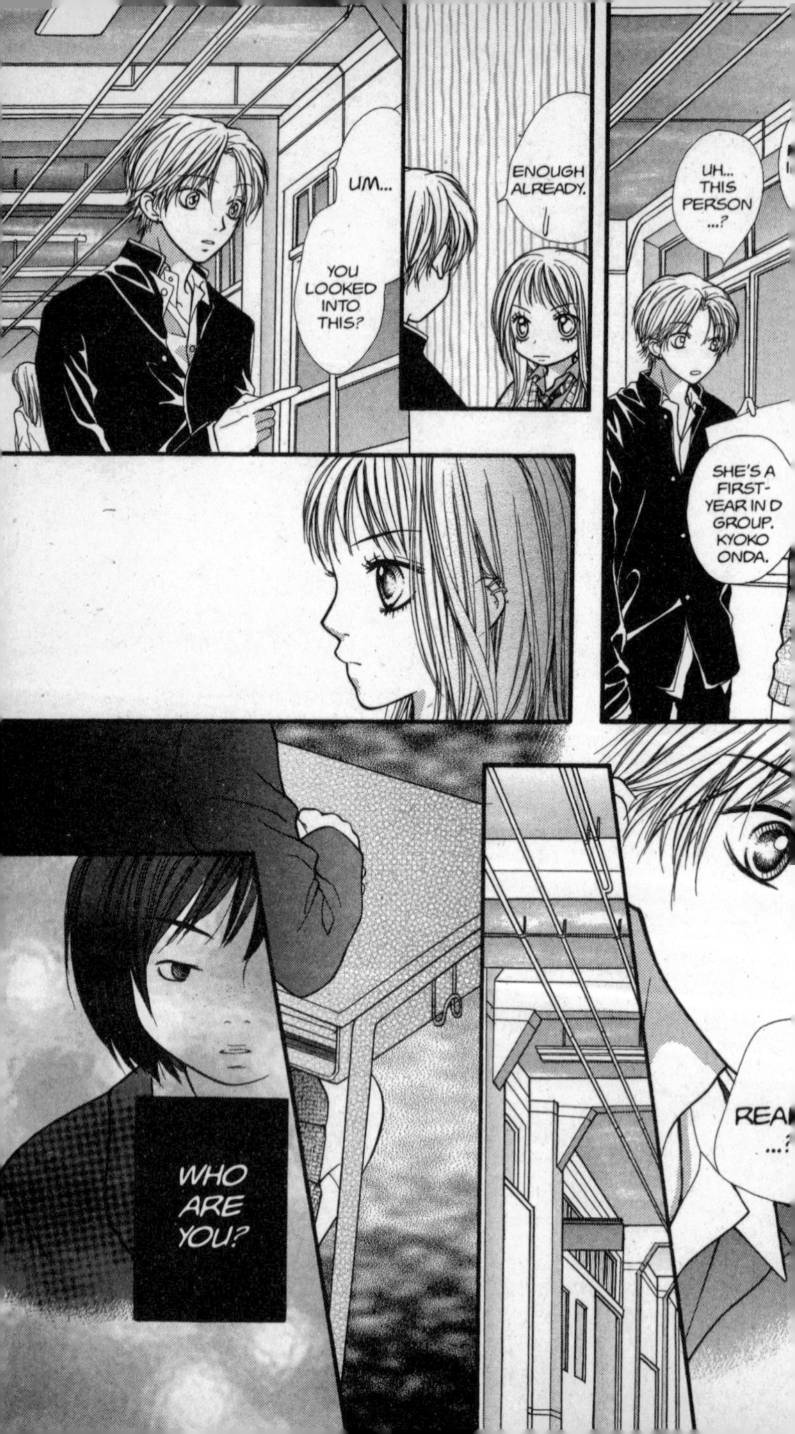
UH... THIS PERSON ...?
SHE'S A FIRST-YEAR IN D GROUP. KYOKO ONDA.
ENOUGH ALREADY.
UM...
YOU LOOKED INTO THIS?
REA
...?
WHO ARE YOU?

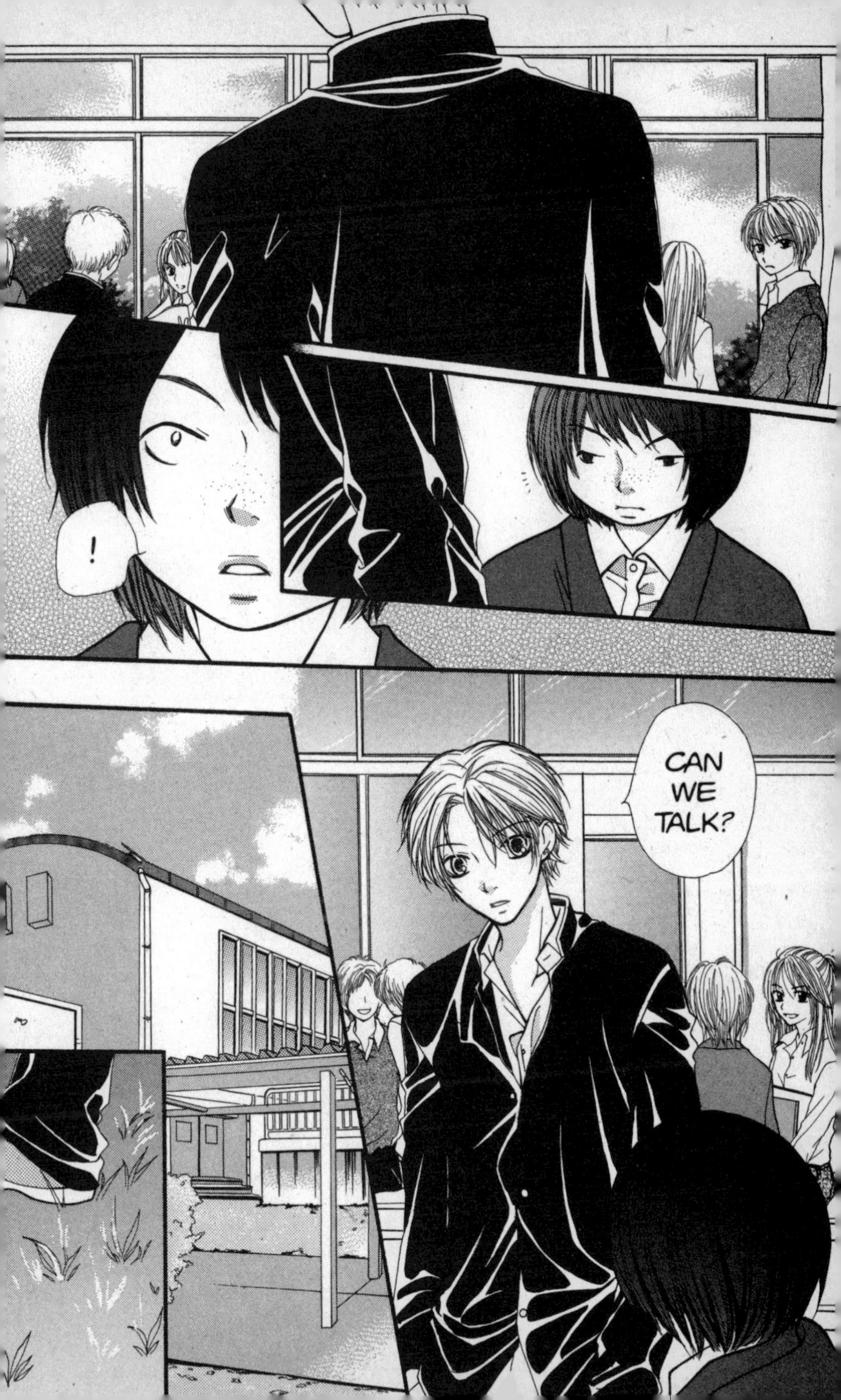
!
CAN WE TALK?

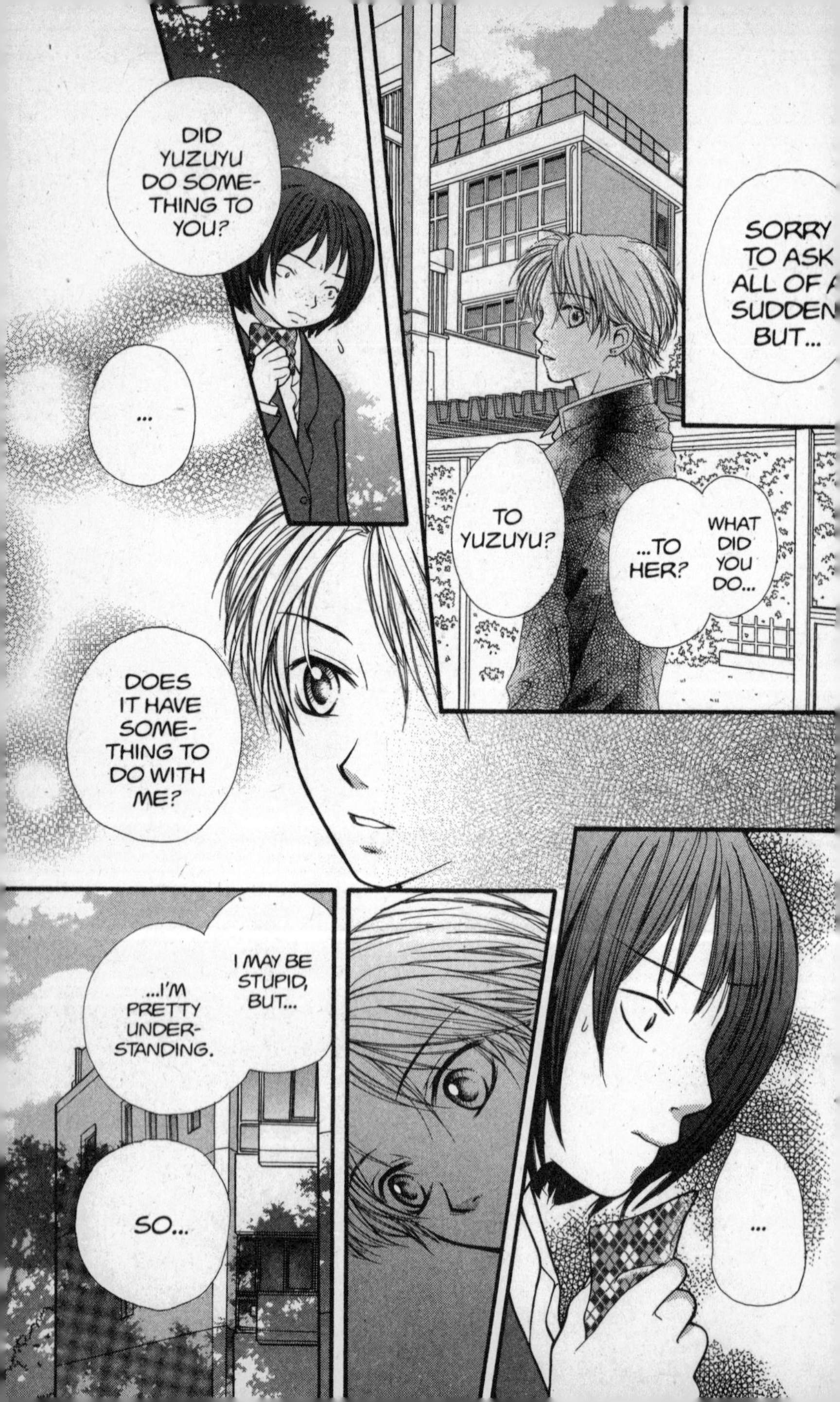

SORRY TO ASK ALL OF A SUDDEN BUT...
WHAT DID YOU DO...
...TO HER?
TO YUZUYU?
DID YUZUYU DO SOME-THING TO YOU?
...
DOES IT HAVE SOME-THING TO DO WITH ME?
...
I MAY BE STUPID, BUT...
...I'M PRETTY UNDER-STANDING.
SO...

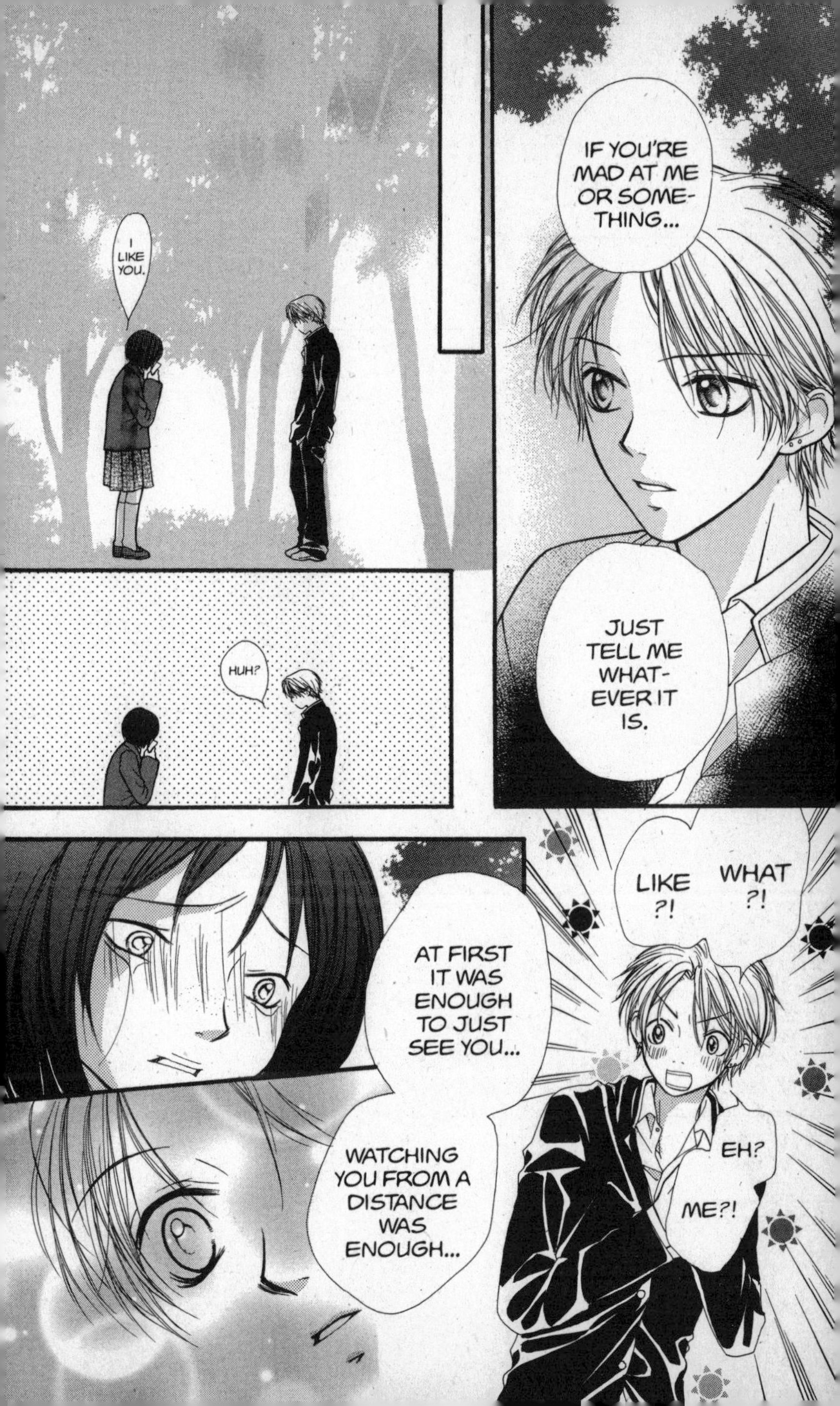
IF YOU'RE MAD AT ME OR SOME-THING...
JUST TELL ME WHAT-EVER IT IS.
I LIKE YOU.
HUH?
WHAT?!
LIKE?!
EH?
ME?!
AT FIRST IT WAS ENOUGH TO JUST SEE YOU...
WATCHING YOU FROM A DISTANCE WAS ENOUGH...

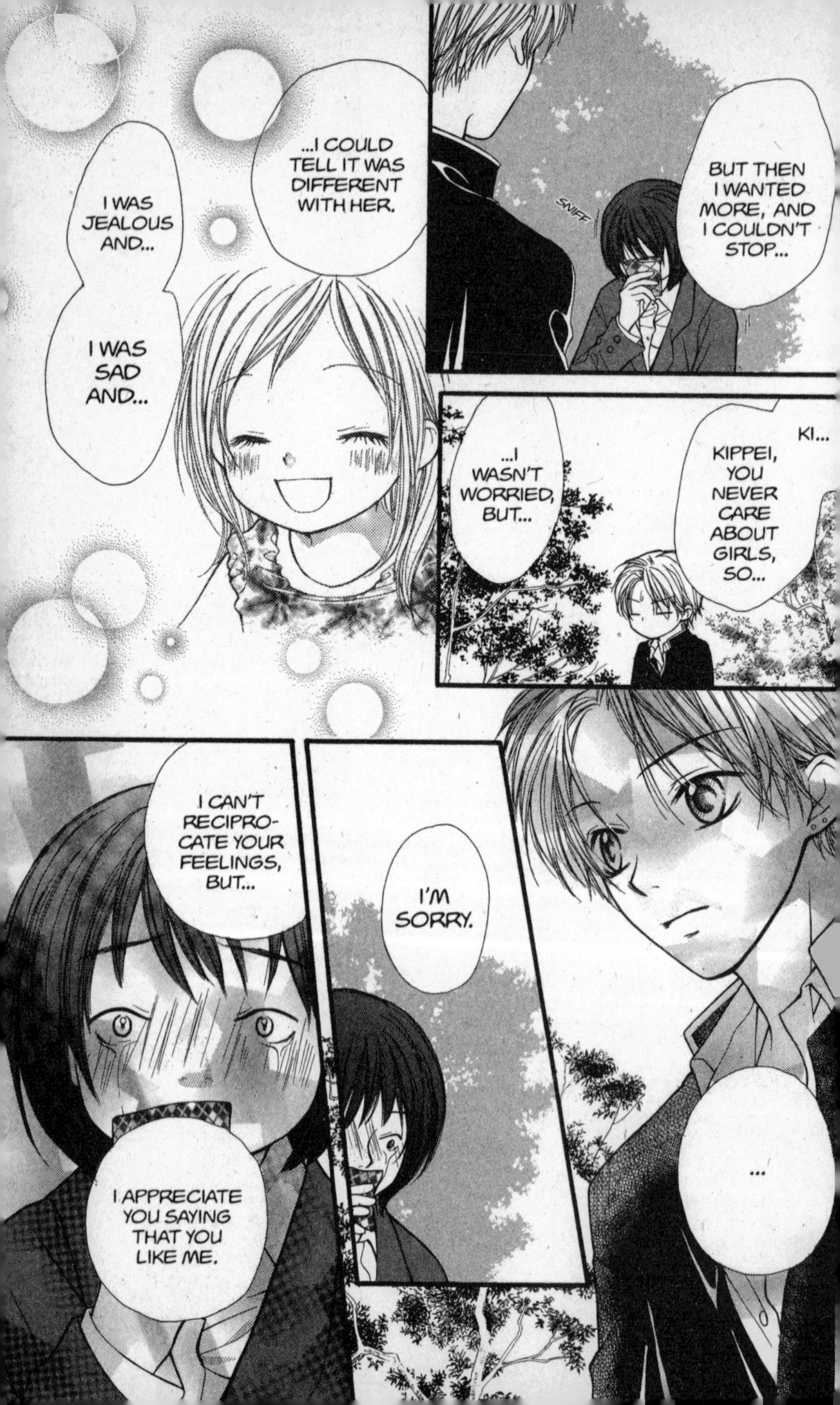
BUT THEN I WANTED MORE, AND I COULDN'T STOP...
SNIFF
KI...
KIPPEI, YOU NEVER CARE ABOUT GIRLS, SO...
...I WASN'T WORRIED, BUT...
...I COULD TELL IT WAS DIFFERENT WITH HER.
I WAS JEALOUS AND...
I WAS SAD AND...
...
I'M SORRY.
I CAN'T RECIPROCATE YOUR FEELINGS, BUT...
I APPRECIATE YOU SAYING THAT YOU LIKE ME.

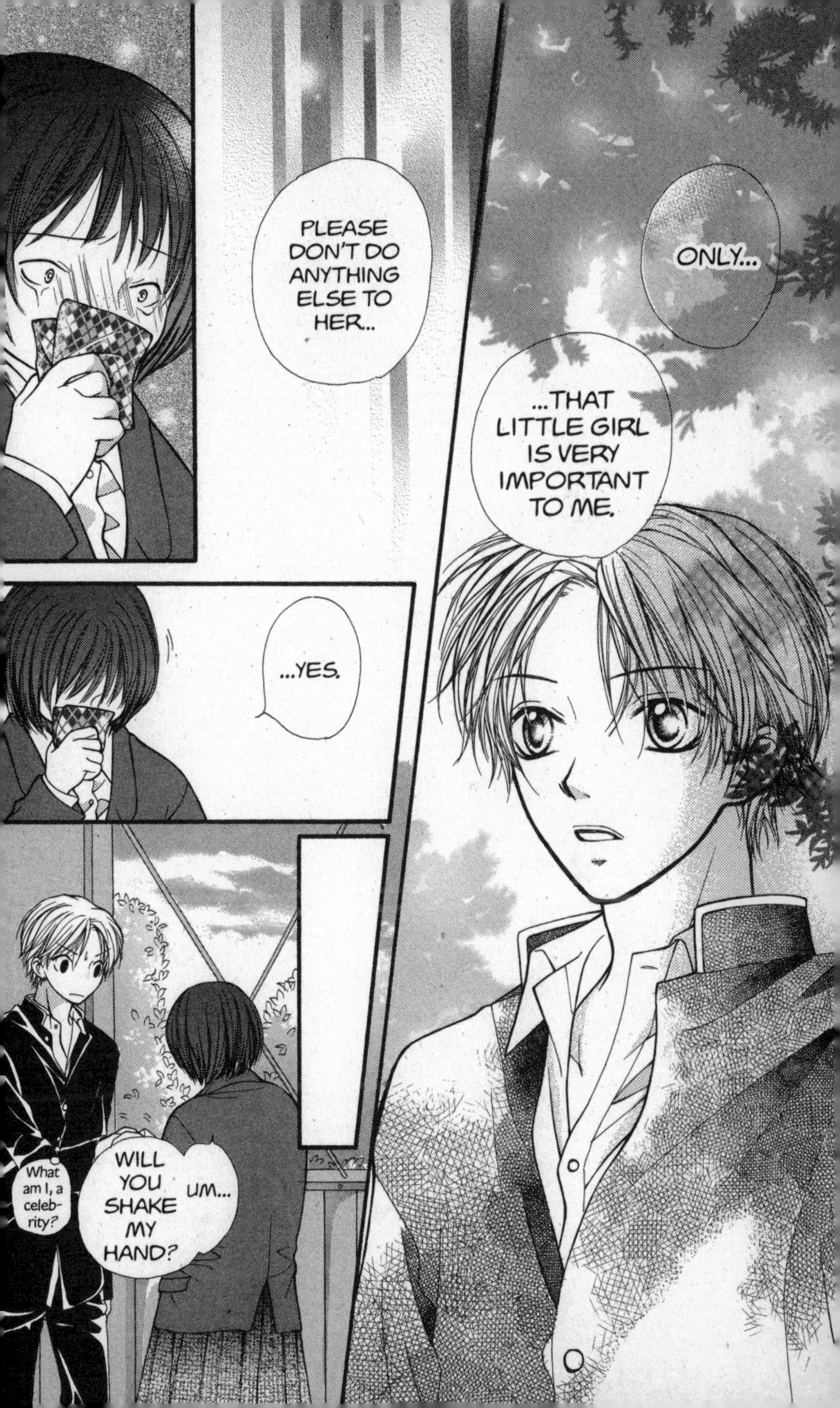
ONLY...
...THAT LITTLE GIRL IS VERY IMPORTANT TO ME.
PLEASE DON'T DO ANYTHING ELSE TO HER...
...YES.
UM...
WILL YOU SHAKE MY HAND?
What am I, a celebrity?

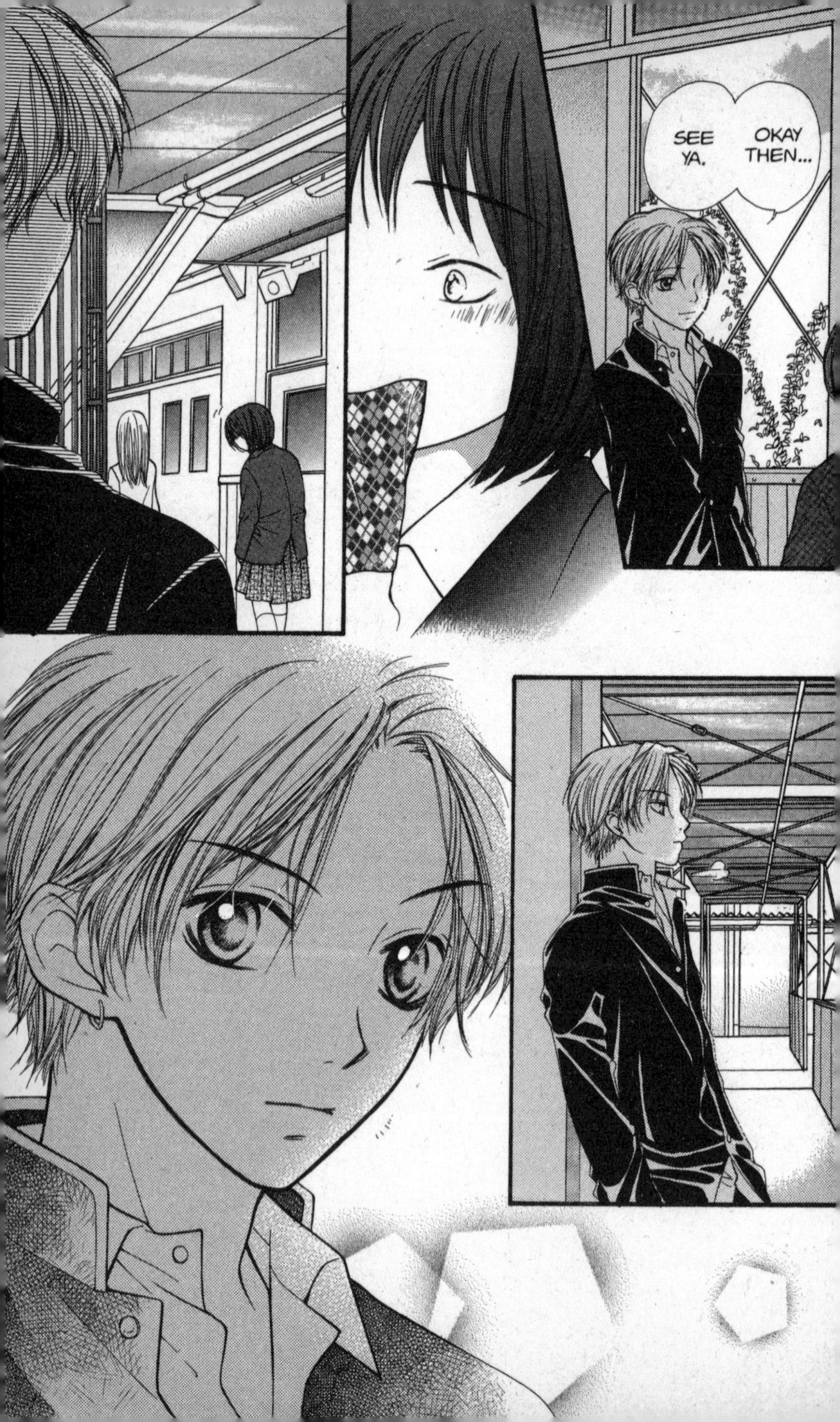
OKAY THEN...
SEE YA.

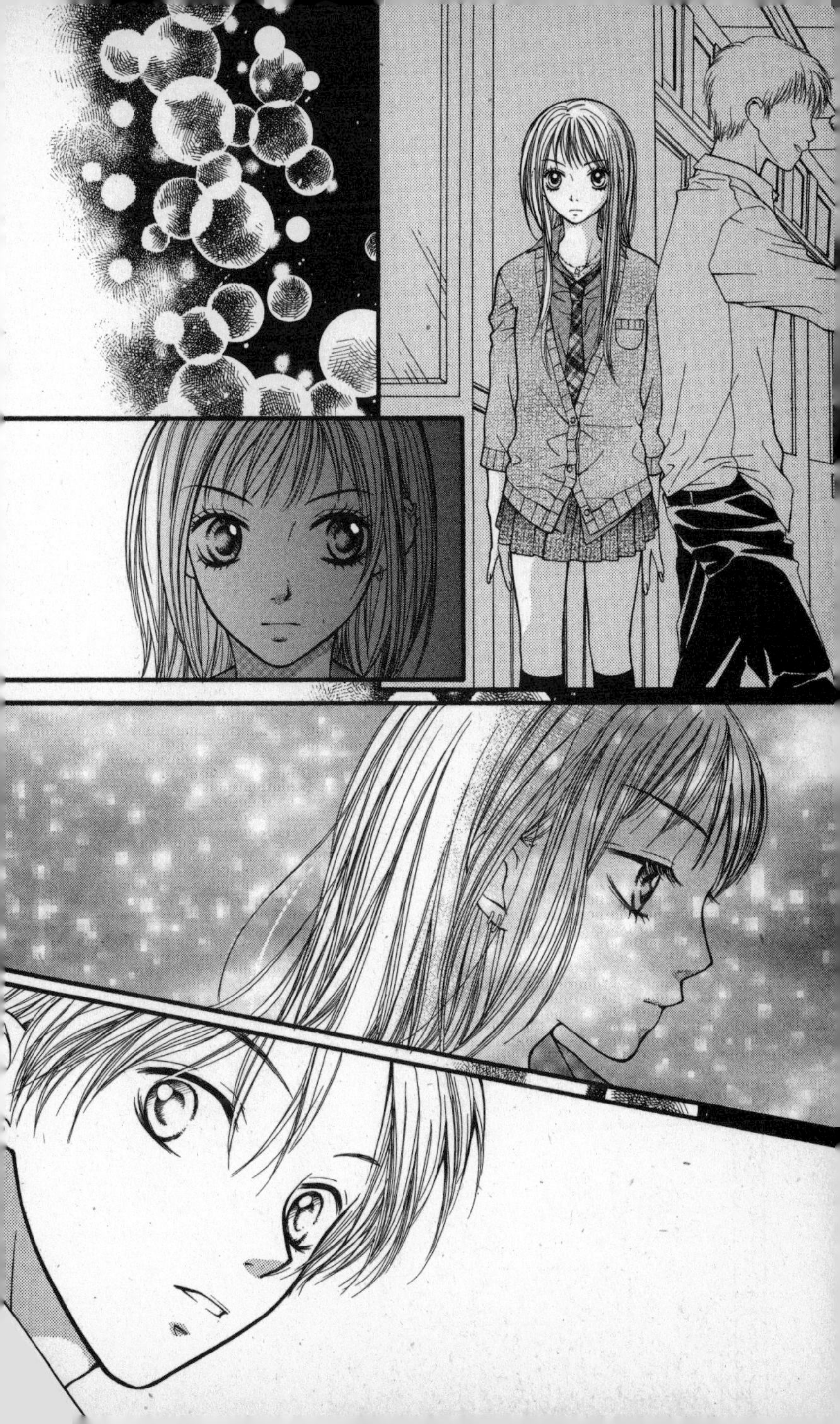

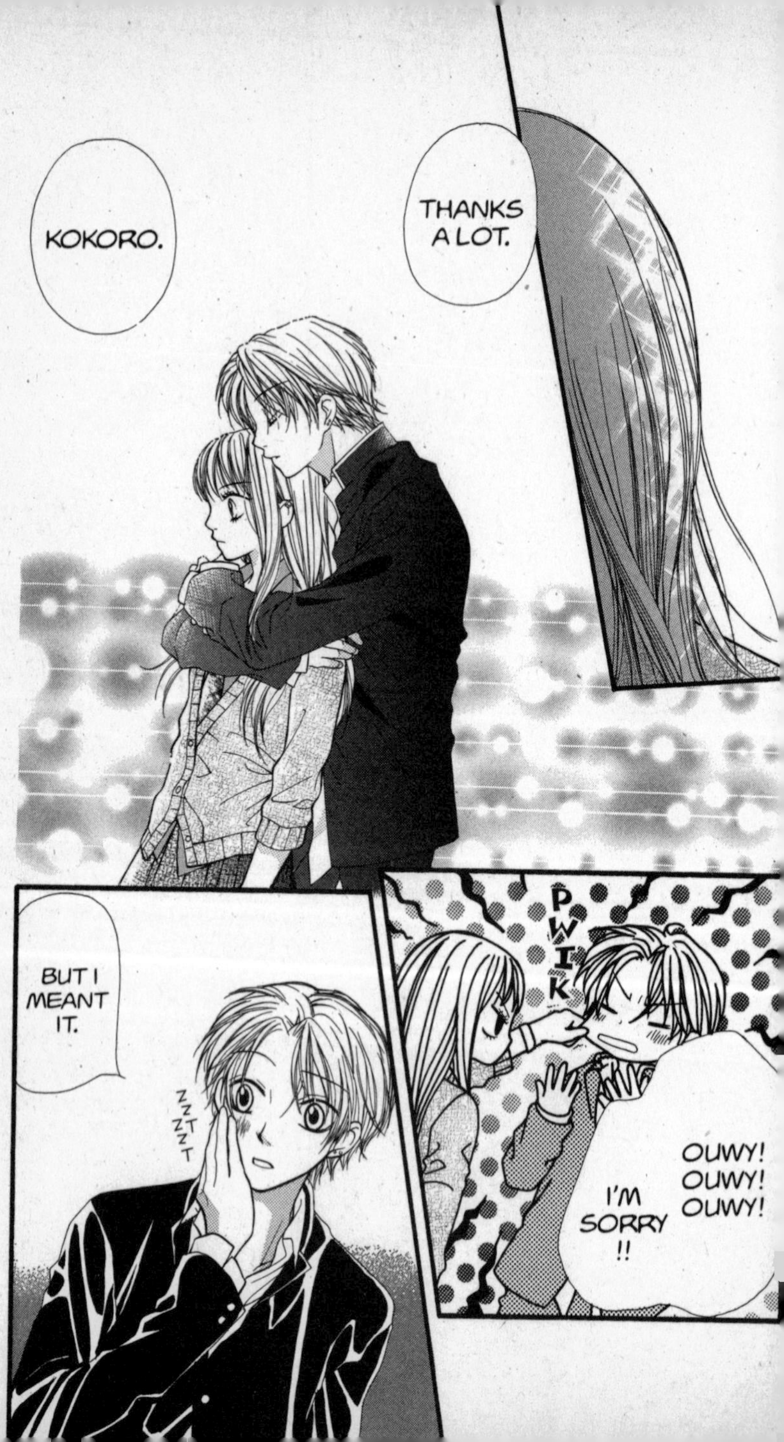
THANKS A LOT.
KOKORO.
PWIK
OUWY! OUWY! OUWY!
I'M SORRY!!
BUT I MEANT IT.
ZZT ZZT

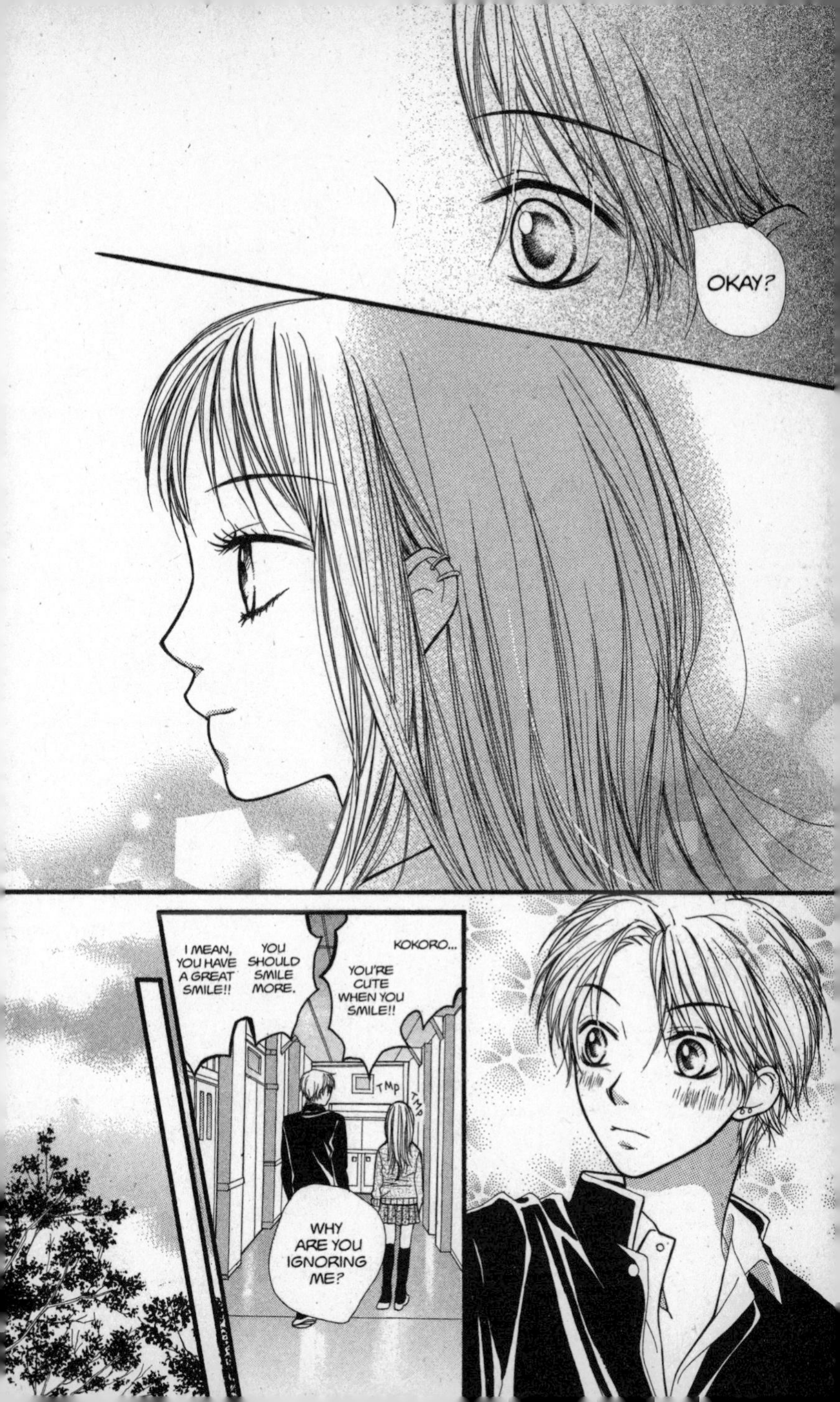
OKAY?
KOKORO...
YOU'RE CUTE WHEN YOU SMILE!!
YOU SHOULD SMILE MORE.
I MEAN, YOU HAVE A GREAT SMILE!!
TMP
TMP
WHY ARE YOU IGNORING ME?

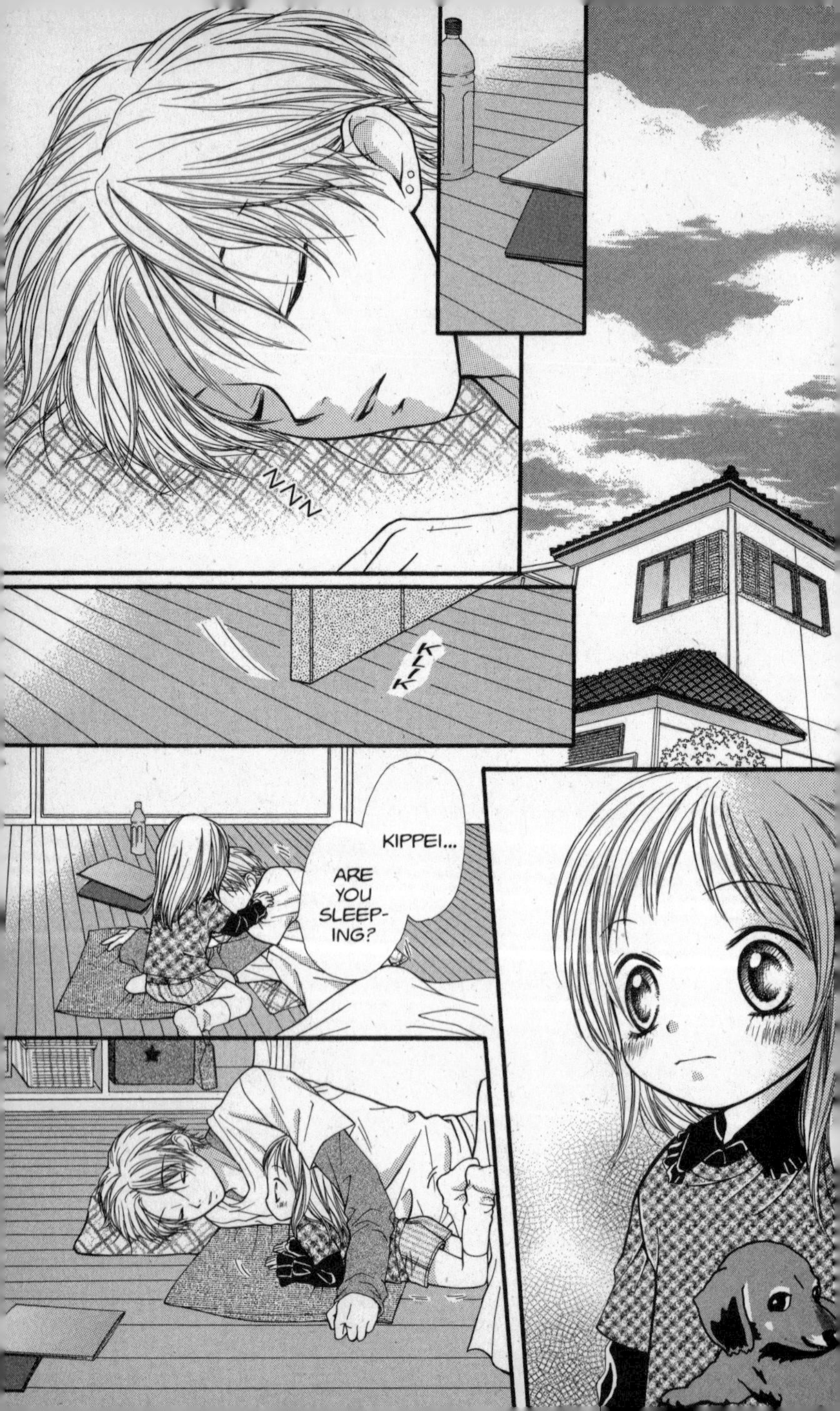

NNN
KLIK
KIPPEI...
ARE YOU SLEEPING?

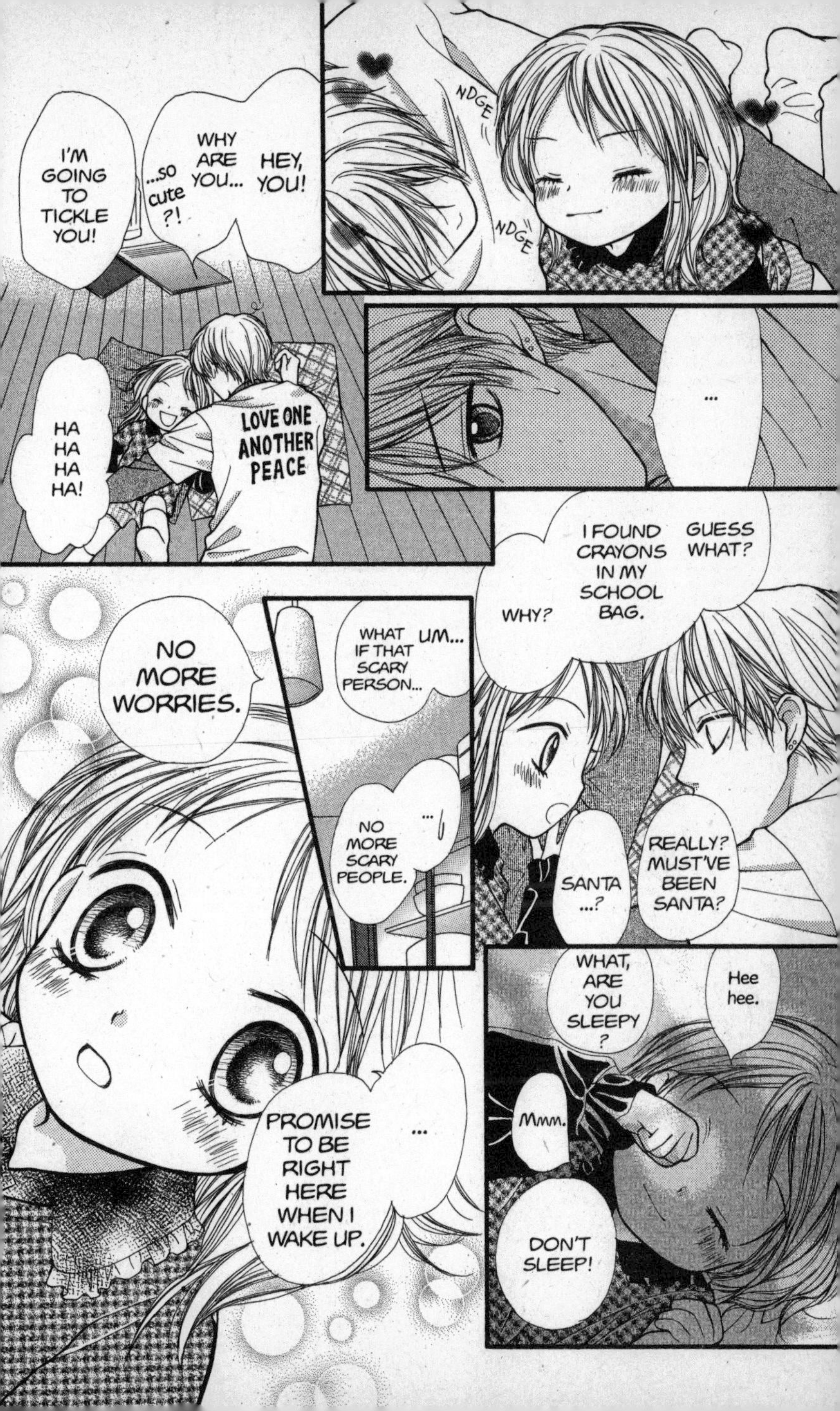
NDGE
NDGE
...
HEY, YOU!
WHY ARE YOU...
...so cute ?!
I'M GOING TO TICKLE YOU!
HA HA HA HA!
LOVE ONE ANOTHER PEACE
GUESS WHAT?
I FOUND CRAYONS IN MY SCHOOL BAG.
WHY?
REALLY? MUST'VE BEEN SANTA?
SANTA ...?
UM...
WHAT IF THAT SCARY PERSON...
...
NO MORE SCARY PEOPLE.
Hee hee.
WHAT, ARE YOU SLEEPY ?
Mmm.
DON'T SLEEP!
NO MORE WORRIES.
...
PROMISE TO BE RIGHT HERE WHEN I WAKE UP.

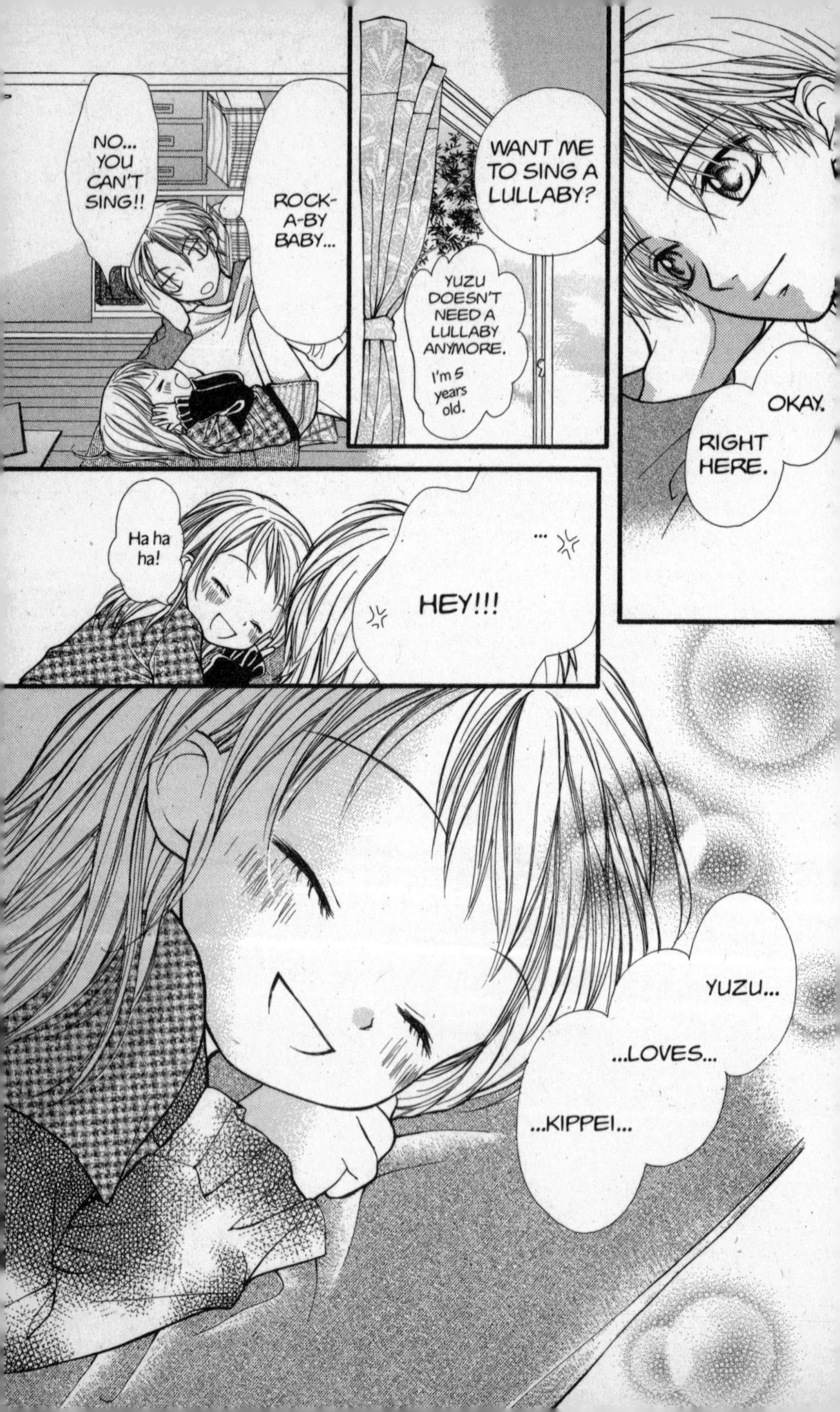
OKAY.
RIGHT HERE.
WANT ME TO SING A LULLABY?
YUZU DOESN'T NEED A LULLABY ANYMORE.
I'm 5 years old.
ROCK-A-BY BABY...
NO... YOU CAN'T SING!!
... HEY!!!
Ha ha ha!
YUZU...
...LOVES...
...KIPPEI...

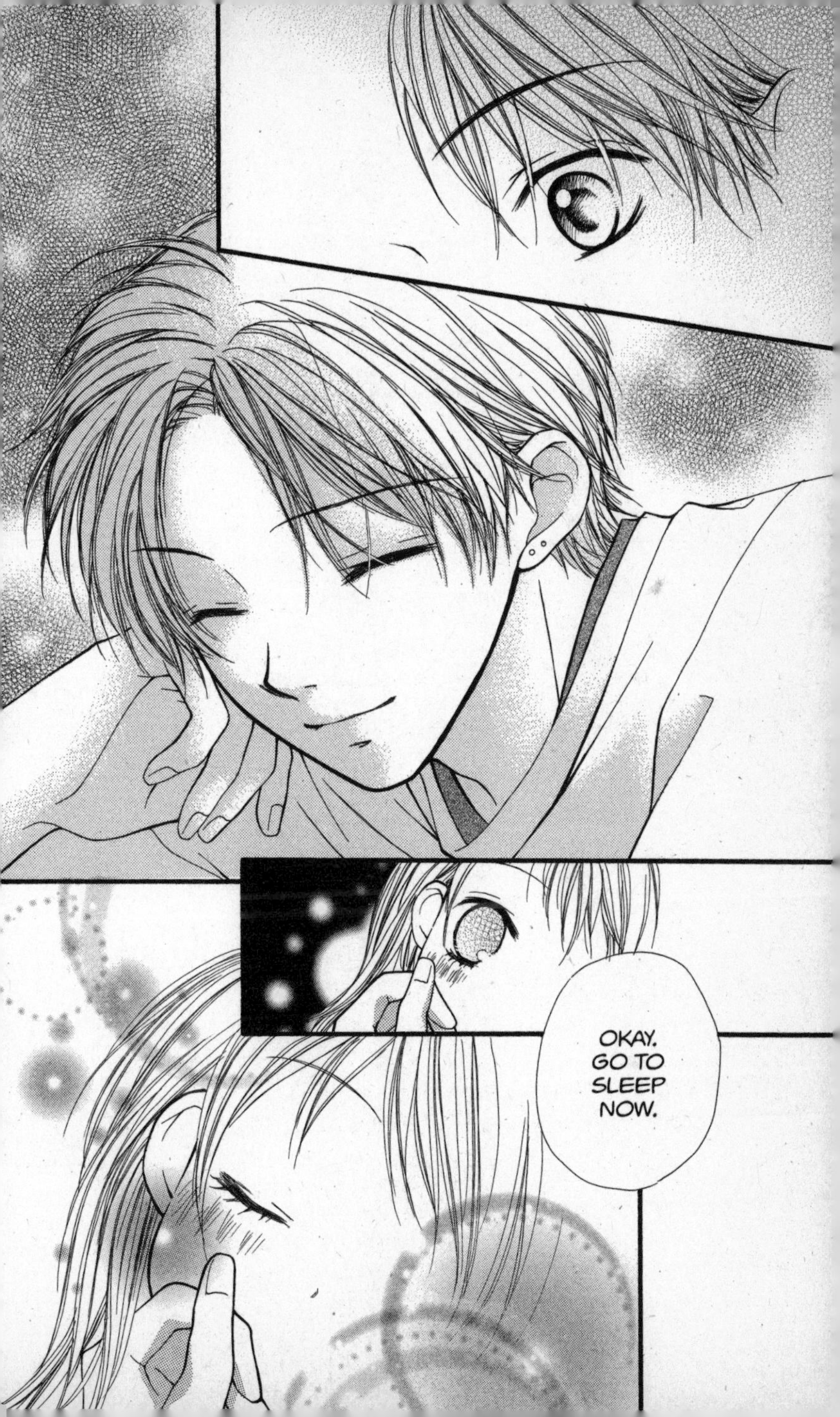
OKAY. GO TO SLEEP NOW.

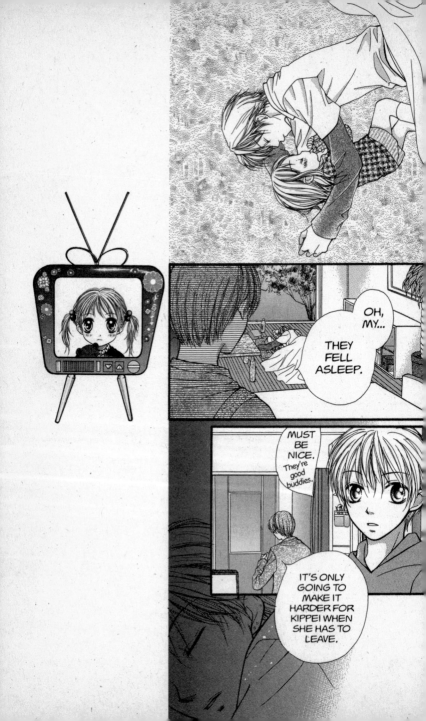

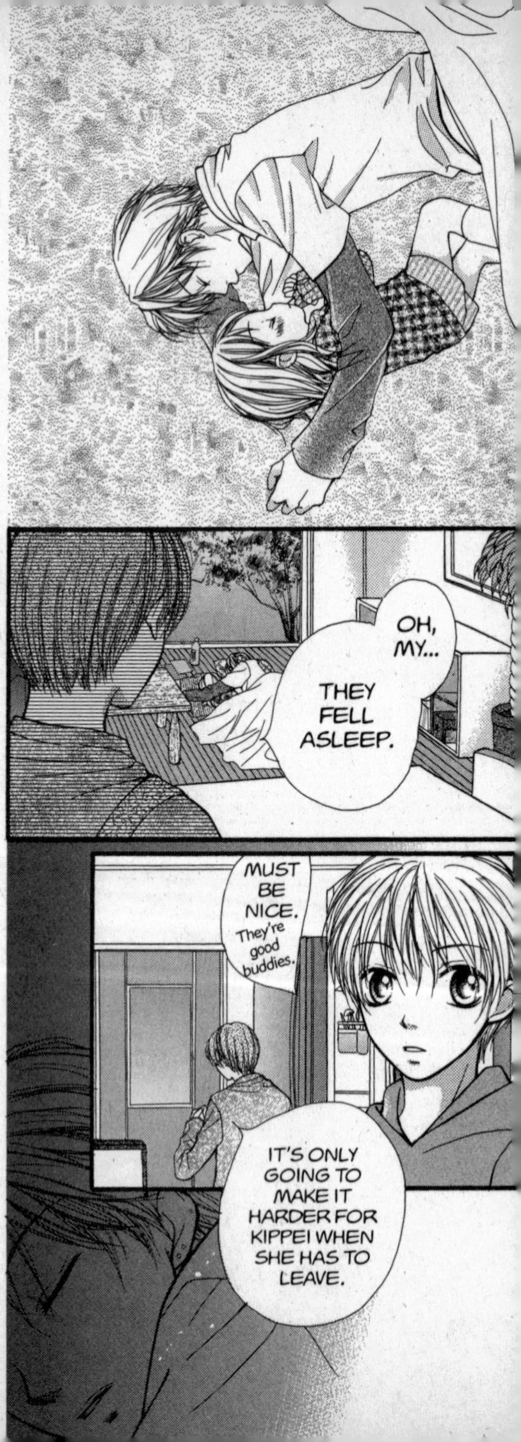
OH, MY...
THEY FELL ASLEEP.
MUST BE NICE.
They're good buddies.
IT'S ONLY GOING TO MAKE IT HARDER FOR KIPPEI WHEN SHE HAS TO LEAVE.

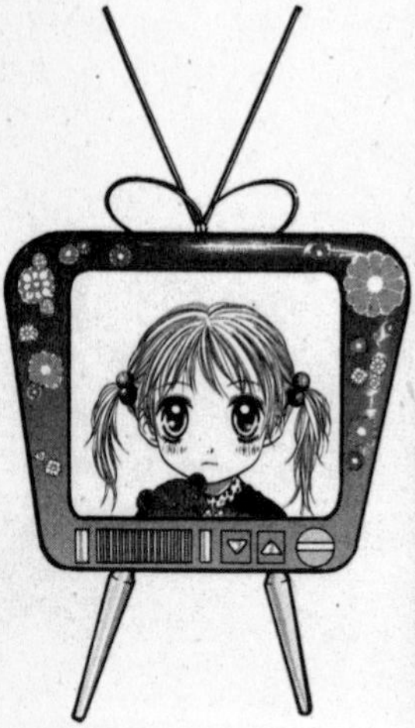

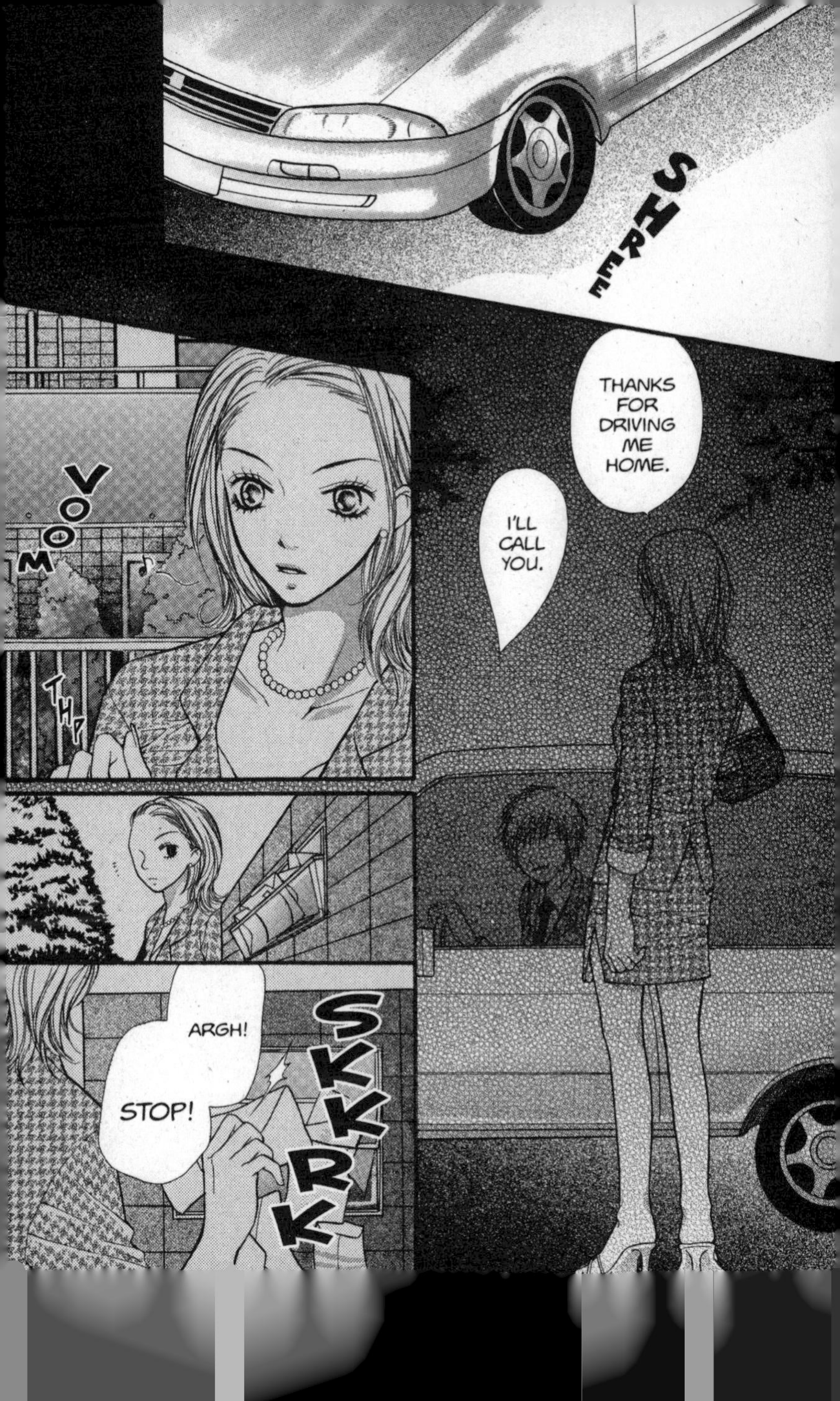
SHREE
THANKS FOR DRIVING ME HOME.
I'LL CALL YOU.
VOOM
THP
ARGH!
STOP!
SKKRK

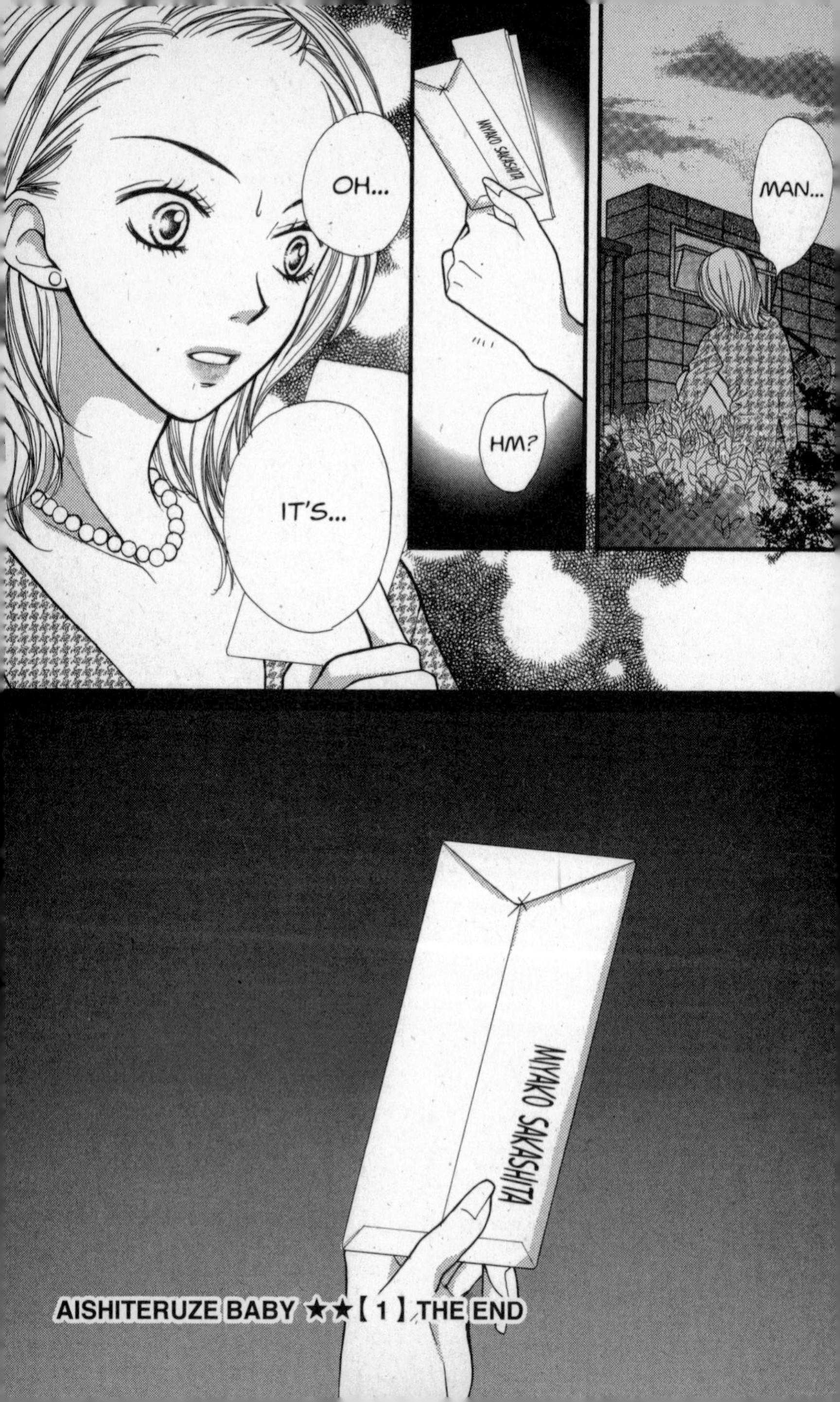
MAN...
MIYAKO SAKASHITA
HM?
OH...
IT'S...
MIYAKO SAKASHITA
AISHITERUZE BABY ★★【 1 】THE END

BABY DIARY

Now, this is where I, Yoko Maki, write a diary when I feel like it (and when I have time to) while drawing "Baby."

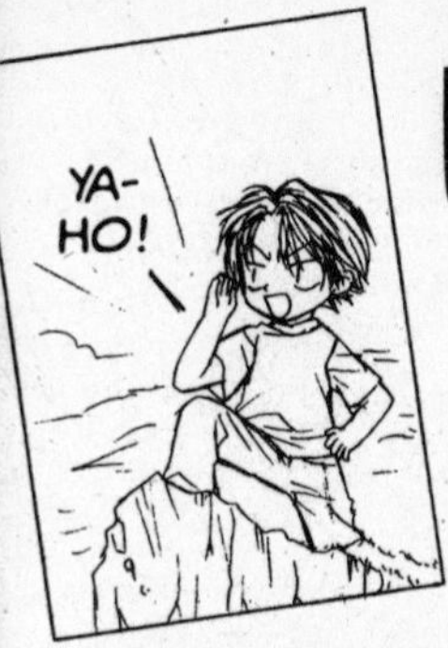
YA-
HO!

↑ I am currently coloring the playing cards. (This is one of the sketches.) I'm going to finish it off ASAP! Yeah!
3.21.02

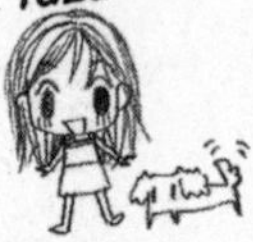
YUZU

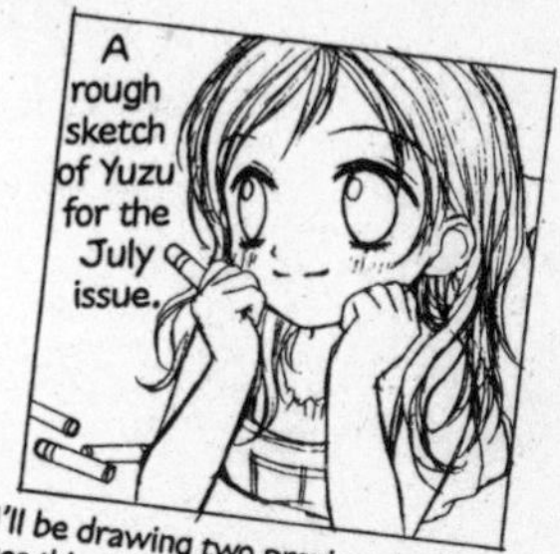

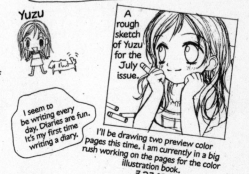

A rough sketch of Yuzu for the July issue.

I'll be drawing two preview color pages this time. I am currently in a big rush working on the pages for the color illustration book.
3.23.02

I seem to be writing every day. Diaries are fun. It's my first time writing a diary.

Due to a miscommunication, I had not even touched the pages that were due today—oops! Well, sometimes things do happen... Oh, man!
3.22.02

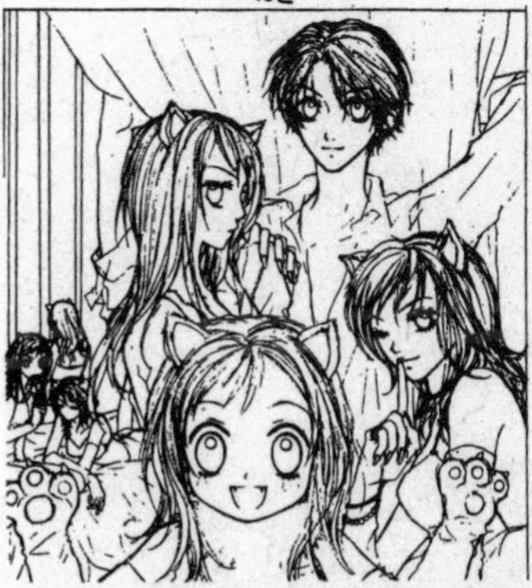

↑ This is the poster (rough draft) that came with insert 6. It shrunk quite a bit.

I finally finished the color illustration book yesterday, so I went to sleep right after and woke up very early. I feel great! I can finally get back to the manuscript. It's just the additional pages, so I'll work hard on them! Lately, I'm in good shape (healthwise) and am able to work exactly how I want. I'm having fun.
3.27.02

I've been putting a lot of effort into my work lately. My Rep said, "You worked hard!" Yes. The cherry blossoms are in full bloom right now and I took a brief break to enjoy the cherry-blossom viewing. I also held Leo as I walked so that he could see the cherry blossoms as well. He was heavy. But it was beautiful.
3.26.02

Today, I had a dream where I was all excited with Norika Fujiwara about "becoming an apartment superintendent at least once in our lifetime." It was a dream where I thought how commendable Norika was for thinking about things like that. Right.
3.28.02

Man... I want to eat some bamboo shoots...
5.1.02

Today, I drew illustrations for some sort of summer event goods. When I looked over at Leo, he was under the chair where my TV is, thinking intently about something. He ignored me even when I asked him, "What's wrong?" I guess he has a lot to think about as well.

Um, it's been a while, Diary. It is Golden Week right now. Since my schedule didn't permit me to travel, I have no choice but to be working right now. I did get some rest, though. On my days off, I try my hardest—that is, I always go outdoors. Since I work at home, I don't feel like I'm taking a break if I wind up staying home on my days off. Oh, I found a really good coffee shop in Shibuya!! It was so good I screamed!
4.30.02

When I was watching TV in the middle of the night, I suddenly felt a dizzy spell come creeping on and I thought, "Oh, that's right—I only had 2 rice crackers today!" I immediately went out to buy some food. I was wobbling as I peddled my bicycle. I think I'm a little better since I ate a little. Man, was I surprised. It happens to me sometimes, but it's been a while since it has happened. Whew!
5.2.02

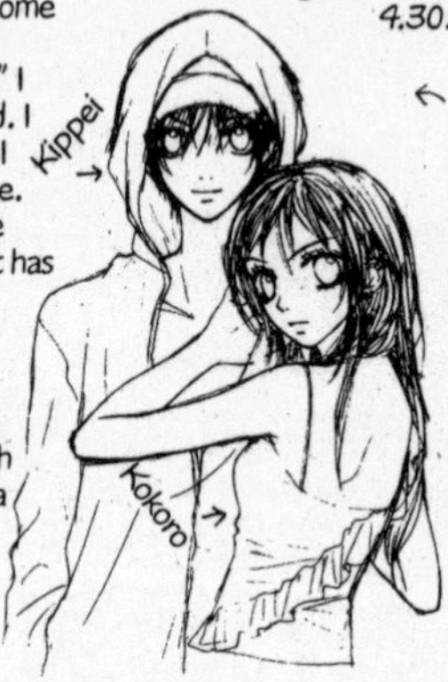
Kippei
Kokoro

← This was also for some event. Kippei turned into some other person after I colored him in. But I like how Kokoro turned out, so this is just fine. As you can tell from the way Kippei's Big Sis and Kokoro talk, I have a bad mouth. I somehow became boyish as I sped through life, so I've decided to wear more skirts this year! That I should finally become a girl...
5.5.02

Yesterday, Hiura-sensei, Yoshikei-sensei, and Akari Hayano gave me a "Yoko-chan Party." Man, it was great! It was so much fun—I felt blessed. I went to Daikanyama for the first time in a long time.
5.6.02

I finished off the manuscript for chapter 4 and met up with some friends from high school. We went to Nikko with my grandparents. Nikko was quite fun—all my friends were working and everyone around seemed happy, so it was kind of nice. Well, back to work for me again.
5.20.02

They bought me a dragon lighter at Nikko, although I could probably get one anywhere...

Today, I had to draw the cover picture for the August issue, plus drawings for the HP game... I'm exhausted so I'm going to sleep now. By the way, when I take my manuscripts to the editing department, I go out with the editing staff and it's kind of nice because I am able to confirm what I want out of life and what I want to do by talking to them. Oh, I changed to a fun cell phone. It has a camera—it's great!
5.22.02

"Gyah!! Yuzu's hair is green?!!" This is what I think sometimes when I see the color pages. Yuzu's hair color doesn't come out right when printing. It's irritating. Not that I can do anything about it...

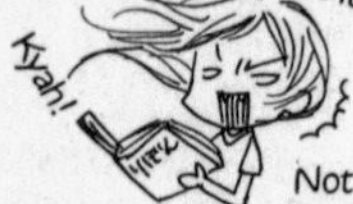
Kyah!

Not brown. Not blue. I really like such a subtle color...
5.23.03

Let's see, I am working on the title page for chapter 5. I am currently waiting for the plaster. Witch Barbie looks so adorable that I thought, "I want Yuzu to wear it too!" Now it is of witch Yuzu. I must start the manuscript immediately... I had so much time this month to enjoy myself that I am now running a little later than usual.
5.30.02

Let's see, day before yesterday, I saw "Spiderman" and "Panic Room." They were really good. And then, yesterday, I went to my cousin's field day. It was fun. I frolicked, etc. But, as expected, children were scarce.
5.27.02

Excuse the abruptness, but my extreme "sluggardness" has been cured!! One reason is that, well, I love natto and I decided to eat it every day! Then, by having rice and salads and such, I was cured. I hate it when my kitchen is a mess, so I clean it now. I even got to the point where I hate my room being messy! Wow! I have become a complete blood type A personality! ✄✄ Woo hoo!
5.31.02

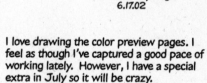

Right now I am working on the stalker conclusion in chapter 5, so let me tell you a little about it. Does everyone dislike the stalker, Onda? (smile) I never portray a character as an enemy. Each person has his/her own feelings, but the world is not easy enough to accept the differences of opinion in everyone—that is why those characters cannot become the heroes... This is what I think when I am writing such characters.
6.05.02

Tomorrow is a drinking party in Shinjuku. Yeah!!! I'm gonna finish my work before then. Excuse the abruptness, but the most popular title page so far is from chapter 2. Apparently, the paint colors were fresh. I have become fond of it as well. I am currently thinking about the manga cover. I can't wait to get to work on it. Apparently, the manga will come out in November or December.
6.19.02

Yesterday, I went to Maruku 109 and bought up a storm. There were so many cute tops. I was so satisfied. I showed my family what I bought, and then my mother approached me because there was apparently a top that she liked too. When I told her she could have it she was so happy, and she wore it. Mm...she's so young...
6.17.02

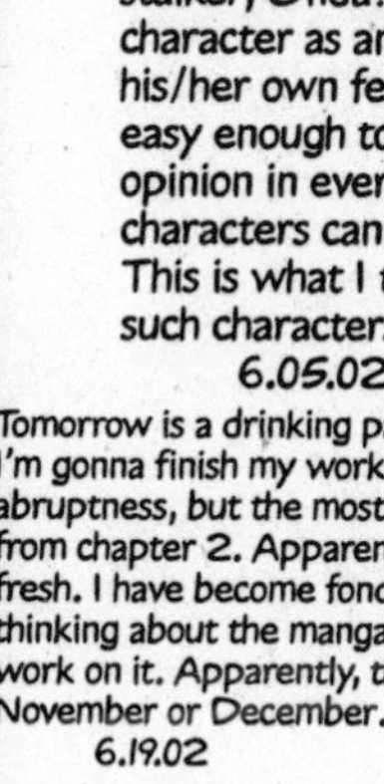

Rough sketch of the September preview page ←

I love drawing the color preview pages. I feel as though I've captured a good pace of working lately. However, I have a special extra in July so it will be crazy.
6.22.02

Right now, I really want to eat some avocado. Wohhhh.
6.28.05

Recently, I purchased a manga. It's called "Onna no Mondai Teiki" (Female Concerns). There is just a tad of this in my manga, but I enjoy manga that show the world is a bit in trouble. It takes energy to read and write love and adventure stories. Right? (Or is it only me?) I am able to enjoy these—they're not unrelated. That's why I am able to portray "Baby" so close to myself in comparison to the other stories I've done up to now.
6.27.02

Although mine are a bit silly.

In the Mainichi Newspaper (July 16 edition), there was a critic's article about "Baby." It was done quite well. Hiro-ne sent me the article by FAX. Man, I am so happy, but I am even more pleased to see my relatives buy out all the newspapers! When I say "wow" to the editorial staff, they say "Wow is you!" Hiro-ne was all fired up.
6.17.02

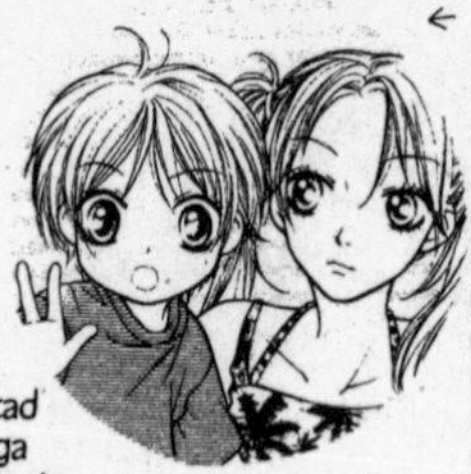

← This is the 2002 special extr (summer) preview page. Kip (left) and Big Sis (right). Ac when I was being indecisive a which preview drawing to us because there were so many I got a job offer to do the pre page (what a surprise it was) chose the one that was the cl my mind. It is a drawing of th them when they were younge though they are still young. I Big Sis looking adult-like bec most of the kids today look so older than they are.
6.25.02

I just received my fan letters, so I will take a break and read them. They are all so much fun. When I wrote that I drink tea like crazy, someone sent me some tea!! How hot!! I love people that are hot like that!! I'm so happy!!! Now, back to my manuscript...
6.29.02

That doesn't mean that I'm asking you to send me tea.

"Hiro-ne" is my new Rep. Please call her "Hiro-ne."

Now then, I have written my diary as I please, and finally, "Baby's" first book is about to come out. (It's out already, isn't it...) Finally. Really.

I will continue writing the diary, so please continue to read it.

Oh, yeah, I have not written asides in the manga this time. I didn't want to stop the rhythm of the manga with words, so that's why. Accept my regrets. I wasn't slacking off.

I am pleased that I am able to draw more girls even though I made the main character a boy.

Kippei: The side dish for today is deep-fried oysters.
Yuzu: Yeah! I can't wait!!!

It has that feeling. Silly? By the way, this is a preview drawing (rough draft).

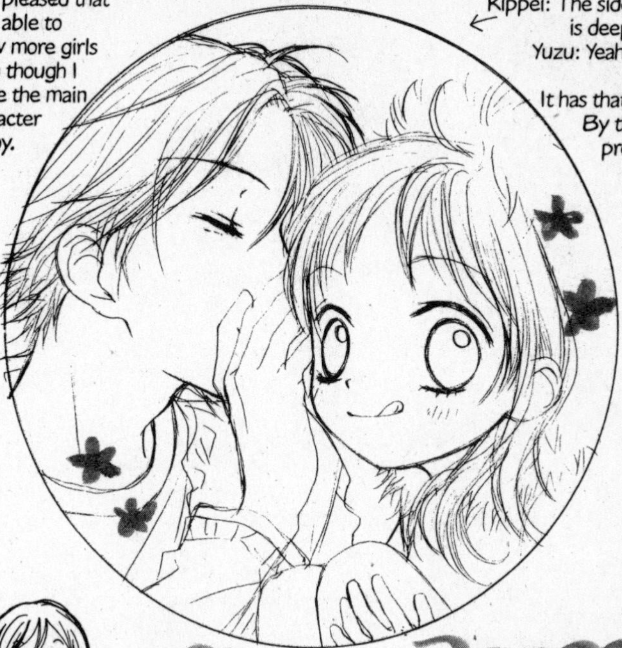

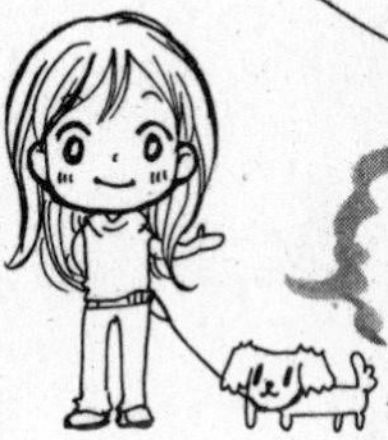

• The latest on Yoko Maki •

❀ I want to grow out my hair, so I died my blond hair black. It has calmed down profusely. Now it's rather Japanese-style.

❀ Leo jumped on my knees today, which was quite a surprise. Then he dashed out the door. How cute.

Lately, I have been going to the gym to run, swim, and lift weights. It feels good to exercise. For letters with comments about my work or "Hey, Yoko Maki, listen up!": (Of course, I do enjoy comments.)

Yoko Maki
C/O Aishiteruze Baby
P.O. Box 77064
San Francisco, CA 94107

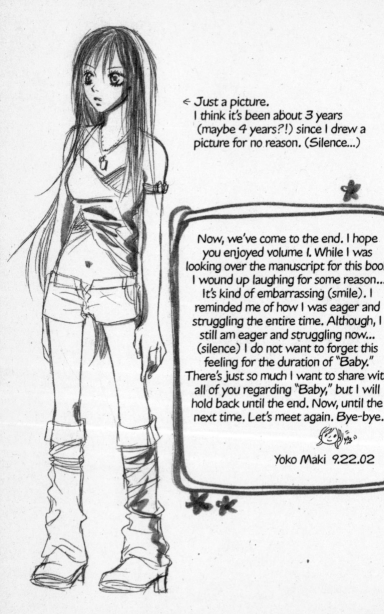

⇐ Just a picture.
I think it's been about 3 years
(maybe 4 years?!) since I drew a
picture for no reason. (Silence...)

Now, we've come to the end. I hope
you enjoyed volume 1. While I was
looking over the manuscript for this book,
I wound up laughing for some reason...
It's kind of embarrassing (smile). I
reminded me of how I was eager and
struggling the entire time. Although, I
still am eager and struggling now...
(silence) I do not want to forget this
feeling for the duration of "Baby."
There's just so much I want to share with
all of you regarding "Baby," but I will
hold back until the end. Now, until the
next time. Let's meet again. Bye-bye.

Yoko Maki 9.22.02

Aishiteruze ABCs

***A**ishiteruze* is a casual, masculine way to say "I love you" in Japanese. The title, *Aishiteruze Baby*★★, refers to Kippei telling his 5-year-old cousin that he loves her.

***B**ento* is a boxed lunch. Making someone a homemade bento is a way to show affection.

***C**ray-Pas* are oil pastels used for drawing. They are referred to as "crayons," but they're much nicer.

I often have a sore back.

When the stories that have been in my head for a long time are finally on paper, I think, "Oh, I'm so happy to be drawing manga right now!" "Baby" is one my creations that is filled with those kind of feelings. So, I want to share all my feelings! Or something like that. I'm not making sense anymore. Well, see you in Volume 2!

-Maki

Yoko Maki was born on July 11 and is originally from Kagoshima Prefecture in the south of Japan. She has a pet dog named Leo. Her hobby is blowing soap bubbles. Maki claims that one of her skills is passing quickly through a crowd of people. She debuted in 1999 with "Love Service!" in *Ribon Original* magazine.

Aishiteruze Baby★★
Vol. 1
The Shojo Beat Manga Edition

STORY & ART BY
YOKO MAKI

English Translation & Adaptation/Marie Cochrane
Touch-up & Lettering/Gabe Crate
Graphics & Cover Design/Yukiko Whitley
Editor/Nancy Thistlethwaite

Managing Editor/Megan Bates
Production Manager/Noboru Watanabe
Vice President of Publishing/Alvin Lu
Vice President & Editor in Chief/Yumi Hoashi
Sr. Director of Acquisitions/Rika Inouye
VP of Sales & Marketing/Liza Coppola
Publisher/Hyoe Narita

AISHITERUZE BABY★★ © 2002 by Yoko Maki. All rights reserved.
First published in Japan in 2002 by SHUEISHA Inc., Tokyo.
English translation rights in the United States of America and Canada
arranged by SHUEISHA Inc. The stories, characters and incidents
mentioned in this publication are entirely fictional.

Printed in Canada

Published by VIZ Media, LLC
P.O. Box 77064
San Francisco, CA 94107

Shojo Beat Manga Edition
10 9 8 7 6 5 4 3 2 1
First printing, April 2006

store.viz.com

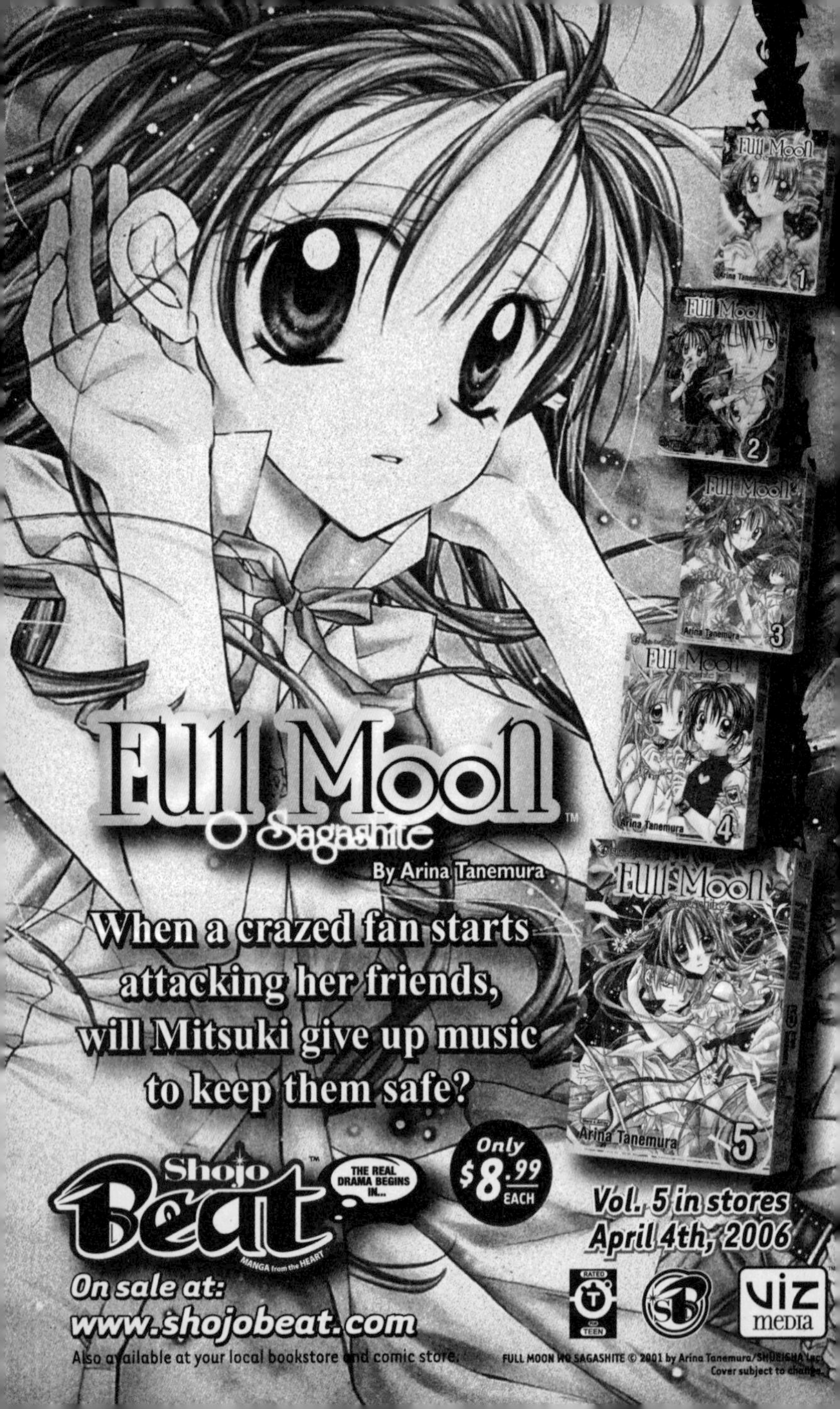

Full Moon O Sagashite™
By Arina Tanemura
When a crazed fan starts attacking her friends, will Mitsuki give up music to keep them safe?
Shojo Beat™ MANGA from the HEART
THE REAL DRAMA BEGINS IN...
Only $8.99 EACH
Vol. 5 in stores April 4th, 2006
On sale at: www.shojobeat.com
Also available at your local bookstore and comic store.
RATED T TEEN
viz media
FULL MOON WO SAGASHITE © 2001 by Arina Tanemura/SHUEISHA Inc.
Cover subject to change.

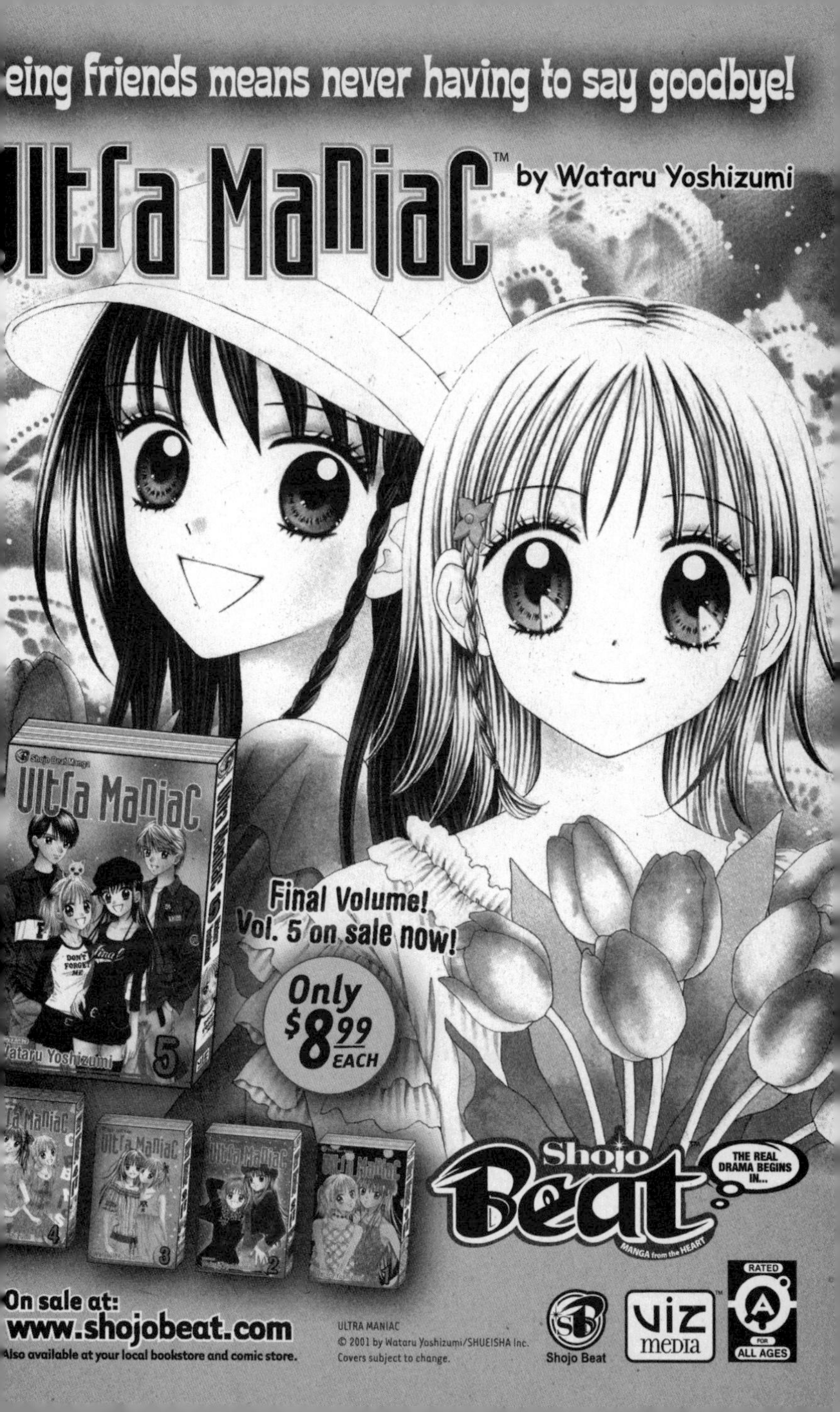
eing friends means never having to say goodbye!
Ultra Maniac™ by Wataru Yoshizumi
Final Volume! Vol. 5 on sale now!
Only $8.99 EACH
Shojo Beat™ THE REAL DRAMA BEGINS IN...
MANGA from the HEART
On sale at:
www.shojobeat.com
Also available at your local bookstore and comic store.
ULTRA MANIAC
© 2001 by Wataru Yoshizumi/SHUEISHA Inc.
Covers subject to change.
Shojo Beat
viz media
RATED A FOR ALL AGES

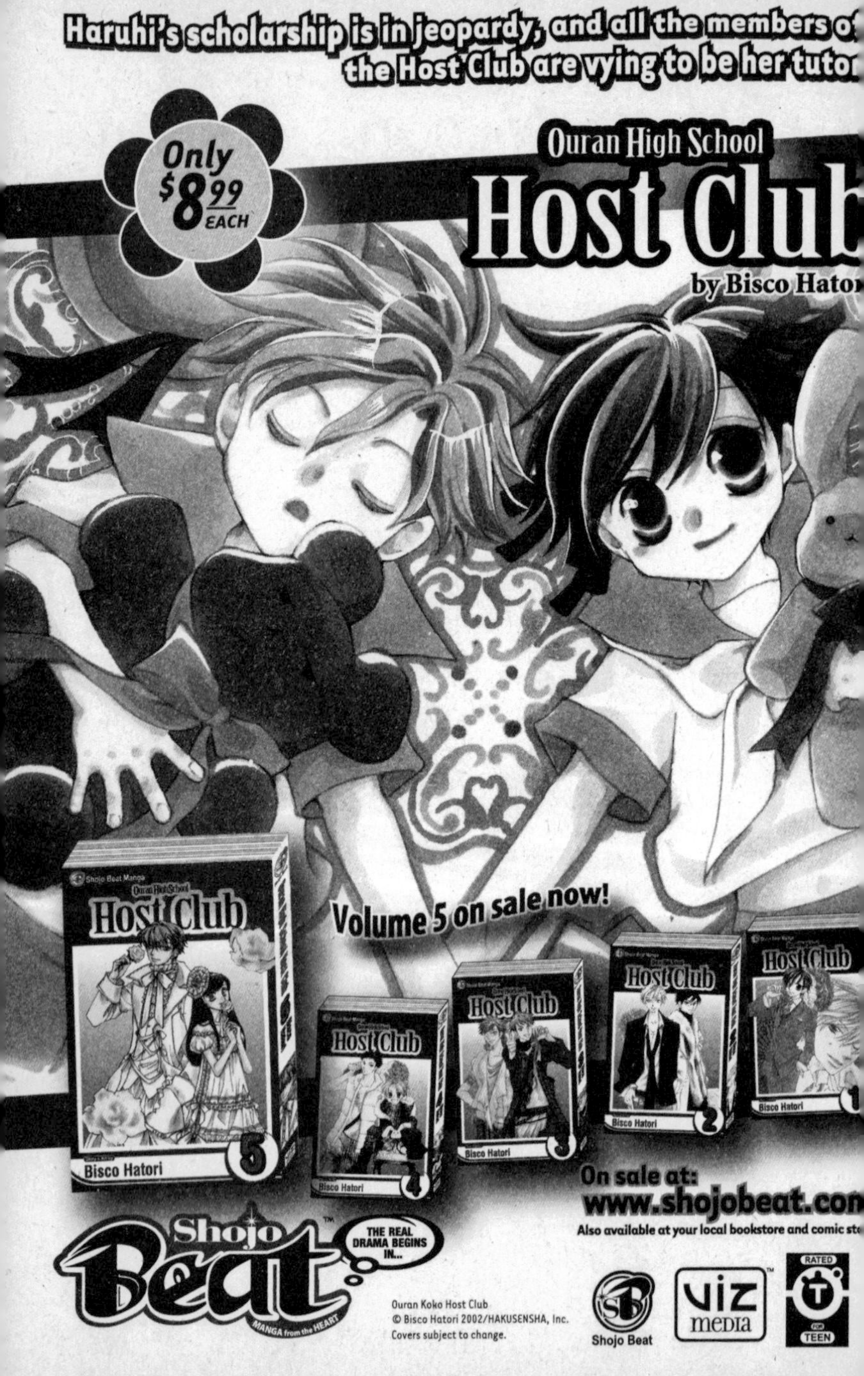
Haruhi's scholarship is in jeopardy, and all the members o
the Host Club are vying to be her tuto
Only $8.99 EACH
Ouran High School
Host Club
by Bisco Hato
Volume 5 on sale now!
Shojo Beat Manga
Ouran High School
Host Club
Bisco Hatori
5
4
3
2
1
On sale at:
www.shojobeat.co
Also available at your local bookstore and comic st
Shojo Beat
THE REAL DRAMA BEGINS IN...
MANGA from the HEART
Ouran Koko Host Club
© Bisco Hatori 2002/HAKUSENSHA, Inc.
Covers subject to change.
Shojo Beat
VIZ media
RATED T FOR TEEN

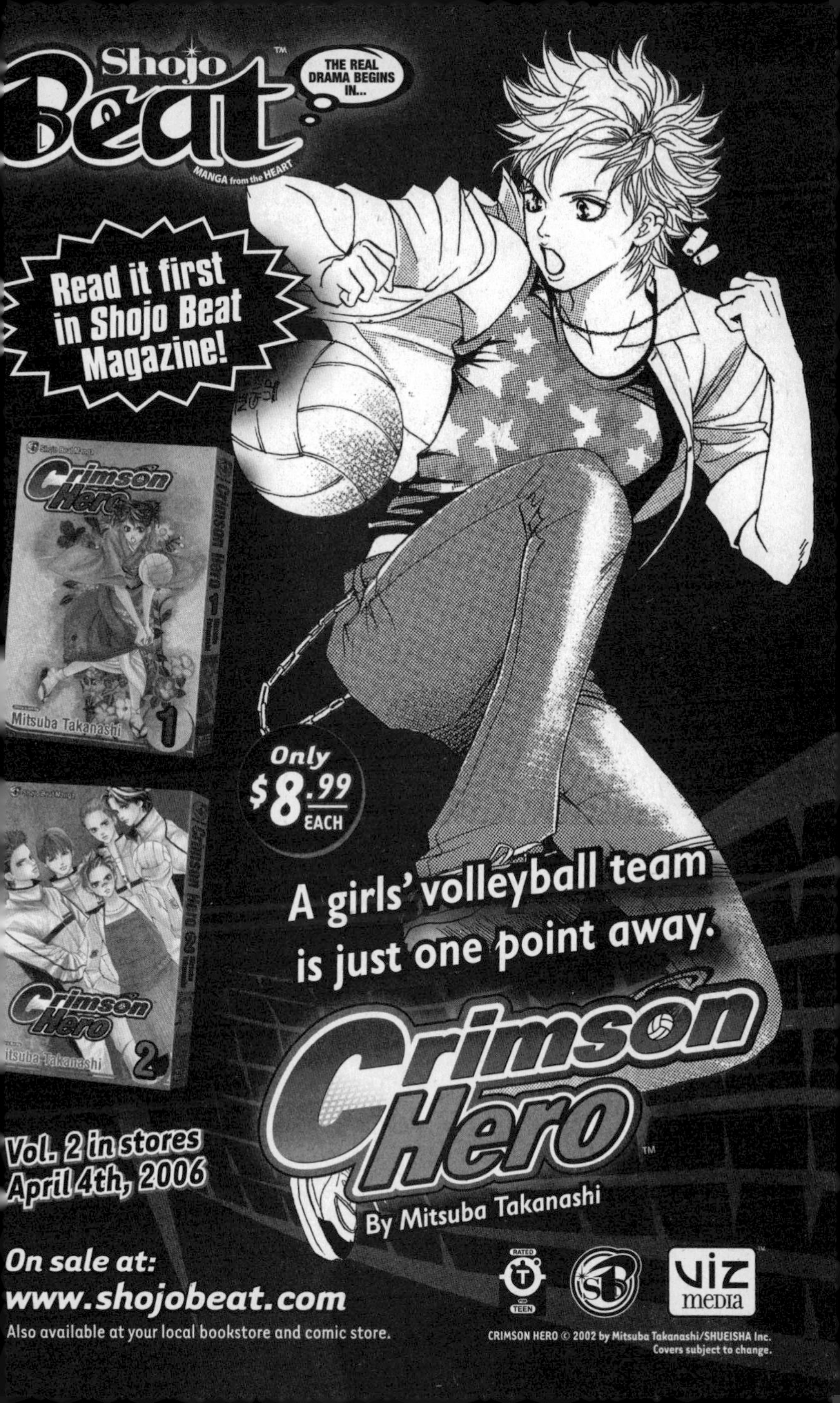

Shojo Beat™
THE REAL DRAMA BEGINS IN...
MANGA from the HEART
Read it first in Shojo Beat Magazine!
Crimson Hero
Mitsuba Takanashi 1
Crimson Hero
Mitsuba Takanashi 2
Only $8.99 EACH
A girls' volleyball team is just one point away.
Crimson Hero™
By Mitsuba Takanashi
Vol. 2 in stores April 4th, 2006
On sale at:
www.shojobeat.com
Also available at your local bookstore and comic store.
RATED T TEEN
viz media
CRIMSON HERO © 2002 by Mitsuba Takanashi/SHUEISHA Inc.
Covers subject to change.

Get the Beat online!
Check us out at
www.shojobeat.com!

COMPLETE OUR SURVEY AND LET US KNOW WHAT YOU THINK!

☐ Please do NOT send me information about VIZ Media and Shojo Beat products, news and events, special offers, or other information.

☐ Please do NOT send me information from VIZ Media's trusted business partners.

Name: _____

Address: _____

City: _____ State: _____ Zip: _____

E-mail: _____

☐ Male ☐ Female Date of Birth (mm/dd/yyyy): ___ / ___ / ___ (Under 13? Parental consent required)

❶ Do you purchase *Shojo Beat* magazine?

☐ Yes ☐ No (if no, skip the next two questions)

If **YES**, do you subscribe?

☐ Yes ☐ No

If you do **NOT** subscribe, why? (please check one)

☐ I prefer to buy each issue at the store. ☐ I prefer to buy the manga volumes instead.

☐ I share a copy with my friends/family. ☐ It's too expensive.

☐ My parents/guardians won't let me. ☐ Other

❷ Which particular Shojo Beat Manga did you purchase? (please check one)

☐ Beauty Is The Beast ☐ Full Moon ☐ Fushigi Yûgi: Genbu Kaiden

☐ MeruPuri ☐ Ouran High School Host Club ☐ Socrates In Love

☐ Tokyo Boys & Girls ☐ Ultra Maniac ☐ Other _____

Will you purchase subsequent volumes?

☐ Yes ☐ No ☐ Not Applicable

❸ How did you learn about this title? (check all that apply)

☐ Advertisement ☐ Article ☐ Favorite creator/artist

☐ Favorite title ☐ Gift ☐ Recommendation

☐ Read a preview online and wanted to read the rest of the story

☐ Read introduction in *Shojo Beat* magazine ☐ Special offer

☐ Website ☐ Other _____

4 Do you plan to purchase Shojo Beat Manga volumes of titles serialized in SB magazine?

☐ Yes   ☐ No

If **YES**, which one(s) do you plan to purchase? (check all that apply)

☐ Absolute Boyfriend   ☐ Baby & Me   ☐ Cri~ Hero
☐ Godchild   ☐ Kaze Hikaru

If **YES**, what are your reasons for purchasing? (pleas~

☐ Favorite title
☐ I want to read the full volume(s) a~ ~ead it over and over again
☐ There are extras that aren't in the ~   ☐ Recommendation
☐ The quality of printing is better than the magazine
☐ Other _____

If **NO**, why would you not purchase it?

☐ I'm happy just reading it in the magazine   ☐ It's not worth buying the graphic novel
☐ All the manga pages are in black and white   ☐ There are other graphic novels that I prefer
☐ There are too many to collect for each title   ☐ It's too small
☐ Other _____

5 Of the titles NOT serialized in the magazine, which ones have you purchased? (check all that apply)

☐ Beauty Is The Beast   ☐ Full Moon   ☐ Fushigi Yûgi: Genbu Kaiden
☐ MeruPuri   ☐ Ouran High School Host Club   ☐ Socrates In Love
☐ Tokyo Boys & Girls   ☐ Ultra Maniac   ☐ Other _____

If you did purchase any of the above, what were your reasons for purchase?

☐ Advertisement   ☐ Article   ☐ Favorite creator/artist
☐ Favorite title   ☐ Gift   ☐ Recommendation
☐ Read a preview online and wanted to read the rest of the story
☐ Read introduction in *Shojo Beat* magazine   ☐ Special offer
☐ Website   ☐ Other _____

Will you purchase subsequent volumes?

☐ Yes   ☐ No   ☐ Not Applicable

6 What race/ethnicity do you consider yourself? (please check one)

☐ Asian/Pacific Islander   ☐ Black/African American   ☐ Hispanic/Latino
☐ Native American/Alaskan Native ☐ White/Caucasian   ☐ Other

THANK YOU! Please send the completed form to: **Shojo Survey**
42 Catharine St.
Poughkeepsie, NY 12601

VIZ media

All information provided will be used for internal purposes only. We promise not to sell or otherwise divulge your information.

KU-592-236